J. ARTHUR RANK AND THE BRITISH FILM INDUSTRY

J. ARTHUR RANK AND THE BRITISH FILM INDUSTRY

Geoffrey Macnab

Routledge London & New York

First published 1993
Paperback edition first published in 1994
by Routledge
11 New Fetter Lane, London EC4P 4EE

Simultaneously published in the USA and Canada
by Routledge
29 West 35th Street, New York, NY 10001

© 1993, 1994 Geoffrey Macnab

Typeset in 10/12 pt Times by Florencetype Limited, Kewstoke
Printed in Great Britain by Butler & Tanner, Frome

British Library Cataloguing in Publication Data
Macnab, Geoffrey
J. Arthur Rank and the British Film
Industry. – (Cinema & Society Series)
I. Title II. Series
791.43092

Library of Congress Cataloging in Publication Data
Macnab, Geoffrey
J. Arthur Rank and the British film industry / Geoffrey
Macnab.
p.   cm.
1. Rank Organisation – History. 2. Rank, J. Arthur, 1888–1972.
3. Motion picture industry – Great Britain – History. I. Title.
PN1999.R37M33   1993
384′.8′0941-dc20   92-24832

ISBN 0-415-07272-7
0-415-11711-9 (pbk)

CONTENTS

PLATES

GENERAL EDITOR'S PREFACE

The pre-eminent popular art form of the first half of the twentieth century has been the cinema. Both in Europe and America from the turn of the century to the 1950s cinema-going has been a regular habit and film-making a major industry. The cinema combined all the other art forms – painting, sculpture, music, the word, the dance – and added a new dimension – an illusion of life. Living, breathing people enacted dramas before the gaze of the audience and not, as in the theatre, bounded by the stage, but with the world as their back drop. Success at the box office was to be obtained by giving the people something to which they could relate and which therefore reflected themselves. Like the other popular art forms, the cinema has much to tell us about people and their beliefs, their assumptions and their attitudes, their hopes and their fears and dreams.

This series of books will examine the connection between films and the societies which produced them. Film as straight historical evidence; film as an unconscious reflection of national preoccupations, film as escapist entertainment; film as a weapon of propaganda – these are aspects of the question that will concern us. We shall seek to examine and delineate individual film *genres*, the cinematic images of particular nations and the work of key directors who have mirrored national concerns and ideals. For we believe that the rich and multifarious products of the cinema constitute a still largely untapped source of knowledge about the ways in which our world and the people in it have changed since the first flickering images were projected on to the silver screen.

Jeffrey Richards

PREFACE

The vicissitudes of the British feature film industry arouse a wider
and deeper public interest today than any but the most outstanding of
its products. To some, its achievements, disappointments and
betrayals have the Wolseyan quality of Shakespearian tragedy; to
others, it is a Chaplinesque figure of comedy, reeling drunkenly from
crisis to crisis, elaborately supported, in mock solitude, by its constant companion, the Government, which is in nothing so competent
as picking its pocket . . . there has been no dearth of doctors,
students and temperature charts in the sick bay, and the patients
themselves have diagnosed and prescribed for each other and the
doctors.
              (Professor Arnold Plant, writing in *The Times*, 22 May 1952)

It is a commonplace to say that, since its very earliest days, the British film
industry has been enmeshed in crisis. There was a crisis in 1926, shortly
prior to the first Cinematograph Films Act, when the British awoke to the
fact that over 90 per cent of pictures shown in their cinemas were reckoned
to be American. There was a fresh crisis in the late 1930s, when investors
suddenly developed icily cold feet, and the whole fragile edifice of British
film production came tumbling down. There was a crisis in the Second
World War just as there had been in the First: briefly, it looked as if the
government would close the industry for the duration. There was a new
crisis in the late 1940s, when dollar shortages persuaded the Attlee administration to introduce swingeing taxes on Hollywood imports, thereby
provoking a Hollywood embargo which, in turn, helped set off Rank's
crisis of 1949, when his ambitious programme of films – conceived to
counterbalance the embargo – saw the Rank Organization's overdraft
escalating to in excess of £16 million. There were crises throughout the
mid- to late 1950s, when television started to drain away cinema audiences.
There was the crisis of the late 1960s, when the Hollywood investors who
had pumped money into 'runaway' productions in London packed their
bags and left. There was a crisis in the 1970s, as the rate of British

production plummeted, and another crisis in the 1980s, when Mrs Thatcher abolished the Eady Fund, a levy on box-office receipts which had helped buttress British filmmakers for nearly forty years. In the 1990s, for all the bold talk of Britain as the 'Hollywood of Europe', there is still a crisis.

Despite the well-nigh permanent state of siege in which it exists, the industry wobbles on. British exhibitors and distributors have traditionally managed to inoculate themselves against the bugs which affect their colleagues in production: the UK, in the late 1980s, after the efforts of British Film Year (1985) and the rise of the multiplex, was the one country in Europe where attendances were on the rise. Any talk of 'crisis' in the industry must, therefore, be tempered: it is the producers who have faced crisis after crisis, and production is only one part of the film process. It is hardly surprising that Hollywood hegemony has remained largely unchallenged for the last sixty years. The British industry is severely hampered by its own will-to-destruction, and by its never-ending capacity to generate internal feuds, fissure and division. Hollywood has helped divide and rule the industry, has ensured that renters and 'showmen' are always at loggerheads with producers, mainly because they have no great desire to handle British movies when they know they can make more money for less effort with transatlantic imports.

Just as in Preston Sturges' film *Hail the Conquering Hero!* the conquering hero in question turns out to have been a coward with hay fever, the British industry's putative saviours, who emerge at the rate of about two a decade, make a lot of fuss and noise before leaving British cinema in the same mess that it was in when they started. The pages of the film journals abound in panaceas for the tottering business today, and have done so since the journals began. One thing seems clear. However downtrodden, battered and bruised it might be, the British film will never quite become extinct. And, as Professor Plant's words quoted above suggest, there is a large measure of tragedy, pathos and comedy in the industry's ongoing struggle for survival – there is almost richer drama in the anxious battles being fought behind the screen than there is in the 'British Film' itself.

The purpose of this study is to chart some of that drama; to try to move the focus away from the films themselves, and to consider other facets of the industry – such as training, politics, newsreels and animation. I have tried, in short, to analyse a whole film culture and not just a handful of first features. In the process, there is an attempt to restore the reputation of, I would argue, the single most influential figure in British film history, namely J. Arthur Rank. Rank managed to tie all the discrete strands of British film culture together. In his bid to set the industry on its feet, he intervened on every level. He pioneered technical research and developed equipment. He invested in 'B' pictures. He started up a 'charm school' to generate stars. He financed the making of children's films, newsreels, cartoons and educational shorts as well as features. He even bought a meteorological company so that his units on location would know when it was going to rain. For a brief moment in the mid-1940s, it seemed as if he had managed to introduce a measure of harmonious sanity to the schizophrenic organism which the British film industry has traditionally been. He provided unheard-of creative opportunities to a host of filmmakers.

My book sets out to chart the many different facets of the Rank Organization. It does not purport to offer a comprehensive biographical portrait of Lord Rank. Indeed, it is only fair to mention at the outset that Rank's daughter Shelagh Cowen, who saw an early draft of the introductory chapter, was not happy with the portrayal of her father. As she pointed out in a critical letter, 'there is very little mention of his endeavours with the Methodist Church and his work toward a joining of the Methodist Church with the Church of England, and nothing about his philanthropic work and his founding of the Rank Foundation'. Cowen professed herself distressed that 'people will never know of his great wisdom, concern for other people in every aspect and his great humanity'. My concern, however, was not with flour, religion, or hagiography, but with the Rank Organization's influence on the British film industry. I have sought to revise the standard model of British film history which dismisses Rank as a Croesus-figure with little knowledge of cinema, and instead celebrates the contributions of a handful of dynamic producers, ranging from Alexander Korda and Herbert Wilcox to Michael Balcon and David Puttnam.

I wanted to show that without Rank's enthusiasm and investment, British film culture might well have collapsed in the 1940s. He came closer than anybody, before or since, to establishing a market for British films in the United States, and, for a short period, seemed to have united the warring factions – the sellers and producers who rent the industry apart – under his banner by establishing a truly integrated company, where the competing demands of 'art' and 'business' were both accommodated.

ACKNOWLEDGEMENTS

In this work, when it shall be found that much is omitted, let it not be forgotten that much likewise is performed; and though no book was ever spared out of tenderness to the authour, and the world is little solicitous to know whence proceeded the faults of that which it condemns; yet it may gratify curiosity to inform it, that the *English Dictionary* was written with little assistance of the learned, and without any patronage of the great; not in the soft obscurities of retirement, or under the shelter of academick bowers, but amidst inconvenience and distraction, in sickness and in sorrow.

(Preface to Johnson's *Dictionary*, London, 1755)

I am indebted to countless friends. I thank Rebecca Barden at Routledge for her goading; Nick Thomas for reading an early version of the manuscript; David Tibballs for his encouragement; Kevin Macdonald and Adrian Driscoll. I also express my gratitude to the various film industry veterans who allowed me interviews: Betty Box, Sidney Cole, Jill Craigie, John Davis, Olive Dodds, Weston Drury, Anthony Havelock-Allan, Peter Rogers, Donald Sinden, Charles Staffell, Hugh Stewart, Norman Wisdom, John Woolf, Sydney Wynne and (by telephone) Bob Monkhouse. I am grateful to George Helyer and Derek Long for giving me access to the files on 'This Modern Age' in the Rank Film Archive. I thank the film historian Mark Glancy for furnishing me with figures of Rank's earnings in the US market. I also thank J. D. Hutchison, Rank's nephew, and the Hon. Mrs Shelagh Cowen, Rank's daughter, for speaking to me; and Robert Philippi for providing me with a cartoon of Rank and Spyros Skouras. Last of all, I should thank my parents in Fife and my brother in Edinburgh who, at various times during the writing of the book, offered me the use of a bed and a desk. I would like to dedicate *J. Arthur Rank and the British Film Industry* to my nieces, Alice and Emma.

INTRODUCTION
OF FLOUR AND FILM

In April 1946, when it held its first, grandly styled 'World Film Convention'[1] at the Dorchester Hotel in London, the Rank Organization was huge, even by Hollywood standards: it could boast five studios, two newsreels, a great many production companies, making everything from feature films to cartoons and educational shorts, and close to 650 cinemas in Britain alone. It had twenty-four managing directors, a staff of 31,000 – by comparison, the National Health Service employed 34,000 people on its inception – and a turnover of £45 million. Bombardier Billy Wells,[2] longest-reigning British heavyweight boxing champion before Henry Cooper, was the brawny man walloping the gong: Rank's immediately recognizable motif, which prefaced movies produced or distributed by the organization, and which would eventually be seen on everything from photocopying machines to bingo halls, from motorway service stations to ten-pin bowling alleys, was already as familiar to cinemagoers as MGM's roaring lions or RKO's bleeping pylons.

Who was J. Arthur Rank and how had his company come into being?

From behind the awesome façade of the organization which bears his name emerges a genial, if enigmatic, Yorkshireman, driven in business by an unshakeable religious faith, who had entered the industry circuitously thirteen years before, in 1933, when he had decided to equip various Methodist halls and Sunday schools with film projectors. Like the Wizard of Oz, surprisingly vulnerable and diminished when removed from his carapace and forced by Dorothy out into the open, Mr Rank didn't entirely live up to Wardour Street's expectations: he was a very mild-mannered magnate, lacking the arrogance and flamboyance then considered *de rigueur* amongst movie moguls. The press releases, endless features and interviews generated by Rank's industrious publicity machine, which was spending over £1 million a year promoting the company, reveal him as a scrupulous, paternal man. He was homely – with an informal, down-to-earth way of expressing himself – and even shy. These were not traits associated with film tycoons. Journalists took advantage of Mr Rank, portraying him as a bluff, slightly eccentric figure, as a sort of ingenuous

1

and affable Colonel Blimp, meandering into the cut-throat world of film from his office in the City. Rank is 'a man of the utmost integrity'.[3] Even detractors admit as much. Integrity is hardly the stuff to build a film empire, which was what Rank had done by 1946.

There is a cartoon on the front of a 1946 issue of the *Cine-Technician*, journal of the Association of Cine-Technicians (ACT), drawn by David Low, who had 'fathered' Blimp and provided many debunking images of the politicians of the era,[4] which shows Rank clutching an alabaster statue,

Figure 1 Cartoon featured in the *Cine-Technician*, 1946
(By courtesy of Low of the *Evening Standard*)

smiling at a film camera, as three baseball-cap-wearing Hollywood executives, Mr Spitz, Mr Spatz and Mr Spotz, give him directions. The statue, representing British culture, and bearing an uncanny resemblance to Anna Neagle, is deemed 'not sultry enough' for American tastes. Rank, stiff and awkward, hardly cuts a dash as a leading man: he is no Stewart Granger. Dressed in dark suit and dark shoes, English city-gent outfit, he looks every bit the bashful, conventional British businessman, whereas the

American executives, in creased and crumpled white, bespectacled, cigar-smoking, are at their ease, snapping out instructions to him. This was the pivotal year of Rank's great drive to establish British films in the American market. In certain quarters, his policy brought him criticism and ridicule. On the left, in the pages of *Tribune*[5] or of the newly formed *Penguin Film Review*,[6] it was felt that he was betraying the robust British film culture of the war years, epitomized by pictures with such patriotic, consensual titles as *Millions Like Us*, *The Way Ahead*, or *In Which We Serve*, whose champions claimed that they had managed to blend the true grit of 'documentary realism' with the compelling narrative dynamo of the popular feature film.[7] Rank, these critics suggested, was sacrificing all this. He was trying to make ersatz Hollywood movies, importing American directors and stars, and neglecting the home-grown talent. Low's cartoon infers that he is jumping to Hollywood's bidding and that the antiquated representations of British culture he presents his transatlantic partners with (grass, statue, Arcadian bandstand) are at odds with the crass vulgarity of the Hollywood movie. Under the guise of making Anglo-American features, the Americans are taking Rank for a ride.

Throughout his career, whatever his policies, Rank was liable to be caricatured. He was rich, influential and yet so far removed from the popular conception of a film magnate that he was bound to be an immediate target for satirists. He was once likened to an ant-eater by the American press.[8] When he visited the United States in the summer of 1947 *Time* magazine characterized him as follows:

> Joseph Arthur Rank is a burly grandfather-clock of a man, at 59 tick-tock solemn and sure and rather bumblingly humorous when wound up. He stands 6ft 1in. with his limp brown hair stuck down flat, and bulks a solid 15 stone (210 lbs). He resembles General De Gaulle, except that he does not share the look of a supercilious camel. His great tired nose droops even lower than De Gaulle's. It curls under just in time to disclose an uncertain mustachelet which changes position with each shave.
>
> (*Time*, 19 May 1947, p. 31)

Ian Sinclair-Phail, a journalist writing for the *Yorkshire Post*, charted the US media's fascination with the magnate. Again, his Chaplin-like moustache comes in for particular scrutiny:

> One American woman columnist notes that 'he wears a moustache which he alters frequently from "tooth brush to handle bar" and then back again. His face is bony and his smallish shrewd eyes are set narrowly.' A Canadian woman sums it up like this: 'his large face reveals so little of brilliance or even shrewdness that many people feel his bland expression is a mask.'
>
> (Ian Sinclair-Phail, *Yorkshire Post*, 5 December 1946)

If his appearance was not enough for the satirists, his background added extra grist: when he entered the film industry, he was a middle-aged Methodist flour-miller, living in Reigate, the heart of the Home Counties, and commuting daily to his office in London. He taught in Sunday school: on trips to Hollywood, he would alarm the cigar-chewing American studio executives by interrupting what they at least felt to be important business to write postcards to his Sunday school charges. During the war, when petrol was short, he used to ride off to the Reigate Sunday school – a veritable Jacques Tati – on an old bicycle. By all accounts, he was a ferociously competitive bridge player.[9] Breeding pointer dogs and labradors, shooting grouse, pheasants and partridges, and playing golf with his old war comrade, now his farm factor, Colonel Hake, were his weekend and holiday pastimes. Outside film, Methodism and business, a crowning ambition, which was sadly to remain unfulfilled, was to win with one of his dogs at Cruft's. (Nor was he any luckier in his attempts to walk off with the top 'coursing' greyhound trophy, the Waterloo Cup.) Rank ate prodigious quantities of chocolate and, for most of his life, smoked in eleven months of the year. (During February, the shortest month, he generally chose to abstain from tobacco in the name of self-discipline.) Politically, he was a staunch Conservative. He turned down a peerage from the Attlee government in the late 1940s,[10] averring that he would never accept such an honour from a Socialist, and waiting a decade for a Tory prime minister, Harold Macmillan, to repeat the offer. He had held a low opinion of the Attlee regime from the outset, and was sure that it would find some way of 'messing things up'.[11] (His fatalism was indeed rewarded. As we shall see, the Attlee government's 1947 ad-valorem tax dealt the Rank Organization an almost mortal blow.)

On the face of it, Rank did not seem a very likely 'saviour' of the British film. A gentleman farmer, a keen Methodist who enjoyed country pursuits, and went for holidays twice a year, in unseasonable March and November, in Cornwall, Rank was renowned for his generosity; he kept copious quantities of alcohol for his guests, although he had signed the 'temperance pledge' and stuck to ginger beer himself. This greatly endeared him to Ealing boss Michael Balcon:

> Lord Rank is the most tolerant of men. He is a teetotaller, but when entertaining he will drink ginger ale and lime because it looks like a real drink and guests don't find it uncomfortable.
>
> (Michael Balcon, writing in *The People*, March 1968)

Before he entered the industry in 1933, he was not especially keen on cinema. As his daughter Shelagh Cowen testifies: 'he wasn't a film addict at all. . . . Before he got into films, we didn't go to the cinema much.'[12]

The Reigate squire had little in common with his Hollywood counter-parts: with the Schenck brothers, with Spyros Skouras, or Louis B. Mayer, or Barney Balaban. Often, at least as legend has it, rags-to-riches American archetypes, former 'showmen' and hustlers, steeped in film culture, who had been in the industry since the days of the nickelodeon, the Hollywood magnates had shimmied their way to the top and, once there, displayed exemplary ruthlessness and ostentation. Nor was Rank in any way akin to his great British predecessor Alexander Korda, the Hungarian-born maverick, who had wended his way into British film via Hollywood and France. The contrast between the two characters Rank and Korda is drawn by the latter's nephew, as if each represented a mutually exclusive strand of British film culture:

> He [Korda] was a gambler who had staked too much and lost. J. Arthur Rank, by contrast, though his financial difficulties were at least as acute, escaped criticism. Since he was dull, reticent, devout, a prudent businessman who lived modestly, his financial problems were accepted as part of the normal risk of business. Perhaps he had made mistakes. Which businessman did not? But he had never put himself forward as a miracle worker, whereas Alex had been delighted to accept that role when it had been offered him.
>
> (Korda, 1980: 349)

This antinomy, Rank v. Korda, stolidity v. flair, has generally been allowed to stand. Over the past decade or so, as British film, like every other part of British culture, from the country house to punk music, from the Battle of the Somme to the railway engine, is made a focus for nostalgia, complete with its own museum, the Museum of the Moving Image (MOMI), and bolstered by myriad 'star' biographies and TV retrospectives; as *The Red Shoes* and *The Four Feathers* are lovingly restored by the National Film Archive; as monographs on Powell and Pressburger, Launder and Gilliat and Gainsborough melodrama, re-evaluate British cinema and society of the last ninety years; as ingenious critics make adversary readings of *Genevieve* or *Expresso Bongo*, the Rank Organization is shunted to the margins, and is seldom granted the cultural respectability of, say, Ealing Studios, although it was responsible for distributing and financing Ealing pictures from 1944 onward. While there are studies of crusading British producers from Michael Balcon to David Puttnam, who are celebrated for resisting Hollywood oppression, and for trying to carve out a national cinema in the face of enormous odds, J. Arthur Rank is largely ignored. To supersede thumbnail-sketch dismissals of one of the most influential figures in British film history as 'dull, devout – a Methodist', a look at the inner workings of Rank and his organization is long overdue.

As it was religion that brought Rank into the industry, his desire to furnish Methodist halls with projectors and to establish a 'Cinema for Christ', it is worth assessing Rank's peculiar brand of crusading Christianity, his evangelism, at the outset, as well as charting the background from which he emerged. In interviews throughout his career, Rank always insisted that he was guided by God, that his every decision was taken in consultation with the Almighty. As his daughter remembers:

> He had the most extraordinary simple faith which he tried to make us understand. 'If you've got it,' he used to say, 'it's a most wonderful thing, but it's very hard because you can't ever gainsay it. You know what you have to do and you do it. . . .' He went every morning of his life and used to walk around the garden and say his prayers. Or if we were in Scotland, he would walk along the river and talk to God. And he wouldn't do a thing, even business-wise, without talking about it and thinking about it.[13]

While his faith certainly galvanized him, and no account of Rank's part in the British film industry can overlook it, it none the less presents an awkward obstacle: faith, by definition, is inscrutable. In so far as it affected the decisions which led to the forming of Rank's empire, this faith must be addressed, however awkward and elusive a concept to somebody who doesn't share it. It is easy to impugn such a faith, particularly when its proud possessor was a sometimes ruthless businessman who derived great personal profit from his dealings. In negotiations with the ACT or in board meetings, the faith could present a problem – Rank was a positivist, convinced his every decision had been sanctioned by a higher force. Union representatives or board directors who disagreed with him were in danger of being regarded as apostates. With God on his side, Rank brooked no disagreements. This inevitably riled his opponents. As former vice-president of the ACT, Sidney Cole, no friend of the Rank Organization, caustically observed:

> he [Rank] assumed that he was more acquainted with God than other people were, which is always a doubtful proposition.[14]

Rank's beliefs did not spring from nowhere. In his meshing of business and religious goals, he owed much to his family, in particular his father Joseph, and to a well-documented nineteenth-century tradition.

JOSEPH RANK

To describe him bluntly, Joseph Rank, one of the foremost philanthropists of his day, was an unreformed troglodyte of a Victorian capitalist, a 'man of facts and calculations',[15] who would have doubtless defined a horse as a graminivorous quadruped, and who would not have been out of place in Charles Dickens's Coketown. His biographer R. G. Burnett, while professing to admire him, none the less concedes that Joe Rank was the produce of a harsh, entrepreneurial age, where only the fittest survived and prospered. Social Darwinism combined with God, hard work and thrift to form this dour industrialist. What was Rank senior's credo?

> If I am asked to state the guiding principles of my life . . . I think it would be: firstly, attention to business, and secondly, living within one's income.
>
> (Burnett, 1945: 34)

Having pulled himself up by his own socks, Rank believed implicitly in competition: 'We cannot get away from the law of the survival of the fittest,' he is reputed to have said, 'it is a natural law and human nature without competition would become effete.'[16]

Before becoming flour-millers, the Ranks were farmers in the East Riding of Yorkshire. There are records extant of the Ranks as a farming family from the mid-sixteenth century onward. It was in 1825, when Joseph's grandfather John rented tenancy of a windmill in Sproatley, not far from Hull, that the Ranks first started 'grinding'.

Despite being from moderately prosperous Yorkshire stock, Joe Rank saw himself as a self-made man who had started close to the bottom rung. Born in Hull on 28 March 1854, he was lame in both feet and, as a child, showed an aptitude for little other than cricket. Leaving school at 14, and after a brief apprenticeship in Aberdeen, he began to work in his father's mill. It used to be said of him that 'he found no pleasure in the mill' (*The Master Millers*, 1955: 17). His father considered him lazy and dull, and would pay him only a small allowance. On one notorious occasion, his father offered him to a visiting customer: 'Take the lad as well as the bran. . . . He's good for nowt' (ibid.: 19). When the father died, he did not pass on the family mill to Joe: 'James Rank left a moderate fortune, more than £30,000 – a large sum in real value in 1874. The share of it bequeathed to Joseph was £500', wrote Burnett. Joe struggled to put his portion to work, buying and running his own tiny mill. Milling in nineteenth-century Britain was backward, still dependent on wind: on flat calm days, the whole business would grind to a halt. Joe set out to change this state of affairs and, in doing so, helped lay the foundations of his own future prosperity. First, he introduced portable gas engines 'to help drive the stones when the wind was idle'. Then, at his Holderness corn mill, opened on All Fools' Day 1885, he helped pioneer the 'roller mill'.[17] And, finally, in 1891, he staked everything he had on his thoroughly modern Clarence mills: 'They were driven by a triple expansion engine, one of the earliest type to drive a flour mill in this country. It proved both effective and economical' (*The Master Millers*, 1955: 33).

The ascent took time and effort – no Victorian success story would be complete without these two components, and Joe Rank worked awesomely long hours, sometimes even sleeping in the mill, although he would never raise a finger on a Sunday, which remained the sacred day of rest. (His mills used to close at 11.59 p.m. on a Saturday night and open again at 12.01 a.m. on a Monday.) Eventually, Rank's innovation paid dividends, and his flour empire began to grow. Burnett points out that Rank's religious conversion came at just about the moment he started to make money. As his business expanded, his Wesleyan fervour flamed. This was not unusual. The 'virtues' encouraged by Methodism, by, for example, Wesley's 'General Rules of Employing Time'[18] – central to which were avoiding 'idleness, freedom with women and high-seasoned meats' – were consistent with Victorian capitalism: diligence and frugality were the bed-rock for both. 'Methodism, mill ownership and the new industrial wealth went hand in hand',[19] Glynn Hughes wrote in his recent book, *Yorkshire*. However, the northern industrialists, with their spartan personal habits and their knee-jerk dislike of alcohol, forever associated with idleness, squalor and the workhouse, sometimes made Wesley into an unnecessarily severe patron. Plays, dancing and novels may have been taboo for Methodists and mill-owners alike, but Wesley is on record complaining, like any stalwart of the Campaign for Real Ale, about the adulteration of 'honest English ale'.[20] While he eschewed extravagance and encouraged early rising and hard work, and appreciated that such a life-style could bring fortune in its wake, he was vehemently opposed to the making of money for money's sake: acquiring a fortune was an occupational hazard, not a goal in itself, for the assiduous Methodist. Wesley believed the only justification for personal wealth was that it enabled its bearer to give generously to worthy causes. Joe Rank, however, found the competitive urge chafing against the charitable instinct. For his business to succeed, he had to make sure he produced his flour more cheaply than his rivals. He had little compunction about driving competitors out of the market, but, once he had bankrupted them, his will to charity would quickly blossom: nobody was more conscientitious about providing for ruined millers than Rank. And he saw no contradiction in his behaviour. In 1933, he set up a trust to administer a benevolent fund for 'the poor but worthy people of Hull'. As his great-nephew recalls, he lived frugally himself, and devoted much of his time and money to furthering the cause of Methodism in Britain: 'after making what he considered ample provision for his family, he turned a great deal of his accumulated wealth into a series of trusts for the benefit of the Methodist Church and other charities.'[21]

As his fortune grew, and as he moved his base from Hull to London, he embarked on a two-pronged crusade. Part of his ambition was to convert the people of Britain, in particular his ever-increasing workforce, to Methodism. (It used to be said that he was more interested in preaching to his workers than in paying them well.) He invested in the building of dozens of Methodist halls, where his workers could take their families on a

Sunday. (But he refused to install lifts in any of his mills or offices.) The second part of Rank's grand scheme was to recapture the home market for British millers. His protracted battles with the American flour industry anticipate those his son would wage a generation later against Hollywood. In both cases, flour and film, the Americans had the same competitive advantage, based on resources, technology and size of market, that they have been able to exercise over the British in so many other spheres.

In the Midwest of America, as every schoolchild and *National Geographic* photographer has long known, the fields are full of fine-quality wheat, millions of acres of the stuff. Joe Rank quickly discovered that US farmers were only too ready to use their easy access to such abundant crops as a means of destabilizing the British flour market. They could afford to do this – to 'strike the averages', as it was called – because their own market was protected by a 20 per cent tariff, effectively excluding foreign flour; any shortfall caused by cost-cutting abroad could thus be offset by raising prices at home. British millers couldn't match the artificially cheap US export prices. They had to pay more for their wheat, which was often imported and of a lesser quality. Before Joe Rank's innovations, their mills were not mechanized. Their market was not protected. (This was closely akin to the scenario confronting Britain's beleaguered filmmakers in the 1920s and 1930s, when Hollywood pictures, already having paid for them-selves at home, were offered at knockdown prices to British exhibitors, who would book them in preference to UK movies.)

Joe Rank, driven by Wesley, patriotism and the love of capital, though not necessarily in that order, sought to erode American domination of the British market. He was renowned for his knowledge of the world's wheats, and insisted that British bread, baked with flour from his own mills, was better than anything the Americans could provide. His tactics were to import high-quality wheats from outside the USA – he found ample, cheaper resources in India – and to build up an organization large enough to compete on equal terms with the biggest of the transatlantic flour moguls. The problem with Joe Rank's expansion was that it squeezed rival British flour-millers out of the market. It was a matter of supreme indiffer-ence to them whether they were competing with Rank or with the Americans: either way, they were bound to lose.

J. Arthur Rank's trials and tribulations as he sought to wrest control of the British film industry away from Hollywood bear an uncanny resem-blance to the type of problems confronted by his father. Like Joe, J. Arthur upheld the sacred principles of economy of scale and centralization, and like Joe, J. Arthur found that he was inadvertently squeezing British independents out of the frame.

Born on 22 December 1888, the youngest of Joseph's three sons, J. Arthur Rank was educated at private school; found early and 'character-building' employment sweeping the floors of his father's mills; underwent a thorough apprenticeship with W. Looker of Exchange Roller Mills, Luton; studied every aspect of the family business, spending six months at the Mark Lane corn market, eighteen months in London, and a year in charge of one of Joe Rank's mills in Hull. He joined the board of Joseph Rank Ltd in 1915; served as sergeant in the First World War; set up his own business, Peterkins Self-Raising Flour, and when that business failed, came to work for his father. Eventually, he would become chairman and managing director of Joseph Rank Ltd and a life president of Rank Hovis McDougall Ltd, and would play a leading part in the restructuring of the flour industry during the time it was emerging from the government controls applied during the Second World War. In the early 1930s, however, he was an affluent, suburban businessman, already well into middle age, who had briefly owned the *Methodist Times* in 1925, but had otherwise shown no tycoonish tendencies. In this period, he purchased Sutton Manor, a large estate in central Hampshire, which soon became one of the best-known sporting estates in Britain. Rank managed to reconcile his Methodism with an irrepressible enthusiasm for blood sport, and soon established 'one of the best partridge shoots in the country and a wonderful kennel of gun dogs'.[22] He was renowned for his shooting ability, and used his estate for entertaining his family, friends and business associates, as well as for holding endless field trials for dogs. J. Arthur Rank was 'just as religious as his father', but was a 'more broad-minded and liberal man'.[23] Joseph had been a strict, somewhat austere parent, who disapproved of his children going to the theatre or to public dances. While he did take them once a year to the circus in Hull, and while he had no objection to their watching cricket (he was a long-standing member of Yorkshire County Cricket Club), he was no fan of the cinema, and was suspicious of his son's dalliance with the medium. However, J. Arthur Rank was always on the look-out for ways of adding brio and colour to his Sunday school lessons in particular, and to the sometimes rather dour presentation of Methodism in general. After long discussions with the sagacious Colonel Hake, who shared his conviction that film could add a new dimension to religion, he began to think about buying projectors to liven up Sunday school and church services.

THE CINEMA FOR CHRIST

Those who have exploited the cinematograph . . . have deliberately appealed to the jungle instincts which lurk beneath the surface of Western Civilization . . . they have applied to their art the cynical ideas of the vulgar peep-show . . . why should not the cinematograph be adapted for church needs?

(Burnett, 1934: 15)

In 1933, Hitler came to power in Germany, Alexander Korda made *The Private Life of Henry VIII*, and the Religious Film Society, 'an offshoot of a body for religious propaganda called the Guilds of Light',[24] a voluntary body presided over by the Bishop of London, was formed. At first, the Religious Film Society confined its activities to work in churches, Sunday schools and temperance organizations (Burnett, 1934: 67). J. Arthur Rank was the joint honorary treasurer of the new society. He had been drawn to the cinema by his conviction that 'pictures would get through to people whereas church and that sort of thing wouldn't'.[25] Disheartened by the poor quality of religious films then on offer, he had decided that buying projectors was not enough: he needed something worthwhile to show. He hoped the Religious Film Society might provide it.

The society had been set up in opposition to mainstream cinema, which it abhorred. The previous year, 1932, R. J. Burnett, Joe Rank's biographer, who was on the society's committee, had expressed his fear and loathing of the commercial film industry in *The Devil's Camera: Menace of a Film-Ridden World*. Dedicating this grim, hyperbolic tract to the 'ultimate sanity of the white races',[26] Burnett opens the study with an account of a young schoolboy and schoolgirl 'huddled together in the darkened, stuffy, erotic atmosphere of a London super-cinema'.[27] The boy becomes so caught up in the 'sensationally realistic production' he is watching that, as soon as the film is over, he promptly drags the young schoolgirl down a darkened alley and, in imitation of the offending movie, stabs her to death. When film falls into the wrong hands, Burnett avers, it can quite literally have fatal consequences: it is 'the greatest crime-producing agency of this generation'.[28] In his lurid, anti-Semitic vision of the contemporary cinema:

> Most of the actors and actresses seem ready to go to any length in decadence and nakedness to earn the salaries doled out to them by the little group of mainly Jewish promoters who control the greater part of what is now one of the most skilfully organized industries in the world.
>
> (Burnett and Martell, 1932: 11)

Rank's old newspaper, the *Methodist Times*, edited by the Reverend Benjamin Gregory, also on the committee of the Religious Film Society, shared Burnett's distrust of mainstream film. Its critic Mr G. A. Atkinson pointed out that 'crimeless and sexless films' had not been given a chance since the arrival of the talkies.[29] He offered an image of the Hollywood denizens as fiendish scientists who had carried out every manner of research on young people with a view to

> ascertaining their pulse, salivary and glandular reactions while they are watching a drama of erotic emotion. There is nothing haphazard

about it. What you see on the screen is the factory principle in the commercialization of sex.

(Atkinson, quoted in Burnett and Martell, 1932: 12)

Threatening factory metaphors, which cast consumers as automata, responding to film or to music as if to Pavlovian stimuli, have always been used by opponents of mass/popular culture. From Chaplin's *Modern Times* to Richard Hoggart's *Uses of Literacy* and the Frankfurt School's critiques of 1950s America,[30] the commercialization of culture is seen as impinging on individuality and as standardizing response. Take, for example, Theodor Adorno's assessment of the behaviour of jazz fans, an assessment which sounds uncannily like Atkinson's:

What is important is the sense of belonging. . . . As girls, once they have trained themselves to faint upon hearing the voice of a crooner . . . they call themselves 'jitter-bugs', bugs which carry out reflex movements, performers of their own ecstasy.[31]

By a neat irony, the Methodists, so distrustful of the Hollywood film's effect upon its viewer, the physiological reactions and changes of behaviour it appeared to provoke, were themselves prey to similar accusations. The established church was not kindly disposed towards Wesley's methods of preaching. The Reverend Mr Downes, writing in the mid-eighteenth century, comes close to accusing the Wesleyan preachers of making jitter-bugs out of their congregation:

They [the Methodists] have darkened religion with many ridiculous fancies, tending to confound the head and corrupt the heart. . . . A thorough knowledge of them would work in every rightly disposed mind an abhorrence of these doctrines, which directly tend to distract the head, and to debauch the heart, by turning faith into frenzy, and the Grace of God into wantonness . . . we pronounce them *filthy dreamers*, turning faith into fancy, the gospel into farce, thus adding blasphemy to enthusiasm.[32]

While drawing parallels between Adorno's, Chaplin's and Hoggart's attacks on mass culture and debates surrounding Wesley, the Religious Film Society and the *Methodist Times* is doubtless a laboured and tenuous endeavour, it is none the less true that both factions set up a rigid opposition between some aspect of mainstream culture, which they deplore, and a preferred antidote: for Adorno, the atonal music of Schoenberg is infinitely preferable to the contrived spontaneity, with its 'machine-like precision',[33] of American jazz; Hoggart holds up the 'authentic' working-class culture he remembers rather hazily from his childhood, a culture

predicated on brass bands, home and hearth,[34] in opposition to the meretricious triviality of 1950s commercial British television; the Religious Film
Society offers its own low-budget religious pictures, aimed at select
audiences, as an alternative to the scourge of Hollywood. Within little
more than a decade of the founding of the Religious Film Society, Rank,
its treasurer, would be identified with precisely the kind of popular culture
attacked by Adorno and Hoggart. As sponsor of *The Wicked Lady*,
overseer of Britain's own studio system at Pinewood and Denham, and
owner of a great many cinemas, some of which would mysteriously trans-
mogrify in the late 1950s, becoming bingo halls, ten-pin bowling alleys and
even casinos, he fits (at least with the benefit of hindsight) somewhat
uncomfortably into his role as religious film patron. This tension stands, in
miniature, for an essential contradiction at the heart of the Rank experiment, for a confusion between religious and commercial instincts, which
will be explored at length later in the book but is worth observing at the
outset.

The Religious Film Society was, perhaps, jealous of the cinema's influence, an influence which it deplored in Hollywood's hands, but which it
would have liked to exercise itself: the problem was not so much with the
medium as with the message – Hollywood, according to Burnett, had
ignored religion as a subject, or had 'caricatured and misrepresented it'.[35]
This was not strictly true. Some of the American industry's greatest box-
office successes of the previous decade, the 1920s, had had religious
themes: *Four Horsemen of the Apocalypse* grossed $4.5 million in 1921; De
Mille's *The Ten Commandments* had also proved extremely lucrative.
Filmmakers all the way from Griffith (*Intolerance*) to Scorsese (*The Last
Temptation of Christ*) have made at least a loose use of religious subjects.

J. Arthur Rank, not an ardent cinemagoer himself, was on the periphery
of these debates. He wasn't setting out to counter Hollywood, but wished
to use film in a relatively modest way, as a vehicle for religious education in
Sunday schools and Methodist halls. The zealous fringe of the Religious
Film Society had more ambitious, and sometimes even fascistic, plans for
the medium. Burnett had written:

> How can we expect our young people to apply themselves seriously to
> national reconstruction when they revel night after night in such
> orgies of squandermania, idleness and loose living?[36]

and had gone on to list a series of suitably edifying 'shorts' for the young
people to see. These included films quoting from Mussolini, among others,
for use at temperance gatherings. The short *Our Wonderful Body* was to be
prefaced with the following fine words from *Il Duce*: 'I abstain rigidly from
all alcoholic beverages, even from the lightest wines. Wine is never bought
for my household.'[37]

SELLING GOD

John Wesley had been a thoroughly energetic evangelist, travelling thousands and thousands of miles to preach the 'good message', and, with his brother Charles, writing a series of rousing hymns to stoke up the fires of faith. The nineteenth-century industrialists also travelled far and wide, selling commodities as well as God. And Joseph Rank, more than most, had taken a mercantile attitude towards his religion: he saw the converting of souls as being directly akin to the selling of bags of flour. Making the comparison between commerce and religion to his Methodist colleagues, he explained that he had little time for sit-at-home priests who spent (wasted) their days in intricate theological surmising. He preferred a more muscular approach to his Christianity:

> Every Friday I have my travellers before me, and I go over what they have done during the week. If they have done well I urge them to improve on it; but if their account is down, I say, 'You had better do better than this, Mr —, or you and I shall have to part company.' That's what you should say. Ask him how many people he has saved, and if his report is unsatisfactory, get rid of him.[38]

Given the emphasis that the Methodists put on selling, whether in religion or in business, it was highly appropriate that the first picture completed by the Religious Film Society, *The Mastership of Christ*, should star Lax of Poplar, the Nonconformist preacher and evangelist from London's East End, an expert at 'hawking God to the masses'. Costing £2,700, and featuring more than a hundred actors and actresses in the crowd scenes, it was directed by Aveling Ginever, a journalist and advertising man, later to make the far from classic *Cross Beams*, which would receive this tart appraisal in the Rank Viewer's Report:

> Not much can be served by this crude attempt to spread Christianity via the screen. Religious groups may be uncritical to its feebleness, bad direction and indifferent acting, but as a proposition for houses of entertainment, it is of little use.[39]

Mastership as it came to be known, was a modest success. Shot in a week at Merton Park Studios, and premiered in the spring of 1934, it was, as Burnett quickly pointed out, 'avowedly a cinema sermon which could be incorporated in any religious service of any denomination'.[40] Primarily shown in churches and halls, *Mastership* eventually travelled further afield, arriving in the Far East with a missionary expedition, where the film was directly responsible for converting six dissenting Communists to Christianity.[41]

Fiscal and theological differences soon led to a parting of the ways between Rank and Ginever. Rank reckoned that Ginever had overspent on the film and, moreover, didn't like his newfangled approach to the gospels. He therefore found himself another producer, John Corfield, commissioning him to make two shorts, *St Francis of Assisi*, starring the 'unknowns' Greer (*Mrs Miniver*) Garson and Donald (actor-manager) Wolfit, and *Let There Be Love*, for a combined cost of £4,500.[42] Through Corfield, Rank met his new business partner, a 'regal, grey-haired Scotswoman', Lady Yule. Widow of an Anglo-Indian jute baron, a woman with religious convictions to match Rank's own, a great deal of money and an enthusiasm for all manner of equestrian pursuit, Yule had meandered into film as a means of combating boredom, apparently a constant scourge since her husband died. She and Rank joined forces, and fortunes, to form British National in October 1934. The first British National film, *The Turn of the Tide*, released in 1935, turned out to be a landmark, the picture that drew Rank from the fringes into the mainstream of the British industry. Its very title is emblematic, serving as a crest for Rank's bold endeavour to restore the British film industry to former glories. Directed by Norman Walker (an industry veteran, army captain and long-time collaborator with Rank, who would later manage Pinewood Studios as well as make Rank's highest-budget religious picture, *The Great Mr Handel*) and edited by Ian Dalrymple and an uncredited David Lean,[43] the film told of two warring families of 'fisher-folk', the Fosdykes and the Lunns, with the religious elements astutely downplayed. As Norman Walker had observed:

> If the message of the Kingdom of God is to succeed in the cinema it must conceal itself under the guise of entertainment.[44]

Boasting a strong gallery of British character actors, including Moore Marriott, the grey-bearded loon of several Will Hay films, and Geraldine Fitzgerald, later to work with Orson Welles at the Mercury Theater in New York and to be Oscar-nominated for her performance in *Wuthering Heights*, *The Turn of the Tide* won third place at the 1935 Venice Film Festival. The picture was to be distributed in Britain by Gaumont-British, the foremost producing and renting organization of the period. Unfortunately, Gaumont-British proved dithering and dilatory, and did little to promote the film, which consequently sank at the box-office. Rank was stung by this experience of what he estimated to be Wardour Street double-dealing. Chastened, he resolved to set up his own sales outfit and to find his own cinemas:

> He couldn't make good films, films which would entertain people but which would be of reasonable moral value, unless he was in the business.[45]

Through Corfield again, he was introduced to C. M. Woolf, probably Britain's top film executive. A few months before, Woolf had been joint managing director of Gaumont-British, but he had fallen out with other members of the board. Encouraged by Max Schach, the renegade *émigré* producer of *Abdul the Damned*, Woolf decided to set up on his own.[46]

Lord Portal and J. Arthur Rank were the backers behind Woolf's new company, General Film Distributors (GFD), when it was formed in May 1935. Under Woolf's tutelage, Rank left the Religious Film Society behind him. Rather than simply furnishing Methodist halls with projectors or making 20-minute, £2,000 religious shorts, Rank now began to invest in distribution, exhibition and even studios.

1

ON THE WAY TO AN EMPIRE

I am a plain Yorkshireman without the gift of the gab but I am out to do the best for my shareholders.[1]

If I could relate to you some of my various adventures and experiences in the larger film world, you would not only be astonished, but it would, I think, be as plain to you as it is to me that I was being led by God.[2]

Right from the outset, 1933, when he first became involved with the Religious Film Society, Rank's had been a Janus-faced endeavour, a curious collision between business and missionary enthusiasm, a mixture of prudence and recklessness. Within eight or nine years, the somewhat haphazard transformation of the middle-aged suburban businessman from Reigate into the single most influential figure in the British film industry was complete. It was a gradual and unlikely metamorphosis, with no one deal, merger, or acquisition effecting the change, but a steady accumulation of assets leading to the foundation of a film empire as expansive as any in British cinema history.

The film industry into which Rank had dipped his toes when he bought his first projector for Sunday school use was a dense and murky pool. The period has been written about exhaustively elsewhere, but to sketch it in brief, it was the era of the 'quota quickie',[3] the low-budget, rapidly shot films which were made more to fulfil the terms of government legislation than to please audiences, but also of Korda's lavish, international epics which presented British imperial history in a quirky Technicolor light: *The Four Feathers* and *Sanders of the River* were making phlegmatic British colonialists and soldiers into the equivalent of cowboys, with the colonies as the Wild West. On a less warlike footing, the domestic cinema was dominated by that holy trinity of British popular film: George Formby of the gormless smile and twanging ukulele, Gracie Fields, the spunky Lancashire lass, and Jessie Matthews, the 'dancing divinity'. Fields and Formy were purveyors of cheap and cheerful comedy, rooted in community, films like *Sing As We Go* or *Keep Your Seats Please*, which did

17

tremendous business in Britain without ever threatening to crack the American market. By contrast, from the regions of the Strand and Shaftesbury Avenue were emanating high-brow, hidebound West End farces and operettas, whose very titles haughtily hint at their rarefied and rather limited appeal: films like *Be Mine Tonight*, *Bitter Sweet*, *Night and Day* and *After the Ball* transferred woodenly to the screen, offering an illusion of sophistication to snobbish, metropolitan audiences.

In a bizarre and accentuated parody of the Marxian model of the capitalist system, the British film industry rapidly shoots through cycles, boom-crash, boom-crash, with the crashes seeming to last infinitely longer than the booms. Of no decade in British film industry is this more true than the 1930s. The early to mid-1930s witnessed unprecedented expansion and investment: more than 200 features were made in 1936 alone. Never before, never since, have British filmmakers reached this pitch of productivity. However, this proved to be a false dawn: the Wardour Street bubble burst, and the industry lurched back into a severe depression. Producer Michael Balcon later remarked that hardly a film made in the period 'reflected the agony of the times'.[4] While this may have been true, the trials and tribulations of the industry towards the end of the decade, when unemployment stood at over 80 per cent, were quite in keeping with the seismic political upheavals affecting the rest of Europe as it toppled into a second world war.

The 1930s production boom screeched to a halt because the industry's economic foundations were far from stable. Most 1930s movies were funded through borrowing. An elaborate, and ultimately disastrous, system evolved, whereby insurance companies used guarantee policies as security for bank loans to producers. Naive financiers threw money for a whole series of films at producers before the first project in line had either been completed or turned into a profit. Understandably, some of the less scrupulous producers took the money and ran, leaving the insurance companies and banks to pick up the pieces. The Westminster Bank managed to lose more than a million pounds while one small production company, with capital of less than £100, was able to persuade backers to advance it £200,000 for its never-to-be completed endeavours.[5]

The sudden, if belated, realization that they were being fleeced led the financiers to cut short the easy flow of credit. The City shut up its coffers and the entire industry was tainted by the ensuing scandal. Even Alexander Korda, who had started the decade with such *élan*, making the supremely successful *Private Life of Henry VIII*, achieving full-member status of United Artists along with Chaplin, Pickford and Co., and sweet-talking the Prudential Building Society into helping him build his own studios at Denham, was in a financial morass by 1938.[6]

For an insight into the schizophrenia and merry extravagance of the decade, one need only read Jeffrey Dell's satirical novel of 1939, *Nobody*

Ordered Wolves, which lampoons Korda, renaming him Napoleon Bott, the chief of Paradox Film Productions. By the book's end, packs of wild dogs, unused extras for a jungle movie, are scavenging through Bott's studios. The image is apposite: the industry had indeed 'gone to the dogs', an impression reinforced by the Crazy Gang's 1937 vehicle, *Okay for Sound*, which achieves a similar pitch of mayhem as the six madcap music-hall stars run riot on the sound stages while a studio boss, again based on Korda, desperately tries to keep his creditors at bay for long enough to complete the films which will stave off bankruptcy.[7]

With such creative and fiscal anarchy to the forefront, a little *gravitas* was needed. It was an opportune moment for Rank to appear on the scene, in the company of his new partner, Lord Portal.

RANK, PORTAL AND THE GENERAL CINEMA FINANCE CORPORATION

> Wyndham, you're surely not going to interest yourself in that awful film industry?
>
> (Wilcox, 1967: 107)

In 1936, the General Cinema Finance Corporation (GCF) was formed. As *Tribune* journalist and inveterate critic of the Rank Organization, Frederic Mullally later observed, GCF was a bastion of capitalist endeavour. He listed the company's directorate:

> we find ourselves face to face with some of the most outstanding personalities in the world of English finance capital. Lord Portal of Laverstoke . . . Lord Luke, Chairman of Bovril, and with other interests ranging from gold mines to banks and publishing companies . . . Paul Lindenburg, director of vast financial concerns in Britain, Canada, Austria, Rumania and the Netherlands. Leslie William Farrow, holder of four chairmanships, three deputy-chairmanships, and 17 directorships in paper and other interests. And . . . Mr Joseph Arthur Rank.
>
> (Mullally, 1946: 12)

Wyndham Portal, GCF's chairman, was an appropriate figure to head a film finance outfit. His family firm, Portals Ltd and Wiggins Teape, 'made' money, literally as well as figuratively: they were paper manufacturers, supplying material for banknotes in Britain and throughout the world. Portal had enjoined Rank to invest in British film to save it from 'one of its oncoming collapses'.[8] GCF was essentially a consortium of patriotic financiers, a 'league of gentlemen', to borrow the title from a picture Rank would help to finance twenty-five years later. The corporation had a clear affinity with American film-financing outfits. It resembled, for example, the Cinema Finance Corporation set up in 1921 by a group of Los Angeles bankers, who knew precious little about film, but were keen to invest in the new medium, to provide 'outside capital', because they were lured by the glamour of cinema and, more pertinently, the chance of making some easy money.[9]

One of GCF's more surprising interventions in the business was its bold 1936 swoop for a quarter-share of the ailing Hollywood outfit Universal, which had off-loaded most of its theatres in the wake of the depression, and had glumly fallen into receivership by 1933, but was none the less part of the cartel, one of the 'big eight' studios who dominated the American film industry. Barely managing to prop itself up in the grim years of the early 1930s, when all the studios were still reeling under the enormous cost of converting to sound, Universal was notable for its 'horror cycle', a series of pictures existing in bizarre counterpoint to the company's financial plight. (Bela Lugosi, a contract star, had taken his first draught of blood as Dracula in 1930, while Boris Karloff, the definitive screen Frankenstein 'monster', made his initial, tottering steps, with obligatory bolt through neck, in 1931.) Despite Dracula and Frankenstein's best efforts, studio boss Carl Laemmle, one of the original Hollywood pioneers, was obliged to put the studio on the market in 1936 to stave off bankruptcy. A consortium of New York businessmen, led by John Cheever Crowdin (president of Standard Oil), bought the majority of the stock, but Rank, Portal and Co. also invested. (Had Laemmle been able to hold his creditors at bay for a little longer, he would have obtained relief from an unlikely source. Deanna Durbin, 'the spirit and personification of youth', who had been passed over by MGM, was signed by the studio: much to everybody's surprise, her blend of singing neighbourly sweetness immediately caught on – her very first film, *Three Smart Girls*, was a world-wide hit.) Universal was not one of the 'majors'. Without a cinema circuit of its own, the company lacked the resources to compete with MGM or Warner Brothers blockbusters. None the less, from 1936 onward, it turned out a steady stream of popular and accessible movies, epitomized best by Durbin's musicals in the 1930s and by Abbott and Costello's untaxing comedies in the 1940s.

Almost since before the Lumières were born, Hollywood had been investing in and exploiting British cinema. It was rare for the British to buck the trend and buy into the American industry. (That was like the prey investing in the predator.) Rank's subsequent attempt to secure himself a niche in the US market, an endeavour which stirred up controversy on both sides of the Atlantic and which he pursued as if it were a fully fledged moral crusade, had its origin in this early deal with Universal. Not that he was yet the dominant partner in the General Cinema Finance Corporation. (It would take him until 1942 to acquire a majority holding.)

Montagu Norman, governor of the Bank of England and a close friend of Portal, expressed considerable misgivings about GCF's plans to invest in Universal. A haughty and eccentric man, who was so scared of being assassinated that he donned outlandish, but always transparent, disguises when he travelled abroad; an economist whose fiscal plans in the 1930s were far from successful – as Rank's colleague, the former banker, Richard Norton, put it, 'there seems little doubt that his policy of deflation in Britain and pouring money into Germany was disastrous'[10] – Norman held the film industry in some contempt, displaying against cinema a prejudice typical of his class and profession. Portal and Herbert Wilcox, the showman, publicist and producer maverick of British and Dominion Films, a company closely affiliated to GCF and Rank, had approached Norman, hoping to win his support for the proposed raid on Universal's stock. Norman's response is instructive:

> Introductions over, Portal started to outline the Universal deal when Norman broke in with: 'Wyndham, you're surely not going to interest yourself in that awful film industry?' Portal caught my eye and tried to make out a case, but Norman was adamant: *'It's no good, Wyndham, it's unsound. And those dreadful people are not your class. Keep out of it!'*[11]

Wyndham Portal and J. Arthur Rank, the paper magnate and the flour-miller, respectable British capitalists with friends in high places, were indeed unlikely figures to find in the film industry of the late 1930s. The former was chairman of the 1936 Berlin Olympics and the latter was a driving force behind Reigate Sunday school and the 'Cinema for Christ'. Lofty Olympian ideals, religious fervour and patriotism seemed to propel these two forward in their bid to rescue that endangered species, the British film: they both shared the conviction that if they applied sound business practices, like doctors did poultices, they could steer the industry away from crisis. Before GCF's intervention, the most prominent producers, from Alexander Korda to Max Schach, were 'foreign'. This, combined with the fact that they had managed to lose foolhardy investors large lumps of capital, only confirmed the City in its prejudices: its little spasm of confidence in British cinema was long since spent. Assistant Postmaster-General Sir Walter J. Womersley begged the bankers to reconsider their decisions, arguing that the underlying conditions for filmmaking were better than they had been during the short-lived boom:

> We have all the assets except one: we have studios equal to any in the world, first-class producers, artistes and technicians . . . and a beautiful and historic background on which to project ourselves. . . . All we want is money . . . the City unfortunately has not regained the confidence in films which they lost through their experiences a year or two ago.[12]

On the whole, Womersley's pleas were ignored. Film was still regarded by the great and the good as a bastard medium, the 'result of an unholy liaison between the magic lantern and the novelette', as Anthony Asquith had called it[13]: it was not a business which seemed likely to attract much support from traditional/conservative backers who had witnessed the various film finance 'scandals' of the decade. However, Rank and Portal, who entered the industry when most financiers were keen to quit it, were able to prise funds from otherwise reluctant sources. With their secure City backgrounds, their easy access to potentates such as Norman, and their confirmed moral pawkiness, not to mention their own extensive resources, they were given plenty of leeway by the National Provincial Bank, who oversaw Gaumont-British's debts; by the Prudential, Korda's main creditor; by Eagle Star Insurance, who helped fund Odeon Theatres; and by the few remaining institutions prepared to prop up the British film business. They already owned the country's top renting outfit.

GENERAL FILM DISTRIBUTORS

Throughout the 1930s, distributors dominated British films, manipulating the purse-strings at will. They were 'virtually in charge of production, story, cast and presentation'.[14] Before a picture was started, they reserved the right to vet the script and propose stars. Once that picture was complete, they were the first to see it, and were never slow to suggest wholesale changes in producers' cherished would-be masterpieces. Ruefully looking back on the cut-throat decade from the more sheltered vantage point of 1946, David Lean writes of nerve-racking afternoons spent in Wardour Street viewing rooms when the distributors would survey the 'rough cut' of a film, and then, as likely as not, demand it be rejigged.[15] Renters and filmmakers had widely divergent ideas as to what constituted a 'good film' or what would be box-office, and the renters were in the ascendant:

> People who sell and exhibit think that the producers and directors are wild and woolly men who don't know what the public wants.[16]

As most films were financed through distributors' advances, the producers rapidly learned to kow-tow: they suppressed notions of creativity and authorial control, and devoted most of their efforts to pleasing their paymasters.

C. M. Woolf, the doyen of distributors, quickly became Rank's mentor, and was credited with guiding him through the dark vale of Wardour Street, the street where there were rumoured to be 'shadows on both sides'.[17] The image is almost picaresque – the sharp and hardened salesman leading the well-intentioned but bumbling and naive Sunday school teacher along the dangerous Babylonian corridors of Soho film-land as the various rogues and spivs, skulking in doorways, leap out and importune Rank, demanding money for shady film projects. Woolf turns them all down, hurrying his charge on his way.

In his Gaumont-British days, Woolf had already displayed the abrasiveness and intolerance towards producers and directors that were the hallmark of the 1930s British film renter. Alfred Hitchcock was frequently on the sharp end of Woolf's acerbic tongue. *The Lodger*, for example, was deemed 'unshowable' by Woolf.[18] As John Russell Taylor describes in his biography of Hitchcock, Woolf regarded the director as 'a dangerous young intellectual who would ruin the industry given half a chance',[19] and topped his critical demolition of *The Lodger* with an even more destructive appraisal of *The Man Who Knew Too Much*: he 'gave as his considered opinion that it was appalling, absurd, and they could not possibly put it out as it was'.[20] When the film was released, to great critical acclaim, Woolf insisted on showing it as the bottom half of a double bill. The net result: audiences flocked to see it, but it still ended up losing money; second features were always hard pressed to turn a profit.

Given his disdain for Hitchcockery, it is doubtful that Woolf would have had any interest in promoting religious films. However, Woolf and Rank managed to forge a strong business alliance. Woolf taught Rank the ropes, and Rank continued signing cheques; the empire was stuttering into being.

In March 1936, General Film Distributors (GFD), already backed by Rank and Portal, was fully taken over by the General Cinema Finance Corporation (GCF). The advantages for Woolf in his new parent were obvious. In exchange for his 'independence', always a doubtful blessing anyway, he benefited from the tie-up with Universal, whose renting organization in the United Kingdom GFD now absorbed. A steady stream of top-notch material, starting with *Showboat* and the first of the Deanna Durbin vehicles in 1936, helped establish GFD as Britain's prime distribution company. Moreover, GCF, a massive, lumbering and passive entity, with a fully paid-up capital of £1,165,594, could help Woolf in other ways. Most importantly, it provided security for GFD's production programme. Using it as a guarantor, Woolf was able to borrow money from the bank to invest in whichever films he chose.

A cautious man, above all a salesman, who had a horror of extravagance in filmmaking, and had had no qualms about turning down Powell and Pressburger's *One of Our Aircraft Is Missing*, which he judged to be 'too defeatist' for wartime audiences, or refusing to finance Del Giudice's *In Which We Serve*, Woolf was resolutely unadventurous in the type of films he allowed GFD to support. He tended to steer Rank away from prestige, big-budget pictures, instead concentrating on comedies, musicals and spy thrillers, the unchallenging and staple fare of British cinema in the 1930s. Only after Woolf's untimely death in December 1942 would Rank embrace a more expansive, and infinitely more expensive, production policy. (It is inconceivable that the hard-nosed renter of Wardour Street would have countenanced the expensive fripperies of Pascal's *Caesar and Cleopatra* or the Sid Field musical *London Town*, two films to which we will return in later chapters.)

Unlike his boss, who briefly vested his trust in the filmmakers them-selves, Woolf was implacably wary of the artists and creators – 'long hairs' and characters in 'corduroy' as they were dismissively described in the trade press. He thought they lacked all fiscal responsibility and, if given their heads, would do their best to bankrupt their benefactors. He regarded them as wilful children to be kept on short leashes. 'We won't be buggered about!' was his constant refrain,[21] and producers were the ones he was worried were going to take advantage of him. He viewed (British) filmmaking as an occasionally necessary adjunct to distribution and exhi-bition, acceptable if done cheaply and discreetly, but, like most of Britain's renters and cinema-owners, he would probably have been quite content to abandon it altogether, and to show only American movies: distribution and exhibition, the service industries, were infinitely more lucrative, and infi-nitely less risky, than production, which remained a lottery. A confirmed free marketeer, Woolf was perplexed by the government's awkward attempts to animate the cadaver of British cinema through the shock therapy of protective legislation. As *Kinematograph Weekly* reported, he was quite confounded by the plans to maintain quotas in the 1938 Films Act:

> Mr Woolf suggested that it must be obvious that it could not be good for any industry for manufacturers to be forced to make a product; distributors forced to handle it; and the retailer to retail it; when there was no compulsion on the public in any part of the world, including this country, to pay their money to see that product.[22]

However, his appetite whetted by *The Turn of the Tide*, Rank was committed to production, and had already invested in his own studios.

PINEWOOD STUDIOS

In collaboration with the wealthy Sheffield building tycoon Sir Charles Boot, who had originally found the property, and his old partner from British National Lady Yule, J. Arthur Rank acquired Heatherden Hall, a country house in Buckinghamshire which had formerly belonged to Grant Morden, Canadian financier and erstwhile MP, now fallen on hard times. Heatherden Hall boasted the largest private swimming pool in Europe. Soon it would be the site for the most up-to-date film studios.

Pinewood was built at great speed, and at a cost of more than £1 million: 'the first brick had been laid in late January, 1936; and the first picture began in September, 1936'.[23] As Alan Wood observes, Rank was keen to bring factory principles to bear in the wayward craft of filmmaking, and having seen the wastage and delay entailed in shooting *Turn of the Tide* at a studio, Elstree, with only one sound stage, resolved to build a thoroughly modern complex. 'When the studio was finished, it had 72,490 square feet of floor space in five stages.'[24]

Despite being blessed during an unusual ceremony by Dr Gregory, a senior figure in the Methodist Church, who was later to lend his initial and his spiritual expertise to Rank's religious outfit, GHW (Gregory/Hake/ Walker); despite its name, with its conscious evocation of Hollywood; despite its décor (complete with Turkish bath, bar and fruit machine, it was half-way between country club and health spa); despite being state-of-the-art (Charles Boot had visited Hollywood to ascertain what a modern film factory should look like); and despite British National's commitment to use one of the sound stages: the studios soon ran into difficulty. As their managing director Richard Norton, and his assistant Anthony Havelock-Allan, quickly found out:

> When you run a studio, two things happen: there are periods when you have to turn away customers and there are periods when you have empty studio space. It's much more variable than a hotel. There aren't even seasons when people make or don't make films.[25]

Pinewood's opening neatly coincided with the beginning of the film slump of the late 1930s, when production seemed to go out of season. Matters weren't helped by the 1938 Films Act: now, in its bid to rid the screen of the notorious quota quickies, the government introduced a 'treble quota' system, which encouraged producers to make fewer, but 'better' – or, at least, more expensive – British films. If a picture cost three times the prescribed quota minimum, it counted, for quota purposes, as three films. This, combined with the burgeoning wariness of investors, led to a dramatic downturn in production, a consequent rise in unemployment and slow, slow business at Pinewood, when depended on its bookings from outside producers to make money on four of its five sound stages.

A 'convenient' fire at Elstree Studios in early 1936 had persuaded Herbert Wilcox to transfer the British and Dominion (B&D), production programme to Pinewood, but British National and B&D between them could not fill the sound stages. (At the time of the Elstree blaze, B&D's assets were frozen: although Wilcox had won a contract to make quota films for Paramount, and although he was one of the few consistently bankable producers of the period, he invariably over-extended the company, committing its every spare penny to production. The fire thus came as something of a relief. As Norton, a B&D executive at the time, recalled in his autobiography, 'When I got to Elstree I found that everything had gone up in flames except, by some miracle, the vaults and cutting rooms, which would have involved dangerous explosions. B&D got a large cheque from the insurance company, representing more cash than we had ever had for years.'[26]

An aristocratic, monocle-wearing ex-banker, injured in the First World War, who had achieved a certain notoriety in his youth by running up personal debts in excess of £40,000,[27] and who was as well known for his motor-racing stunts as for his financial dexterity, the Hon. Richard Norton arrived at Pinewood via United Artists and B&D, and straightaway came up with an ingenious solution for keeping the studios busy and the staff and technicians employed. He set up a small subsidiary company, Pinebrook, which was designed to make low-budget films when there were gaps in studio bookings. Havelock-Allan cut his teeth as a producer on these 'fillers', which ranged from the instantly forgettable, films such as *A Spot of Bother* or *Lightning Conductor*, to popular musicals like *The Lambeth Walk* (adapted from *Me and My Girl*, the successful West End play) and an inventive comedy thriller, *This Man Is News*, shot for £14,000 but which made ten times that amount at the box-office. Pinebrook was a hazardous experiment which spawned a major innovation in film finance: however cheaply the pictures were made, Norton generally found it a struggle to pay the wages. Every Friday, he remembered, 'I would have to make a dash to our dear friends the National Provincial Bank for a bit more on the overdraft' (Norton, 1954: 184). He therefore persuaded cast and crew to invest part of their wages in the films:

> You took a lesser salary but you invested in the film a part of your salary. Let's say your salary should have been £2,500. You took £2,000 and had £1,000 which would be paid back if the film made a profit.[28]

Nowadays, it is common to give top actors and actresses 'percentages'. Norton, though, was among the first to use the scheme. With the 'Norton Formula', as it became known, Pinebrook never lost money.

In 1937, Rank bought out Lady Yule's share in Pinewood, becoming chairman of the studios, while selling her his 'interest' in British National. His subsequent moves to make his a fully integrated combine, with control over production, distribution and exhibition, were influenced by these early experiences at Pinewood. Just as he had found that the renters selling *Turn of the Tide* were unreliable, he now discovered that if he had to depend on the whims of outside producers to fill his studios, he would be liable to endure long periods of inactivity. Woolf had persuaded his former colleagues at Gaumont-British, still reeling from a disastrous attempt to get their pictures into the American market, to transfer a large part of their production to Pinewood. None the less, it remained a 'rent studio', with Woolf not only steering Rank away from investing in epics, but even expressing disapproval of Norton's tiny Pinebrook experiment, which was making films at a cost of £1 a foot.

DENHAM

Rank's increasing influence in British film was underlined when he acquired his second major studios, Denham, which had been built by Alexander Korda on the back of *The Private Life of Henry VIII* and the goodwill of the Prudential Building Society, Korda's patient and doughty backers, but which had run into serious difficulty by 1938, when Korda found himself £1 million in the red. His big-budget extravaganzas, *The Four Feathers* and *Elephant Boy* among them, had failed to repeat *Henry VIII*'s success in the American market: he was having difficulty in juggling his twin roles as studio chief, in charge of finance, and 'creative' producer. Eventually, even the Prudential's patience wore thin, and Rank combined with the massive insurance company, one of the bulwarks of British film finance, to take Denham out of Korda's hands.

With Hitler and the Second World War on the not-very-distant horizon, and following the advice of Richard Norton, whose days as a banker with Kuhn, Loeb had convinced him that 'you are often better off with a large liability than a small one',[29] Rank pooled his resources, setting up a new company, Denham and Pinewood Studios Ltd (D&P), and, when the army requisitioned Pinewood for storage purposes (the studios also later became the home base for the Crown Film Unit), concentrated all his production at Denham: it was easier to keep one studio full than two, and ownership of both Denham and Pinewood increased Rank's borrowing power. (Eventually, in 1944, he bought out the Prudential's interest in D&P Studios).

Rank's holdings were growing apace. The distribution network was in place. He had access to studios. However, a vital missing link was a cinema chain: the General Cinema Finance Corporation had bought up a string of cinemas in the East End of London, but did not have exhibition outlets to compare with those of ABC or Gaumont-British.

ODEON

As Odeon was to be at the core of Rank's empire, it is worth recapping the company's brief history. The first Odeon was built in Perry Barr, Birmingham, in 1930, and was a grand, spacious picture palace, neo-Egyptian in design. Oscar Deutsch, son of a prosperous Hungarian scrap metal merchant who had made his fortune in Britain, didn't start building Odeons in bulk until 1933, when his mission to entertain the nation, which at least partially explains the acronym – Oscar Deutsch Entertains Our Nation – took shape.

By the mid-1930s, Odeons were popping up all over the place, the cinematic equivalent of rabbits. Like present-day supermarkets, the cinemas created commercial land around them. This helped Deutsch secure finance for their construction. He cleverly played off his backers, Eagle Star Insurance, with local builders, inducing the latter to do £5,000-worth of work on a cinema for 'free' and then persuading the former to advance him £5,000 – which he in turn forwarded to the latter – on the grounds of the work already complete. As Jeffrey Richards explains in *The Age of the Dream Palace*, he was thus able to conjure cinemas out of thin air, without the inconvenience of having to use money of his own to pay for them.[30]

While the Odeons were primarily concentrated outside city centres, in the leafy suburbs – they were, after all, a 'better class' of theatre – Deutsch had bought and demolished the Alhambra, Leicester Square, replacing it with an Odeon, the flagship of his organization and the most prominent cinema in the country, in 1936. By that year, there were already 150 Odeons, and the circuit, valued at £10 million, was still growing. Although it would never be as large as ABC, which had 474 cinemas in 1938, the chain would have doubled in size before it fell into Mr Rank's hands.

Architecturally, the Odeons had a clear identity of their own, fusing modernist and art deco styles:

> The genuine Odeons were supremely comfortable with clear sight-lines, striking exteriors leading to compact auditoriums that were functionally designed to focus attention on the screen. They represented the first clear break with the traditional styles inherited from the theatre and were at the opposite pole from the preposterous but entertaining cinemas that set audiences under stars twinkling in a blue ceiling traversed by cloud patterns.[31]

Like the famous Balaban and Katz theatres in Chicago in the 1920s, Deutsch's Odeons were extravagant in design for a good reason: 'the exterior of each theatre served as a massive outdoor advertising display'.[32] Not only had Deutsch appreciated that the 'rise of the suburbs' – 4 million semi-detached, suburban houses were built in the inter-war years – provided him with a potential new audience:

> One of the reasons for the increase in middle-class patronage was the spread of cinemas to the middle-class suburbs. . . . Oscar Deutsch's promise to put a ring of Odeons round London resulted in the appearance of not less than nine in London suburbs in 1934 and ten in 1936.
>
> (Richards, 1984: 16)

He also realized, as did Rank, that cinemas which did more than merely sell films, which became focuses for local and community events, providing, for instance, low-price Saturday matinees for children, would engender a far greater degree of loyalty in cinemagoers than the average, not inappropriately named, 'flea-pits'.

Deutsch had an ambivalent attitude towards British cinema. Although he professed loyalty to British films, and claimed he wished to see them compete on equal terms, and in equal numbers, with the best of the Hollywood pictures, he wasn't keen to fund their making himself: in 1937, when Odeon became a public company, with a share capital of £6 million, he promised his new shareholders that he would never allow their money to be squandered on film production. Perhaps he made the promise reluctantly, worried that no investors would come forward to support a film finance outfit at a time when British filmmaking was again on the brink of a crisis. Whatever the case, Deutsch's promise to the shareholders that he would steer Odeon clear of production was not one which Rank would feel compelled to keep.[33]

Deutsch was eager to expand overseas. In particular, he was keen to export his cinemas to North America. Such a venture was bound to be expensive. Although he carried on building Odeons in Britain right up till the very eve of war, opening two new theatres, in Elmers End and at Hendon, in the last week of August 1939, it was rumoured that he had over-extended his company. Construction delays, largely occasioned by the shortage of steel and other materials (already, with war imminent, being diverted to the armaments industry), fuelled the rumours further. To quell them, and to attract new money, Deutsch had made a second debenture issue in 1938. It was at this stage that Rank invested, buying 7,000 preference and 4,000 ordinary shares, and moving on to Odeon's board in January 1939. Quite apart from his overseas ambitions, Deutsch had already hinted at his visions of empire by bidding, unsuccessfully, for the ailing giant Gaumont-British in late 1938. Despite being rebuffed, his position was stronger than it had ever been. Not only was he supported by Rank. He was also backed by United Artists, who owned 50 per cent of Odeon Cinema Holdings.[34] If anybody looked likely to establish a stranglehold on the British industry, it was Deutsch. However, the Odeon boss didn't live long enough to realize his ambitions:

> The death of Oscar Deutsch means the passing of another of those paternal dictatorships which have contributed so much to the growth of Kinema.[35]

After Deutsch's sudden death, a victim of cancer aged only 48, in December 1941, his wife and associates overcame their scruples (in some cases, intense ones – Deutsch's partner George Elcock had no liking for the Methodist magnate and wanted to run the company himself) and sold up to Rank. Not only was he inheriting a thriving theatre chain – 1941 had seen record Odeon profits of £1,530,539 – Rank also acquired Deutsch's brilliant young accountant John Davis, later to be chairman and managing director of the Rank Organization, and Earl St John, a 'showman' from Baton Rouge, Louisiana and former pageboy to Sarah Bernhardt, who would head production at Pinewood throughout the 1950s.

Chairman of the General Cinema Finance Corporation, chairman of General Film Distributors, chairman of Denham and Pinewood Studios . . . and king hereafter? Rank's rise to the top of the British film industry was rapid, if erratic, and his pre-eminence was finally confirmed when he acquired Gaumont-British.

GAUMONT-BRITISH

In the late 1930s, everybody was after Gaumont-British: its precarious financial state combined with its ownership of more than 300 cinemas and numerous subsidiary companies, including Baird Television, made it ripe for takeover. The decade had begun promisingly enough for the combine: Michael Balcon and C. M. Woolf were at the helm of a sustained Gaumont-British drive on the American market – Gaumont-British had become the first foreign company to establish a nation-wide sales organization in the USA. However, in spite of some minor successes in the mid-1930s, notably with Hitchcock's *The Thirty-Nine Steps* and *The Man Who Knew Too Much*, the American adventure ended badly, and Gaumont-British was floundering by the decade's end. Both Balcon and Woolf had long since left for pastures new, Balcon for MGM and then Ealing, and Woolf, as we have seen, to set up GFD.

For all its debts and obligations, Gaumont-British proved remarkably resistant to suitors. Founded in 1927, in the wake of the Cinematograph Films (Quota) Act of that year, which seemed to promise protection for British filmmakers (it is no coincidence that British and Dominion, British Lion and British International Pictures all sprang to life at the same time), the various selling and producing branches of Gaumont-British were administered by the three Ostrer brothers, Isidore, Maurice and Mark. Isidore, president of the company since 1929, an economist and occasional poet, a consummate businessman who took pleasure in complexity, in weaving elaborate financial arabesques, had concentrated control of Gaumont-British in a tiny trust, the Metropolis and Bradford. In this trust, which seemed to outsiders to be hermetically sealed, there were 10,000 shares; Ostrer and his colleagues owned 5,100 while Fox owned 4,900. (Ostrer, much to the displeasure of some of his associates, who were terrified that their company might fall into American hands, had sold the Hollywood studio a sizeable stake in the early 1930s to help finance Gaumont-British's conversion to sound.[36])

Rank's chances of broaching the Metropolis and Bradford were slim. As Deutsch had already discovered, Ostrer was not prepared to sell. And John Maxwell, the canny, tough Glaswegian solicitor and head of ABC, had also come to grief in the course of a takeover bid: in 1936, he invested £600,000 in Gaumont-British blithely, but incorrectly, assuming he was purchasing a controlling interest. In fact, he had been hoodwinked into spending his half-million plus on non-voting shares. Although Maxwell didn't realize it, Ostrer had engineered a fiendishly complicated set of checks and balances to deter predators: any aspiring buyer needed Fox approval – in Maxwell's case, this had not been forthcoming. As a token concession for his outlay, Maxwell was allowed a 5-year option on the Metropolis and Bradford shares. Should Fox change their mind and sanction a sale, he was to be given first bid. (This wasn't much of a consolation. Maxwell, on the verge of establishing his own empire, was left grasping nothing, the laughing-stock of Wardour Street. Having been duped by the Ostrers, his health soon deteriorated: he died a premature death in 1940.) Nor were Fox in a much better position. They may have owned 49 per cent of the vital shares, but they weren't allowed representation on the Gaumont-British Board – non-British shareholders had no voting rights. They were little more than the gate-keepers. Nobody could buy Gaumont-British without their consent. It thus came as something of a surprise when, in October 1941, the *Kinematograph Weekly* reported:

> An important development in the British kinema field became known over the weekend when the news broke that the Ostrer brothers were on the verge of selling the control of Gaumont-British to C. M. Woolf, J. A. Rank and Lord Portal, their associates in General Cinema Finance Corporation.
>
> (*Kinematograph Weekly*, 23 October 1941, p. 3)

In the late autumn of 1941, making an outlay of roughly £750,000, Rank bought the controlling interest in the hitherto sacrosanct Metropolis and Bradford Trust. It wasn't as if he had purchased Gaumont-British outright. There were still 5 million ordinary (non-voting) shares belonging to a great variety of shareholders, many of whom were outraged that an outsider could wrest away control of their company. Ostrer, for private as well as business reasons,[37] had agreed to sell, and Rank did not so much circumvent the Fox veto as ignore it. It was probably Rank's most significant coup. As the trade papers were quick to note:

> It can be seen that the ownership of a small fraction of the equity interest carries with it the control of a large company in which the public has invested large lumps of capital. . . . Obviously, it is not income from the investment that is primarily desired.[38]

Rank's disbursement gave him influence over everything from price of admission to production itself. Almost overnight, he established a film empire: when the coils had been untangled and it transpired that he owned two of the three major circuits, Gaumont-British and Odeon (an aggregate

31

of over 600 theatres), the prime renting organization, GFD, and the best available studio, Denham, as well as Pinewood and Gainsborough, there was a general state of amazement. One has only to read the journals of the time to register Rank's 'shock effect'. Before late 1941, his appearances in the pages of the *Kinematograph Weekly* and the *Daily Film Renter* are relatively fleeting: he is one among a whole host of names, and is nearly always mentioned in conjunction with Portal or Woolf. After he takes over at Gaumont-British, he is an ever-present: it is rare not to find his name emblazoned across the front page. By 1945, a journalist was able to write the following about the magnate who had previously been characterized by his relatively low public profile:

> One day somebody with a sense of humour will have to try and produce a film trade journal without mentioning the name of Arthur Rank in it . . . Rank remains the chief news centre on both sides of the Atlantic.
>
> (*Kinematograph Weekly*, 2 August 1945, p. 4)

Rank's frequent refrain that he was 'guided by God', his sense that his own progress through the labyrinth of the British film industry was preordained, was viewed rather more sceptically by his critics, who attributed his rapid acquisition of a fully fledged film empire to luck as much as to divine intervention. Rachael Low has detailed the new vistas of opportunity which opened up with astonishing regularity for the Methodist film magnate,[39] veritable partings of the Red Sea. A spate of deaths in the upper echelons of the industry caused a vacuum,. John Maxwell, potentially a fearsome rival at ABC, died in 1940. Deutsch died in 1941. C. M. Woolf, who would doubtless have modified Rank's production policy, died in 1942. Lady Yule, whose commitment to film was somewhat intermittent, chose to follow her own furrow at British National. Korda, temporarily, was on the decline. Rank's business partners, Lord Portal, Lord Luke and the others, gradually dropped out of the scene. And Isidore Ostrer's wife was ill: Ostrer no longer wanted the full-time responsibility of running Gaumont-British. The benighted state of the industry in the early years of the war, which led to a terrific decline in the share prices of British film interests, also helped.

There are two competing narratives: one has Rank as the saviour of a business close to collapse, who put his money where his faith was – in the British film – when all others were battening down the hatches; the other, less mythic, depicts him as an opportunist who took advantage of exceptional circumstances – the deaths of his rivals, the downturn provoked by Hitler – to buy up what he could at bargain basement prices. A certain schizophrenic quality in the attacks on Rank which soon began to appear in the Press, perhaps as indicative of Rank's own confused motives (that war in his psyche between business and benevolence) as of any prejudice on the part of the journalists, blurs matters further, Rank is, at once, 'a gentle man as well as a gentleman',[40] the indulgent, warm-hearted evangelist who brought all his Methodist enthusiasm to bear on the film industry, and the scheming, reactionary capitalist philistine. Much to the vexation of commentators, Rank manages to be both wolf and lamb.

There is no denying that Rank was capable of ruthlessness. In 1939, for instance, he swooped under Maxwell' and ABC's noses to buy the newly completed amalgamated studios at Elstree,[41] writing a six-figure cheque himself, from his private account, to avoid the delays that setting up deals with bankers and investors would have entailed. And what did he do with these brand-new studios? He promptly leased them to the government for storing records. As Richard Norton put it:

It was a nice stroke of business, as Rank had got a Government security for an investment which checkmated a rival.[42]

If he really had a commitment to production in general rather than to the narrower interests of his own group, critics argued,[43] he would surely have allowed Maxwell to buy (and use) Elstree: already, as the state commandeered studios left, right and centre, space was at a premium, and here he was, wantonly sacrificing it, merely to thwart a rival.

Shortly after the war, as the film empire had continued to expand, the *Daily Express*'s city editor Stewart Gillies had calculated that 'for an investment of around £1,700,000', Rank carried control of assets valued at £50 million, a case of 'a very little tail wagging a very large dog' (*Daily Express*, 4 March 1945). Gillies had gone on to detail Rank's various holdings and how they were organized. Just as Gaumont-British had been controlled by the Metropolis and Bradford, a tiny institution by comparison with the company as a whole, Rank's interests were all directed by the shareholders in a private £100 company, Manorfield Investments, which was 96 per cent owned by Rank and his wife. The phenomenon of £96 controlling several million, of so much influence being concentrated in a single figure, was as alarming to critics as the speed with which the value of Rank's holdings had increased. He seemed to have the Midas touch. As Moore Raymond put it in the *Sunday Dispatch*:

It isn't what Rank has done that they're worrying about – it's what he *might* do if he felt so inclined.

(*Sunday Dispatch*, 6 August 1944)

In only nine years, from 1933 to 1942, Rank had laid the basis of his film empire. The achievement is all the more remarkable when one remembers that cinema was not his primary interest in this period: he was still a managing director at Joseph Rank Ltd, a full-time executive in the family flour business. Somehow, almost unconsciously, he had cut a swathe through the dense and impenetrable thicket of the 1930s film industry. However, his flexibility, ruthlessness and imagination had been applied exclusively to film 'business': the exigencies of film production he left to others. As his daughter puts it, 'he was a man of action and great thought, a man of vision, though not aesthetically . . . but then he bought the brains to do that for him'.[44]

Rank was an anomaly, a hugely powerful film mogul who, by all accounts, had no particular liking for the medium with which he had become involved and certainly didn't profess to understand it, but none the less insisted that it was more than money that motivated him. It was his policy not to comment on any films made under his auspices, 'he didn't feel qualified to judge';[45] his attitude, though refreshingly downbeat and honest, aggrieved critics and producers alike – the producers were liable to get upset, and ask what they had done wrong, when Rank walked out of screenings without making so much as a murmur about the films he had seen: the critics, for their part, would impugn Rank's motives, which were as mysterious as his movie preferences. If he wasn't in the film business for love, it must have been money he was after. Religion and patriotism weren't at all convincing as concepts to Wardour Street sceptics.

Against the backdrop of a country at war, Rank loomed large. As soon as he took over Gaumont-British, the first quibbles about his 'monopolistic tendencies' began to be heard.

2

WAR AND MONOPOLY

> The fronts are everywhere. The trenches are dug in the towns and the
> streets. Every village is fortified. Every road is barred. The front lines
> run through the factories.[1]

Throughout the war, British film production had been running at a fraction
of its capacity, rarely producing more than fifty films in a year. However,
there was a consensus, both critical and popular, expressed in fans' box-
office preferences and in the lengthy film columns of the 'highbrow'[2]
papers and magazines, that the industry was making up in terms of
accomplishment for what it lacked in quantity. Roger Manvell, the influential critic and editor of the *Penguin Film Review*, wrote in 1946 of 'The
great quality of British cinema, its independence and variety of style'.[3]
Manvell attributed this quality to the fact that British film was a micro-
industry, small and intimate: filmmakers possessed 'an individuality of
style contrasting strongly with the rubber-stamp Hollywood
entertainment'.[4]

British films, the critics claimed, were 'crafted' whereas Hollywood
movies were manufactured. The key recurrent phrases in the *Observer*,
Sight and Sound and the *New Statesman* include 'sincerity', 'realism' and
'integrity'. Film historian John Ellis, writing in the mid-1970s, combs
through these critical texts, suggesting that a certain 'radical humanism',[5] a
mild, suburban iconoclasm, which would play its part in electing the Attlee
government, galvanized the critics. While Ellis risks homogenizing a discrete collection of individual writers (Whitebait, Manvell, C. A. Lejeune,
Dilys Powell and Richard Winnington among them) who cannot always be
banded together as happily as he suggests, and while he might profitably
have looked outside the narrow band of critics represented by the so-called
quality press and examined what was being written about cinema in the
popular press, he none the less offers a useful analysis of how the idea and
discourse of the 'quality' film became fixed during this period, establishing
an immediate point of reference against which any other kind of picture,
which did not conform at least roughly with these critics' tenets, could be
measured.

For Rank, the operative term was not 'quality' but 'prestige'. He even named the subsidiary company that distributed *Henry V* in America as Prestige Pictures.[6] As we shall see, on every level, economic, critical and political, there was a tension between these two conceptions, 'prestige' and 'quality'. Only occasionally did they mesh.

THE WAR YEARS AND THEIR AFTERMATH

The war years, 1939–45, are probably the most documented in British film history, and for obvious reasons: they marked a 'golden period' when the British cinema broke out of its Hollywood shackles and discovered an identity of its own. The story of the transformation has assumed almost mythic proportions, running in tandem with celebratory narratives of the war as a whole, which have the British snatching victory from the jaws of defeat at Dunkirk as the brave young knights of the air, in their Spitfires,[7] shoot down improbable numbers of Nazi planes and cheery East Enders have a knees-up in the underground shelters despite the cataract of German bombs raining down on London throughout the blitz.

In September 1939, the government had temporarily closed all places of entertainment, a 'very craven measure' as Sidney Gilliat described it.[8] Studios were rapidly requisitioned by the armed forces, and filled with sugar and other vital provisions. For a brief period, there was a very real danger that British feature film production might be abandoned altogether: shortages, rationing, which affected every part of filmmaking from set construction to costumes and make-up, the lack of studio space, the enforced absence of up to two-thirds of the technicians, who had been 'called up', and the voluntary absence of those select few who had hot-footed it to Hollywood as soon as hostilities were announced,[9] threatened to destroy the industry or, even worse, expose it to Hollywood takeover. (Warner Brothers had already invested heavily in ABC, and MGM and Fox had holdings in Gaumont-British, while some of United Artists' money was in Odeon.) However, the industry was 'saved', with a host of names stepping into the breach, ready to take credit for the rescue. Some argue that Anthony Asquith's mother Margot, with a well-placed word or two in the ears of prominent cabinet members,[10] preserved the British cinema for her son's sake: Anthony 'Puffin' Asquith was president of the ACT, and the union also took some credit for the rescue. Then there was Gabriel Pascal, way over schedule on *Major Barbara* and determined to keep Denham Studios open until his film was finished regardless of the prying attentions of requisitioning British army officers and the constant interruption of German bombers. Frantic lobbying; Korda's quick completion of an effective propaganda film, *The Lion Has Wings*, 'shop-made, edited and directed in less than a month' (Powell, 1987: 335), which juxtaposed images of Britain's brave footballers on sacred Wembley turf with those of goose-stepping Nazis; Lady Yule' and Rank's commitment to production through British National and GFD: these were other factors contributing to the industry's preservation. Soon, the early government assertion that feature film production during a time of crisis was an unwonted luxury was rebuffed. Industry veterans still remembered how British cinema had been devastated by the First World War,[11] and they didn't want the same thing to happen again. More than anybody, Ealing Studio boss Michael Balcon trumpeted the importance of film to the war effort, exhorting technicians to keep to their craft and not to feel guilty about being away from the 'front line'. In early 1941, when the industry was still under threat, he wrote these feisty words in the *Kinematograph Weekly*:

> Realize the potential importance of your work and be proud of it. Don't be ashamed of it. . . . While this fight for recognition goes on it is essential that the hardcore of the industry be preserved. Stick to it! The time will come during this war when a man behind a film camera will command the same respect as a man behind a gun.[12]

In spite of an increase in seat prices, largely brought about by the government's upping of entertainment tax, a subject to be dealt with later (see chapter 7), and in spite of the continuing threat to safe spectatorship presented by German bombs, attendances at cinemas rocketed, eventually reaching the point where, it was calculated, everybody in Britain under the age of 40 went to at least fifty-three feature films a year.[13] Cinemagoers were too phlegmatic to be put off by Hitler: 'The threat of death was soon generally accepted as a normal risk; audiences slipped back into their old routine of entertainment'.[14] They would sit still as an intertitle appeared on the screen, warning about bombing and announcing: 'The show will go on but if you wish to leave please do so QUIETLY.'[15] Not only did they defy the blitz – and the potentially alarming statistic that a full 160 cinemas had been destroyed – this new, hardier breed of cinemagoers began to show a preference for British film over American product:

> One of the most marked phenomena of these later stages of the War was the genuine and unforced interest in British pictures.
>
> (Morgan, 1948a: 72)

There was a variety of reasons for this sharp, though sometimes over-stated, swing in loyalties. Before the war, in the troubled 1930s, Hollywood had held almost uncontested dominion over the cinemas of the UK. Now, at last, British filmmakers had found a theme, a genre – the war picture – which was all their own. For understandable reasons, the French and Russian industries, potential rivals, had more or less closed down shop; there were few pictures depicting the siege of Leningrad or the Resistance in Paris. British films of the 1930s may have been conspicuous by their failure to address the social issues of the day or to reflect the 'agony of the times', but a world war was too monstrous a phenomenon to pass over in favour of West End farce, Edgar Wallace spy thrillers and cheap and cheerful seaside comedies. The war was a universal, affecting everybody: as a subject for movies, it could easily overcome the class and regional barriers which had previously split British audiences. Just as the war was, in Angus Calder's phrase, 'a People's War', so the cinema, at least to a degree, became a people's cinema.[16]

Without equipment, with technicians obliged to use creaking, elderly cameras, booms and cranes, the filmmakers had to learn to improvise. Like their colleagues in other fields, the brilliant 'boffins' and scientists busy inventing radars and bouncing bombs;[17] or like the fashion lovers, starved of cloth, colour and material, but who none the less managed to patch themselves together extravagant costumes; or like the fat bald man in the famous Ministry of Information short who discovers he can have just as good a splash in a bath with only 5 inches of water as in one which was full; or like Dadaist Kurt Schwitters, interned on the Isle of Man, who 'made collages out of everything to hand',[18] including stale porridge and cigarette packets: British film producers learned to improvise, and came up with some surprisingly successful solutions to some thorny problems. Take, for instance, Powell and Pressburger's response to the shortage of extras when they were filming *The Life and Death of Colonel Blimp*: in 1942, spare bodies were hard to come by. Those who weren't at war were busy on the Home Front, in the fields or in the armaments industry. In *Blimp*'s prison camp scenes, which in normal times would have required a small army of extras, Powell and Pressburger filled the field outside Denham Studios, where the action was being shot, with dozens of dummies, sacks of straw in tattered army uniforms. Even today, with the film restored in a spanking new print, nobody notices that half the prisoners are not 'real'.

In the discourse of the 'quality film', *realism* is probably the key term. Yet the very exigencies of wartime production, when you had to 'make do and mend'[19] if you couldn't afford or find the *real* thing, seemed to legislate against it: Britain's wartime cinema is often (literally) characterized by its fabrication. Lean and Coward's *In Which We Serve*, perhaps the most famous war film of all, was shot in a tank of water at Denham; Coward, Mills and the other survivors in the lifeboat were never actually at sea at all. While the opposite was true of Pat Jackson's *Western Approaches*, a drama-documentary which cast real fishermen on a real sea, the *realism* critics cling to, the kernel of their new-found faith in British cinema, seems to be more a feature of the story-lines chosen, the style of acting and the arduous working conditions, than a fully fledged aesthetic aim of the filmmakers. (Even in documentary, in the many films made by the Crown Film Unit and the Ministry of Information, the term remains problematic.[20]) However elusive as a concept, 'realism' did serve as a means of distinguishing British pictures from their American counterparts, thus helping to carve out a new, discrete identity for British filmmakers: the 'realist' British film sets itself squarely in opposition to Hollywood, which Rank always called 'Fairyland'.[21] American exhibitors acknowledge the difference between the two film cultures, some of them going as far as to attribute the style of British filmmaking to the British weather:

> The British weather is one reason why British features have duller, and also more *realistic*, hues . . . outdoor colors in England are generally duller. To maintain consistency, directors usually make their indoor scenes conform.[22] (emphases added)

As British filmmakers were finding their footing, Hollywood was losing its touch. Anthony Havelock-Allan, a prominent figure in the British revival, recalls:

> American pictures were slightly out of tune, not so many, not so good, not containing the kinds of names that took people into the cinema. Because the country was feeling patriotic . . . things about English people, that were funny about them or dramatic about them, they wanted to see them. . . . If there had been stronger competition, maybe they wouldn't have . . . it was a very good period, when the odds weren't against us, as they nearly always are, now particularly.[23]

(Havelock-Allan's emphasis on 'English' is apt: British films never achieved quite the same popularity north of the border as they did in England: throughout the war, the Scots, who were ardent cinemagoers, remained as resistant to domestic fare as they had always been. This is hardly surprising when one considers how infrequently Scottish characters or themes were ever aired on the screen.)

Hollywood in sunny California, thousands of miles removed from war-torn Europe, and chagrined to lose several of its foreign markets to the conflict, was out of sync, at least until about 1943, when it too began to experience a 'war boom'.[24] American filmmakers were hard pressed to achieve that inscrutable element of 'realism' so cherished by British critics and fans alike. Their estrangement from their primary foreign client is underlined by their response to documentary. Hugh Stewart, an officer in the Army Film Unit, recalls being somewhat surprised by the last-minute American intervention on his project *Tunisian Victory*. Originally mooted as a US/UK co-production, the documentary had been made in its entirety by the British, and was already late in the editing stage; Roy Boulting, Hugh Stewart and James Hodson, the trio behind the picture, were making the finishing touches: 'We were sitting in the theatre dubbing when a telegram came. Colonel Capra would like to see you at the Grosvenor House Hotel.'[25]

Capra's rushes were grafted on to the film, which was re-edited, presented as an Anglo-American co-production and distributed by MGM. Ultimately, the film comprised some not very effective battle footage from Africa taken by Hugh Stewart and the British team (wars, haphazard, hard to light, tend to be notoriously difficult to film; as Stewart puts it, 'You can't say to a German tank, "Would you mind doing that again?"'[26]) and some immaculate scenes shot by Capra and the Americans, who, however, hadn't even bothered to visit the site of battle, getting no closer to Tunisia than London, but had shot their 'documentary' scenes back in Hollywood.

A comparison between *Mrs Miniver*, Hollywood's saccharine vision of Britain at war, and the stiff upper-lips of 'our boys in the lifeboat' in *In Which We Serve* suggests Hollywood had gotten the emotional brew all wrong: more salt, less sugar was needed for British heroics.

Still, it is easy to over-estimate the shift in the balance of power. Although Hollywood was producing fewer pictures, had lost some of its top filmmakers (Capra, George Stevens and others) to the armed forces, and was generating less money abroad, the latter part of the war proved immensely profitable (MGM made a record $166 million gross in 1944) and American films still held sway over British cinemas. Whatever the quality of British films, and whatever the degree of enthusiasm for them, there were too few produced to upset American domination of UK cinemas. In 1944 only thirty-eight British features were released, less than one a week. And they had some tough competition. *Gone With The Wind*, which prompted a rare family outing to London by the Ranks,[27] ran for most of the war in Leicester Square. *Citizen Kane* provoked debate in the pages of the ACT journal, the *Cine-Technician*, where opinion was firmly divided as to whether it was a work of genius or of meretricious sophistry. The letters page of *Picturegoer*, always a useful litmus for fan reactions, fluctuated between fervent jingoism, demanding that British films should not be 'cast in the Hollywood mode', and pleas from pro-American fans for less British movie propaganda. The split is even more evident in the letters of respondents to J. P. Mayer's *British Cinemas and their Audiences*,[28] where the proselytizers of British film are outnumbered by the fans of Hollywood. British exhibitors were not immediately 'sold' on the idea of the British film, which remained a risky proposition for them. Writing in the *Kinematograph Weekly* in 1940, a Mr Greenhalgh, chairman of the Bolton branch of the Cinematograph Exhibitors Association (CEA), had lashed out at the quota system, which compelled him to sacrifice a mere 15 per cent of his screen time to pictures that neither he nor his customers wished to see:

I see no reason why I should bolster up incompetence by being forced to give 15 per cent of my screen time for British films on which I know I shall lose money. The British public, in the main, does not like them, and shows its dislike at the box-office as my records prove.

Those people who claim to like British films are those who only see the much boosted films, and their views do not represent the views of our patrons as a whole.[29]

Perhaps Greenhalgh's remarks are not representative. Perhaps he modified his views later in the war, when British pictures began to rival Hollywood's in popularity. However, his splenetic outburst points up an essential lack of harmony, a clear schism between the various parts of the industry, between producers and critics on the one hand and renters and exhibitors on the other. Not even Rank, who owned interests in production, distribution and exhibition, would be able to bridge the gulf between producers, sellers and consumers.

A little less than five years after Greenhalgh's letter to the trade press, T. H. Martin, an RAF man from Burma, wrote in to *Picturegoer*, praising British films with a chauvinism and an enthusiasm which belie Greenhalgh's assertion that the public, in the mass, did not like them. His letter, offensive, even racist in tone, epitomizes the new-found sense of ebullience that at least some of Britain's cinemagoers shared:

We are sick and tired of having American films (chiefly second-rate) rammed down our throats, and please don't say: 'Do you have to go? There's plenty else to do.' They may be slick of production and technically sound, but they are filled with Oomph-oozing women, their bodies covered or uncovered so as to stimulate the sexual rather than the artistic senses; not forgetting the immaculate negro either depravedly drooling inarticulate dirges or attempting to knock seven hells out of a valuable piano.

Imagine, therefore, what refreshing contrasts are provided by British films, full as they invariably are, of superb acting by people full of character, and in which one can almost exist, so realistically and vividly are they portrayed.[30]

Despite their temporary switch of allegiance from Hollywood's pictures to Britain's, which was at its most pronounced in 1946, the *annus mirabilis* in British film history, 'this momentous year' as *Picturegoer* called it, when British movies outgrossed their American counterparts, the fans' new-found loyalty was contingent: they came to the cinema in their droves because there was little else for them to do. The watering-down of beer combined with the wartime upheaval of other traditional leisure activities and geographic dislocation (much of the population was 'billeted' far from home) made the cinema an obvious refuge, whether it was showing the latest from Ealing or the new one from RKO.

Two of the main beneficiaries from the boom in attendance were the government, creaming off revenue in the form of entertainment tax, and J.

41

Arthur Rank, whose Odeons and Gaumonts were packed full seven days a week, even on Sundays.[31]

Through his very presence, Rank had a destabilizing effect on the industry, not least on the critics, whose newly defined notions of quality and craftsmanship –

> In these [war] films there was a clue both to the method and the character of the self-supporting British film – it should be small-scale and hand-made
>
> (Winnington and Davenport, 1951: 11)

– were immediately threatened by the looming shadow of his organization, a vertically integrated mammoth the size of MGM. Whereas the rest of the industry had been contracting since the beginning of the war, Rank had been expanding. Regardless of Rank's 'good intentions', and regardless of the many films he helped finance, he was quickly demonized as a monopolist: he was introducing almost Fordist practices to film production,[32] and his influence, even if he claimed to be using it benevolently, was all-pervasive: everything from the price of admission, to cinema seats, projectors, screens and more than half the available studio space came under his jurisdiction. On both psychological and ideological levels, this eruption of 'big business' was worrying for the critics, who were trying to carve out an identity for themselves by making film 'respectable', and hence a legitimate object for criticism. No sooner had the British film been fixed – it should be small-scale, crafted and concerned with 'real' people – than Rank threw the definition off its axis.

Whereas the American market was large enough to accommodate a 'mature oligopoly' of eight studios,[33] the British market, less than a quarter of the size, was barely big enough for one 'combine', even at the best of times, when the studios hadn't been commandeered by the government and the war hadn't lured away many of the technicians. Now, inevitably, the imbalance caused by the size of the Rank Organization was exacerbated by restrictions: there were severe shortages of everything from raw stock to studio space, and Rank seemed to have the lion's share of what was on offer. Parrying opponents, Rank sought to justify his group's expansion by saying he was merely doing what was necessary to set the business on a 'sound' footing: it was a question for him, as it had been for his father, of centralization and economy of scale. The Rank Organization, he argued, needed to be big if it was going to service its filmmakers and provide them with everything from celluloid to play-dates:

> We have laid the foundations of an industry by providing the practical means of survival – the vital facilities of production, distribution and a proper flow of equipment.[34]

This was not an argument likely to impress the ACT or the independent producers, or any of the crusading journalists, who saw at least part of the reason for the revival of the film industry in its disavowal of straightforward business aims, and who were striving for a cinema of 'public service', which, like the BBC or the documentary movement, would educate as well as entertain. In wartime Britain, there was an unprecedented level of general interest in the way the country was being run, and in how it was going to be run once the war was over: books on town planning were bestsellers; nutrition, clothing, housing, transport were all areas of intense public debate. The Army Bureau of Current Affairs (ABCA) helped 'politicize' the forces with its regular meetings, encouraging soldiers to debate the issues of the day. In an essay on the Festival of Britain, held in 1951,[35] Michael Frayn distinguishes between two warring factions in 1940s Britain: on the one hand, there are the 'herbivores', the gentle revolutionaries, keen to reform society and culture, who would lend their support to the Attlee government, with its plans for nationalization, its Education Act and its introduction of a National Health Service; on the other side of the coin are the 'carnivores', the brutal, *laissez-faire* capitalists, keen to maintain the status quo, and with it their vested interests. In the war years, the years of the coalition government, and their immediate aftermath, the herbivores, with their irrepressible enthusiasm for committees, were to the forefront. Cinema was one area of public life which they scrutinized. Rank was an enigma. Was he a herbivore with carnivorous tendencies, or a carnivore with herbivorous tendencies? The government, grown concerned at his breakneck expansion and at the dominant position he and his rivals held in British cinema, commissioned a panel of academics, led by Dr Albert Palache, to investigate the state of the industry.

In 1944, the Palache Committee delivered its report, *Tendencies to Monopoly in the Cinematograph Films Industry*.

THE PALACHE REPORT

> The British public are vitally concerned that the British cinematograph industry should not be allowed to become either a mere reflection of a foreign atmosphere or a channel for disseminating the ideas and aspirations, no matter how worthy in themselves, of one or two dominating personalities in this country.
>
> (Board of Trade, 1944: 6)

At first glance, the Palache Report seems singularly ill-timed. Commissioned in the middle of a war, when there were surely more pressing concerns than the well-being of the film industry, its very purpose, namely to devise measures to check the development of monopoly, was undermined by the government's own position in the business. Not only was the Exchequer sucking revenue out of film through entertainment tax, but most of the studios and more than two-thirds of the technicians were out of action as a direct result of state intervention. What remained of the industry was largely administered by the government: the Ministry of Information was supervising and vetting scripts, and, along with the British Council and the War Office, was a main source of funds for filmmakers. The industry was already semi-nationalized. Furthermore, it was enjoying a rare boom period. With record audiences and an increased self-respect, it didn't seem in need of introspective government reports. None the less, Hugh Dalton, President of the Board of Trade, concurred with the widespread belief that film was far too important to leave to the filmmakers, and that it had political, economic and cultural ramifications which made it a fit subject for scrutiny and legislation, even in the middle of the war. The Cinematograph Films Council, set up in the wake of the 1938 Films Act, had been meeting regularly, chewing the fat, advising the government. Now, under Dalton's instructions, it appointed a committee of four independent members, and set them investigating the new phenomenon, 'monopoly'. Distributors, screenwriters, producers, technicians and mandarins from the Ministry of Information were all interviewed. Rank himself gave evidence to the committee.

The Palache Report was finally delivered in July 1944, and, although its language was circumspect, it provided a scorching indictment of the stranglehold Rank was felt to be exercising on the industry.

'Monopoly', like 'realism', was a keyword in film debates of the period, and was notoriously difficult to define in any but the loosest terms. Palache's assertion that the industry was under the thumb of 'one dominating personality' – an oblique way of referring to Rank – was belied by statistics. According to the Palache Committee's own calculations, the 50 per cent of available sound stages controlled by the Rank Organization was not a representative figure: once the dozen or so studios put out of action by the looming spectre of Hitler, and closed down or commandeered by the government, had reopened, the holding would dwindle to 41 per cent of the total space. This hardly constitutes a monopoly in any strict sense. Furthermore, he owned only 600 cinemas of the 4,000 in the country as a whole. As Anthony Havelock-Allan was at pains to put it:

> Unless he [Rank] owned all the studios, unless there was only one distributor and he owned it, it is bollocks to talk about a monopoly. It's the kind of left-wing idiocy you would expect.[36]

Although Rank's interests continued to increase, with his numerous subsidiary companies branching out into every crevice of the film business, Rank could plausibly argue that his group was no bigger than any of the Hollywood majors, who were, after all, his main competitors.

The Palache Committee's primary concern was that there could not be a 'sound British cinematograph industry' unless independent production was safeguarded. The report posits an antinomy, monopoly v. independence, which itself harks back to the British realism–Hollywood whimsy opposition which some of the 'quality' critics sought to draw. Monopoly is associated with big business, inertia, a lack of creative imagination: it is the force for the bad. Independence, by contrast, is linked with flair, imagination and integrity. Independent producers are the Davids to Rank's Goliath.

What constituted independence? Again, the report is a little vague:

> By independent, we have in mind both freedom from foreign domination and freedom from dominating British control.
>
> (Board of Trade, 1944: para. 3)

Independence without resources was meaningless in practical terms: the resources were controlled by the majors. The filmmaking process, from the receipt of the raw material to the completion of the picture, was a complex and expensive affair, and any consideration of the various steps involved reveals how problematic the conception of 'independence' was in the 1940s British films industry. (A later government paper, the Gater Report of 1948, acknowledged the difficulty in defining this somewhat protean term by substituting a more flexible alternative, 'freelance'. As Gater was quick to note, there were producers whose independence was 'fitful . . . at one period they are independent, at another they have continuing associations with one of the major distributing companies'.[37])

A nominally independent producer in wartime Britain, without a studio, reliant on a renter's advance for production money, was in a precarious position: if that producer's film flopped, he or she would be hard pressed to prise finance for subsequent pictures from the notoriously fickle distributors, whose philosophy is perfectly summed up in the age-old cliché, 'You're only as good as your last film'.[38]

All too frequently, independent producers were obliged to tailor their production policy to suit the unreasonable demands of the renter. The independents lacked creative control. By contrast, the Rank Organization, with its own studios, renting facilities and cinemas, could sustain individual losses and, within certain perimeters, could even afford to gamble. Rank's stable of producers pursued a far more adventurous policy than any independent could have countenanced. Ironically, the talented bunch of filmmakers who operated under his auspices at Denham in the war years called themselves Independent Producers Ltd. For Powell and Pressburger, Launder and Gilliat, and David Lean, independence was defined as lack of interference from the front office. And such independence could be guaranteed only by a major combine like the Rank Organization.

Still, the Palache Committee had pointed up an essential flaw in the business. The British film industry was lop-sided, tilted in favour of the distributors and exhibitors. It was generally reckoned that a medium-budget British feature had to run for at least a fortnight in London to recoup its negative costs. As Rank and Warner-ABC owned two-thirds of the best London theatres, this wasn't always easy . . .

Distributors, well aware that the independents were desperate to get their pictures into London cinemas, charged astronomical prices for their services, often taking up to 35 per cent of the producer's box-office cut. The cut would be further reduced by entertainment tax and by supplementary costs – advertising, publicity and prints – all of which were shunted on to the producer. When a distributor agreed to handle a property, this didn't mean that it would be sold energetically. (Rank's experiences with *The Turn of the Tide* in 1935 underlined the lethargy which periodically afflicted even the most assiduous of renters.) General Film Distributors, a prime source of production money, were more enthusiastic about promoting films in which they had invested than pictures from 'outsiders'. Block-booking was as prevalent in Britain as in America, and it was only too likely that an independent producer's 'gem', which all the cinemas were clamouring for, would be used as part of a package to help sell a distributor's 'duds'. Even the exhibitors, no angels themselves, felt exploited by their renting brethren: they had quota obligations to fulfil and resented the high price they were charged for British films, which they sometimes had no choice but to hire. Hollywood, of course, offered its wares at a much cheaper rate. And, generally, the customers preferred Hollywood pictures.

Wearing his various hats, Rank was a member (and president) of the British Film Producers' Association (BFPA), the Kinema Renters' Society (KRS) and the Cinema Exhibitors Association (the CEA). He soon discovered that the three arms of the industry were far from united. All keen to protect their vested interests, they were engaged in well-nigh permanent quarrels and feuds. The renters and exhibitors were convinced that they had exclusive knowledge of what the public wanted, while the producers saw their colleagues in the service industries as philistines, who neither had the first clue about filmmaking nor were prepared to allow their 'creative peers' their due reward. The Palache Committee was inclined to take the producers' side, arguing:

> The finance of feature film production should be placed on a healthier and more permanent basis. The terms of distribution contracts should be adjusted to ensure that a reasonable share of the proceeds from exhibition find their way back to the producer.
>
> (Board of Trade, 1944: para. 32)

The Report was especially wary about Rank. Obviously, in his own cinemas, he would give his own films pride of place. That was only to be expected. But, Palache feared, he was also liable to tilt the rest of his scheduling in the favour of the American companies with whom he had reciprocal arrangements.

Palache's stated aim was to protect the industry from American competition while encouraging filmmakers to 'think small', to make films for domestic consumption. Alexander Korda, who shared Rank's commitment to internationalism, was predictably scathing about such narrow ambition:

> The Films Council Committee wants a large number of mediocre films and Hollywood will make bigger and bigger films and if we do not then it will be the end of the British industry.[39]

Rank, for his part, countered accusations of monopoly by saying that he provided 'all-the-year-round employment' for studio workers, something which the independent producers would never be able to guarantee:

> Continuity of production is the desirable end which such an organization as mine can and does achieve.[40]

Little immediate action was taken on the report. Warner-ABC and Rank were asked to give a 'gentleman's agreement' that they would not buy further cinemas without first receiving permission from the Board of Trade. Korda and Rank had frantically lobbied civil servants to oppose Palache's recommendations, and they found the civil servants responsive. As Street and Dickinson observe in their exhaustive survey *Cinema and State*, the Board of Trade and the film expansionists had much in common: both parties wanted to promote Britain culturally and commercially, and to earn dollars in the process.[41] As far as Korda and Rank were concerned, the Palache Report was an enormous red herring, written by academics and dealing with abstractions, with 'tendencies', which served only to obfuscate matters. The indictment of distributors was all very well, and it was quite fair enough to draw attention to the unfair 'competitive' advantage held by the two combines, who had renters and cinemas on their side, but attendances were booming: the theatres were full to overcrowding. And there was ample evidence of an appetite for British movies. Korda suggested that striving for monopoly was a 'suicidal policy. . . . In the absence of healthy competition the standard of production will decline, and there will then be no independent production to keep the interest of the public alive.'[42] Given the range and quality of British pictures being made while the Palache Committee was in session, it hardly made sense to impeach Rank. There was no evidence that he was interfering in production policy, using his influence to make his films reflect his own political or religious beliefs. As for independent production, it was not an area likely to be prospering in wartime. Inevitably, feature film output fell from 1939 to 1945, but the decline had more to do with Churchill and Hitler than with Rank.

British cinema history is cyclical, with the same kind of crisis seeming to repeat itself each decade. The central question, the be-all and end-all of nearly all British film debates, which was again posed by the Palache Committee,[43] was whether the British should concentrate on making relatively low-budget films for consumption in the domestic market, or whether they should risk more lavish productions, which would need to find a foreign market if they were to have any chance of recouping their costs but which, by the same token, might hit the jackpot and net a fortune. In the 1930s, Korda and Gaumont-British had tried to break into America. Now Rank was about to attempt the same thing.

The Palache Report deemed his tilting at the world market an abandonment of 'quality', of 'independence', of 'realism', and of all the other ineffables which had made British wartime cinema so distinct. Moreover, it was a betrayal of the British cinemagoer:

> It would be an unsatisfactory outcome of years of special encouragement for British film production, if, while this country still continued to be served with mainly foreign product, British production in its turn should become more and more dominated by the desire to appeal first to the foreign market. Ultimately, indeed, the sale of a picture to a renter for overseas distribution (under the provision of the alternative quota clauses) might seem a more attractive prospect to the British producer than exhibition to cinema-goers at home.
>
> (Board of Trade, 1944: para. 108)

Rank, by contrast, considered that the only way to set British production on a sound basis was to export. In an interview with the *Cine-Technician* in late 1943, he sought to repel charges of monopoly while setting out his vision for British film, and the part he was to play in its revival, in detail. His comments, paternal in tone, are worth quoting in full:

> There has been a great deal of loose and uncritical talk about this monopoly that I am said to be trying to establish. I am not trying to establish anything of the kind. I certainly have a position in the industry, and a certain power, which I admit I am trying to build up, not in order to secure a monopoly or for the questionable pleasure of playing with power, but in order to do a service to the trade which I consider I *must* do. My position imposes certain obligations which I accept gladly enough at the moment because I think I am doing a service to the industry in Britain as a whole, but at the same time obligations which I will drop tomorrow if the Government decides it has other plans in which I have no part. It is all very well to talk of being able to make good pictures here without bothering about American or world markets, but in all honesty the continued existence of British film production depends on overseas trade. And to get that trade you must have power . . . the whole future of British films

is bound up in the question of overseas trade. Without it we must be resigned to a position as bad as – or worse than – the position before the War. I feel a great sense of responsibility to the industry and to the technical staffs. . . . Granted that entry to foreign markets on a suitable basis, most of the other things we hope for will follow – trade agreement, apprenticeship and so on. Without that foreign trade, all other things are idle dreams.

(Rank, quoted in the *Cine-Technician*,
November–December 1943, p. 124)

In the piece quoted above, Rank suggests his role in the British film industry is one of duty and obligation: he is doing something which he 'must' do. Distinctions between business and evangelism are blurred. 'Power', rather than being a means to consolidate his hold over the British box-office and to secure optimum earnings from his wide portfolio of film interests, is presented as a necessary evil: he claims he needs to be powerful if he is to have any chance of getting playing time in US theatres and thereby setting the British industry on a sound basis. As he puts it, he 'must be in a position to bargain'. He fails to appreciate that while his 'power' in the industry may give him the capacity to fulfil his God-given obligations to the British film, critics fear that it allows him to exert an undue influence over his rivals.

In his statement, Rank seems more concerned with the long-term good of the industry than with any goals of his own. Yet he issues a quite palpable threat to the government: if legislation is introduced to curb his power, he will have no qualms about dropping his obligations, whatever the consequences. That familiar blend of visionary enthusiasm (the sense of a crusade against the Hollywood infidels) and business pragmatism characterizes his remarks. He does not talk of British films in cultural or aesthetic terms; trade is his primary concern. He paints himself as the man of destiny. He alone is in a position to effect a turn-around in British film's fortune because he alone is powerful enough to trade on level terms with the Americans:

If I can't do it – nobody else can, no *British* producers making *British* films.[44]

He expects the rest of the industry to rally to his standard. It is hardly surprising that producers, technicians and journalists alike should bristle with resentment at seeing their business's fate in the hands of one man, and, moreover, a man with no specialist knowledge of or enthusiasm for British cinema. Nor is it surprising that Rank should feel aggrieved to bear the brunt of so much criticism. After all, as he saw it, he was stepping into the breach and committing himself and his millions to the rescue of British cinema.

Convinced, by recollections of his father's trade battles against the US millers and by his own observations of business, that size, centralization and access to the American market were the key to setting the industry on its own feet, Rank embarked on a prolonged export drive. However controversial, draining and frustrating it proved, his bid to carve British film a sizeable niche of the US market was more thorough, was better financed, and came closer to success than any attempts made on America by his predecessors or, indeed, successors.

J. Arthur Rank with two of his beloved dogs. (Courtesy of the Hon. Mrs Shelagh Cowen)

C.M. Woolf, founder of General Film Distributors in 1935, and the man responsible for guiding Rank through the dark vale of Wardour Street until his premature death in 1942.

Stewart Rome, an actor brought out of retirement by Rank, played Dr Goodfellow, a wise religious cove who leaned over a gate and imparted a 'Thought for the Week'. Audiences sometimes responded by throwing (rationed) tomatoes at the screen.

The Turn of the Tide (1935), a tale of warring fisher-folk, brought Rank into the mainstream of the British Film Industry.

'Not bloody likely!' Wendy Hiller caused quite a stir as Eliza Doolittle in Gabriel Pascal's production of *Pygmalion* (1938), the first big success made at Pinewood.

Anthony Havelock-Allan was one of the earliest producers at Pinewood. A founder member of Cineguild in the 1940s, he also made pictures for Rank in the 1950s.

The Great Mr Handel (1942) directed by Norman Walker, was the most expensive of Rank's religious films, and was notable for its early and expert use of Technicolor.

Shot for £14 000 at Pinewood Studios, *This Man is News* (1938) made ten times that amount at the box-office.

Michael Balcon, one of Rank's most outspoken critics in the early 1940s, later to join the Rank board and make Ealing's pictures under Rank's auspices, with his arm round the dancing divinity of 1930s British cinema, Jessie Matthews.

The Lambeth Walk (1939), one of Havelock-Allan' and Norton's low-budget Pinebrook winners.

The Rank Laboratories at Denham Studios.

George Elvin of the Association of Cine-Technicians, with whom Rank was to have many run-ins.

3

TILTING AT THE WORLD MARKET

If one factor more than another is to be designated as chiefly responsible for increases both of schedules and cost this is the prolonged
effort of the Rank group to break into the American market.

(ACT memorandum, quoted in *Kinematograph Weekly*,
12 May 1949)

Export or die applies as much to the film industry as it does to the
nation.

(Harold Wilson)

Don't let Mr Rank wave his Union Jack at me!

(Louis B. Mayer)

Now that he was indisputably the single most powerful figure in British
film, Rank set about developing a production policy of appropriate scope
and grandeur to go along with his massive holdings. In 1933, he had been
inspired by a mission to put religious pictures on the map. It wasn't that he
had abandoned the mission: 'the Religious Film Movement', as it was now
known, had continued to grow throughout the 1930s and had reached a
point where it could successfully hold summer schools. In 1940, Rank had
formed GHW, a religious film unit, to shoot *Better Than Light*, a film
based on the King's Christmas broadcast.[1] GHW took its name from an
unlikely trio: Canon Benjamin Gregory, Rank's old ally from the days he
owned the *Methodist Times*, provided the 'G'; Home Guard Colonel
'Hakey' Hake, Rank's estate manager and golfing partner, came up with
the 'H'; and Captain Norman Walker, industry veteran, director of *The
Turn of the Tide*, was behind the 'W'. GHW kept busy throughout the
early 1940s. As Peter Rogers, a young journalist and publicist on the
group's staff, recalls, there were certain hazards confronting religious films
which the mainstream cinema managed to avoid. For instance, depicting
Christ was problematic: 'Because there were so many denominations
around the table who couldn't agree what Christ looked like, they still used
a shadow.'[2]

GHW films, mainly shot at the small Gate studio in Norwood, were shown in Methodist halls and in army and navy camps. They were a commercial proposition – even when spreading the gospel, Rank made sure he was paid a fair rent for his films. From time to time, GHW attempted to cross over and reach a general cinema audience. For instance, its series 'Sunday Thought for the Week' hit Odeon screens in late 1942, serving the dual purpose of promoting Christ and helping Rank to justify opening his cinemas on a Sunday. (He could rebuff the hordes of irate Christians who were vehemently opposed to Sunday screenings by claiming that he wasn't only showing films shot with the 'devil's camera'.) Rogers recalls that the format of the 'Thought for the Week' didn't always appeal to spectators:

> He [Rank] brought out of retirement an old silent films actor called Stewart Rome who called himself Dr Goodfellow and who leaned over a farm gate and told the audience what to do next week and what to think about . . . at Edgware one Sunday night they started to throw things at the screen, so he decided to stop 'Thought for the Week'.[3]

Perhaps GHW's most ambitious undertaking was its 1942 biopic *The Great Mr Handel*, directed by Walker and shot in full Technicolor, with Wilfrid Lawson, who'd also been in *The Turn of the Tide*, taking the role of the *Messiah*'s anguished composer. Rank, called into a production meeting and asked if he liked what he had seen of the picture, explained to the director what was wrong with it: there was not enough 'Rita Hayworth'.[4] Earnest and handsome, and one of the best early British stabs at Dr Kalmus' much cherished three-colour process,[5] it none the less failed to capture the public imagination as either war propaganda or escapism. Rank's criticism was borne out by its disappointing box-office performance. The film lacked glamour and failed to make clear whom it was addressing. As *Observer* critic C. A. Lejeune put it in her review:

> Just why the British producers decided this was the moment to linger over the debts, doubts and diet of the eighteenth-century-born German composer I do not know, but since they did so linger (103 min.) they were wise to give us good things to look at and listen to . . . the art director . . . managed the most gracious and intelligent arrangement of Technicolor ever introduced to any film anywhere.
>
> (C. A. Lejeune, *Observer*, 27 September 1942)

By the end of 1942, when his empire was intact, Rank's mission expanded somewhat. No longer would he be satisfied with promoting religious pictures and sponsoring a piecemeal selection of British feature production through GFD. Now, his new aim was to promote British film throughout the world. To justify investing large sums in research, equipment and facilities, in making 'big' films in terms of budget, cast and crew, he would need to reach beyond the British market: it was a matter of economic necessity as well as an evangelical goal in itself. The profits that were generated by natively produced and natively consumed cinema were minimal in comparison with the profits that America made in Britain and that Britain, if the example of Alexander Korda was anything to go by, could make in America: Korda's *The Private Life of Henry VIII*, which opened at the Radio City Music Hall, New York, in October 1933, made $18,400 on its very first day of exhibition and went on to accrue takings in excess of half a million pounds during its first world run, a healthy return for a production cost of well under £100,000. While such success had since proved elusive, defiant producers were bound to try to emulate it. To accept that British filmmaking was a micro-industry in comparison with the macro-industry of the USA was to reduce Britain to a secondary status in its own market. The alternative was to compete. But the economic logic was daunting. For the British to be able to afford lavish, big-budget productions that would have a chance in the American market, they would have to make lavish, big-budget productions. And the downside, the risk of losing a fortune, was the inevitable price to be paid for the opportunity to tilt at Hollywood.

Films are 'infinitely exportable'.[6] Once a picture has been made, it costs very little extra to strike prints. As Walter Benjamin observed in his essay 'The work of art in the age of mechanical reproduction', the film work, unlike old sacral art, is divested of its aura.[7] It is no longer specific to a time or place, but can be reproduced anywhere. This has enormous economic as well as cultural implications. It has paved the way for an era of 'mass culture', and has helped to facilitate American cultural hegemony. By the end of the First World War, a conflict which, quite apart from its other catastrophic consequences, managed to arrest British film in its tracks,[8] America had moved from being 'a debtor to being a creditor nation',[9] while the British had slid in the opposite direction. While 1913 saw the USA export 32 million feet of film, and while in the pre-war years European movies had had some success in America, by 1925 the USA was exporting 235 million feet and importing next to none.

Appropriately, given that the Americans were knocking the British off their imperial perch, the UK was Hollywood's prime export market. Wim Wenders' famous epigram, from *Kings of the Road*, 'Hollywood has colonized our subconscious',[10] has added poignancy when applied to 1920s Britain. Now the former imperial power experienced the trauma of colonization itself as its film industry was ruthlessly undermined and taken over by the Americans. This painful process is charted in full in Street and Dickinson's *Cinema and State*, a compendium of invariably depressing statistics and facts dealing with British films legislation, which points out that before the 1927 Cinematograph Films (Quota) Act afforded a measure of protection to the industry, more than 90 per cent of pictures shown in British cinemas were American.[11] Hollywood, like the American flour industry, was able to hawk its wares at a generous discount: because its domestic market was so huge, American producers, managing to recoup their 'negative' costs at home, were in a position to offer their films at disarmingly low prices. They undercut their competitors so effectively that British exhibitors often found it cheaper to buy American than to buy British:

> American films could be hired for as little as thirty-six shillings at a time whereas the economic rent for a British film was about twelve pounds.[12]

Stark figures reveal the gulf between the respective industries. Whereas about 20 million people a week visited British cinemas in the 1920s, generally to see American films, over 80 million Americans visited US cinemas, and always to see American films. The average return per film in America was ten times greater than its equivalent in Britain. The producers could therefore afford to spend more on their films. Because British cinemas were so saturated with American product, and there was a shortage of screens anyway, British producers often found themselves in the invidious position of going slowly bankrupt while they waited for their features to get exhibited. Until their previous ventures had shown a profit, they could not afford to embark on new shoots. The interest rate on the money borrowed to finance their films in the first place could see them lapse catastrophically into the red as long as those films remained on the shelf.

As Rank would quickly discover, there was a traditional animosity between British producers and British renters and exhibitors. The latter felt themselves under no compulsion to 'push' British films just because they were British. On the contrary, it was to their advantage to show American movies. Hollywood, keen to 'divide and rule', did its best to foster the dissent. Journalist Peter Burnup observed in 1946:

> Exhibitors know for their part that their prosperous businesses have been built up, and are now maintained, by Hollywood's outgivings. They appreciate that any summary pruning in the number of American films brought here – Hollywood's films currently occupy some eighty percent of the country's screen time – would result in an equally summary closing down of their theatres.
>
> (*Motion Picture Almanac*, 1946/7, British section)

Hollywood's force seemed irrepressible. Will Hays, head of the Motion Picture Association of America (MPAA), had set the American film industry the modest task of 'Americanizing the world', and the Motion Picture Division (MPDA) of the US Bureau of Foreign and Domestic

Commerce declared that every foot of film exported and exhibited 'yielded one dollar in foreign purchases of American goods'.[13] Not out of any love that they had for British films *per se*, but because they had seen the scope and influence of Hollywood, industrialists and politicians helped force through the 1927 Cinematograph Films (Quota) Act. On the one hand, they wanted to counter what they regarded as all-pervasive US propaganda. The secretary of the Empire Marketing Board, Stephen Tallents, was jingoistically blunt about this matter:

> It is horrible to think that the British Empire is receiving its education from a place called Hollywood. The dominions would rather have a picture with a wholesome, honest British background, something that gives British sentiment, something that is honest to our traditions, than the abortions we get from Hollywood. . . . the American film is everywhere, and is the best advertisement of American trade and commerce. Trade follows the film, not the flag.[14]

On the other hand, they wanted to emulate Hollywood: the legislation was motivated by fear and loathing in equal parts.

The 1927 Act introduced quotas. Initially, 5 per cent of all films exhibited were to be British. The quota was to have risen to 20 per cent by 1936, when the Act was due to be revised. (One option that the government had considered was insisting that for every American film allowed into Britain, a British film should be allowed into America. However, it was feared that such a measure would merely persuade Hollywood to invest in Britain, and that Britain would end up with an American-owned industry.) On a cosmetic level, the Act was successful. Within a decade, Britain was second only to America in film production. But this ostensibly healthy state of affairs belied the true condition of the industry. No significant inroads were made into the world, or, more importantly, the US, market. A large proportion of the new production consisted of the notorious 'quota quickies' which did so much to compromise British filmmakers' reputations. Often financed with American money, shot on tiny budgets and at breakneck pace, their primary function was to enable exhibitors to circumvent government restrictions and to screen as many Hollywood films as possible at peak times. Although shown in cinemas, the quickies were rarely made with audiences in mind, and could go more or less unseen – early mornings were considered prime slots for these offerings, which were measured by length and not by quality. (Cinema owners wanted to 'honour' their quota obligation to show British movies, as quickly, discreetly and efficiently as they could, while preserving their prime slots for Hollywood's output.) Michael Powell cut his teeth as a director on quota pictures, and almost ruined his career in the process; as a *Kinematograph Weekly* correspondent later recalled:

55

Mickey . . . made a picture for Gerry Jackson called *His Lordship*. At its Sunday night screening at the Dominion, it was booed off the screen. Next morning the press gave the incident so much unwanted publicity that it is something of a miracle Powell ever survived as a director.[15]

The quota films were useful as a training ground for British talent, allowing novices to learn their craft in the most straitened of circumstances. They helped maintain high levels of employment. They even provided an outlet for 'Mother Riley'[16] to display his/her wares. And some of them – unexpectedly – turned up trumps at the box-office. None the less, the government's low opinion about their merits was quickly made clear. Further legislation was introduced in 1938,[17] insisting that all films for quota should cost at least a certain 'minimum' amount to make. This revealed that the government regarded 'quality' in film as something intimately entwined with cost. The quickies were no glowing advertisement for the new-found prowess of British filmmakers. There was precious little chance that they could find audiences outside Britain. Compared to the worst of them, even a Hollywood 'B' feature was a gem.

In the 1920s and 1930s, Hollywood continued to set the agenda for British filmmakers and British film legislators alike, and still does today. Contemporary producer Steve Woolley's comparison between the respective industries of Britain and America in the 1990s,

It's like comparing the space programme with people in the Hebrides knitting scarves[18]

hints at the problems which will always bedevil British producers who want to show their films in the USA. When America already has British production in a stranglehold, when the dominance of Hollywood movies undermines the chances of the British capturing a significant slice of even their own market, what chance does British film have of crossing the Atlantic?

For Rank, as for Korda before him, competing in the world market in general, and in America in particular, was the essential prerequisite to competing in the home market. To have a successful national industry in a relatively small country like Britain, Rank estimated, it was necessary to make international films. However, the USA was resistant not merely to British cinema but to British culture in general.

BRITISH CULTURE AND PROPAGANDA IN AMERICA

After the initial flurry of interest before 1920, American audiences showed a definite distaste for foreign films, including those from Britain.[19]

US society of the 1920s was characterized by its isolationism. Britain was blamed for luring 'Uncle Sam' into the war against the Kaiser. Now, America wanted to cut itself off from Europe and was immediately suspicious of any attempt to catch its cultural or commercial ear. As Philip Taylor suggests in his study of British overseas publicity and propaganda, *Projecting Britain*, aggressive British propaganda, whether in the form of film, news, or commerce, risked running aground on the rocks of American public opinion:

> The self-respecting American is down on all propagandists, as the self-respecting housewife is down on vermin.[20]

None the less, it remained important for Britain to court its transatlantic neighbour. The British ruling class took a curiously ambivalent attitude towards self-promotion. In the pin-striped halls of power, 'showing off' was considered vulgar, and the government was wary about financing institutions such as the British Council, whose *raison d'être* was to brag, however subtly, about the glories of British living. With the Armistice in 1918, the British Ministry of Information had been closed down, and most of the wartime propaganda machinery disbanded. While news agencies such as Reuters, the Northcliffe and Beaverbrook Press, and the British Official News Service, which provided a stream of news exclusively for the benefit of foreign journalists, did their best to counter the anti-British propaganda emanating from the aggressive totalitarian regimes coming to power in post-war Europe (Hitler in Germany, Mussolini in Italy), Britain was slower than competitor countries to realize that trade no longer 'followed the flag'[21] and that culture, in the form of books, newspapers and films, could play a vital part in the projection of a nation: it was a question of the country putting its goods in the world's shop-window.

Even when the importance of commercial propaganda was belatedly appreciated, America remained a thorny problem: the country where the hard sell originated was remarkably resistant to being sold anything by anybody else. While the British Travel Association, formed in 1929,[22] was able to promote Britain vigorously throughout the rest of the world, luring tourists to the kingdom by the sea and developing a taste for British culture and goods, it had to cease its trumpeting and become more circumspect when approaching the USA. The association fell back on oblique and cautious marketing techniques. Rather than soliciting Americans, and trying to bamboozle them with British 'hype', envoys sat back and made themselves 'available for consultation'. The British Library of Information in Washington did not dispense news; it held its news in waiting, and coyly allowed 'writers, speakers, students and others'[23] to make the first move. An inevitable problem of such a low-key approach was that the propaganda only ever reached a small elite. Targeted at the so-called 'opinion-formers,' this mild-mannered proselytizing would never set the prairies on fire: 'British propaganda supported by those who live on Fifth Avenue will always be regarded with deep suspicion by the mass of the American public'.[24]

British film in America risked being similarly marginalized. American renters and exhibitors considered most British movies as suitable only for smart theatres and smart audiences. The British picture was metropolitan and sophisticated fare. It might achieve limited success in Los Angeles or New York. It might be fêted by the critics. It might play to enthusiastic audiences on the college or art-house circuits. But it was unlikely ever to breach the cinemas of the small towns in the Midwest and to make serious money: there was no way past the gate-keeper, the American 'showman'. Hiding behind the ideology of free trade and the competitive market, this 'showman' (in both British and American trade press of the period, cinema exhibition seems to be an exclusively male business) was, in fact, a rigorous censor, guarding public taste, monitoring the flow of foreign films into American theatres and turning away anything outlandish on behalf of his customers. 'He' could claim that his criteria for booking movies were strictly commercial, that he would hire anything he thought might make him money: 'in almost thirty years, this watchtower has never encountered an exhibitor who gave a second thought to labels. He'll take product from Bombay if he can buy it right and make a profit',[25] wrote Red Kann, the editor of the showman's bible, the *Motion Picture Herald*. The illusion of an open market with which US exhibitors tantalized British producers was far more effective in excluding foreign competition than a government-instituted quota system. Hollywood was able to claim the moral high ground, to criticize 'protectionism' in foreign industries, all the time boasting that its own system was fair and deregulated. The fact that this fair and deregulated film market seemed to be hermetically sealed against outside encroachment was, or so the showmen protested, only an indication of the superiority of US movies. If British or Indian pictures were as 'good' or as relevant to the lives of midwestern audiences as their American counterparts, they would have free access to US cinemas.

Even as he protests that American showmen are fair-minded paragons of virtue when it comes to booking, swayed in their decisions by nothing so base as nationalism or protectionism, ready to take product from anywhere in the world, if only it will make them a profit, Kann acknowledges that a quite palpable anti-British bias exists among several midwestern exhibitors. In the article quoted above, Kann goes on to bemoan 'Ill-considered criticism which urges theatre operators in small towns not to buy foreign films at any price because British films are "poison" and because Hollywood's poor "B" pictures are better than British treble "A"s'.[26] British producers had long been aware of an inveterate American resistance to their wares. Michael Balcon, part of the abortive blitzkrieg on the US market in the mid-1930s, wrote – as Rank was about to embark on his own grand export drive – that 'it was easier for a camel to go through the eye of a needle than for a British film to be shown in America'.[27] Hugh Stewart, producer of *Tunisian Victory*, recalls an unsavoury meeting he had with Louis B. Mayer in Hollywood towards the end of the war:

> I did have the honour, if that is the word, of seeing Louis B. Mayer . . . the little bastard wandered up and said to me, 'Don't let Mr Rank wave his Union Jack at me!' There was a deliberate attempt to put British films out of business. Nothing will convince me that wasn't so.[28]

Since the early 1930s, the time of Korda's initial success, America had been regarded rather fancifully by British filmmakers as an El Dorado, a promised land full of milk and honey and brimming with box-office receipts that was well-nigh impossible to reach. Many bankrupted themselves in the attempt to get there. Vice-president of the ACT Sidney Cole presented the argument against heading westward with exemplary clarity. As early as 1943, before Rank's export drive was fully under way, he pointed out that it was

> a matter of simple logic that we cannot 'crash' the American market. If we make bad pictures, obviously the Americans don't want them: we don't want that kind ourselves. If we make good ones, the Americans want them still less, for then they are in direct competition with their own, and so reduce their profits.[29]

A random survey of a selection of the so-called 'Showmen's Reviews' in the back of ancient – 1933 – editions of the *Motion Picture Herald* offers stark examples of the many different ways British films failed the 'quality test' set them by American exhibitors on behalf of their audience, and goes some of the way to explaining why the British have traditionally performed so badly in the US market. The cultural and economic prejudices that Rank would have needed to overcome before his pictures won their way into the affections of small-town, midwestern, corn belt cinema-owners and the communities they served were considerable. The survey, which focuses on 1933 because that was the year of Korda's phenomenal American success with *The Private Life of Henry VIII*, is, of necessity, selective. However, trends do not take long to emerge.

Take, for example, the following review of the Gaumont-British picture *Be Mine Tonight*:

> When the rolling title of this picture flashed on the screen indicating it was a foreign made production and with a cast none of which, apparently, was even remotely familiar, the preview audience moved restlessly. . . . Fine as *Be Mine Tonight* is its American release may

possibly meet an obstacle in the fact that it is of foreign make, and of course there's the absence of known cast names.

(*Motion Picture Herald*, 18 February 1933)

The image of the audience moving restlessly at the sight of a non-American film suggests that US cinemagoers do not merely dislike foreign movies: they are physically alarmed by their 'difference'. The reviewer doesn't hesitate to express what a low opinion American exhibitors had of their audience's range of tastes and depth of comprehension. Although claiming to have enjoyed the movie himself, he worries that it will be above the heads of most American spectators, who will be fatally disenchanted by the lack of familiarity of the actors. Stars are a crucial marketing device, and the absence of an established star system is constantly cited as a key factor in the failure of successive waves of British filmmakers to carve out a slice of the American market. British producers, from Michael Balcon and Victor Saville in the 1920s, who brought over Betty Compson to star in *Woman to Woman*, to Goldcrest's benighted supremo in the mid-1980s, James Lee, who imported Al Pacino at a cost of several million dollars to bolster the American profile of the ill-starred *Revolution*, would try to get round the lack of native firepower by hiring from Hollywood. On the whole, however, Hollywood stars cost more than British filmmakers can afford; the ones who are prepared to work in Britain tend to have passed their 'sell-by' date and are on the wane. Moreover, as Rank would discover, one of the quickest ways to offend film and acting unions was to import personnel from abroad: to the disgruntled, home-grown talent, such a gesture always seemed to betoken a lack of confidence in their ability.

A review of the Gaumont-British picture *Ghost Train* in the following week's *Herald* highlights the single greatest obstacle the British were obliged to negotiate, namely the linguistic one: 'At times the English accent causes the dialogue to become almost obscure to the American patron' (*Motion Picture Herald*, 25 February 1933). The unfathomable quality of the English middle-class accent, British slang in general and the pace of British speech make up a constant complaint of US exhibitors and audiences. Again and again, showmen confronted with British pictures protest that their patrons cannot understand the dialogue. They consider the majority of British productions as suitable for only for the smart city theatres which make up a tiny proportion of America's 20,000 cinemas. As the showmen's review of *After the Ball* observes: 'The wit in the dialogue suggests that the appeal of the film will be more particularly to the sophisticated audiences of the big cities' (*Motion Picture Herald*, 25 March 1933).

It was into this metropolitan ghetto that most British films were destined to be thrown. For American cinemagoers as a whole, they were baffling,

and even incomprehensible. Quite apart from any reservations the spectators might have had about the pictures in terms of production values,
genre, or lack of stars, they couldn't understand what was being said:
British and American cinema were 'divided by a common language'.[30]
That BBC nasal whine, considered to be as clear as a bell by the mandarins
at Broadcasting House, confused midwestern audiences, who associated
the ringing timbre with 'bit' parts, unctuous butlers in the main. Abram F.
Myers, a typically forthright American exhibitor with a healthy xenophobic
dislike of British pictures, wrote in to the *Herald* with the following
injunction:

> British producers will have to learn . . . that among Americans,
> [English] accents of such thickness are associated with character bits,
> butlers and comics – not with principals.
>
> (*Motion Picture Herald*, 23 March 1946)

Americans were disconcerted to see the household help in starring roles.
(That this preconception lingers to the present day is testified to by the
casting of Sir John Gielgud as a butler in the 1981 hit movie *Arthur*: one of
Britain's most celebrated Shakespearian actors is reduced to bringing
Dudley Moore drinks in the bath.) Conversely, 'non-posh' vernacular
accents were also deemed impenetrable. Although Will Hay built up a cult
following in the United States, George Formby and his ukulele never
found their niche in this most precarious of markets. As Michael Balcon
recalls in *A Lifetime of Films*:

> Between 1934 and 1941 Formby played in eleven films with enormous
> success in every country of the world including the USSR but ex-
> cluding the United States of America. The Americans could not
> come to terms with this type of comedy.
>
> (Balcon, 1969: 118)

Gracie Fields, hugely popular in Britain throughout the 1930s,
attempted to modify her 'Lancashire Lass' persona for a foray into the
USA: the *Motion Picture Herald* noted of *This Week of Grace*:

> Julius Hagen . . . produced this picture with an eye on the USA. . . .
> He minimized the dialectic and idiomatic features which usually
> characterize this artist's work.
>
> (*Motion Picture Herald*, 28 October 1933)

But it was to no avail. Fields never managed to repeat her British success in
America. (After moving to Hollywood at the outbreak of war, Fields did
moderately well in two American pictures, *Molly and Me* and *Holy
Matrimony*, but these weren't a patch on her British work.) Neither
Norman Wisdom, Rank's top box-office star of the late 1950s and a
comedian with a following everywhere from Kuala Lumpur to Albania,

whose films were especially admired in Hong Kong, Holland and Iran, where they were dubbed into Farsi,[31] nor Sid Field, the outstanding music-hall comedian and star of *London Town*, was popular in America. The very fact of a film being English seemed to put off the showmen before the audience had a chance to see the picture for itself. Take the *Motion Picture Herald* review of another 1933 movie, *The Men They Couldn't Arrest*, for example:

> Insofar as winning the attention of the American audience to the picture is concerned, its definite 'Englishness' must be taken into consideration. Accents of the English that is England, no matter how much more accustomed the average audience is here today than yesterday, are still strange, the choice of idiom sometimes less than understandable. . . . By playing down the English origin and English flavor of the picture and concentrating on the Mystery and Romance elements, the exhibitor may do something with the picture. It is fairly good entertainment.
>
> (*Motion Picture Herald*, 25 March 1933)

As has already been observed, British cinema suffered from American cultural imperialism. The endless moaning of the *Motion Picture Herald* that the English do not speak English properly, that their accent is obscure and their idiom 'less than understandable', marks an ironic reversal: the British would insist that it was their parvenu American cousins who were mauling and distorting the 'mother tongue'; the American exhibitors, however, cite Hollywood, and not the king or queen, as the source of correct speaking – the commonly held cultural stereotype of Americans genuflecting at the merest mention of Shakespeare is thrown into relief by these exhibitors' confidence in Hollywood's voice.

Quite apart from cultural and linguistic misgivings about British films, the American showmen perceive foreign production to be inferior to Hollywood's, an attitude which is articulated in the following review of the musical *Maid of the Mountains*:

> Because it is set in the romantic Balkans – the Prisoner of Zenda country – and because most of its musical numbers are world-wide in their fame, it has a certain charm about it which may excuse its shortcomings in more material aspects.
>
> (*Motion Picture Herald*, 22 April 1933)

As far as the showmen were concerned, the British did not have the set designers, the camera operators or even the hairdressers to compete with Hollywood. Although related to budget, it was not only a question of money: Hollywood personnel were considered more skilled in every aspect of the craft of filmmaking. Continuity of production allowed them to hone and practise their techniques. By sorry contrast, British technicians, subject to long lay-offs, were liable to grow rusty: Sidney Cole, a film editor as well as a prominent ACT man, remembers the terror he felt on the first day of shooting for Thorold Dickinson's *Gaslight*; he nervously assembled the rushes, frightened that he might have 'lost the knack': this was the first feature that he had edited in two years.[32] It is inconceivable that top Hollywood editors would go so long between jobs.

Often, American showmen felt, British films were weighed down at the outset by the unnecessary *gravitas* of their titles. *Counsel's Opinion* was a case in point:

> Here is a British production that ought safely to negotiate the American audience, although a new title will be needed. While lacking in obvious selling points, the picture is a well-made comedy that will help the intelligent patron kill a pleasant hour. There is comment that it packs more talk than action, but there's a section of the community that likes it that way.
>
> (*Motion Picture Herald*, 22 April 1933)

There are countless other examples of British pictures finding new names as they crossed the Atlantic. Powell and Pressburger's sombrely titled *A Matter of Life and Death* was leavened, becoming *A Stairway to Heaven* before it reached the American screen. And their geometric-sounding *49th Parallel* was given a fiercer edge, appropriate for a British film trying to break into the American market, eventually being rechristened *The Invaders* for US audiences. The Ealing classic *Whisky Galore* was shown on the American circuit as *Tight Little Island*, and the rather staid-sounding *London Town*, Rank's stab at a brash musical, became *My Heart Goes Crazy*. *Counsel's Opinion*, suggests the showman, needs a similar rejigging. None the less, it is a quintessential example of the UK film that can be marketed on its snob appeal. Just as American television has a public service channel, which, in a series called 'Masterpiece Theatre', tries to woo anglophiles with stuffy, 'tasteful' adaptations of English novels, bought in from the BBC or Granada, showmen quickly appreciated that there was a clearly identifiable audience, albeit a limited one, for this specialized kind of film, which they labelled 'smart comedy'.

British film fare can be curiously insubstantial, not hearty enough to satisfy the voracious appetites of midwestern cinemagoers, who want something big and full-blooded and not just a 'light piece of work'. The showman refers dismissively to *Marry Me* as typical of the British trend to make throwaway movies:

> This is another of those light pieces of work held together by a liberal supply of musical interpolation that the British studios have been manufacturing freely for so long a period.
>
> (*Motion Picture Herald*, 22 April 1933)

The review of *Radio Parade* reinforces the impression that the showmen considered British film culture to be in some way effete: suitable, perhaps, for enervated anglophiles but not for the average hick:

> As far as the US market goes, the whole thing would have benefited immensely from a drastic pruning of gags, many of which are of that naivety that misses fire on full-blooded Americans.
>
> (*Motion Picture Herald*, 13 May 1933)

British musicals were unlikely to be able to compete in America. After all, the musical is often regarded as the 'all-American genre'. The flamboyance and expertise of Busby Berkeley were hard to emulate. As British director Carol Reed put it in an interview with *Variety*:

> We haven't the songwriters, the hairdressers, the elaborate costumes or the studio facilities to compete with Hollywood musicals.[33]

A film like *Radio Parade*, derived from American paradigms – Lloyd Bacon's great musical *Footlight Parade* was made in the same year – but using entertainers from a specifically British music-hall tradition, had little chance of finding an American audience.

The *Motion Picture Herald* reviews are far from consistent in their responses to British movies. The showmen might advise their colleagues not to go near anything British or, alternatively, suggest that exhibitors 'play down the English origin' of one film and 'avoid too strong an indication that another is a London-made production'.[34] Astute omissions in publicity and advertising, the passing-off of the pictures as American-made, can, the reviewers proclaim, lure spectators to the theatres, even for British pictures, which in a subsequent sentence they might say are inherently incomprehensible to US audiences. Sometimes, the showmen concede that the best of the British efforts are 'fairly good entertainment', in spite of the foggy English accents and the feeble songs and jokes. They don't acknowledge the contradiction in their own perspective: on the one hand, they are stating, quite baldly, that their audiences have an aversion to foreign product; on the other, they are claiming that the skilled and imaginative exhibitor will be able to do some business, even with woebegone British films. This begs the question: is their 'dislike' of foreign pictures genuine, or is it manufactured, a subtle form of censorship and isolationism? How fairly are they representing US cinemagoers' tastes, and what are they doing to manipulate those tastes?

In the mid-1940s, as British fans grew more patriotic, there were fervent letters to *Picturegoer* magazine, expressing bewilderment at the fact that the Americans claimed to find the British accent so incomprehensible, and yet had no difficulty in understanding British actors when they were drafted into Hollywood films.[35] After the war, a galaxy of top British names was bought up by the studios, James Mason, Stewart Granger and

Jean Simmons among them. (And, as John Russell Taylor's *Strangers in Paradise* reveals, the American film industry had little difficulty in absorbing foreign talent, whether from Universum Film Ag (UFA) – Jannings, Lang, Lorre, Murnau *et al.* – or from Sweden – Sjöström, Stiller, Garbo, etc. Hollywood sought to emasculate its rivals by pilfering their top talent.[36]) The drain continues today. Weston 'Budge' Drury, former casting director at Pinewood Studios, suggests that the paradox is as pronounced as ever: the Americans still can't seem to understand British actors in British productions, but they are quite comfortable with British stars in American vehicles. Drury opines that contemporary British stars in Hollywood, like their predecessors, have learned the basic precepts of acting for the mass American audience: speak slowly and clearly. Sean Connery, Michael Caine and Bob Hoskins he cites as prime examples of British actors who have managed to mould their techniques, to achieve that degree of simplicity and clarity in their performances that makes them immediately acceptable to American audiences.[37] There was a time in the mid-1940s when Rank's actors made a conscious attempt to modify their speech for America's benefit. Briefly, the experiment seemed to work. The editor of *Picturegoer* suggested that by 1946 the language barrier had been overcome. As traditional class barriers in British society as a whole seemed to be breaking down, British cinema moved out of its safe Mayfair enclaves:

"No, Mr. Skouras, I hardly think teaching all our stars to play the zither will put the film industry on its feet."

Figure 2 Giles cartoon from the *Daily Express*, 15 November 1949

For years, the greatest reproach against British pictures . . . was that American picturegoers could not understand what our actors were saying. The accusation was not altogether unreasonable when we consider that many of our pictures were unintelligible in large areas of these islands. It was indeed an alien tongue that was so often spoken, so we can hardly wonder that until recently, US exhibitors have complained of our pictures being so 'excessively native'. Fortunately, without sacrificing character and ideas, many of our producers and directors are now obtaining an English that is acceptable to American ears. There is no more of the so-called Oxford accent. Lines are not being 'thrown away' in the Mayfair manner. And America is beginning to understand us. One of the main objections to British pictures is being swept away.

(*Picturegoer*, 25 May 1946, p. 3)

Sadly, *Picturegoer*'s optimism was not justified: British films and their accents might have changed but the showmen's attitude to them had not. Only occasionally did a British picture break through the determined defences. Balcon's adaptation of Priestley's *The Good Companions* was a case in point: 'Because its different types are basically as representative of the average American citizen as the normal Briton, it should be excellent material for good class and family houses' (*Motion Picture Herald*, 29 April 1933). The film's decent, homely values were as strong a selling point in post-depression America as in Britain.

Another vehicle the showmen responded kindly to was the speedway drama *Money for Speed*:

If British productions can maintain the entertainment standard of this one they will soon become a force to be reckoned with.

(*Motion Picture Herald*, 15 July 1933)

Of all the films so far mentioned, this is the only 'action' drama. Motorbikes do not have English accents. A speedway movie thus avoids most of the pitfalls and pot-holes awaiting British musicals and romantic comedies. Sometimes, instilling American themes in British pictures was a way to win the approval of the showmen. Take, for instance, the 1933 Gaumont-British picture, written by Sidney Gilliat, *Orders Is Orders*, which charts the happenings when an army barracks is thrown into upheaval by the arrival of a Hollywood film company; the *Motion Picture Herald* enthused about this one:

For long enough we have had to say that British film producers had no sense of comedy; probably no sense of humor either. Now we get a rich, scintillating screen affair . . . we begin to see now that there is nothing inherent against the making of screen comedy in England

. . . it's such a lovely, polished satire, without a concession to the highbrows.

(*Motion Picture Herald*, 19 August 1933)

Korda's *The Private Life of Henry VIII* was another picture which the showmen (correctly) surmised could do good business:

There is room for wide-open selling and exploitation in the title and its indication of the Bluebeard of kings who married six women and caused two of the six to pay for their infidelity with their deaths under the axe of the executioner . . . it's a costume piece, but *only in its setting*.

(*Motion Picture Herald*, 22 September 1933; emphases added)

It is easy to assume that the American popularity of Korda's film was due to its pomp and circumstance, its invocation of British history. (Herbert Wilcox was also successful in America with 'regal' projects: his two Queen Victoria/Anna Neagle films did excellent business.) The review hints at something different: the picture was successful in spite of its historical setting rather than because of it. It was the 'private life' aspect rather than the 'Henry VIII' angle which attracted audiences, who were eager to follow Charles Laughton's amorous adventures. Historical accuracy was of as little importance to the showmen as to the filmmakers: Henry VIII's wives were executed not so much for their infidelity as for their failure to provide the gluttonous king with male heirs.

In the wake of Henry VIII's success, American exhibitors briefly became more favourably disposed towards British films, and were almost, if not quite, prepared to overlook their 'Englishness'. An earlier Korda picture, *The Girl from Maxim's*, was given a US release:

There is a freshness about the atmosphere and the usual Korda brilliance about the treatment . . . it is an easy laughter-maker, playing any place, although the talk is distinctly English.

(*Motion Picture Herald*, 14 October 1933)

Korda's 1930s crop of movies was less British than 'super-British'. Hungarian himself, he had his brother Vincent as production designer, Georges Perinal, a Frenchman, as camera operator, and Harold Young, an American, as editor on *Henry VIII*. Only with this polyglot crew was he able to concoct a vision of England that flattered and tallied with US audiences' rather quaint notions of the country. Although his films had but a tenuous link with British culture and society of the period, he regarded himself as better qualified than native filmmakers to shoot British films:

An outsider often makes the best job of a national film. He is not cumbered with excessively detailed knowledge and associations. He gets a fresh slant on things.[38]

The fragments from assorted 1933 *Motion Picture Herald* reviews quoted above indicate the range of preconceptions and barriers Rank would have to overcome if his films were not merely to be dismissed by the Americans as 'foreign' and 'box-office poison'. The occasional flickerings of enthusiasm for British product evinced by the showmen, who were, after all, relentlessly upbeat about everything, even pictures they ostensibly detested, at least offered a mirage of a market for British product. But piercing US screen defences was always going to be an uphill battle: the British Board of Trade, well aware of the fact and patiently monitoring the reception of UK films in America, used to cut out and clip to the office walls the most negative reactions it encountered in the American trade press. As Paul Swann points out in his study *The Hollywood Feature Film in Post-War Britain*, the reactions could be caustic and barbed,[39] ranging from a North Carolinan's remarks about *The Adventurers* – 'These English pictures are getting very poor. I would hate to think I had to play their pictures to make a living' – to dismay about Powell and Pressburger's punchily retitled *Stairway to Heaven*:

> The newspapers gave this four stars. My customers gave it four Bronx cheers. Color, beautiful. This type might be good for class houses but they are poison to the guy with the average 'thinker'.
>
> (Quoted in Swann, 1987; 95)

Powell and Pressburger had their share of bumps and mishaps at the hands of the Americans. Despite their success with *49th Parallel/The Invaders*, which won Pressburger a Best Screenplay Oscar, and regardless of the phenomenal performance of *The Red Shoes*, which garnered more than $5 million at the US box-office, the Archers were frequently given a mauling by renters and showmen alike. This happened most notoriously with *The Life and Death of Colonel Blimp*, whose multi-layered narrative and span of generations were too much for any self-respecting showman to endure. United Artists tried to sell the film as a ribald tale of a lusty old soldier, a sort of Colonel Bluebeard. One the posters, the slogans read as follows:

> The lusty lifetime of a Gentleman who was sometimes Quite a Rogue! Duelling – hunting big game – and pretty girls – life's a grand adventure with Colonel Blimp![40]

So as not to try the patience of their customers, United Artists reduced the picture in length somewhat, chopping it down till it was only a little over a tidy hour. The net result was a court case: they were called to appear in front of the Federal Trade Commission. How could they defend desecrating the sacred text, tampering with what is still felt to be one of the 'masterpieces' of British cinema? They evidently felt no qualms, contending that their cutting had improved the film, which otherwise would have been hard to follow. United Artists' chief witness, Harold Austen, held the film in some contempt: he claimed that *Blimp* had not even paid for its printing and exploitation costs, and went on to declare that 'British pictures contained too much padding and too much tea drinking' (*Kinematograph Weekly*, 13 January 1949, p. 24).

Powell and Pressburger's Scottish island fable *I Know Where I'm Going* was an unlikely victim of the pro-Zionist lobby. It wasn't immediately apparent what relevance Wendy Hiller and Roger Livesey's high jinks in the Highlands had to British foreign policy in Palestine, but the picture was picketed none the less when it was already well into its run at the Trans-Lux Theater, New York (*Kinematograph Weekly*, 10 June 1948, p. 7). The Palestine issue inflamed tempers, and helped drive a wedge between British and American film industries when Ben Hecht, the celebrated scriptwriter and former Chicago journalist, took out a full-page advertisement in *Variety* magazine to announce that there was a 'song in his heart' every time a British soldier died in Palestine. This led to his films being blacklisted in Britain.

The Legion of Decency attempted to have *Black Narcissus* banned. Fortunately for Powell and Pressburger, the gesture backfired, and soon the steamy tale of nuns in the Himalayas was attracting 'queues early in the morning and late at night' (*Kinematograph Weekly*, 11 September 1947). In his autobiography *Silver Spoon*, Richard Norton writes of Catholic Ladies Associations who would find all sorts of (unintended) *double entendres* in the British and Dominion comedies he was trying to sell in the USA in the 1930s.[41] He also had his share of trouble with the Hays Office:

> I set off for America to set about selling *Bitter Sweet* and *Nell Gwynne* there. I found they were both being held up by the Hays Office – later known as the Breen Office – on the most ludicrous pretexts: the dresses were a little too low-cut, and so on.
>
> (Norton, 1954: 70)

In 1930, Will Hays, a Republican and former lawyer, had established the so-called Production Code, a self-regulatory charter for the film industry. The Hays Code was always a tricky obstacle for British filmmakers to negotiate. Hays, infamously, took exception to the use of the term 'bastard' in Olivier's *Henry V*, thereby provoking the ire of a great many of Britain's Shakespeare scholars, who seemed to feel the Bard had been insulted personally by this slight. Hays also expressed considerable misgivings about the low-cut necklines of *The Wicked Lady*, but in this instance his complaints provided useful oxygen of publicity for the movie.

Given that British films are deemed to be 'emotionally repressed' when compared to their more robust Hollywood counterparts, it is surely surprising that they managed to cause so much offence to American audiences. After all, the showmen were inclined to protest that British pictures, at least as far as comedies are musicals went, weren't full-blooded enough for American tastes. Even British melodrama was adjudged to be inferior and lacking in gumption. *Madonna of the Seven Moons*, considered risqué by the British, was tartly dismissed in the *Motion Picture Herald* as a

> polite and rather demure adventure story . . . the melodrama is treated rather too reverently – without the customary brash and dash that American audiences expect. It's just a little too well bred and distant.
>
> (*Motion Picture Herald*, 26 January 1946)

Similarly, *Variety* upbraided *Hungry Hill*, a 1947 Margaret Lockwood vehicle, for 'its lack of heart'. Another Lockwood picture, *Bedelia*, had its rather brutal British ending, in which the heroine poisons herself, softened for transatlantic consumption. For America's benefit, Miss Lockwood merely gave herself up to justice.

Surveying the variety of levels on which their films were attacked, it is quite understandable that British producers should feel that America was prepared to use any excuse under the sun for not showing their wares. Whether the Zionist Sons of Liberty, the Catholic Ladies Associations, the Hays Office or the midwestern showmen were being appeased, the result was always the same: the British film was excluded. Moral, aesthetic and religious judgements were conflated as the Americans strove to keep their market for themselves. Exporting British cinema to the USA was like walking on eggshells: there were a myriad different parties waiting to be offended. Lean's version of *Oliver Twist* is a case in point: Alec Guinness's portrayal of Fagin was condemned as anti-Semitic; the film was picketed and did only a fraction of the business of its predecessor, *Great Expectations*, which had been a popular (metropolitan) hit. Lean argued that the film portrayed Fagin in the same way Dickens had: he wasn't a sympathetic figure. (When the Americans remade the movie for TV in the mid-1980s, they cast a popular Irish-American actor, George C. Scott, in the role, and allowed his 'Fagin' to enjoy several moments of redemption. Such equivocating with villainy may have been at odds with the Dickens novel, but was, at least, more acceptable to US audiences than a depiction of the man as a monster.)

Frank Launder, back in Britain after a Rank-sponsored fact-finding tour of the States, reported that he had encountered strong anti-British feeling from exhibitors throughout America:

> One exhibitor, for example, has gone on record that the day he has a British film in his kinema, he will get out of the business.[42]

Despite overwhelming evidence to the contrary, the Americans scorned accusations that they were running anything other than an open market.

David Rose of Paramount bemoaned British filmmakers' complete lack of understanding of American tastes.[43] He proposed that the British should do their fieldwork: they should find out what the Americans liked, and then provide it. If they were not prepared to undertake this basic research, they had no right to complain about the disappointing reception afforded their movies. (Rose conveniently overlooks the fact that Britain did not have the resources to conduct large-scale surveys of US audience taste patterns. Anyway, research, as Rank found out, merely revealed that the Americans liked American films. For the British to try to 'ape' Hollywood would have been prohibitively expensive, and unlikely to work anyway.)

The British puffed and stuttered while Hollywood claimed its movies were popular abroad only because it had closely monitored its clients' foibles, and was providing appropriate pictures for its various markets. On one level, this was true – Hollywood has always been expert at tailoring its product for foreign consumption. In the classical studio days, it wasn't unusual for the Americans to add footage to a negative intended for German distribution: the Germans traditionally liked long films. By contrast, the Swiss preferred to cram two features into a 2-hour show, and for their convenience Hollywood would trim the negative.[44] When it came to villains, Hollywood took peculiar pains not to offend its customer countries. It would, for example, be economically club-footed to feature a Brazilian baddy in a film that might be sold to Brazil. Interviewed by Volker Schlöndorff, Billy Wilder recalled that he split with Paramount in the 1950s because they tried to make him change the nationality of the 'baddy' from German to Polish in his prison camp drama *Stalag 17*, so that the film would do better business in Germany. This mollifying brand of censorship didn't always seem to extend to Britain. From Sydney Greenstreet in *The Maltese Falcon* to the devil in *The Last Temptation of Christ*, the British accent has had sinister connotations.

For all its skill at fitting films to clients' needs, Hollywood also resorted to more nefarious underhand activities to protect its share of foreign markets. David Rose's chastisement of the British makes no mention of the part that undermining foreign production plays in Hollywood export drives.[45] Nor does he talk of the assistance that the American film industry has always received from the State Department, which, working in cahoots with the Motion Picture Export Association (MPEA), is able to bring considerable diplomatic and economic muscle to bear on opponents. And, thanks to the tireless work of the showmen, its own market remains watertight. No competitor country can broach it.

This, then, was the background to Rank's attempt to carve himself a niche in the USA, and a sisyphean task it proved to be: armed with a cheque book, various distribution deals from Hollywood studios, a clutch of promises and a handful of prestige films, he sought to spend his way into America.

CITIZEN RANK

In the summer of 1945, William Randolph Hearst, newspaper magnate and model for Welles's *Citizen Kane*, entertained J. Arthur Rank as one of the weekend guests at his famous Californian ranch. The two moguls had important business to discuss. Throughout the war, the Hearst press had either ignored or attacked British films. Now, Hearst agreed to instruct his columnists to treat the British picture with less hostility while Rank gave his undertaking that he would 'spend big money'[46] in American advertising. The inference was clear: if Rank had something to barter, or dollars to spare, the Americans would do business with him.

Rank had been a source of great fascination since his arrival in the States at the end of May. Hollywood had turned out in force to greet and scrutinize him. There are reports of lunches and dinners with Louis B. Mayer and Sam Goldwyn, with David Rose of Paramount and Nate Blumberg of Universal; stars such as Myrna Loy, Cary Grant and Constance Bennett were in attendance. Rank even managed to strike a deal with the quicksilver David Selznick, a coup which both impressed the American film community and earned its envy: Selznick agreed to set up Selznick International Pictures of England just so he could combine with Rank to make a movie about Mary Magdalene in Britain. It would have been quite an achievement for Rank to have secured the services of *Gone With The Wind*'s producer for a religious picture, a real feather in the cap of the Reigate Sunday school teacher. Although the project later fizzled out, as did Rank's endeavour to film *The Pilgrim's Progress* (with Michael Powell pencilled in as the director), Rank had established his credentials. Anybody invited to stay with Randolph Hearst and to parley with David O. Selznick was worth taking seriously.

W. H. Mooring, Hollywood correspondent for both *Picturegoer* magazine and the *Kinematograph Weekly*, sent copy back to London, relating how Rank had confounded the American press. Few of the journalists knew anything about him. Not only his manner and appearance –

> He didn't fit into their pigeon-holed pattern of a tycoon. His language and gestures were stilted when compared with the flourish of a typical American businessman.[47]

– but also the extent of his holdings surprised the American film hacks: Rank seemed to control everything: when ingenuous journalists asked him if his company had any tie-up with Baird Television, he was able to reply, in typically terse fashion, that he owned Baird TV. Whether from an innate sense of modesty, or because he was aware of the counter-productive effect that strident British propaganda tended to have on Americans, he did not, however, boast about the scope of his film interests. Instead, he adopted a low-key, and even self-deprecating, approach: rather than proclaiming the merits of his own pictures from the pulpit, he asked his hosts to tell him frankly what they thought was wrong with them. This they did with alacrity – the Americans were not at all reluctant to air their reservations about British cinema. Reprising the perennial complaints of the *Motion Picture Herald* showmen, they identified five basic weaknesses of the British picture in comparison with its Hollywood counterpart:

> 1) The action was too slow. 2) There was too much dialog. 3) The actors talked too fast and their accents and slang words were difficult to understand. 4) The actresses looked dowdy and the actors seemed effeminate. 5) The physical quality of the films often looked inferior to American productions.[48]

There was a world of difference between a 1930s screen version of a West End farce and a 1940s stiff-upper-lip movie along the lines of *In Which We Serve* and *49th Parallel/The Invaders*, both of which had enjoyed critical and popular success in the States, and had helped convince Rank that there was indeed an audience for British pictures to be found on the far side of the Atlantic. The general Hollywood perception that all British movies, regardless of genre, director, period, or stars, fell down on the above criteria, revealed how ineffective the British had been at broaching the American market. Although these five planes of damnation hardly seem appropriate for judging the wartime industry, Rank quietly made note of the criticisms, and even seemed to accept them as just. Red Kann wrote a condescending editorial about the British magnate in the *Motion Picture Herald*:

> When he [Rank] admitted British accent was a barrier on his side, when he recognized British tempo was too slow for American audiences and when he bowed to the American demand for glamor, it totals the same thing. When he told of employing American stars for future production, it was an oblique acknowledgement of the lack of marquee power of his own starring roster in the United States.[49]

Rank's disavowal of his own films and stars, and his fraternizing with the denizens of Hollywood, provoked a small storm at home, where British technicians and journalists felt that he was in league with the 'devil' and would quite willingly sacrifice the new-found integrity of the British picture simply to get himself bookings in the Midwest. George Elvin, president of the ACT, witnessed Rank's progress from afar, bitterly observing that 'he was becoming part of the American film industry'.[50] But Rank had no choice but to humour Hollywood. It was vitally important for him to get his films into the American market, and he was prepared to stoop to do it; to use American stars if necessary and to modify scripts so that they might appeal to American audiences. He appreciated that control of theatres was at least as important as the quality of pictures that he brought with him, but he still went through an elaborate rigmarole of consulting, flattering and deferring to his Hollywood hosts. Earlier in 1945, he had boldly stated:

> I do not want to get into America if I have to be half-American to do it.[51]

Now, at least as far as the ACT was concerned, his words had a hollow ring.

There was a fine line between making 'sensible' amendments to scripts which would enable US audiences to understand them and destroying a film's native identity by tampering with it. Tiny linguistic quibbles encapsulate the dilemma. Rank instructed his filmmakers to use the term 'fill'er up' when depicting car and garage scenes. This was a compromise, avoiding the American 'gasoline' and the British 'petrol', but seemed so trifling as to be worthless: surely the sense of the scene could be conveyed visually, without recourse to such semantic fudging. Rank thought otherwise, claiming that the British film's future in the USA rested on such trivial issues: he certainly didn't want his big-budget, prestige pictures to be excluded from the American market because they had slipped up and used British slang or broken one of the rules of the Production Code. Sydney Box's experiences with *The Bad Lord Byron*, a film he intended as a tribute to an important literary and historical figure, were symptomatic of the problems the British faced. As Box recalled:

> It is not difficult to imagine what a stunning blow we received when we heard from Hollywood that the Motion Picture Association, after reading our preliminary script, had decided that, in the form in which they had read it, our film was unacceptable from the standpoint of the Production Code.
>
> (Box and Cox, 1949: 12)

The problem, it seemed, was as much to do with Byron as a figure as with Box's script. As a saucy historical hero, the lecherous, limping bard was sure to stir up trouble with Will Hays' successor, Mr Breen.

In America, Rank met with Hays in person, asking him to explain the intricate details of his regulatory charter. Eventually, he would even persuade his filmmakers to submit their scripts to the Hays Office before starting shooting: for some critics, this was a craven capitulation to Hollywood censors. For Rank, it was a painful, but pragmatic, step to ensure that his pictures would not be banned on 'moral technicalities'.

Before coming to Hollywood, Rank had already conducted his own local surveys into American taste patterns by inviting the son of Fox boss Spyros Skouras, a GI based in Britain during the latter part of the war, to come and spend weekends in Reigate, and to bring his friends with him. Rank would grill the young American soldiers about their cinema preferences, paying particular attention to their remarks about British films. However, he realized that pandering to American taste was not really the key to opening up the USA to movies: economic control, on every level from raw material to training facilities and theatres, would have to come first. As a businessman, he would have to engineer the film assault on the world market.

During his time in America, Rank was shown round Universal Studios, in which he was still a major shareholder. Astounded by the efficiency of the American studio operation, he resolved to make more use of his influence at Universal by sending technicians, producers, directors and even stars to study American filmmaking at first hand. As his emissaries confirmed, Hollywood made its films quicker, 'nine weeks as opposed to our twelve weeks' being the average shooting schedule; had extensive research facilities ('MGM has an International Department of about 16 people whose sole function . . . is to see that all their pictures are palatable and understood in foreign markets'; and kept their studios in spruce conditions: 'the first thing you notice when you enter one of the big American studios is the extreme cleanliness and newness and tidiness of everything. Even before the War there always seemed to be a lot of litter and muck and odd bits of props lying around our studios.'[52]

Although Rank didn't feel he had achieved much with the Hollywood moduls ('How can you achieve anything in Fairyland?'), he was certainly taken seriously by his hosts. For all his deference to the Americans, he seemed to have an unshakeable faith in British cinema:

> In America, they like to make pictures about things that might happen once in twenty centuries. We like to make them about reality.
> (Rank, quoted in Wood, 1952: 117)

The newly robust state of British cinema allied with a fear of recession in the American industry gave him a strong bargaining position. By the end of the war, Hollywood was worried. The eastern European market was closed. Much of western Europe had done without US films from 1939 to 1945, and could continue to do without them unless America provided its cash-starved economies with the means to pay for such luxury goods. Television was on the not-very-distant horizon. (By 1949, 40 per cent of the US population would have access to television.) The cartel, the 'mature oligopoly' run by the eight Hollywood studios, was under threat from government legislation, soon to put an end to such time-honoured practices as block-booking and price-fixing, and to compel the moguls to separate their production and exhibition interests. Against this grim backcloth, the British market assumed a new importance. A decade before, in 1936, at the time of the Moyne Committee – another government-sponsored excoriation of the British film industry – the producer Simon Rowson had submitted memoranda on the need for reciprocity with Hollywood: 'It is probably impossible to contemplate the production of large-scale pictures otherwise than under the protection of a reciprocal plan' (quoted in Street and Dickinson, 1985: 84).

It seemed that 'reciprocity' was precisely what Rank was in a position to achieve. As Spyros Skouras observed, Hollywood was now as dependent on Britain, its prime foreign market, as Britain had always been on it: mutual back-scratching was quite in order:

> The cost of American production is so high that we must have the English market to maintain profitable Hollywood production. If a market that has returned $80 million to us last year is lost because the English could not afford to market our pictures, either American pictures of quality would suffer or the American theatregoer would have to pay more for his entertainment.
>
> (*Motion Picture Herald*, 5 July 1947)

Desperate to keep its export channels open, the American industry was ready to make concessions to its foreign competitors, a state of affairs underlined by the rapidity with which Hollywood jumped to trade with the Rank Organization. However, the fact that the studios were prepared to do business with Mr Rank didn't mean that the showmen were any more eager than before to show his films. It wasn't as if the Americans had suddenly discovered an enthusiasm for Rank's pictures. They were dealing with him only because they wanted to protect their market share in Britain.

RANK AND FOX

Spyros Skouras, son of a poor Greek shepherd, former busboy in a St Louis hotel, who had progressed, via running his own theatre chain in St Louis, managing the Warner Brothers circuit and briefly working for Paramount, to one of the top positions in the American film industry – since 1942 he had been president of Fox – was, on the face of it, an unlikely friend and ally for Rank in Hollywood. After all, Rank had 'poached' Gaumont-British from under Fox's very eyes, neglecting to seek the American company's approval – which he legally required – for his take-over in late 1941. Fox had close to $20 million invested in Gaumont-British, but was without representation on the board. The company had had to sit back and watch as Rank swooped for the controlling shares in the British combine. The war was raging, and Rank claimed he had more pressing matters to attend to than appeasing the American studio: in the early 1940s, scheduling business meetings between British and American film interests, who were thousands of miles apart, was far from easy, and Rank let the matter slip. It wasn't until 1944 that he and Skouras finally came face to face in London. To everyone's surprise, they quickly reached a satisfactory agreement: alarming his shareholders, Rank rearranged Gaumont-British's tangled affairs and allowed two Fox representatives to take their place on the board. (This went against Ostrer's cloak and dagger policy of the 1930s, which was to encourage Americans to invest in the company, but not to allow them any executive influence.) There were murmurings of dissent. Sceptics were worried that now Fox would be in a position to buy up Gaumont-British for itself, an impression reinforced when they discovered Rank was to provide Skouras with production facilities in Britain. In return, Fox was to help him distribute his pictures in the States, and there was even talk of co-productions. This cosy arrangement – and the opposition to it – highlighted one of Rank's fundamental problems: he may have owned a vast film empire, but that empire was far from integrated.

Kinematograph Weekly announced in 1944:

> Three pictures are to be made annually by one of the companies within the Rank production set-up for Fox . . . they will contribute toward the Fox requirements in this country, but will be distributed in America by Eagle-Lion Film Distributors.
>
> (*Kinematograph Weekly*, 23 March 1944, p. 3)

Eagle-Lion was Rank's new world sales outfit: the Gaumont-British shareholders, prickly as ever, failed to see why the deal with Fox, which was struck on their behalf, should benefit another Rank company. What might have been to Mr Rank and Eagle-Lion's advantage was not necessarily to theirs; they resented the way Rank made decisions affecting them without any prior consultation. Rank ignored their carping, holding up the agreement as a concrete example of the improved relations between British and American industries. It was psychologically reassuring for him to deal with a major Hollywood company on equal terms. Besides, Spyros Skouras and his brother Charles, fellow golfing enthusiasts, soon became his firm friends. They remained on good terms although their business partnership was conspicuously unsuccessful; as Robert Murphy observes:

> Little came out of the joint production plans and Fox distributed only a handful of British films in America.[53]

UNITED ARTISTS AND EAGLE-LION

Of the eight Hollywood studios, United Artists was the most favourably disposed towards British films. Not only was one of its founder members, Charlie Chaplin, English, with two of the others, Pickford and Fairbanks, confirmed anglophiles; the company's own position within the American industry was similar to that of the British. United Artists were first and foremost independent producers, who had splintered off from the majors so that they could exercise a greater degree of creative control over their projects and, more venally, so that the found members, Griffith, Chaplin,

Fairbanks and Pickford, could realize their full box-office potential. United Artists did not own a cinema chain. However, they had a reasonable distribution and sales outfit, and were always on the look-out for lucrative foreign movies to rent. It was they who had sold *The Private Life of Henry VIII* so successfully in the US market. As a consequence, they already had a 'British' producer on board: Korda had been granted full-member status of United Artists in 1935. Relations between Korda and his new colleagues soon deteriorated as the producer failed to repeat his earlier triumphs and as it transpired that the American company's lack of theatres was a serious drawback:

> Most Korda films never reached the sophisticated city audiences: they were shown in little out-of-the-way small-time cinemas to precisely those audiences who were likely to be puzzled by them.
>
> (Wood, 1952: 63)

United Artists were no more successful in distributing Herbert Wilcox's British and Dominion films than they had been with Korda. Whether or not there were theatres available, 'the man out in the field did not want to sell them'.[54] English pictures seemed to spell the kiss of death at the box-office. Even to resemble them was bad news for Hollywood: Godwell Sears' letter to Jack Warner about a Bette Davis film, *The Private Lives of Elizabeth and Essex*, highlights the danger:

> They say that it smacks of Alexander Korda and that in the south, Midwest and small towns particularly, it will be confused with an English picture, which, as you know, do very little business over here.[55]

Despite all the unhappy precedents, Rank was eager to find an outlet for his films in the USA, and he had targeted United Artists as a potential vehicle on which to carry his pictures to the Americans. His financial representative Barrington Gain had been sounding out US distributors. It was known that Korda was keen to sell his stock in United Artists, but only if he could get a top price. Rank seemed an obvious candidate to replace him. United Artists were already linked with the Rank Organization through their holdings in Odeon Cinema Holdings. Furthermore, Rank was committed to building and acquiring theatres throughout the world. An alliance with the British magnate would guarantee United Artists commonwealth as well as UK outlets for their own production. Unfortunately, United Artists was a far from harmonious outfit at the time the deal with Rank was mooted. For a start, Pickford and Chaplin were barely on speaking terms, and were liable to vote against one another in board meetings out of sheer enmity. And Alexander Korda, already irritated at having his mantle of 'saviour of the British film' pinched by the Methodist flour-miller, wasn't keen to have Rank march off in his shoes.

Selznick (who had signed an 8-picture deal with United Artists in 1935) and Pickford were dubious about the benefits in replacing 'one stockholder who is 6,000 miles away only to turn around and acquire another stockholder who has the same problem'.[56]

Rather than find a replacement for Korda, the partners wanted to buy out his share. Korda, though, was demanding an ever higher price for his holding: initially, he had said he would be willing to accept about $600,000 for his stock, but soon his asking price had risen to a million dollars. Chaplin, notoriously mean, refused to countenance such an outlay. In his book *United Artists*, Tino Balio paints a picture of confusion and dissent in the board room and beyond, of crossed telegrams and contradictory decisions.[57] United Artists' supervisor of foreign affairs and vice-president, Arthur Kelly, was wired by salesman Teddy Carr with the news that Rank wanted to buy a 50 per cent share in United Artists, and to create an Anglo-American distribution company. In the mayhem of crossed lines, Rank was turned down flat. It wasn't clear whether this was because Selznick and Pickford didn't want him as a partner or because Kelly had blundered. Whatever the reason, Rank was offended. He had helped increase the value of United Artists' holding in Odeon Theatres. Since he had become chairman of Odeon, the share prices had shot through the roof:

> The film investment public has definitely got it in its mind that J. Arthur Rank and others are going to obtain a place in the sun for British films.
>
> (*Kinematograph Weekly*, 13 January 1944, p. 31)

Furthermore, he was providing United Artists with British play-dates. Alienating him was not something they could afford to do. With the ABC circuit saturated with Warner Brothers' and MGM movies, they desperately needed space in his Odeon and Gaumont cinemas. As Balio puts it: 'at stake was UA's very existence in Britain.'[58] Rank seemed well and truly peeved by this carry-on in the early months of 1944. He refused to supply United Artists with films for their quota requirements, but went further, saying that he 'had no further interest' in the company, and felt that he had been betrayed by a 'staunch friend'.[59] Now he resolved to set up his own distribution agency, along American lines and with top American personnel: bizarrely, both Arthur Kelly and Teddy Carr, who had been at the hub of his protracted and abortive negotiations with United Artists, were now lured away to manage Eagle-Lion Distributors on his behalf.

'A distribution organization on the American model',[60] Eagle-Lion Distributors Ltd was registered in London on 1 February 1944. Rank had set Kelly and Carr an awesome brief. They were to put British film on the map by selling it to all five continents of the world. To challenge

Hollywood, Rank reckoned, it was not sufficient simply to sell films in America. He intended to compete in every foreign market.

Teddy Carr, former managing director of United Artists in Britain, had a natural affinity with his new boss. Born in Hull, and with a reputation as Britain's first 'super-salesman' (and a salary to match), he soon began to echo Rank, adopting flowery, evangelistic language to describe Eagle-Lion's goals. Profit-making, he insisted, was not the main consideration:

> I like to think of it not so much as a commercial mission as a crusade.[61]

Carr even managed to capture Rank's strange mix of prudence and extravagance in his statements to the Press:

> My Chief says that our films must show the British way of life, what we represent, where we stand and why, and what we mean by what we say. . . . I can tell that none of the films on our schedule will cost less than £225,000. We have already paid £480,000 on *Henry V* and have budgeted for *Caesar and Cleopatra* no less than £500,000. . . . We shall make no 'B' films. America doesn't want them. We don't want American 'B' films either. . . . while cautioning me not to waste money, Mr Rank told me that even if it cost £10 million he was determined to establish Eagle-Lion as a world influence.
>
> (*Kinematograph Weekly*, 11 January 1944, p. 27)

The list of countries that Eagle-Lion targeted is lengthy and impressive. Exhibitors in France, Portugal, Iraq, India and China expressed an interest in showing British films. There were Eagle-Lion offices in Denmark, Holland, Finland and Sweden. Rank's films were shown with great success in Czechoslovakia, although wartime currency restrictions prevented any money coming back to London. Carr had put out his feelers in Greece, Yugoslavia and Rumania. His main Middle Eastern office was in Cairo, with sub-offices in Syria, Palestine and Abyssinia. There were offices on the west coast of Africa, in Lagos and Freetown. While Skouras and Fox had undertaken to distribute Rank's films on Eagle-Lion's behalf in South Africa, Australia and New Zealand, Eagle-Lion had a sister company, British Distributors Ltd, in India, and there were Eagle-Lion offices in Singapore, intended to cover the whole East Indies.

As Eagle-Lion grew apace, Rank's canny accountant John Davis was travelling round the world, buying up theatres. He bought into the Great Union Theatre Chain in Australia (where he also invested in studio development); he invested in Canadian Odeons, buying as well as building theatres; he secured an interest in the South African Schlesinger Group. He invested in South America. There was a de luxe cinema in Cairo, and another one in Lisbon. There were even theatres in Ireland. There was an interest in the Kerridge Circuit in New Zealand. The Rank Organization was engaging in its own bout of cultural imperialism and had, Davis felt, stolen a march on Hollywood in its exploitation of global markets:

> We subscribe wholeheartedly to the policy of free trade on the screen . . . . Indeed we can perhaps claim to have anticipated our American friends in this acceptance of the right of access of the good films of all nations to world screen time.
>
> (*Kinematograph Weekly*, 19 December 1946, p. 33)

Rank's own innate modesty and frugality clashed headlong with a deliberate films policy of extravagance. To raise British cinema's profile, he was prepared to escalate budgets, wilfully to exaggerate them to Fleet Street, and to engage in a bout of free spending, even wastage, which hardly sat naturally on his Methodist shoulders. Interviewed in early 1944, as his plans for Eagle-Lion crystallized, he had told the *Manchester Daily Dispatch*:

> To secure a world market for British films they must be well produced and the stars given adequate exploitation before the film is released, so that there is a ready-made audience, their interest aroused by advance publicity. Publicity costs money, but money must be spent to make money.[62]

However well-oiled his renting, sales and publicity outfits were, however extensive his range of world-wide interests, in the end, his attempt to secure the British industry a place on the map would be dependent on the films he was producing. How would they compare with their Hollywood counterparts?

4

RANK AND HIS PRODUCERS

I don't think Rank had the slightest idea – after all, he was not a
filmmaker – what would be a prestige film, and what wouldn't: he just
said 'Go ahead, go ahead, go ahead.'

(Anthony Havelock-Allan)[1]

The producers whom Mr Rank employs have never in the history of
the cinema enjoyed so much artistic independence or so little interference with their methods of work. The objective or technical quality of British films has never been better than it is in the more
ambitious efforts produced under these auspices: the subjective or
thematic value never more adult.

(Dallas Bower, *New Statesman*, 2 September 1944)

Perhaps not since the time of the Renaissance Popes have a group of
artists found a patron so quick with his wallet, so slow with unsoli-
cited directions and advice.

(*Time*, 19 May 1947)

I know I have no talent for making films, but I can help you get what
money you want.

(Rank, quoted in Wood, 1952: 127)

Rank's plans to expand production in the wake of his acquisition of
Gaumont-British in late 1941 led to a brief vision of Shangri-La, a 'celluloid utopia',[2] for the select group of filmmakers he backed. Sidney Gilliat,
for example, talks of the 'remarkable freedom' given him by Rank, and
refers to the break-up of the Independent Producers group as 'tragic',[3]
while his colleague Michael Powell, never one to underestimate his own
glowing contribution to British cinema, described his brief liaison with
Rank as 'one of the most glorious partnerships in the history of British
films'.[4]

Although he had been involved in the industry for well-nigh a decade
before embarking on his huge prestige production drive half-way through
the war, Rank professed an ignorance of filmmaking, and made a virtue

out of it. Claiming, a little disingenuously, that he had no knowledge of their craft whatsoever, he placed his trust in the producers, and gave them free rein. He saw his role as 'taking care of business', in providing his newly recruited creative personnel with an environment in which they could flourish: he made sure his charges all had shared and easy access to the facilities they needed.

Never before, never since, have British filmmakers experienced anything like it. Such unfettered freedom would not have been countenanced by Rank's old mentor, C. M. Woolf. However, after Woolf died at the end of 1942, Rank began to listen to a flamboyant Italian producer who felt that filmmakers should be handled with kid-gloves: Filippo Del Giudice is credited with selling Rank the idea of production, with convincing him to place his faith in the imagination of the writers and directors, even if it meant swallowing business scruples and disregarding the strictures of the rapacious Wardour Street distributors.

DEL GIUDICE AND TWO CITIES

'A very big man who smoked Havana cigars',[5] Del Giudice entered the British film industry in a circuitous way. He was born in Trani, Italy, in 1892, and, after studying at Rome University, had established a successful law practice. An ardent anti-Fascist, he was compelled to leave Italy in 1932 to escape the Mussolini regime. He fled to London, where he supported himself initially by giving Italian lessons to well-heeled English children before re-establishing his law practice. In 1937, he set up Two Cities Films with Mario Zampi, an erstwhile juvenile lead from Italy, who had been working as an editor at the Warner Brothers British outfit. Del Giudice was to be legal adviser to the company, which made an auspicious debut with an early Asquith–Rattigan collaboration, *French Without Tears*, in 1938. Inventive, low-budget expatriate comedies such as *Spy for a Day*, which combined the talents of Anatole de Grunwald and Emeric Pressburger in concocting a far-fetched tale about an English farm labourer (Duggie Wakefield) who is kidnapped by a German pilot while tending his turnips, typified Two Cities fare before the war. The company's very existence was jeopardized in 1940, when both Zampi and Del Giudice, Italian and hence enemy aliens, were interned on the Isle of Man. (Angus Calder has written of the rich cultural life the island enjoyed during the war: the Amadeus Quartet was founded by four musical internees,[6] who, grateful for the chance to practise, went on to become a world-famous ensemble. However, there was nothing romantic about being locked away and the island provided no filmmaking facilities. Del Giudice, who had come to Britain to escape Fascism in the first place, was incensed to be incarcerated.) Released in late 1940, Del Giudice teamed up with Anthony Havelock-Allan, Richard Norton's assistant at Pinewood and a successful producer of quota pictures. (The unfortunate Zampi had been sent to Canada.) Del Giudice and Havelock-Allan's first collaboration was a patriotic film about newspapers carrying on in the blitz, *Unpublished Story*, with Valerie Hobson and Richard Greene. Then the Italian resolved to find a great writer – 'I can't have Shaw because Gabriel Pascal has Shaw'[7] – and a weighty theme for another propaganda pitch. He settled for Noël Coward and the Royal Navy.

In Which We Serve, loosely based on the early wartime exploits of 'Dickie' Mountbatten, was the first British war film to make a significant impact on the American market. (The US National Board of Review voted it the top picture of 1942.) It was shot for £240,000 at Rank's Denham Studios, but was not directly financed by the Rank Organization: C. M. Woolf, wary of Del Giudice's credentials and, like Jack Beddington at the Ministry of Information,[8] sceptical that a film which cast British sailors into the sea could help boost wartime morale, turned down the project, which in the end was mainly financed by Sam Smith of British-Lion, who supported the picture because he had never yet lost money on a film about the Royal Navy. (His previous forays into the genre had been comedies.) Rank provided 'topping-up' money and had a hand in the film's distribution.

Like Rank, Del Giudice was largely ignorant about film. He brought to the industry an inherent belief in the 'tal-ented', assembling around him, in best Diaghilev fashion, a stable of filmmakers he referred as his 'tal-ents'. (As his contemporaries recall, his pronunciation always managed to sever 'tal' and 'ent', making them into separate words.) His self-appointing role was that of the butler to these filmmaker aristocrats. Anthony Havelock-Allan is curiously ambivalent about his old partner:

> The creative people had to be cosseted and allowed to make the dreams they dreamt. This was Del Giudice's great contribution, but having made that contribution he didn't make any contribution himself. He didn't know about film costs. He didn't know about scripts. Del never appeared in the studios while we were making films. He didn't see rushes or rough cuts.[9]

The directors and producers were flattered by his personal attention and lack of professional interference, and derived confidence from it. (While Americans were saying that British films were technically inferior to their own, and while British directors were subject to the kind of xenophobic criticism later vented on them by Satyajit Ray and François Truffaut,[10] who accused them of being temperamentally incapable of holding movie cameras, confidence was a very scarce resource. Del Giudice may have exaggerated the scope of his protégés' abilities, but in doing so he helped free them of a crippling diffidence.)

Keen to foster screenwriting talent, Del Giudice played a major part in developing the Scenario Institute in London:

Screenwriters were to be invited to become members of a sort of club in which producers might be encouraged to look for screenwriting talent and the Institute might acquire screenplays by direct purchase from members or by matching any genuine 'outside offers'.[11]

This bright idea inadvertently antagonized the Palache Committee, the ACT and the Screenwriters Association, who all suspected the institute was designed to extend Rank's monopoly by giving him first choice and right of rejection over every new script. The Screenwriters Association took particularly badly to the concept, accusing Rank and Del Giudice of being parasites preying on the creative talent and calling them 'merchants and middlemen of a profitable business'. This was unfair. Del Giudice was one of the first film executives in Britain to draw attention to the importance of scripts. (The screenwriters themselves were constantly to be heard complaining that their contribution to film production was overlooked: 'The writer's experience is that he is regarded as a necessary evil rather than as the maker of the blueprint from which the film is to be made, and without which nothing in a studio can even commence. The only exception to this rule are the playwrights and novelists with big names who are employed to write a script, and who, with remarkably few exceptions, are without the technical knowledge to do so.'[12]) Furthermore, Del Giudice also highlighted the impact of music in movies by putting composers under contract. Film scores were a useful source of income for even the most distinguished music-masters, most of whom were not especially well paid. Amongst others, William Walton (*Henry V*) and Arthur Bliss (*Men of Two Worlds*) worked for Two Cities. Some, though, were doubtful about the extent of the Italian maverick's music knowledge:

> Del Giudice would never have known Vaughan Williams from a cabbage.[13]

To begin with, Del Giudice's relationship with Rank was informal: *In Which We Serve* was shot at Rank's studios and GFD helped sell the picture, but there was no contractual agreement between the two parties. When *The Gentle Sex*, a Two Cities/Leslie Howard collaboration about seven young women, all from different backgrounds, who were drafted into the war effort as army recruits, ran over budget, Del Giudice turned to Rank for help:

> My friend Arthur had the vision to understand the potential merits of the film. He wrote me a nice cheque.[14]

American receipts from *In Which We Serve* enabled the producer to pay back Rank promptly. Again, when Olivier's *Henry V* went over budget shooting in Ireland, Del Giudice prevailed upon Rank for assistance. As GFD were distributing the picture anyway, and had provided the initial funding, Rank dutifully wrote another cheque. But after *Henry V*'s completion, Rank insisted on formalizing the arrangement, taking over as chairman of Two Cities himself.

Del Giudice always was liable to be a controversial figure. His production policy was diametrically opposed to that advocated by the ACT and, by implication, the Palache Report. Rather than cutting costs and upping output, he believed that the British should concentrate on making a select series of prestige pictures with 'the Rolls-Royce stamp'.[15] He placed great emphasis on the literary, viewing the respectable writer, whether it be Noël Coward, Shakespeare, or F. L. Green (the novelist behind Reed's *Odd Man Out*) as a useful piece of cultural baggage to attach to a production, but also was keen to nurture new talent. By using established musicians, writers and composers, by purveying a brand of cinema which meshed traditional British 'high' culture with the strong visual impact of popular film, he hoped to breach the American market; with specialized distribution and long runs, his pictures, he thought, would reach out to sophisticated metropolitan cinemagoers whose tastes were not catered for by mainstream Hollywood fare. The films he was involved with may have been wordy, but they generally managed to combine spectacle with ideas. Del Giudice was prepared to make basic concessions to American audiences: he advocated that Hollywood provide the UK with dialogue experts 'so that British idioms and expressions which made our films unintelligible to American audiences could be eliminated'.[16] This was bound to infuriate the champions of a national cinema, the documentarists of the Crown Film Unit and Michael Balcon's staff at Ealing Studios, who believed that British idioms and expressions, whether or not they were familiar to the Yanks, were precisely what gave the British industry its new-found sense of identity: with Del Giudice in the 1940s as with Korda less than a decade earlier, there was the fear that British film would go 'international', that it would become a loose, mid-Atlantic hybrid, with no discernible appeal in either the UK or the US market.

Del Giudice's personal extravagance, combined with his expansive film production strategy, made him an unpopular figure not only with the journalists and intellectuals associated with the ACT and the *Tribune*,[17] most of whom were avowedly anti-American and wanted no truck with Hollywood, but also with the pragmatists and accountants, the grey-suited businessmen coming to prominence in the Rank Organization, who cared less about saving British film than showing a profit on the yearly balance sheet. A former colleague recalls that Del Giudice magnanimously waived his salary from Rank,[18] resolving to live on expenses alone. As the expenses came to more than £1,000 a week, this was not quite the selfless gesture it appeared. Del Giudice had bought himself a large country house, Sheepcote in Beaconsfield, and divided his time between there and the Grosvenor House Hotel, where he kept a service flat. He installed a private theatre at Sheepcote, threw riotous parties, and was not averse to giving his mistress, the Oslo-born actress Greta Gynt, the occasional jewel bought on Rank credit. While he possessed an influential friend in the President of the Board of Trade, Stafford Cripps, he had an even more influential enemy at Odeon Theatres in the person of John Davis, Rank's chief accountant, who was sidling his way up the organization, and was now second in influence only to Rank himself. Cripps is associated in popular memory with his time as Chancellor of the Exchequer in the Attlee government: he presided over a gloomy moment in post-war British history, the so-called Age of Austerity,[19] when the frozen drains and the food and fuel shortages of 1947 helped push the national towards despair, killing off the optimism and idealism which had elected Attlee in the first place:

> The snow fell and fell, and went on falling. By January 29th, the entire country was paralysed by the appalling freak winter of 1947: the worst winter of our century, which chose the worst possible year in which to arrive.[20]

During this time of shortage, Cripps, in charge of the purse-strings, assumed the mantle of the nation's Scrooge, renowned for his frugality in almost every area of public life. However, his successor at the Board of Trade, who was not kindly disposed towards Del Giudice, suggested Sir Stafford was prepared to make undue allowances for the Italian, even as he introduced swingeing cuts elsewhere:

> The truth was that Sir Stafford was not austere when it came to the financing of films. More accurately, Stafford was a soft touch when his wife Isobel came on to the set. She was a warm-hearted lady, a devoted supporter and indeed leader of many good causes. Amongst these was encouragement in season and out for an immigrant film producer named Del Giudice. Cripps, who was counting every penny for the welfare state . . . was ready to raid the tills for Del.[21]

Unlike Cripps, Harold Wilson would not lift a finger to help Del Giudice.

Del Giudice's expensive brand of prestige patriotism had found a ready audience in the war years: *The Way to the Stars*, *This Happy Breed* and *The Way Ahead* all raked in money. None the less, his position was precarious. Rank, never one to flaunt wealth, was known to disapprove of his lifestyle, and John Davis, accumulating more and more power within the organization, was his inveterate enemy. Davis regarded Del's extravagance as a betrayal of the trust placed in him by Rank and as a dangerous example to other producers, who might attempt to emulate his wastrel ways in the mistaken impression that extravagance and creativity went hand in hand. As early as 1946, it was obvious that Davis was chipping away at Del Giudice's authority. He had had himself and Josef Somlo[22] drafted on to the Two Cities board. (Richard Norton was also employed by Rank to curb Del Giudice's worst excesses. He achieved limited success, persuading Del to shelve expensive plans for filming Winston Churchill's torpid life of Marlborough.) More and more of Del Giudice's projects were being abandoned. Films made, such as *Men of Two Worlds*, lost money. Davis was not averse to using underhand means to sabotage reception of Two Cities pictures: he could open movies at awkward moments in out-of-the-way cinemas. *Henry V* was previewed in the East End, where tomatoes and eggs – which were then rationed – were thrown at it. As we shall see (pp. 157–60), Jill Craigie's *The Way We Live* suffered a similar fate before being rescued by crusading critics.[23]

On one level, Del Giudice's 'high living' was an astute piece of public relations. The film industry may have been castigated for its extravagance, but Two Cities first nights were always 'splendid and lavish occasions'.[24] Del Giudice had hired Major 'Fruity' Metcalfe, ADC to the former Prince of Wales, for the express purpose of disinterring high society figures from their drawing-rooms, of persuading the ermine-draped upper classes to come to the cinema. Rank's newsreels were able to make capital out of these occasions, which conferred a snobbish veneer of respectability on the industry. And they were useful for impressing visiting Hollywood executives. But, for all the publicity Del Giudice generated, both at these first nights, and with his grand visionary statements to the press,[25] he was rapidly falling out of favour. By the spring of 1947, his position at Two Cities was no longer tenable. His films weren't making money; his tal-ents were being denied the creative freedom he felt they needed. Worst of all, Davis was established as Rank's favourite. One of Del Giudice's young protégés has described the struggle between the Italian maverick and the dour Odeon accountant as a 'fight for Rank's soul'.[26] Each seemed to encapsulate competing characteristics within Rank himself. Had he plumped for Del Giudice, Rank would have been embracing a policy of flair and extravagance, of granting unbridled licence to the filmmakers: his evangelical side warmed to the Italian. Davis, by contrast, represented prudence and hard work. As Rank publicity chief Sydney Wynne recalls, Davis arrived at his desk by eight in the morning, and would probably still be there fourteen hours later. At all times, he attempted to apply sound business principles to the film industry: as a *Kinematograph Weekly* correspondent noted in 1946:

> All businesses, Davis argued with me, are essentially the same. The engineers, the technicians and the creative men can look after the product while the executive accountant can co-ordinate the whole organization and see that it is running on sound lines.[27]

The idea that you had to spend money to make money was anathema to the accountant: he wanted every single film produced under Rank's auspices to be shot as cheaply as possible and to turn a profit, and he showed little compunction about slowly squeezing Del Giudice out of the Rank Organization when Two Cities output ceased to be either cheap or profitable. In April 1947, after enduring almost two years of incessant sniping from Davis, Del Giudice admitted defeat and resigned from Two Cities, setting up a new, and chronically underfunded, outfit, Pilgrim Pictures, in its stead. Even as he quit, he protested, with some justification, that his reputation for going over budget was unwarranted. He claimed he had spent

> not more than £6½ million for the thirty-one films for which I have been responsible since the inception of Two Cities[28]

and that had not it been for the distorting effect of entertainment tax, he would have turned a tidy profit. However, his insistence that his films were 'no good for general audiences' and that they needed specialist marketing, pointed to his central problem: after the war, as audiences declined, it would become more and more difficult for big-budget, prestige pictures, without the hook of war subjects, to recoup their costs. Del Giudice had novel ideas for cutting out the distributors – he regarded them as unnecessary intermediaries, jackdaws preying on producers' profits – and showing his films for long runs in selected cinemas. The problem with such a method was that even when an individual film made money, it took an eternity to do so. Witness the case of *Henry V*: distributed by Prestige Pictures (American renters for Rank's more rarefied movies), Olivier's vehicle was 'roadshowed': C. M. Woolf's son John, back with GFD after his war service, was in charge of selling the movie. Rather than approach the main circuits, he negotiated with the Theater Guild, run by Lawrence Langley and specializing in tours of plays, for the picture to be shown on a series of one-night bookings – like a travelling Shakespearian epic – in a variety of college towns. The film was booked into halls so small that it invariably sold out every time it played. Gradually, as word of mouth spread the message, it was booked into slightly larger halls, and eventually managed to reach a fairly wide audience. Although the marketing of *Henry V* was held up as a triumph, a prime example of how to lure unwilling Americans to a 'highbrow' British movie, it cost time and effort (and money) to generate the box-office returns: it would be prohibitively expensive and tortuously slow to market all films on this basis.

After the collapse of Pilgrim Pictures (bought, in the end, by John Woolf), Del Giudice fell on hard times, 'he ended up in the gutter, poor fellow',[29] eventually retiring to a monastery, where he died destitute in 1962. Various faltering attempts to rekindle his film career in Britain had foundered: he wasn't even granted a visa to stay in the country in the 1950s.

Half venerated, half execrated, one of the truly flamboyant personalities in British film history, Del Giudice was responsible for luring Rank into production on an expansive scale. Without his impetus, Rank might have heeded C. M. Woolf's advice and steered clear of big-budget, prestige filmmaking. However, Two Cities' success in America, with both *In Which We Serve* and *Henry V*, persuaded Rank that it was possible for British films to compete with the best of Hollywood. Altogether, Del Giudice produced thirty-five films in Britain, working with Olivier, who said of him, 'I know no one else in British films so kind, generous, imaginative and courageous',[30] and with David Lean, Thorold Dickinson, Peter Ustinov and the Boulting brothers amongst others: he may have been guilty of hubris and extravagance –

> He gave his filmmakers such a heady draught of self-importance that they were soon understandably giddy . . . the wine was stimulating before it proved dangerous.[31]

– but he was unique in having the courage to stand up to the front office and to move the balance of power from the renters and exhibitors, with their ready-built formulas for pleasing the public, to the filmmakers themselves:

> Del Giudice is Italian for Judge. A good judge provides protection for the innocent. Del has provided protection for a large number of filmmakers who believed that a native film industry was a possibility. Today the industry is in existence. Nothing can diminish the extent of his contribution.[32]

INDEPENDENT PRODUCERS

> We of Independent Producers can make any subject we wish, with as much money as we think that subject should have spent on it. We can cast whichever actors we choose, and we have no interference with the way the film is made. No one sees the films until they are finished, and no cuts are made without the consent of the director or producer, and what's more, not one of us is bound by any form of contract. We are there because we want to be there.
>
> (David Lean, *Penguin Film Review* 4, 1947: 35)

David Lean's oft-quoted panegyrics in the *Penguin Film Review* belie the experiences of his colleagues at Independent Producers who, while acknowleding the extraordinary freedom they were given, paint a much less rosy picture of the outfit, particularly in its latter years. Had everything been as idyllic as Lean suggests, Independent Producers would never have broken up. None the less, Independent Producers Ltd (IPL) marked a pinnacle both for its constituent members and for its unlikely sponsor, Mr

Rank. This unique experiment in British film production, which bears testament to Rank's confidence in British filmmakers, spawned several classic pictures as well as one or two clunking catastrophes.

Structurally, Independent Producers bore a loose similarity to United Artists, the company set up by Griffith, Pickford, Chaplin and Fairbanks in 1919, but, rather than pooling together the resources of four major stars, IPL assembled producer/director teams, and did so under Rank's banner. The teams were 'independent' because of the major studio, not in spite of it.

Michael Powell and Emeric Pressburger, the Archers, were the first aboard. As Pressburger noted in his diary in early 1942:

> Mick and I went at 4 to Odeon's Central Office on Park Lane to meet Woolf, Rank and Woodham-Smith [Rank's lawyer]. It was a triumph! We agreed on making two pictures for them in the next year, subject to our discretion (first *Blimp*) with £15,000 per picture plus ten percent from the net profit.
>
> (Pressburger's diaries, 27 January 1942)

Rank had approached the duo in 1941, after *49th Parallel*, made for Lady Yule's British National, with backing from the Ministry of Information, proved successful both in Britain, where it did an estimated £250,000 worth of business, and in America. He was keen to back the follow-up, *One of Our Aircraft Is Missing*. However, as he reluctantly told the Archers, he had been overruled by C. M. Woolf: 'he thinks it is a defeatist picture. He doesn't think it will be box-office' (Powell, 1987: 388).

Despite his misgivings about 'intellectuals', into which category both Powell and Pressburger fell, and notwithstanding his failure to answer a succession of letters they had written him,[33] Woolf eventually relented. By early 1942, he was as keen as his boss to sign up the Archers. Powell and Pressburger were to form the nucleus of Independent Producers.

Eight months later, when the formation of IPL was announced in the trade press, Marcel Hellman of Excelsior Productions, Leslie Howard, the dashing Pimpernel himself,[34] and Alfred Watkins were named as the other 'producer' members, although none of these three was destined to have much impact on the group. The initial aim of IPL, hardly earth-shatteringly ambitious, was to centralize production facilities, to avoid waste, 'to promote business co-operation between the various producers concerned, and to provide the machinery to enable them to make the best use of the available manpower and studio space.'[35] The growing demand for British films abroad, in particular the mirage of a market in America, was advanced by Rank as justification for setting up the operation, which proved costly at the outset. The terms offered the producer members were generous. While they still had to submit proposals to GFD for films, and while GFD retained the right to 'cut alter sub-title and dub' pictures for foreign distribution,[36] GFD were not permitted to make 'any substantial alter-ation' in a picture without the consent of the filmmakers.[37] As at Two Cities, the balance of power had swung away from the front office and towards the producers. So long as the producers didn't go more than 20 per cent over their agreed budget, which was likely to be a generous one anyway, they could do pretty much as they liked. Furthermore, Rank was prepared to concede percentages of profits.

To swell IPL's ranks, the Archers were encouraged to recruit 'creative producers'.[38] Cineguild, the outfit formed by Ronald Neame, Havelock-Allan and David Lean, was invited to come aboard in the summer of 1944. At roughly the same time, Individual, the company formed by Launder and Gilliat, joined the fold. For all these young filmmakers, the offer of a cut of the profits proved to be alluring bait. The Cineguild team had splintered off from Two Cities precisely because the trio felt that they had not been fairly rewarded for their work on *This Happy Breed* and *In Which We Serve*: once the distributors had been reimbursed and all the loans paid off, and once Del Giudice and Noël Coward had taken their slice, there was precious little left to nibble for Messrs Lean, Neame and Havelock-Allan, who were, after all, the key creative figures behind the Two Cities pictures, photographing, writing, co-producing and directing them. Likewise, for Launder and Gilliat, the top screenwriting team of the 1930s, who had penned such classics as Hitchcock's *The Lady Vanishes* and Carol Reed's *Night Train to Munich* before graduating to director status them-selves, IPL had obvious attractions. Fresh from their successes for pro-ducer Ted Black at Gainsborough Studios, notably the Home Front propaganda piece *Millions Like Us*, and the wartime love triangle *Waterloo Road* (which Mrs Rank had felt to be immoral), the duo would relish the chance to work with bigger budgets and on longer schedules.

All these filmmakers had cut their teeth in the frenetic and hurried 1930s, the 'quota quickie' decade, when, as Michael Powell put it – with becoming lyricism – 'retakes were as rare and unattainable as wild straw-berries'.[39] At long last, as members of the Independent Producers co-operative, they would be freed from the duresses of breakneck £1-a-foot production: after their turbulent apprenticeships, they would formally be recognized as 'artists' and allowed to experiment. They were outside the scope of C. M. Woolf, dead since the end of 1942, and were yet to encounter the 'Davis aesthetic'. (When John Davis was restructuring the company in the wake of its massive production losses of 1947–8, he put a ceiling of £150,000 on a first-feature budget.[40] The Independent Producers liked, on average, to spend about twice as much as that.)

For good measure, IPL recruited its documentary man: Ian Dalrymple. Executive producer of the Crown Film Unit from 1940 to 1943, Dalrymple had worked on such quintessential war documentaries as *London Can Take It*, and the two most famous Humphrey Jennings pictures, *Fires Were*

Started and *Listen to Britain*. With his company, Wessex Films, he now branched out into feature filmmaking. (Unfortunately, none of his projects would make Rank money, but as soon as he defected to Korda at London Films, he struck box-office gold with *The Wooden Horse*.)

At the outset, IPL was a loose affiliation of producer/director teams without a clear identity of its own. However, the profile of the group was changing. Leslie Howard died in a plane crash in 1943, shot down by Nazis who were convinced he was travelling in tandem with Churchill. Marcel Hellman made two undistinguished films at IPL, *They Met in the Dark* and *Secret Mission*, before his company, Excelsior, left Rank, and Alfred Watkins, 'the lone wolf of Denham', did little more than offer his services as an adviser on special effects. Those remaining, the Archers, Cineguild, Wessex and Individual, came as close to complete artistic and economic freedom as British filmmakers have ever been. (And only Orson Welles, let loose to play with 'the electric train set' at RKO in 1941 while making *Citizen Kane*, has enjoyed a similar degree of licence in the American industry.) From 1944 till late 1947, IPL was operating at full throttle. Arguably, the set-up suffered from fundamental structural weaknesses right from the outset. It was inevitable that the experiment would be abandoned sooner or later, but, as Sidney Gilliat explains, the filmmakers were able to ignore contractual, budgetary and logistical shortcomings, and blithely get on with making their pictures, even as the front office gradually sought to reassert its position: 'Independent Producers was a case where the honeymoon was almost longer than the marriage.'[41]

Initially, there were few curbs put on the filmmakers. They had their own managing director, George Archibald, a Glaswegian who had started life sweeping the floors of Glasgow cinemas and would end it in the House of Lords: 'He was to be our servant and not our master.'[42]

There was also a production manager, James B. Sloan, a longtime associate of Mr Rank, who had been the first general manager at Pinewood Studios, and had also worked for the Religious Film Unit, GHW. Like Archibald's, his role was functional and administrative: he was there to help the filmmakers, not to hinder them. With Pinewood Studios unavailable because of the war, the producers were based at Denham. Each of the individual companies became a member of IPL, with a seat on its board, which had Rank as chairman. Not that this board had much relevance in the early years. The filmmakers were given a free rein. They submitted a project with tentative name, story idea, proposed stars and proposed maximum cost. It was as simple as that. As long as everything was in order, they were allowed to proceed:

> Finance was supplied for each company up to a named figure and providing the budget was within that amount, then each company was independent and could – in theory – make any film it wanted.[43]

There were two tiers of control: a production meeting every fortnight, chaired by Archibald and attended by representatives of all the companies – this was a basic, low-key meeting in which the various producers offered progress reports and addressed their day-to-day problems; and the monthly meeting, chaired by Rank himself and consisting of the full board of IPL, which (according to Gilliat's memo of 22 May 1991) 'would summarize the production policy for the Chairman and discuss general policy, relations within the business, technical points such as the procuring of new, up-to-date equipment and the like'.

Casting himself as the benevolent patron of an artists' studio, Rank tried to encourage a cross-fertilization of ideas. He had hoped that his stable of filmmakers would provoke and chide and stimulate one another: ideally, the Archers might offer constructive criticism of Cineguild's scripts or Individual recommend actors to Wessex: David Lean might wander on to the set of a Michael Powell film and suggest an idea for a set-up, or vice versa. This did not happen. The Independent Producers were determined to stay independent of one another, and would have felt it more than a little presumptuous to criticize a colleague's work: a 'helpful' suggestion could easily be misconstrued as a veiled attack. Moreover, the filmmakers approached their craft from a variety of different angles; there was no consensus as to how to make a successful film, as Havelock-Allan recalls: 'What David and Ronnie Neame and I might have thought was a good script might to Launder and Gilliat have seemed a not very good script.'[44]

Rank was likely to accept any proposal put forward to him by his trusted Independent Producers. In the years after Woolf's death, he was also remarkably indulgent to his other production companies. He held weekly conferences in his Park Lane offices where Archibald, Del Giudice and Maurice Ostrer argued the cases for, respectively, Independent Producers, Two Cities and Gainsborough. It was rare for him to block a project proposed to him by any of the above. While this attitude may have pleased the production chiefs, it infuriated business colleagues, who didn't share his faith in the filmmakers. There was an almost touching naivety in Rank's philosophy about making pictures. Contemporaries remember that he always insisted

> he was non-creative and could not therefore comment on the creative processes of film producers, directors, artistes, etc. Since the success of the final film depended on their creative artistry he could not and would not stand in their way. If they felt that financial restrictions would hamper their creative ability then they must have their way. Although, he added, his own mind never worked like that.[45]

His reluctance to 'cap' his filmmakers allowed Cineguild and the Archers in particular to follow a bourgeois/romantic creed of the creative individual artist: Powell and Pressburger, Lean and Co., were no longer hired hands churning out product for quota pruposes: at IPL, they were cine-poets, making 'art' films within the mainstream. They achieved some startling results. They also helped to fuel the rumours of waste and extravagance which began to bedevil Rank from late 1944 onward. (In 1944, Rank's renegade producer Gabriel Pascal, a late recruit to Independent Producers, had embarked on his epic adaptation of Shaw's *Caesar and Cleopatra*, a vast, ill-fated endeavour which did more than anything else to besmirch the reputation of the outfit, casting the filmmakers, at least in the eyes of a hostile Press, as profligates in an age of austerity.) Schedules for Independent Producers pictures tended to be long drawn out, both by Hollywood standards and by comparison with British movies of the 1930s. The Archers' Scottish island fable, *I Know Where I'm Going*, for example, clocked in at twenty-two weeks of shooting, while *Caesar and Cleopatra* went on for well over a year. Less favoured Rank producers, particularly those at Gainsborough, who were working in much more stringent circumstances, complained at the preferential treatment IPL was receiving. Betty Box, for one, while admiring many of their films, was sceptical about the leeway given her Independent Producers colleagues at a time when she was making at least six pictures a year:

> You can bet your bottom dollar that Cineguild never did anything under twenty weeks, and what they were doing for twenty weeks with some of their pictures I do not know. . . . Cineguild were always the clever boys of the Organization. . . . I have seen David Lean sit on the set the whole of the day and not shoot anything and say, 'Oh, God! Give me inspiration!' It's all very well, isn't it! Why didn't he get the inspiration before he started shooting?[46]

With the resources made available to them, the Independent Producers were bound to be ambitious: they might re-create the Himalayas in Horsham (*Black Narcissus*) or transfer Canterbury Cathedral to Denham Studios (*A Canterbury Tale*); they might experiment with blending monochrome and Technicolor photography (Jack Cardiff's cinematography on *A Matter of Life and Death*); or they might make their films on location in Ireland (*I See a Dark Stranger*) and on remote islands off Scotland (*I Know Where I'm Going*); they might make costume dramas (*Esther Waters*), adapt Dickens (*Great Expectations* and *Oliver Twist*) or Arnold Bennett (*Dear Mr Prohack*). Poppa Day, in charge of special effects, a brilliant artist and master of every screen technique from hanging miniatures, split screen and wind-back to painted backdrops and matte photography, brought his craftsmanship to bear at IPL: Day was a former apprentice of George Méliès, and Michael Powell called him 'the greatest trick photographer and double-exposure merchant that the movies have ever seen' (Powell, 1987: 239). Then there was Alfred Junge, a production designer who arrived in the British film industry via the Berlin State Opera and UFA Studios, and who had worked with Powell since the 1930s; there was Hein Heckroth, a compatriot of Junge, who would win an Oscar for his costumes in *The Red Shoes*, and John Bryan, who had designed René Clair's *The Ghost Goes West* and Korda's *The Shape of Things to Come* before joining up with Cineguild at Independent Producers. Rank was spending vast amounts on research in general, and on a production technique called Independent Frame (see pp. 122–31) in particular. He sent most of the Independent Producers on jaunts across the Atlantic to study production methods in Hollywood and to assess exhibition practices – 'showmanship' and how it affected British films – on the east coast and in the Midwest. The producers were also given instructions to earmark new, up-to-date equipment that Rank might purchase. Launder and Gilliat, Lean and Neame, Powell and Pressburger, all went to the States on Rank business, delivering lengthy reports of their findings on their return. Not that their advice was always taken . . .

The Independent Producers films have been written about extensively elsewhere, and this is not the place to extol their formal and aesthetic virtues. Suffice it to say that 1944–7 was an extraordinarily rich period, both in the range of subjects broached (everything from the magnified intimacy of *Brief Encounter* to the epic grandeur of *A Matter of Life and Death*, one of the few British films bold enough to move off the earth and represent 'heaven') and in the depth of talent in every department from special effects to set design, from cinematography to scripting and directing.

The war years may have been characterized by the cross-fertilizing of documentary and feature, by the films that were coming out of Ealing and that were being sponsored by the General Post Office and the Crown Film Unit. *San Demetrio, London*, *The Foreman Went to France*, *Went the Day Well* and *The Big Blockade* – the very titles of much of Ealing's war output suggest courage and self-deprecation beyond the call of duty. But at Two Cities and Independent Producers, the filmmakers were not at all hampered by notions of realism and restraint. There had been an explosive flamboyance in British cinema seeking expression since the cash-starved 1930s, when Lean and Powell were doing their routine work. The 'imp of the perverse' wasn't only Eric Portman squeezing glue on women's heads in *A Canterbury Tale*: it was there in Cavalcanti's films at Ealing; in Launder and Gilliat (*The Rake's Progress*) and in the Gainsborough melodramas: all of their work chafed against the pudeur and restraint of the 'documentary/realist' tradition, at least as it is defined in its narrowest form. Del Giudice's 'tal-ents' and the Independent Producers couldn't be constrained by what Gilbert Adair has called 'Grierson's slightly dour ideological high-mindedness'.[47]

The 'quality' press critics initially supported IPL output, tending to neglect Rank's part in providing the filmmakers with an environment in which to work, and instead suggesting that the pictures were successful because they were made by small, autonomous units with creative freedom. However, relations quickly soured: too much 'creative freedom', the critics decided, allowed the filmmakers to become 'prima donnas' and to roam in the 'realm of fancy'.[48] The Archers' excesses were much frowned upon. *A Matter of Life and Death* was deemed whimsical, while the glue scenes from *A Canterbury Tale* were judged to be a shocking lapse in taste. IPL pictures, for all their finery, were compared unfavourably with the neo-realist films coming to prominence in Europe after the war. Rossellini and De Sica were addressing the 'problems of peace',[49] whereas Rank's bushy-tailed protégés had turned their back on issues of social and political import; had abandoned the central tenets of the 'quality' film, and were indulging in far-fetched fantasies.

Richard Winnington, writing in the *News Chronicle*, is quite acerbic about Independent Producers' tendencies towards 'self-indulgence'. He refers to

stillborn epics conceived and made in the sort of individualistic romp
Mr Rank was led to encourage in the name of Prestige[50]

and goes on to accuse Rank and his motley crew of pushing 'all the tentative character out of British films'. As the war ended, the critics seemed to lose faith in the British film revival which they themselves had attempted to foster: there was an almost palpable sense of disappointment that talents like Lean and Powell and Pressburger, lauded and encouraged by the journalists, should veer off from the tracks laid down for them and hoist British cinema in an altogether inappropriate direction. Not that Winnington, Whitebait, Manvell and their colleagues were having much impact on cinemagoers' tastes as a whole: the circulations of magazines like *Sight and Sound* and the *Penguin Film Review* were small by comparison with those of mass market fanzines like *Picturegoer*. While the critics were railing against Rank's policy of sponsoring 'scores of ridiculously expensive minor films',[51] and somehow vitiating the quality quota in the process, fans were beginning to protest that British pictures were too highbrow. On both popular and critical levels, Rank's experiment was running into difficulty:

For some time now it has seemed to me that here in England we are making films for a small group of long-hairs rather than for the public. Worse, a pride is being taken in this kind of film and we speak rather pompously of Hollywood's efforts. . . . Let the British film industry comb some of the arty dead weight it is carrying out of its hair; then, and only then, will we find ourselves with a worldwide market.

(Letter in *Picturegoer*, 24 May 1947, p. 14)

The very image of the gong was putting some cinemagoers off:

Slowly the caption came into view – J. Arthur Rank presents. From behind me came a muffled yawn and a peculiar remark. 'Oh dear, now we are going to be educated.' The unseen commentator behind me seemed to have the impression that Mr Rank's name on a picture meant that it was a dose of factual information slightly sugared. The horrible word 'propaganda' springs to mind. Are the products of the Rank Organization too highbrow?

(*Picturegoer*, 7 June 1947, p. 9)

Rank's attempts to spend his way into the US market with glossy, prestige productions grated against the celluloid sensibilities of patriotic fans and critics alike:

I am one of the many who, by eating bread and seeing films, have put J. A. Rank in a position to disregard their wishes. In planning films to fit the Hays Office, with American stars and producers, he should remember that these films have also to be shown in Britain. . . . Money would be better spent on films for the home market than thrusting our films into America. Anyhow, has America all of the world's filmgoers? What of the British Empire and Europe? No, Mr Rank, you want to do your best for British films but you are looking in the wrong direction.

(*Picturegoer*, 29 September 1945, p. 14)

The disparate strands of British film culture, the critics' 'quality' cinema, the fans' 'popular' cinema and Rank's 'prestige' cinema, had briefly come together during the latter part of the war. Now, they were split asunder: there was no consensus as to what form the British film should take. All the old acrimonies, the tensions between critics and fans, filmmakers and renters, surfaced once more. Rather than laying the foundation for a sustained boom in the industry, the wartime harmony now seemed a brief and isolated moment, an aberration. Rank was caught in the cross-fire, managing to please neither the fans nor the critics. And he was still stuck on the horns of his own dilemma: he had set out to put British film on a 'sound' basis by applying 'sound' business formulas to the industry, but he also wanted to give the filmmakers their head. The two goals were not always compatible. Nowhere was the business–art tension more evident than at Independent Producers Ltd. Ironically, the very factors which made IPL work would eventually cause its demise. Instead of liberating the producers, the system, with its emphasis on 'rationalization' and 'centraliz-ation', ended by bogging them down in bureaucracy. Eventually, this halcyon episode in British film history would end in bitterness and recrimi-nation, and with a mass exodus of Rank's best producers to Alexander Korda's newly revitalized London Films. In the course of its existence, IPL underwent a bizarre metamorphosis, starting as an ad hoc, loose arrange-

98

ment – the producers weren't even on contracts – and ending with the putative artists in a bureaucratic tangle: a cautionary tale, perhaps, of the dangers in trying to marry art with business. Rank discovered that the very fact of having an outfit like Independent Producers demanded regulation. While he didn't claim to understand his filmmakers' 'creative processes', he none the less felt impelled to run the studios, first Denham and then Pinewood, along business lines. His experiences with Pascal's *Caesar and Cleopatra* alerted him to the dangers in allowing a producer complete creative and fiscal licence: nothing that Cineguild or the Archers could do, not even the most hideous excesses of the free-spending Del Giudice, were a patch on Pascal.

PASCAL, PIFFLE AND THE DEMISE OF IPL

Caesar and Cleopatra was budgeted at £550,000, and came in at a final cost of a million and a quarter plus bank interest (which the accountants had forgotten to add in!). Although this was the only film made by Pascal for IPL, it cast a late shadow over the operations of its remaining members after he had gone. Just when most of us felt we were not doing sufficiently well financially, after the pictures we had turned out, that we were being increasingly entangled in centralized bureaucracy and that we should be given more freedom, not less, it became ever clearer that the Rank Organization, in the persons of John Davis and Arthur Rank, were of roughly the opposite view in each case, due to what had happened with Pascal.[52]

Why did Rank agree to make *Caesar and Cleopatra*? Had he canvassed the other Independent Producers – and they were supposed to have a say when it came to decisions that affected them – he would have found that they had extreme misgivings about the project. Anthony Havelock-Allan remembers that the subject of Gabriel Pascal engendered a rare unanimity between the filmmakers:

Pascal sold a bill of goods to Arthur. . . . If we'd been consulted, to a man, we would all have said you are raving mad. Do not let Gabriel Pascal attempt to direct anything. He does not know how to direct. It will be a disaster. Let him produce if he must. He's got Shaw. If you think it's worthwhile, do it. But what you must never do is allow him to be in charge of the money or direction.[53]

Perhaps Rank felt some vestigial loyalty to Pascal. After all, *Major Barbara* was credited with saving British film production at the start of the war: Pascal, predictably over schedule, had kept Denham going at a time when Beaverbrook wanted to requisition the studios for the Ministry of Aircraft Production. And *Pygmalion*, free from his directorial touch, but very much a Pascal production, had proved an Oscar-winning success in the USA in 1938. He had George Bernard Shaw on tap, having persuaded the writer that he, Pascal, was the man to bring Shaw's plays to the screen. Like Del Giudice, Gabriel Pascal was a colourful figure with a flair for self-promotion and a nice line in spleen, who once sent a Hollywood agent with whom he was in dispute the following telegram:

> —, Hollywood, I give you my word of honour as a Hungarian Cavalry Officer and an English farmer you are the greatest crook unhung. Gabriel Pascal.
>
> (Quoted in Norton, 1954: 180)

He used to dictate to secretaries while sitting on the lavatory, and couldn't understand why the secretaries all left his employment.[54] A former colleague has vivid recollections of meeting the producer at the Pinewood swimming baths:

> A little man, fat, tubby, Gabriel Pascal was most charming, he would spend money like water. [At the swimming pool] there were these rings you could swing across. He used to get up on the balcony, grab the rings and swing across the pool. He was short, fat, full of hair and looked just like a gorilla.[55]

When Sidney Gilliat pressed Rank about the exorbitant cost of *Caesar and Cleopatra* at an IPL meeting, Rank justified the expense by arguing that Pascal's epic would sell six other British movies in its wake as it burned a swathe across America. As we have seen, Rank was desperately keen to break into the US market: the success of *The Private Life of Henry VIII* and Olivier's *Henry V* had shown that there was an appetite for prestige historical productions which spiced up the past. And even the Americans had heard of George Bernard Shaw, by then probably the most famous living writer in the world.

As a putative director, Pascal had several fundamental drawbacks, not the least of which was that he had no knowledge of cameras or lenses: shown a design for the film, he would automatically protest that it 'wasn't big enough'.[56] Size, he felt, was the key to winning over the USA, but he didn't appreciate that technicians had the ability to distort perspective and that a 6-inch model of an ape could be transmogrified by trick photography into a 50-foot-tall Titan called King Kong. Pascal was a perfectionist, moving at an incredibly slow pace through the script. Scheduled for four months, his picture took more than a year to shoot. This was quite startling and far from politic in the context of the 1944–5 British film industry, when space was at a premium and the Palache Committee had already delivered its damning verdict on Rank's 'tendencies towards monopoly'. Unconcerned at the film's tardy progress, Pascal built his own Sphinx – the one in Egypt wasn't up to scratch – and ignored the growing chorus of critics who were imploring him to get a move on.

In the end, Pascal achieved a pyrrhic victory. His sojourn in the deserts of Egypt (on location) and of Denham (he covered the studios in sand) helped Rank achieve his primary goal: *Caesar and Cleopatra* was a success in the USA. Rumours of its troubled gestation had reached the American showmen, but didn't seem to affect its reception. As Ray Lewis, a Canadian journalist, wrote in the *Moving Picture Digest*:

> In the United States and Canada our critics gave the wealth of good entertainment much praise. The only poor publicity which the picture received on the American continent came from the English press. . . . *Caesar and Cleopatra* . . . is still holding forth at the Astor Theater, New York, where it has been showing for months.[57]

The picture's box-office performance was impressive:

> With £1,790,000 in the till and some 3200 contracts still to be played, *Caesar and Cleopatra* appears to be the British picture industry's all-time top grosser in the USA.[58]

There was no denying that Pascal's film was handsomely mounted: with costumes by Oliver Messel, photography from a selection of top camera operators, including Robert Krasker, Freddie Young and Jack Cardiff, and with set design from John Bryan, the picture at least looked impressive. However, its astronomical budget, combined with its punishing publicity and advertising costs, prevented it from going into profit. In Britain, it was a public relations disaster, forfeiting Rank the goodwill of the ACT and much of the Press, and having a catastrophic effect on IPL in particular and the British industry in general. Rank's reputation would never recover from the battering it was given in the wake of Pascal's folly. Here was prestige filmmaking taken to extremes. Even Rank's 'Viewer's Report' was lukewarm in its assessment of the picture:

> Appeal: chiefly to Shaw fans. It should be a good draw in good class neighbourhood houses. Story is rather thin and scrappy and the picture in consequence may not appeal to all classes.[59]

This is hardly a glowing testimony for a picture which cost more than a million and took longer than a year to make . . .

Rank quickly withdrew his backing from Pascal's new project, *St Joan*, writing off £30,000 of development money rather than allowing the producer/director to carry on his wastrel way. Even Shaw's loyalty was strained: in 1946, the playwright paid a visit to the Welwyn Garden City Embassy to see *Caesar and Cleopatra*. The cinema manager offered him a free seat, but Shaw chose to pay – he was on 10 per cent of the ticket money.[60] In spite of his affection for Pascal, Shaw wasn't remotely

impressed by the picture, which he deemed to be 'very bad'. This chastisement from his patron must have been especially galling for the director:
Pascal had treated G.B.S.'s drama with absolute discretion, refusing to
open it out to make it more cinematic.

Unlike their American counterparts, British critics were openly hostile
to *Caesar and Cleopatra*. Richard Winnington of the *News Chronicle*, most
bloodthirsty of the 'quality' critics, was blunt: 'it cost over a million and a
quarter pounds, took two and a half years to make, and well and truly
bored one spectator for two and a quarter hours.'[61] And even the imaginative revamping of the London cinema where it opened couldn't win over C.
A. Lejeune, the *Observer*'s film pundit:

> Into the Odeon, Marble Arch, newly conditioned as an Egyptian
> temple, with figures of gods in niches, and a drop-curtain enscrolled
> with a map of Alexandria; into the Odeon, with a fanfare of trum-
> pets, comes the million and a quarter pound *Caesar and Cleopatra*
> . . . to my mind, [it] is a singularly cold triumph.
>
> (Lejeune, 1947: 166)

The ACT tabled a motion at its annual conference which would forbid
Pascal from ever working in Britain again. The Hungarian's autocratic
style hadn't endeared him to either cast or technicians. Besides, the union
was incensed that he had gone more than six months over schedule. As P.
L. Mannock acidly observed in the *Kinematograph Weekly* towards the end
of shooting:

> We have Gabriel Pascal monopolizing studio space . . . over what is
> beginning to seem an entire epoch: it is now 14 months since Claude
> Rains arrived to co-star in this epic.
>
> (*Kinematograph Weekly*, 21 June 1945, p. 29)

The policy of hiring top Hollywood stars, like Claude Rains, was also
controversial. Their recruitment seemed to presage a lack of confidence in
British talent, an impression that was underlined by Rank's million-pound
musical of 1946, *London Town*. Big-budget musicals did not come easily to
the British: the brashness, vigour and colour of the Ziegfeld Follies were at
odds with a cinema of understatement. Rather than entrust the project to a
British director, the Rank Organization had brought over Wesley Ruggles
from America. It wasn't clear what qualified Ruggles for this particular
job: he was an ex-Keystone Cop, a journeyman director, whose greatest
claim to fame was his handling of the most lurid of all the Mae West
vehicles, *I'm No Angel*, way back in 1933. A British fan, Audrey Scott of
Bedford, was quick to write in to *Picturegoer*, complaining that the
Hollywood director was more interested in eugenics than filmmaking:

So Wesley Ruggles has arrived. But apparently, his visit is not going to prove as beneficial as we expected. The man has actually brought with him lots of glamourizing make-up to use on our English girls. To add insult to injury, he says they will have to drop their 'Mayfair accents' and learn to speak 'Anglo-American' (whatever that might be). No, Mr Ruggles, it isn't going to work, and we sincerely hope our great naturalistic actors, like Rosamund John, Sheila Sim and Deborah Kerr, will not lose their sensible heads and turn themselves into objects of your horrifying experiments.

(*Picturegoer*, 17 March 1945, p. 14)

Like Pascal's folly, *London Town* was derided by the British critics, again catching Richard Winnington at his most bilious:

I can't see the point of importing an American director and giving him all the time and money in the world to play with when we can make bad musicals on our own, and quicker.[62]

Unlike *Caesar and Cleopatra*, however, *London Town* failed to make any impact in the USA: it wasn't even released in the States until it had been 'hypo-ed',[63] – which is to say doctored and shortened – and had had its title changed to *My Heart Goes Crazy*. Ruggles took the blame for the fiasco, but he had been faced with a host of problems which made even completing the film a minor miracle. For a start, the musical was shot at Shepperton Studios, which Rank had hired for the purpose. The studios were in a shambles after the war: they hadn't been used for years. Furthermore, returning British technicians, unaccustomed to making high-budget musicals at the best of times, were rusty, their skills not exactly sharpened by their many months at the front. Making a lavish extravaganza in a country where clothes rationing was still in force, and where many materials were simply unavailable (however much you were prepared to pay for them) was bound to be a forlorn task. It hadn't been Rank's decision to hire the American director: Sid Field, the music-hall star of the vehicle, insisted that somebody from Hollywood be brought over. None the less, Rank was held responsible for the decision.

Between them, *London Town* and *Caesar and Cleopatra* helped blight Rank's reputation, provoked questions in the House of Commons, and ensured that the Rank Organization lost a small fortune on production. ACT members, politicians, journalists and freelance producers campaigned for medium-budget British films, made by British technicians and aimed at British audiences, to replace the international 'prestige' pictures that were being made at IPL and Two Cities. (Ruggles' and Pascal's failures had a serious 'knock-on' effect on all Rank filmmakers.) Shortly after *London Town*'s release, ACT vice-president Sidney Cole had summed up the opposition to Rank's policy in the *Daily Worker*:

Mr Rank hopes to break into the American market. Yet in trying to do so he starves us of British films. An extravagant picture like *Caesar and Cleopatra* or *London Town* occupies time and space that could be used to make five other pictures intended primarily for our own cinemas.

(*Daily Worker*, 28 June 1946)

Rank's trust in his filmmakers was lessening. He would later call *London Town* 'one of his biggest mistakes';[64] the death knell for Independent Producers Ltd was being sounded. Ostensibly to assist the filmmakers at IPL, and their colleagues at Gainsborough and Two Cities, Rank had set up 'Piffle'.

Production Facilities (Films) Ltd – quickly abridged to 'Piffle' by producers who regarded it as a tiresome nuisance – was founded in 1944: on the surface, Piffle seemed like a sensible idea. In spite of drawing their finance from the same source, Rank's disparate group of production companies often found themselves in open competition for stories, stars and studio space. This competition helped to rocket production prices. Far better, Rank decided, to have a central organization which could deal with exigencies for everybody. Piffle was divided into nine parts: Finance, Central Casting, Contract Artistes, Publicity, Legal, Art Direction/ Research, Stories, Special Effects and Film Library. A nightmare of bureaucracy, Piffle soon backfired. Its primary function was to regulate filmmaking so that the horrible excess of Pascal's folly could not be repeated. This it singularly failed to do. Piffle ended up throttling producers and directors with red tape: witness IMCOS.

Ever solicitous, Rank had bought his filmmakers a weather company, International Meteorological Consultants (IMCOS), so that they would know when it was going to rain. IMCOS joined the Rank fold in the summer of 1946. (Previously, filmmakers had depended on the Air Ministry for their location weather reports.) IMCOS was not a popular purchase. 'It was a waste of time and money and helped nobody, in spite of its claims', was Sidney Gilliat's verdict on the Weather Forecasting Unit. IMCOS had two basic drawbacks in the eyes of British film producers. First, it was staffed by Americans. (Importing Hollywood stars, let alone US meteorologists, was 'bad form'.) Second, and more relevantly, IMCOS never came close to achieving the 90 per cent accuracy rate it had set itself as a target. While Ken Willard and Erving P. Krick had evidently done sterling work on the weather front for General Eisenhower towards the end of the Second World War, their elemental soothsaying failed to impress Rank's producers, who soon decided it was safer to consult local sources, shepherds or regional airfields, about the prospect of rain than it was to trust the hapless Americans. IMCOS was a typical example of a well-intentioned Rank innovation that cost money and ended up causing more problems than it solved. Weather, however, was no trifling matter. It was quite understandable that Rank should strive to track the path of the notoriously evasive British sun. Not only were schedules at risk (many producers went over budget because of bad weather in the summer of 1946), so were cinema attendances: during the freezing winter of 1947, audiences plummeted, a situation which was further exacerbated by the national fuel emergency of that year: to conserve fuel, cinemas were prevented from opening before four o'clock in the afternoon.[65] At a vital moment in his export drive, Rank was deprived of much-needed revenue. To add insult to injury, the searingly hot summer which followed also deterred cinemagoers from their local Odeons and Gaumonts. In its expense and inaccuracy, IMCOS epitomized what was wrong with Production Facilities (Films) Ltd. Not that it was the only thing wrong.

As part of Piffle, centralized workshops were made available to all Rank filmmakers: there were carpenters' shops, electrical stores and plasterers' shops. However, as Sidney Gilliat soon found out, 'the materials cost more to the producer than if he had chartered them outside'. Likewise, Piffle's Stories Department was a source of grievance: if anybody wanted to purchase a 'property', a novel or a play, they had first to register an interest with the department, which then might, or might not, acquire the rights. (Producers were not allowed to bid directly for stories.) When two or more parties[66] expressed an interest in the same title, as happened most notoriously with *Uncle Silas*, the property was awarded to the producer who had lodged the first claim. This was often determined by something as inconsequential as the date on the top of a telegram, regardless of how serious about any given project rival producers might be, or of who was likely to make the better film. There was also a Story Reading Department: this was run by Pat Wallace, daughter of thriller writer Edgar Wallace (the novelist who 'launched' a thousand crime quickies in the 1930s) and involved a small advisory committee, which included the well-known writer Rose Macaulay, sifting through piles of plays and fiction, looking for potential movie vehicles. 'Unfortunately, no one took the slightest interest in anything Pat Wallace threw up. This was most disheartening to her and to her staff for they all worked most diligently' (Gilbert, 1981: 20).

Piffle quickly became an enormous encumbrance: its staff managed to antagonize technicians who had evolved their own working methods over the years and deeply resented having a sort of studio 'secret police' monitor their every move. Charles Staffell, the Oscar-winning special effects man at Denham and Pinewood, remembers Piffle personnel with contempt:

My remembrance of Piffle is of a bunch of people from various studios who claimed to be experts in this, that and the other, brought together, working under one banner . . . they never really did anything expect make themselves a bloody nuisance. . . . when these people came along, they usurped what little piece of knowledge I had

105

. . . I did happen to know where the light came out of a projection machine: it didn't come out of the smoke chimney at the back: it came out of the bloody lens. They didn't know what the lens was, let alone anything else. So I couldn't live with that.[67]

Likewise, Sidney Gilliat's grumbles about Piffle are manifold: 'casting tended to lose any individual quality when one had to deal with a bureau constantly trying to push stars under contract into pictures for which they were not necessarily suitable . . . publicity and exploitation tended to have to take its place on a conveyor belt of all the Rank pictures.'[68]

As Piffle was servicing all Rank filmmakers, not only those at IPL, the Independent Producers soon felt that they were losing their privileged position. They were accustomed to supervising every facet of their pictures, and found the new outfit, which was reckoned to add £60,000 on average to a feature budget, a wearisome interference.[69] F. L. Gilbert, Piffle's original managing director, who had stumbled into the film industry after a stint with Rank's brother at the Ministry of Food, is scathing about the way the servicing organization was run. In an unpublished memo, he characterizes Rank, rather harshly, as 'a man out of his depth and swept along by his associates, who were mostly concerned with personal ambition and gain'. He suggests Rank 'had little idea of structural company organization or the techniques of modern management'.[70]

Piffle is best seen as Rank's benighted attempt to resolve the business–art dichotomy that often threatened to tear his films policy apart: he wanted to allow his producers creative licence, but only within the (business) perimeters he set. Unfortunately, rather than co-ordinating the activities of his various filmmakers, Production Facilities (Films) Ltd ended up leaving them bothered and bewildered: relations between the artists and their patron were soured as bureaucracy began to hold them all in thrall. Piffle was a slow poison:

Undoubtedly from the beginning of 1944 to 1947 filmmaking conditions were good and we had a remarkable freedom in most departments. But you should remember that Piffle took quite a time to grow and penetrate the mind.[71]

There was, though, more to the demise of Independent Producers Ltd than Piffle alone . . .

Whether prompted by excess profits tax,[72] an incentive to escalate production costs, or because creative accountancy could make assets out of nebulous and unnecessary additions to budgets, or through sheer inefficiency, a measure of extravagance had been tolerated, and even encouraged, by the Rank Organization: up until 1947, box-office receipts were high enough to underwrite production losses.

As the 1940s progressed, filmmaking costs, at their apogee in 1945–6, declined rather than increased. This suggests that budgets had been artificially inflated. Rank, keen to lure the Americans to his pictures, wanted to be seen spending money: his seemingly bottomless pockets, into which he dug deeper and deeper for 'brass' (his Yorkshire industrialist slang for cash), impressed and frightened Hollywood. Havelock-Allan remembers that the Rank Organization spent £60,000 simply to acquire the rights to the half-hour Noël Coward playlet *Still Life*, which spawned *Brief Encounter*: Rank bought Coward's entire *Tonight at 8.30* cycle at a vastly inflated price to get hold of this single piece. Similarly, in 1947, when Cineguild were making *Take My Life*, which they envisaged as an interesting 'little' film,[73] more notable for its Winston (*Poldark*) Graham script than anything else, and possibly warranting a budget of about £120,000, they were allowed to run up costs of £210,000. Neither Neame nor Havelock-Allan had had any desire to spend so much. (The maximum that a reasonably popular British picture could expect to make at the domestic box-office was £200,000. As soon as production costs exceeded this figure, export became a necessity.) The overheads and studio rental artifially inflated the price.

When Pinewood Studios were officially reopened in April 1946, Independent Producers moved their operations from Denham and took them over. This proved to be a mistake. Previously, shortage of space had been the problem. Now IPL was under pressure to keep the place busy, even if it meant that each company had to make two films a year:

> The whole thing became topsy-turvy. Rank and Davis saw our films as feeding a machine – producers like ourselves saw the machine as there to feed the films.[74]

George Archibald, supposedly a sort of valet to serve their every need, now began to bully the filmmakers as he was put under pressure by Rank and Davis to make sure projects kept to budget and to schedule. No longer were the Independent Producers the elite cadre of the Rank Organization. Notions of prestige were giving way to commercial considerations. This caused fissure and dissent within the outfit, particularly at Cineguild, where Neame and Havelock-Allan were beginning to feel that Lean's pictures weren't popular enough:

> They said, 'Look, David, we've decided that while your films will bring us prestige, it is our films that will make the money.' And David didn't have the slightest idea what to say. He was absolutely shattered.[75]

A film like *Brief Encounter*, without star names and with an unhappy ending, the story of an affair between a 'matron' and a 'doctor',[76] wasn't particularly good box-office. As Lean acknowledged himself, the film did

107

well in 'better-class' halls in both Britain and America, received its share of critical plaudits, but was no popular success. Lean blamed the audience:

> The greater proportion of film-goers are under twenty-one mentally or physically; they go to the movies as an escape from reality. The big movie executives know this, and have provided a liberal diet of saccharin and silver linings, which has rewarded them with enormous profits.[77]

Havelock-Allan and Neame were eager to reach the mass audience, even if it meant compromising. Havelock-Allan tried to change the Cineguild 'aesthetic' by making *Blanche Fury*, released in 1948; this was an attempt to fuse the tasteful, literary IPL tendencies with the unashamed brashness of Gainsborough melodramas:

> Gainsborough were then making those Barbara Cartland things like *The Man in Grey*, *The Wicked Lady*, etc. . . . I said I wonder if I could make a serious one of these, one that was for real as it were . . . *Blanche Fury*.[78]

It didn't prove to be a happy experience. Havelock-Allan had imported a French director, Marc Allégret, who was in the throes of a domestic crisis, spoke little English, and was hard pushed to find the appropriate idiom, half-way between Victorian 'shocker' and respectful period piece, for the picture. Shortly after its completion, Havelock-Allan left Cineguild to form his own company, Constellation Films, and Neame also eventually quit. Lean, whose loyalty to and enthusiasm for Rank took an eternity to dissipate, stayed at Independent Producers long after his colleagues had left. However, neither *The Passionate Friends* nor *Madeleine*, his two 'solo' vehicles, achieved the critical and popular acclaim of his earlier work. When, eventually, he followed the exodus to London Films, Alexander Korda was able to boast that he had 'gotten Lean on the cheap'[79] because the director was in no position to bargain: by the end of the 1940s, Rank's production plans were in tatters and Lean's stock had fallen.

Sidney Gilliat writes of a 'final acrimonious meeting' at the Dorchester Hotel where Archibald read out the expected revenues from a series of IPL films, 'an act clearly intended to cast doubt on our collective commercial value, especially as all the quoted figures were blatant underestimates'.[80] Archibald 'stormed' out of the meeting. Around the same time, Davis and Rank had 'stormed' out of *The Red Shoes*. In *A Life in Movies*, Powell wryly recollects the preview:

> When J. Arthur Rank and John Davis saw the film for the first time, they thought they had lost their shirts, collective and individual.
>
> (Powell, 1987: 653)

A £700,000 film about ballet – it had come in £50,000 over budget: Rank and Davis saw little prospect of *The Red Shoes* doing much business in the local Odeons and Gaumonts. By the time of its release in 1948, the Rank Organization was already wilting as it tried to cope with the aftermath of the ad-valorem tax and the Hollywood film embargo (pp. 173–80). Rank persuaded Powell and Pressburger, along with the other producer/director teams, to take a cut in salary. Following the Norton formula, he offered them an increased percentage of profits – $37\frac{1}{2}$ as opposed to 25 – in compensation. They accepted the new terms and agreed to stay at IPL. However, Korda was lurking ominously in the background. He had acquired Shepperton Studios; had established a close rapport with the new President of the Board of Trade, Harold Wilson, and was shortly to be given a hefty subvention from the National Film Finance Corporation.[81] He was on the lookout for disenchanted filmmakers. He spent many months prising the Independent Producers away from their one-time bed of roses at the Rank Organization, wining and dining them, flattering them, offering them more money than they were getting at Rank. The Independent Producers weren't happy with their salaries or with the burgeoning degree of interference, 'pressure from the front office',[82] being exercised by Archibald and Davis. As their creative autonomy was undermined, they grew more and more willing to listen to Korda. *The Red Shoes* was the last film that the Archers made at IPL. Davis probably regarded the picture as the final excrescence from a bad old system which would shortly be brought to an end: art for art's sake, indulgent, pretentious – surely, with this ballet film, the Independent Producers had danced themselves into a corner. They needed less freedom, not more.

The Red Shoes was distributed unimaginatively in Britain. It was as if the Rank Organization wanted it to slide quickly into oblivion. (In his autobiography, Powell suggests the 1948 rights issue was uppermost in the executives' minds. They were loath to draw shareholders' attention to what they thought was going to be an expensive flop.[83]) Slowly, after a mediocre performance at the British box-office, the film made its mark in America. (Within six years, it grossed more than $5 million.) Rank and Davis learned, to their cost, that trying to anticipate and regulate the reception of British films in the American market was a hopeless task. Success invariably came when it was least expected. An American executive had told them that Powell and Pressburger's picture wouldn't earn a dollar in the USA, and they had been inclined to agree. There was no evidence that they struggled to retain the Archers' services. By late 1948, Powell and Pressburger had already defected, agreeing to make five films for Alexander Korda:

> Thus ended one of the most glorious partnerships in the history of British films. Perhaps all works of art that necessitate a collaboration between an artist and his patron, contain the seed of enmity.
>
> (Powell, 1987: 670)

The quixotic contradictoriness of Rank's production policy is seen in microcosm in the brief history of IPL. His philanthropic mission to set British production on a firm footing led him to grant, briefly, an almost complete creative licence to the Independent Producers. The same force that had driven him to equip Sunday schools with projectors prompted him to try to sell British production to the world. However, his desire to run an efficient business combined with his vulnerability to a whole range of outside factors, from Gabriel Pascal's extravagance to Britain's chronic post-war debtor status, made sure that he would withdraw the creative licence from his filmmakers almost as soon as it had been issued:

> You will notice that certain producers and directors are no longer with us. I have told our creative artists that they must realize that their creative freedom must be related to the economic side. The two must be blended.
>
> (Rank, quoted in *Kinematograph Weekly*, 17 June 1948, p. 8)

Between them, Olivier's *Hamlet* and *The Red Shoes* won eight Oscars at the 1949 Academy Awards. Rank, evidently, was delighted, hailing this success as a vindication of his production policy. However, by the time the awards were made, the Independent Producers had already fled; Del Giudice had left Two Cities, and this golden, if indulgent, moment in British film history was well and truly over. IPL was no longer in existence. (In the autumn of 1948, the group, shorn of its mainstays, had been reconstituted as Pinewood Films.)

RANK, BALCON AND EALING

> Ealing's films had a more sustained success abroad than anybody else's. This was not achieved by incorporating 'international' stars, themes or production values. While many studios expanded their scale of operations in a 'gold rush' spirit, Ealing maintained the economy and spirit of its wartime productions. While others dealt in superlatives, Ealing in a typical deadpan style took as its slogan 'the studio for good British films'.
>
> (Barr, 1977: 63)

> Unquestionably the appearance on the film scene of Mr J. Arthur Rank has contributed in no small measure to the present healthy state of the industry.
>
> (Balcon, 1947: 9)

In demonologies of British film history, Sir Michael Balcon is often cast as the brave, paternal 'independent' producer, fighting a noble, rearguard battle on behalf of Ealing Studios against an evil army of accountants and financiers who cared not a jot for Ealing's mission to project 'Britain and the British character'.[84] While Rank, like an ancient dinosaur, was trying to secure a slice of the US market for himself with a series of expensive, prestige films, most of them devoid of a sense of national identity, Ealing's modest comedies were quietly winning over audiences on the American art-house circuit that burgeoned in the early 1950s. This, at least, is the way the myth runs: Balcon has been gilded by history, made the subject of retrospectives of British cinema at the Museum of Modern Art in New York, cited by producers and critics alike as 'the central and outstanding figure in the creation of . . . the British film industry'.[85] The pictures he produced at Ealing are celebrated as representing a triumph of the paro-chial, of the 'local', 'small-scale', 'hand-made', 'artisan' approach to the 'craft of filmmaking'. Balcon, we know, voted for the Attlee government in 1945, as did his 'like-minded colleagues'[86] at the studios he ruled over like a stern but indulgent headmaster. Ealing is seen as standing in brave opposition to the free market philistinism of Rank's film executives, led, in a mind-numbingly brutal way, by Rank's heir apparent, Mr John Davis, who is cast as Cain to Balcon's Abel. The closure of Ealing Studios in the mid-1950s, when they were bought by the BBC, is viewed as a betrayal of the game little independent by the callous 'major'.

While the Balcon myth-making process is not entirely wide of the mark, it stands in need of at least mild correction. Ealing's boss had a few warts of his own: he was manipulative, chauvinistic – producer Betty Box recalls that Sir Michael 'didn't really approve' of women behind the camera[87] – and occasionally ruthless: he wasn't above resorting to underhand means to sabotage rivals' productions.[88] Geoff Brown has pointed out that 'the important reality of his career as British film producer remains clouded by cosy nostalgia and easy assumptions'.[89] Balcon is associated with a brand of comedy that was forever England. Although he was active within the British film industry for more than forty years, he is remembered for one moment alone: in 1947–8, he had made a conscious decision to steer Ealing away from the serious drama of its war output. Comedy, as he realized, had been badly neglected in the British wartime film revival. All the mirthy stalwarts of the 1930s, Formby, Will Hay, Jack Hulbert and colleagues, were out of favour, and there was nothing with which to replace them. The music-hall tradition, itself in steep decline, was deemed 'too old-fashioned, too slow and too unsubtle to make a good basis for screen comedy'.[90] Critics were complaining about the lack of laughs in British post-war cinema. Just as he had rallied to the cause when the industry was in dire peril at the start of the war, Balcon leapt into the breach once more: in their wry, gentle, prodding critiques of certain aspects of post-war British society, the Ealing comedies were following the precepts laid down by Roger Manvell in an early issue of the *Penguin Film Review*: 'comedy must grow out of the life of our time, out of the way people face contemporary society and its problems, out of their evasions and subterfuges and their uneasy relationship with each other.'[91]

Perhaps the more misleading of all the 'easy assumptions' made about Ealing is that its post-war production policy was in direct and conscious contrast to that pursued by Rank. There's no denying that Rank and Balcon had very different ideas about the 'golden' American market. Balcon had suffered some turbulent experiences in the 1930s, both competing with Hollywood and, later, as one of its employees[92]:

> Some years before the war, armed with good quality British product and considerable sums of money to promote it, I set foot in America, zealous to turn the people into a nation of latter-day Columbuses who could, in their turn, discover Britain through British films. . . . But fate decreed it was I, and not America, who was to make a discovery; and that discovery was that all the promotion in the world would not open the doors the American buyers had determined to keep shut.[93]

After the Gaumont-British sales drive of the 1930s had floundered, and after two painful years as one of the British hirelings of MGM boss Louis B. Mayer, Balcon had eschewed the US market. Rank still harboured hopes of breaking into it. None the less, the films made at Ealing Studios from 1944 to the mid-1950s complement rather than challenge the rest of Rank's output. Whether comedies, like *Passport to Pimlico*, *Whisky Galore*, *The Maggie* and all, or whether still-upper-lipped adventures, such as Ealing's most expensive picture, *Scott of the Antarctic*, the pictures which Balcon helped to produce were all at least partially financed by Rank: they fitted neatly into the rim of a mixed Rank production portfolio, which ranged from the delusional gradiosity of Pascal at IPL to the quickies being made by Sidney and Betty Box at Gainsborough Studios from 1946 onward.

Since 1944, Ealing Studios had been a satellite of the Rank Organization:

> We have been granted dominion status in the Rank empire but this is not the same thing as self-government.[94]

Like the duchy of Burgundy, that part of London which fractured itself from Britain and declared itself a sovereign state in *Passport to Pimlico*, Ealing Studios occupied an ambiguous place within the Rank empire, teetering between devolution and independence. On the surface, the Rank–Ealing axis appears an unholy alliance, although Balcon was quite happy with his new partner. In 1950, he was elected to the board of Odeon Theatres, and was thus involved in administering other parts of Rank's vast estates. For instance, as the head of Contract Artists, Olive Dodds, recalls,

Balcon was instrumental in changing Rank's policy towards character actors:

> Michael Balcon was very good . . . when he became part of the board, we started to be much more interested in character actors. It was his influence I am sure. . . . The Ealing comedies, which had been doing terribly well, were largely character people.[95]

Invariably generous in his assessments of Rank's influence on the industry, Balcon described his tie-up with the flour magnate in glowing terms which belie the little/large, good/bad dichotomy posited by dewy-eyed British film historians, keen to make Ealing into Avalon and to depict Rank as a capitalist heretic. The terms and conditions Balcon enjoyed were every bit as favourable as those given to the Independent Producers:

> This was a model contract, leaning, if anything, to the generous side on the part of the Rank Organization . . . [it] certainly cushioned Ealing against the possibility of financial disaster, and in terms of achievement those years proved the most rewarding of my life, as it was during them that the best Ealing films were made.
>
> (Balcon, 1969: 154–5)

Ealing's attempts at distributing its own pictures had not been successful: a small renting outfit was hard pressed to survive in an already crowded market-place, especially when Rank and ABC controlled distribution and theatres. It was far more prudent to come under Rank's umbrella than to try to compete with the organization. Rank's servicing and renting facilities, combined with his willingness to guarantee 50 per cent (this would later rise to 75 per cent) of the budgets for Balcon's movies, made him an attractive partner. Of course, there were hitches to the liaison: Ealing's relations with the 'major' were far from perfect. Balcon's enthusiasm for Mr Rank, a figure whom he had regarded with ill-disguised horror and alarm in the early 1940s, when he believed that Rank was not only monopolistic, but was blithely going about repeating Balcon's own mistakes by trying to break into the USA, was not shared by all his staff at Ealing, many of whom felt that they had been colonized. Sidney Cole, an editor at the studios throughout the 1940s, regarded the pact with a loathing becoming any self-respecting ACT member. He suggests it was not entered into willingly, but was a matter of necessity:

> If somebody points a gun at you the only possible way to survive is to go along with what the gun is telling you to do.[96]

Occasionally, Rank's renters distributed Ealing pictures in what seemed a wilfully inept way. This happened most notoriously with Harry Watt's Australian 'western', *The Overlanders*, a cricially acclaimed film, shot on location in the outback, which features Chips Rafferty herding 2,000 sheep from coast to coast to save them from the Japanese. Much to Ealing's chagrin, *The Overlanders* was put on the bottom half of a double bill, while a mediocre Hollywood picture was given first-feature status above it. Ealing's innovative Publicity Department, run by Monja Danischewsky, which had commissioned posters from a host of top British artists, had its wings clipped, and was, as Geoff Brown points out, forced back on the 'conventional'.[97] Ealing's Australian experiment came to an abrupt end in the early 1950s. John Davis, by then executive head of the Rank Organization, had little of Rank's evangelical enthusiasm for making British films in the commonwealth as well as showing them there: there wasn't much money to be made in British–Australian co-productions, and profit was always the dominating factor for Davis. As he told the Australians when Pagewood Studios, the establishment used by Ealing, was closed down:

> I could never understand why it was considered necessary to make pictures in Australia. Arthur [Rank] was always keen on it, but I don't know why. After all, we in England have four or five modern, well-equipped studios and nearly 4,000 people employed. We can make all the pictures you need.[98]

In December 1953, Balcon had renewed his pact with Rank for a further five years. However, even with Rank's support, the studios were hard pressed to adapt to the changing nature of British cinema and society in the affluent Macmillan decade. One of Ealing's longest-standing backers, Stephen Courtauld, had withdrawn his support in 1952. In spite of assistance from the National Film Finance Corporation, the studios were incurring heavy losses. It seemed sensible to 'rationalize' operations: in 1955, Ealing's premises were sold to the BBC for £350,000, and Balcon set out to transfer production and staff to Pinewood, where he had been promised two new stages for, he thought, his exclusive use. However, Davis wasn't prepared to grant the Ealing boss such autonomy. It transpired that Balcon would have to share the stages with other Rank producers, something Balcon clearly would not countenance: the Ealing boss sundered relations with Rank, instead transferring his production programme to MGM's Boreham Wood Studios.

In the end, the Rank–Balcon axis came apart at the seams. Rank, much more immersed in his flour interests since his brother's death in 1952, had lost that crusading zeal to promote British cinema throughout the world, regardless of expense. Under John Davis, the Rank Organization was less concerned with sponsoring British filmmakers than with showing a profit on the 'bottom line'. In the 1950s, as we shall see, the organization began to diversify across a whole range of leisure and service industries, downplaying its film production activities. None the less, between 1944 and 1956, Rank had played a vital part in distributing as well as funding Ealing pictures. Without his support, Balcon's 'mild revolution'[99] might never have taken place.

GAINSBOROUGH STUDIOS

Gainsborough Studios made twenty-two features during the war at a combined cost of £1,360,000, and these features grossed £2,600,000. In other words, the studios' entire programme, over a period of five years, cost no more than Pascal's folly, the swollen, epic *Caesar and Cleopatra*. While Independent Producers and Two Cities were trying to spend their way into the American market, and while Ealing was busy distilling Britain and the British character, Gainsborough steered a middle course, turning out popular, inexpensive pictures which may not have received the plaudits of Rank's prestige films or Balcon's quirky anatomies of post-war society, but were certainly more successful at the British box-office.

The studios had been founded by Michael Balcon in 1924, absorbed by the Gaumont-British Picture Corporation four years later, and had spent the 1930s making a wide range of pictures, everything from Will Hay comedies to Hitchcock thrillers. In 1941, they came under J. Arthur Rank's aegis when he acquired control to Gaumont-British from the Ostrers.

The Gainsborough 'aesthetic', if it can be described as such, was very different from that of either the Independent Producers or the Ealing filmmakers. In the early years of the war, inspired by production chief Ted Black, the studios made medium-budget pictures which often pleased the critics, pictures like Launder and Gilliat's *Waterloo Road* and *Millions Like Us*. Black, from a circus background, was determinedly unpretentious, with a showman's touch and the desire to make films about people outside London high society. He abhorred snobbery and pretension:

'If I mix with the intellectual lot, it'll impair my judgement,' he [Black] said. He had a working code that if you please the people in the Midlands and the North your money is made and if you please London and the South you might just get by. He aimed primarily at audiences between Watford and Newcastle upon Tyne.[100]

Not the least of Black's achievements was his establishment of a British 'star' system: Margaret Lockwood, Phyllis Calvert, Stewart Granger, Eric Portman, John Mills, Patricia Roc, James Mason and Jean Kent were all groomed for celebrity at Gainsborough. Black departed from Gainsborough in mid-1943, just as the company was entering what the critics have called its 'baroque period'.[101] In a bid to provide escapism for war-weary audiences, the studio now began to make their famous melodramas. From the critical, if not the commercial, point of view, this was adjudged unfortunate. In the 'maturity' and 'realism' stakes, the melodramas didn't come up to scratch. Dilys Powell, monitor of good taste for the *Sunday Times*, labelled them

> inferior films on conventional themes, trivially handled, undeserving of the popular success they have won.[102]

The films were attacked for their extravagance as well as for their ostensible triviality. However, the opulence of the melodramas was contrived out of relatively small budgets: it is a compliment to the art directors and costume designers that the critics deplored their prodigality. The melodramas weren't directly akin to their Hollywood counterparts, and were often panned by the American showmen for their lack of heart and gumption. Made in an era of rationing and shortages, they were specifically British, with 'their own cinematic vocabulary, their own repertory of female stars'.[103] Although Gainsborough boss Maurice Ostrer seemed primarily concerned with profit, Leslie Arliss, director of *The Man in Grey*, *Love Story* and *The Wicked Lady*, had ulterior motives in making the pictures. His mission was to defrost notorious British reserve, to take British film out of the emotional deep-freeze:

> He says that British films and players are afraid of genuine emotion on screen and says this is the reason for the supremacy of Americans in human drama. Arliss wishes to challenge this diffidence, and to concentrate on allowing his characters to express themselves and their feelings freely in films without any embarrassment either to themselves or to their audiences.[104]

This didn't seem a project that was likely to endear him to Rank. The Methodist magnate may have tried not to interfere with his filmmakers' 'creative processes', but he baulked at financing movies which he found to be 'morally dubious' in any way. He was often swayed by his wife. It is known that Mrs Rank regarded Launder and Gilliat's *Waterloo Road* with extreme misgiving, and was well-nigh apoplectic at the prospect of their depraved 1945 romp, *The Rake's Progress*. (Gilliat even suggests that the film might have been abandoned had it not already been three weeks into shooting when Mrs Rank got wind of it.[105]) After all, J. Arthur Rank was an old scion of the Religious Film Society, and however far he meandered into mainstream movies, he tried to avoid sponsoring 'exploitative' or 'prurient' projects. His daughter Shelagh Cowen recalls that both he and his wife were scrupulous about the kind of movies they would allow the Rank Organization to finance:

> My mother was also very religious. Not in such an outgoing way. She just had a great belief. She was very strong on what was wrong and what was right. If Father had made a film she thought morally wrong, or an unsuitable story, she would have told him. And he would have

listened to her. He used to bring people to dinner for my mother to meet and see. She was a great judge of character.[106]

Why, then – sceptics ask – was Rank prepared to back Gainsborough pictures like *The Wicked Lady*, whose low-cut necklines were too much for the Hays Office's sense of propriety, or *The Man in Grey*, where a sadistic James Mason bludgeons Margaret Lockwood to death? Rank evidently regarded the melodramas as moral fables: the wicked ladies always got their come-uppance and patriarchal Christian good always prevailed. (As Sue Aspinall observes in her discussion of the films in the BFI dossier on 'Gainsborough Melodrama', the melodramas were consistent: they tended to be based on conflict between two kinds of women, both after the same man, one representing marriage and duty, the other unrestrained libido. Marriage and duty may be tested in the early reels, but always carry the day at the denouement. Sexual desire is always punished. The libidinal women who expresses it is generally of a lower class than the eventual wife. Property relations and the status quo are thus maintained.) Although Rank subsequently vetoed Arliss's plan for making a sequel to *The Wicked Lady*, he was quite happy with the first film. Not only was it a terrific commercial success: its production had been sanctioned by the Almighty:

> It was all wrapped up with his simple faith . . . he was doing the right thing. Quite honestly, if God thought making *The Wicked Lady* was all right, then the rest of the people could go shunned.[107]

On the whole, the melodramas were period/costume pieces, but they had little truck with either historical accuracy or visual 'realism'. The films were determinedly artificial and studio-bound, and thus incensed the critics, one of whom memorably complained that in the 1946 picture *Caravan*, the principal character (a man) existed for months in a cave without any obvious washing facilities, but none the less managed to 'preserve a spotless elaboration of dress'.[108]

In 1945, *Madonna of the Seven Moons* and *Waterloo Road*, with combined production costs of less than £200,000, were runaway box-office hits. The following year, *The Wicked Lady* was the most popular British movie of 1946. Despite the melodramas' popularity, there was a growing tension between Ostrer and Rank, and Rank was looking to change the set-up at Gainsborough. F. L. Gilbert, managing director of Production Facilities (Films) Ltd, writes of the way that Ostrer used to sit, with 'a slightly amused and sardonic smile', at Rank's weekly Park Lane conferences.[109] Ostrer took great exception to Piffle, and seemed to regard Rank as something of an idiot. He knew his market. He and Ted Black had built up a roster of stars. Gainsborough continued to turn in a profit, even as the Rank Organization lost money on production overall. Ostrer's 'bread and butter' films helped subsidize the prestige pictures. Regardless of his success, Ostrer was never given the status of the 'artists' at IPL and Two Cities. His movies were dismissed as potboilers. He was simmering with resentment. In the *Kinematograph Weekly*, there were oblique references to 'stormy Tuesday afternoon sessions with Ostrer vehemently justifying his middle-budget box-office winners against criticism'.[110] Rank was perturbed by the low level of productivity at Gainsborough towards the end of the war. The studios never seemed to complete more than one or two pictures in a year. To balance the slow and expensive artistry of Del Giudice and the Independent Producers, Rank wanted Gainsborough to be cheap and prolific. The melodramas were not in the vanguard of his assault on the American market: in the spring of 1946, Ostrer went on a 'reconnaissance' trip to the USA, and was bitterly disappointed with the lacklustre way in which *Madonna of the Seven Moons* was being promoted by its distributors, Universal. At the time *Madonna* was limping round the USA, another British film, similar in tone, was proving a smash hit. Shortly after his return to Britain, Ostrer resigned from Gainsborough, making way for *The Seventh Veil*'s hyperactive producer, Sydney Box.

Box galloped into Gainsborough Studios in August 1946 with plans to treble output by having at least three productions on the go at any one time:

> A film, like any other birth, takes nine months, three for preparation, three for shooting and three for editing and dubbing . . . as I have to make sixteen pictures a year, the margin for retakes is not very large.[111]

As journalist – a former editor of the *Christian Herald* – playwright and producer, Box had always been energetic and resourceful. To his family, his ascent of the peaks of the British film industry was a matter of destiny. Shortly before his birth, Box's mother visited a fortune-teller, who informed her that her son's name 'would shine over the nation'.[112] She anticipated that young Sydney might be the new messiah, and it was only several years later, when she saw the credit 'Produced by Sydney Box' emblazoned across the screen of her local Odeon, that it finally dawned on her what the palmist had meant. Throughout the 1930s, novels, short stories, reference books and plays had 'poured down his tireless right arm',[113] along with his journalism and a useful volume on 'film publicity'.[114] During the war, he ran a production company, Verity Films, from an office in St Martin's Lane, London, which turned out documentaries, training and propaganda films at an alarming rate. The Ministry of Information, the War Office and the British Council were his patrons. As his contribution to the war effort, he oversaw the production of close to 200 'shorts' on an infinite variety of subjects. He was helped by his younger sister Betty, who shared his ferocious work ethic, and who had thrown in a promising career as a commercial artist to lend her weight to the Box film drive. As Betty Box recalls, these propaganda pieces ranged from the microscopically brief to the very long:

> They varied from 20,000 feet a film – that's twice a feature length really – to about 60-second flashes at the cinema, which were emergency things to warn people about the new measures.[115]

Soon, Betty Box had ten units working for her, some of which were comprised of women directors and camera operators. (The war thus helped make at least a tiny dent in the traditional chauvinism of the industry.) Both brother and sister had become accustomed to making pictures quickly, and on minuscule budgets, excellent training for feature production.

As the war ended, and Verity Films' commissions started to dry up, Sydney took the leap into independent production, leasing space at London's tiny Riverside Studios. Here, with his wife Muriel as co-scriptwriter, and Betty to assist him, he set out to raise the money for *29 Acacia Avenue*, a family saga set in the suburbs. The main strand of the narrative was to concern[116] a young couple who were preparing for their wedding. Seemingly, this was harmless stuff, good 'programme material'. Eventually, the picture was shot for just under £30,000, with Rank providing roughly three-quarters of the budget, and the Box family somehow raising the remainder. In preview, it proved popular with everybody apart from Mr Rank, who was alarmed by the inference that the young couple had sex before their wedding. (They spend an illicit weekend in suburbia while their parents are away.) Rank's reaction was uncharacteristically peremptory and blunt. He refused to distribute the film:

> He [Rank] was absolutely horrified . . . this was against his moral code. This was adultery to him. He said, 'Mr Box, we can't show this film.' We couldn't believe it. It was the end of the war and there had been all sorts of goings-on . . .[117]

In spite of his misgivings about *Acacia Avenue* (which was later handled by Columbia's British outfit) Rank agreed to distribute the Box family's rather more ambitious follow-up, *The Seventh Veil*. It proved to be one of the most successful British films of all time. In December 1945, John Davis was able to announce:

> *The Seventh Veil* has broken the all-time record on its London general release. In our 80 London theatres, the 'veil' has taken over ten percent more than any picture we have played, either British or American, and at 41 theatres created an all-time individual record for the theatre.
>
> (*Kinematograph Weekly*, 13 December 1945, p. 12)

Sydney Box seemed to have stumbled on the elixir. With limited resources – the film was made for under £100,000 – a tiny studio, and two middle-ranking stars, James Mason and Ann Todd, not to mention a first-time director, Compton Bennett, he had managed to fashion a picture which not only did exceptionally well in the domestic market, but also breached the defences of the showmen and found a way into the USA. Distributed by Universal, it won Sydney and Muriel Box a joint scriptwriting Oscar at the 1946 Academy Awards. 'A rich, portentous mixture of Beethoven, Chopin, kitsch and Freud',[118] as Pauline Kael would later call it, *The Seventh Veil* astutely mixed 'high culture' themes – psychoanalysis and classical music – with down-to-earth melodrama. It was little wonder that, in the wake of the film's success, Rank sought to lure Box to Gainsborough to replace Ostrer: if the enterprising young producer was able to re-create the Albert Hall and a huge Grosvenor Square house in the cramped space of Riverside Studios, Rank assumed he could do wonders for Gainsborough at Shepherd's Bush and Islington.

At first, Box was wary about contracting his soul to the Rank Organization, but Rank's terms were too generous to refuse. As Betty Box remembers:

> Rank offered Sydney so much money that he didn't feel he could say no because he had never had any money. He'd always had to jog along from one bit to the next, hoping, like any other entrepreneur. It was a wonderful dream to have all the money you wanted.[119]

However, there was nothing idyllic about Box's time at Gainsborough. During his first year there, he made fourteen films, and during his second year, he 'upped' productivity to sixteen. By 1950, he had completed forty-four films, and had almost worked himself into a nervous wreck in the process. Most of the Gainsborough pictures in the Box era were quickies: Betty Box had taken charge of Islington, and was herself overseeing the production of six pictures per year. Films like *Holiday Camp* and the 'Huggett' series, which prefigure TV sitcom in their repetition of characters and themes,[120] were the mainstays of Gainsborough production. Slightly more ambitious efforts, like *Christopher Columbus* and *The Bad Lord Byron*, Box's prestige films which were shot on a fraction of the budgets of the Independent Producers pictures, performed disappointingly at the box-office. For all his frenetic energy, Box would never again have a success to match *The Seventh Veil*.

This schematic, and far from comprehensive, survey of Rank's production activities in the 1940s none the less offers an idea of the range of feature films Rank was sponsoring, and of the relatively robust British film culture he presided over in the post-war period. Rank was able to provide British filmmakers with unique facilities. He had, after all, been spending a fortune on research.

In Which We Serve (1942), often cited as a classic realist film, was shot largely at Denham studios, and the success of the movie owed much to the ingenuity and artifice of set-builders and production designers.

David Lean and Noël Coward on the set of *In Which We Serve* (1942).

The props department at Denham Studios, complete with wooden fruit.

Filippo Del Giudice, the moving spirit behind Two Cities.

Margaret Lockwood, Gainsborough's great star. Rank was often asked how he could reconcile a film like *The Wicked Lady* (1945), in which Lockwood enjoyed a triumph as an unscrupulous highwaywoman, with his religious convictions. He countered by saying that Lockwood's villainy was ultimately punished.

David Hand, former Disney bigwig and executive in charge of Gaumont-British Animation. 'He was one of the most impressive men I have ever met . . . a super executive.' (Bob Monkhouse)

Some of the tie-in toys and products for David Hand's Gaumont-British Animation films. Sadly, neither Ginger Nutt nor Zimmy the Lion provided much competition for Mickey Mouse and Donald Duck.

Mary Field, Children's Educational Films supremo, surveying a strip of celluloid.

A dramatic battle scene, reminiscent of Cecil B. de Mille in its scope (and in the number of extras used) from Pascal's *Caesar and Cleopatra* (1945)

Gabriel Pascal and Claude Rains at the opening of *Caesar and Cleopatra* (1945). At the time (1945) it was the most expensive film ever made in Britain. Costing well over £1 250 000, it was considerably dearer than *Gone With the Wind*.

The multi-million pound musical *London Town* (1946), directed by Wesley Ruggles, starred the music-hall comedian Sid Field, along with Greta Gynt and a youthful Petula Clark.

Jill Craigie, arm in jacket, directing a scene on location in the rubble of Plymouth for her 1946 drama-documentary, *The Way We Live*, one of the more unusual vehicles which Rank supported.

5

RESEARCH AND INNOVATION
From kids and cartoons to the Charm School

> The secret of the Atom bomb is common knowledge compared with the underground tactics of the little talked about 'Rank Central Research Organization'.[1]

Beleaguered British filmmakers of the 1930s, invariably behind schedule and short of cash, were so enwrapt in the Herculean task of actually completing and selling their pictures that they rarely had the time or the money to worry about such niceties as research and training. Distributors, the avaricious puppeteers in control of the purse-strings, were not inclined to narrow their profit margins by subsidizing apprentice focus-pullers. The government, as it commissioned a spate of film reports and introduced protective quota legislation, may have feigned concern about the lack of new talent coming through, but did nothing to modify the system so that aspiring technicians could learn their craft before being hurled headlong into the cauldron of the commercial industry. The industry which Rank entered in 1933 thus provided few facilities for training. Shooting 'quota quickies' on tiny budgets remained the traditional, and unsatisfactory, way of learning the business.

Outside documentaries and features, there were areas which the British had conceded almost wholesale to the Americans, not having the resources to develop these fields themselves. In everything from equipment manufacture to newsreels, from cartoons to 'B' pictures, Britain was obliged to defer to Hollywood; the British had nothing to compare with Disney or 'The March of Time'. As a consequence, exhibitors were as dependent on the 'Yanks' for their programme material as for their first features.

No assessment of Rank and the British film industry can overlook the part the Methodist magnate played in trying to rectify this state of affairs. Whatever the shortcomings of other aspects of his film policy, his commitment to research and innovation in the 1940s was unimpeachable. Nobody else in British film history has paid such attention to these activities, which promise nothing but financial loss in the short term. When, in his own pious, humble and patriotic fashion, he embarked on a crusade to put

British cinema on the world map, he felt it was as much his 'mission' to try to broaden the base of the industry as it was to fund the 'prestige' pictures with which he quickly became associated. Fifty years before, mechanizing the mills had enabled Joe Rank to rescue British flour, and to carve himself a vast personal fortune in the process. A similar kind of transformation in British film promised equally beneficent results for Rank Junior.

At the Second World War had shown, there was talent aplenty waiting to be harnessed: the technicians and scientists, the 'boffins' working for various wartime ministries, seemed to have a natural aptitude for optics and electronics, for fashioning such brainstorming devices as radar and the bouncing bomb. (Not long after the war, Rank signed up Sir Robert Watson-Watt, the 'father' of radar, as an electronics consultant.[2]) Rank's vision was of a fully fledged film industry, dealing in everything from newsreels to cartoons and optical engineering.

'It was very easy to pull down Arthur's ear,' a one-time colleague of the film magnate suggests, and it remains sadly true that for all his good intentions, few of Rank's research projects paid dividends in the long run. However, for a brief instant, from about 1944 till August 1947, date of the disastrous ad-valorem tax, he at least gave the British film industry the illusion that it was firing on all cylinders as he invested in a wide range of film-related activities.

INDEPENDENT FRAME

This revolution will be as big a step forward and will have consequences as far-reaching on production as the introduction of colour and sound. It can only be an immediate success when it is carried out on a big production, made by craftsmen of established reputation. If we give all our brains and enthusiasm to it, it *will* be done.
(Memo from Michael Powell to Rank on Independent Frame, February 1945)

In late 1944, Rank had assembled a hand-picked team of twenty 'experts', and had sequestered them (in great secrecy) in an anonymous red-brick building in Upper Berkeley Street, deep in the heart of London's West End, where they were set to work developing 'Independent Frame'. For back-up, these experts could call on a panel of outside consultants, specialists in every field from acoustics to industrial design.

At the helm of the operation, a typically wayward English visionary from Kent with a background in architecture and engineering, was David Rawnsley, whose brainchild the new system was. It was Rawnsley's contention, and complaint, fully articulated in the *Penguin Film Review*, that British filmmakers were suffering from a certain creative flatulence: too often, he suggested, they resorted to a pedantic visual literalism when they should have been using their imaginations:

> Oh, the dreary spoon-feeding sequences. A street scene is built to show a taxi arriving outside a house. An actor is engaged to play the part of the taxi-driver. The star steps from her taxi and pays her fare. She knocks on the front door. An actress is engaged to answer the door in a maid's cap and apron. The maid leads the star down a corridor, through a door and into a room where her lover is waiting. Yet all this elaboration, which simply holds up the story, could be inferred from a design of sound.
>
> (*Penguin Film Review 9*, 1949, p. 32)

Rawnsley felt that the whole process of filmmaking had become tedious and unwieldy, with shooting schedules growing ever longer, and costs escalating, as directors insisted on building, and rebuilding, elaborate sets and façades: they were overcome, he opined, by a mild paralysis in the form of an extreme naturalistic fetish for detail – they showed towards their craft all the tiresome diligence of nineteenth-century novelists who regarded their medium as a commodious vehicle in which to cram every available morsel of information, relevant or not. British filmmakers needed to learn brevity.

Not only would Rawnsley's proposed new scheme animate the very business of filmmaking, quickening schedules and narratives alike: it would also save money. At a time when Hollywood pictures still exercised a virtual stranglehold over British cinemas, if only because British production was limping along at a rate of little more than fifty features a year, Rawnsley's plans for slashing costs and upping productivity must have seemed especially appealing to Rank, who was becoming progressively more disenchanted with the perceived excesses of Del Giudice and the free-spending Independents, and who had quota levels to maintain and cinemas to fill.

The germ of the idea for Independent Frame came to Rawnsley when he was working as an art director on Lean and Coward's *In Which We Serve*. For the film, a naval destroyer had been built across stage four at Denham Studios, and the illusion of sea-storms and seascapes given by a 'rocking process screen' behind the ship. The idea continued to percolate in Rawnsley's mind as he helped design Powell and Pressburger's *49th Parallel*; he had been sent to Canada, shooting there miles and miles of background plates, which he brought back to Denham. In the studios, the technicians then 'composited' foreground images of the actors with the backplates of rugged Canadian terrain. As Rawnsley conceived it, Independent Frame was not so much a startling new invention as the application of already existing techniques, such as those used for Powell and Pressburger and David Lean, in an original and efficient way. It was a question of making a better use of the 'grammar' of special effects – matte shots, hanging miniatures, split screens, front projection and back projection were to be at the core of the system.

Rawnsley's main ally in selling the idea of Independent Frame was Powell, who, in February 1945, submitted a memorandum to Rank about the potential importance of the idea. Powell took credit for inspiring the scheme and cast himself as John the Baptist to Rawnsley's Jesus. He explained to his avuncular patron that he had long since been trying to win over a host of dumb and resistant technicians to his grand, anti-naturalistic vision:

> What has naturalism got to do with entertaining the public? Entertainment is based upon illusion: when audiences are asked to create illusion and to use their imagination they are only too ready to do it, if they are interested in the actors and the story and the story-telling.[3]

(The idea of illusionism, of *trompe l'oeil*, was hardly one likely to appeal to the 'quality' critics, then championing Italian neo-realism as a model for British filmmakers to follow: the artifice of Independent Frame was bound to make it a controversial technique to pursue in the context of 1940s British film culture.)

Even Rawnsley, Powell claimed, had had difficulty in grasping the rudiments of his new approach to film production, which harked back to 'the great days of silent film', when 'every great artist in Europe' was interested in the form, but which managed to combine radical formal innovation every bit as startling as that engaged in by the great and quirky animator George Méliès, with sound business sense, promising to slash production costs. Powell's memo continued:

> It took a long time to sink in: then when I was away in Scotland he [Rawnsley] wrote me a long letter, rediscovering for himself everything I had told him and now selling it to me. He went even further in his theoretical use of process shots: my line had been mainly to simplify and to awaken the public's sleeping imagination and love of effect: his line adapted this and went further, changing scale, and even altering the unalterable and inevitable screen proportions, using process backgrounds and foregrounds in the way they should be used, combining actors, settings and cartoons, setting free a whole new world of possibilities in design and startling theatrical effect.[4]

Powell here addresses Rank with friendly familiarity, and doesn't shirk from discussing relatively complex technical details in full. (This helps dispel the notion of Rank as a figure exclusively preoccupied with business, who had no knowledge of, or interest in, film production. He was obviously someone in whom his filmmakers could confide.) Powell talks of Independent Frame, which he refers to as 'New Design for Films', as a theory which can protect Rank from the excesses of free-wheeling producers. (There is a certain irony in one of Independent Producers' most extravagant directors preaching the benefits of good housekeeping which go hand in hand with Independent Frame.)

> In all these activities you, sir, have a finger in the pie: your immediate interest in this theory is that, if proved successful, it will lessen the risk of getting your fingers burned, which we, your associates in these enterprises, grateful to you for a tidiness and a continuity and a strength, which are foreign to our previous experience, are anxious to avoid on your behalf as on our own.[5]

He offers Rank an image of the film industry as one which periodically slips into decline, but 'captures the public's interest afresh' with some form of strategic innovation, whether it be the introduction of sound, or of the star system, or of Technicolor. Now, Powell suggests, the time had come for a 'craftsman's revolution', in which, for a change, the British would be leading the way rather than following Hollywood's tail.

Given the chance to rebel against the wastrel ways of autocratic producers and directors, the craftsmen had the ingenuity to 'defeat the three giants, Labour, Cost and Studio Space': they could make the medium fluid and experimental, compensating for smaller budgets with their powers of inference and imagination. Independent Frame was to be, above all else, a licence for technicians: it would depend for its success on a harmonious blending of the skills of every department, from script to sound, from music and lighting to camera. (Independent Frame was less a single, earth-shattering device than an 'approach' to filmmaking, which hoisted influence away from the directors and producers to the entire production teams.) The system was to involve movable backdrops, interlocking foregrounds and backgrounds, and various specially built cranes and rostrums. All this machinery promised a greatly reduced shooting period of a month maximum: Rawnsley claimed, 'We might make a feature in a fortnight after six months preparation, at a cost of between £20,000 and £30,000.'[6] Instead of the one and a half minutes footage which most units managed in a day, he wanted to up the tempo to at least fifteen minutes per day: the painted backdrops could be wheeled in and out of the studio, thereby saving the time wasted in putting up and pulling down sets.

In a sense, Independent Frame prefigures the 'total cinema' Powell sought to achieve in his musicals *The Red Shoes* and *The Tales of Hoffman*, where every part of production, from colour to design to costume, is integrated. Studio-based, and inevitably stylized, Independent Frame was, as much as anything else, a reaction against a literary/naturalistic tendency in British cinema: as Denis Forman pointed out in his survey, *Films 1945–1950*:

> Only some ten to fifteen percent of British films are made from original scripts. The vast majority find their subject from novels or short stories.
>
> (Forman, 1952: 48)

Given their source material, it was hardly surprising that British film-makers were inclined to privilege dialogue and 'authenticity of representation' above everything else.

Although Powell had the reputation of being exacting and somewhat sadistic on set, his and Rawnsley's 'New Design for Films' emphasized the collective aspects of filmmaking, seeking to erode divisive hierarchies which have the director (Pascal, notoriously) perched at the top of the pyramid in his or her canvas chair. Under the new system, the director's task was less a matter of imposing a creative vision on a film than of enabling all the departments to coalesce. (Just as there was traditional enmity between producers and 'sellers', there was often ill-feeling between the various little cliques – lighting, script, photography – who actually made the films.) In Independent Frame, the emphasis was, above all else, on pre-planning. Before a production every reached the floor, it was to have been worked out in its minutest detail.

Rawnsley, in particular, conceived that Independent Frame would be developed hand in hand with television, and had bold ideas[7] for piping films and sports events live to cinemas. He also had original notions about trailers:

> By the use of Independent Frame, it will be possible to televise an individual scene or scenes within a feature film, thus including in the film leading stars, who will play the scene in actual before the original background. . . . Leading stars will provide their own trailers before the actual settings by the use of Independent Frame.[8]

Every technician employed on an Independent Frame film, from production designer to scriptwriter, would have a 'thorough knowledge of film technique'; would be able to present his or her ideas in a graphic form, understandable to all; and would have both creative and practical technical ability: not only would the technicians have the 'ideas' but they would also have the ability to execute those ideas. The divisions between the 'artists', who never bothered to dirty their hands, and the workers, who gave a form to these artists' visions, were to be shattered. (Like the famous Dutch soccer team of the 1970s, whose every player could swap position at will, and who purported to play 'total football', Independent Frame technicians were supposed to be supremely versatile, as familiar with sound as with lighting.) Rawnsley was out to wage war on the dilettantes he feared were plaguing the business:

Here is a challenge to the efficiency of every filmmaker who must now prove like every good workman that he knows how properly to use the tools of his trade.

(*Kinematograph Weekly*, 6 January 1949, p. 6)

A practical Rawnsley innovation which quickly caught on was the Cyclops Eye, affectionately known as Dr Cyclops: this was a tiny TV screen, affixed to a camera, which enabled director and camera operator to see how any given scene was 'framed'.

At its best, the Independent Frame system ran like clockwork. As special effects man Charles Staffell, in at its inception, remembers:

Independent Frame did speed things up. You would already have the sets built on the Vickers rostrums: they came on the stage – they went to a set position, pre-planned. They do the lights. The artists come in. Rehearse, rehearse, shoot. Over to another set, probably adjacent. This set goes out. Another one's there. Another one is on its way in. In other words, a belt system, and it did work.[9]

All the framework, backgrounds and mounting for the artists to use during shooting had been built independently, prefabricated as it were. Rawnsley felt that the system could facilitate international co-production, with one country providing the projected backdrops while another actually did the studio work:

Those previously unable to participate in feature film production can by contributing the 'frame' part of the picture become participant in ratio to its cost . . . bringing into the studios the real backgrounds from foreign parts without huge abroad location costs.[10]

In late 1947, Rawnsley left Rank's Research Department, setting up his own production company, Aquila Films, with his colleague Donald Wilson, so that he could test his newfangled technique for 'real': the first of the Independent Frame pictures, *Warning to Wantons*, was ready by the end of 1948. At £100,000, it cost considerably more than Rawnsley had anticipated, and at thirty-five days' shooting time, it took rather longer than the envisaged 'fortnight maximum' to complete. However, these were dismissed as mere technical hitches, teething troubles which could soon be resolved. The *Kinematograph Weekly* gave Independent Frame's debut a cautious welcome:

What the audience saw on the screen this week, from the technical point of view, was an ordinary film. There was nothing which looked 'odd'. But a few technicians associated with the 'secret circle' of

Independent Frame operators at Pinewood saw on screen one of the greatest technical advances since the advent of commercial colour photography.

(Kinematograph Weekly, 6 January 1949, p. 6)

There were eleven other films commissioned in the original batch, amongst them *Poet's Pub*, *Stop Press Girl*, and even a Noël Coward vehicle, *The Astonished Heart*. Rank was reckoned to have spent £600,000 developing the technique. Independent Frame's arrival was trumpeted in the press. Rumours about this revolutionary blueprint for filmmaking were leaked to journalists long before the system was ready, and when the first Independent Frame pictures arrived, they did so in a torrent of publicity.

Unfortunately, hopes that Rawnsley's innovation would have the same boosting effect on the Rank Organization as *The Jazz Singer* – the first 'talkie' – had had on Warner Brothers back in 1927 (myth insists that Al Jolson's tremulous renditions of 'Mammy'[11] saved Warners from the very brink of bankruptcy) proved to be misplaced. Rawnsley's brave new invention belly-flopped. Films made using the system were critically reviled and shunned at the box-office. Independent Frame was quickly suppressed. Several of the experts, and most of the techniques, were absorbed by television, and Rawnsley himself absconded to Italy, where Staffell later found him. 'And what was he doing? . . . Pottery!'[12]

In theory, Independent Frame had seemed a cast-iron winner. It was bringing factory principles to British filmmaking. (The efficiency of the Hollywood studio system had long been held up in opposition to the rather ramshackle way the British went about their business. Rawnsley, though, sought to 'outhollywood' Hollywood by automatizing British film, changing it from a haphazard hybrid of art and business into a manufacturing industry. His technicians were to go about their task with all the sure-footed certainty of workers on a car production line, fitting the appropriate parts to the machine. The secret of his system was its emphasis on pre-production. Every eventuality and mishap was to be anticipated long before the cameras began to roll.)

Perhaps the fact that Rank's Research Department, out of which Independent Frame hatched, was affiliated to the detested central servicing organization, 'Piffle', antagonized producers who might otherwise have embraced the 'New Design for Films'. At Independent Producers Ltd and Two Cities, Michael Powell was the only major figure to show any faith in the system. Sidney Gilliat and his colleagues were very sceptical about the claims made on Independent Frame's behalf, and felt that their scepticism was later justified by events:

By the summer of 1948 the sky was black with chickens coming home to roost. A string of Independent Frame pictures were so awful that cynics said they not only kept people out of the cinema while they were showing, but kept the audiences away the week before *and* the week after.[13]

This meant that the process was shunned by Rank's top directors and writers. While Powell had absorbed (and arguably formed) much of the philosophy behind the technique, the Archers never made a direct use of the system. Nor did Cineguild or Individual. At Gainsborough Studios, producers and directors were too busy with maintaining their breakneck schedules to spare the time necessary to learn and adapt to Independent Frame, even if Rawnsley's scheme offered the prospect of saving time and money in the long run. As Betty Box recalls:

> One of the troubles was that we were all working so hard that we didn't have time to absorb a new technique. It was quicker to get on the way you had always done than to sit down and try and learn a different way of doing things.[14]

A common complaint was that Independent Frame, despite Rawnsley's assurance that 'all the mechanical servicing of production has been designed and conceived with one object in mind – to service the creative element with the utmost efficiency',[15] strained creativity out of filmmaking; that it muzzled directors, stifling improvisation and spontaneity, and compelling them to adhere, with minute precision, to camera angles chosen in the planning stage. Rawnsley scorned this complaint, arguing that directors should learn to discipline themselves like everybody else:

> A film composer has to make his musical art fit any film line by line. Our long-haired directors must learn to do the same.[16]

He had set out to eliminate waste and indulgence, but many felt that he had veered alarmingly in the opposite direction, becoming a petty bureaucratic tyrant. He and Powell had originally conceived of the system as something liberating, based on magic and illusionism, which would emancipate the imaginations of producers and spectators alike. In the end, though, he had prescribed a method for making cartoons – but with human beings. Contract actor Donald Sinden recalls the system without affection:

> We used Independent Frame for background shots in a film called *Day to Remember.* . . . They had this strange tunnel out of Pinewood with these enormous back projection screens – a terrifying system. For the actors it had no atmosphere at all. They had a large cinema screen behind you, at the back of you, and from behind that they projected a scene, an interior. It was a railway station in our case. (It's no good just projecting a photograph because it looks dead. But if a film is projected on to the back – you see people moving.) The trial was that you had to get the camera you were using synchronized precisely with the projector because, as you know, the shutter comes

down between each frame and it would have been possible to photo-
graph only the shutter . . . we had to do those scenes time and time
again. . . . The result always ended with a little halo round everything
in the foreground. . . . It was almost a waste of time . . . you've got
to send a film crew out to film the backplates – you might as well just
take the actors with you.

(From an interview with Donald Sinden by the author,
Chichester, 1992)

By 1948, the mood in the British film industry had radically altered.
Rank was trying to cope with the American film embargo provoked by the
ad-valorem tax of the previous year (see chapter 6 for a full discussion of
this). Now the emphasis was on speed and economy, not on research and
experiment. (Around the time of Independent Frame, Hitchcock's film
Rope was released. For this, Hitchcock had pioneered continuous action,
without cutting, through the 10-minute take'. The British industry
regarded his innovation with enormous interest, but not because they saw
it as a radical aesthetic departure from the norms of editing. On the
contrary, the studio bosses were fascinated by the possibility that the 10-
minute take could save them money on their budgets.)

Sadly, the radical 'New Design for Films' brought to J. Arthur Rank by
Rawnsley and Powell at the end of the war, was caught up in the seismic
events of 1947–8, when the industry again became as unstable as it had
been in the 1930s: Independent Frame was bungled and hurried, misma-
naged, put into operation before it should have been, and adjudged a
failure far too peremptorily.

Charles Staffell suggests that the technique itself was fine. The problem
came with the second-rate scripts and the third-rate directors who shot
those scripts:

What went into it wasn't worthy of it, wasn't worthy of the system.
It's like anything else, isn't it? If you have a Rolls-Royce and give it a
Ford engine it's not going to work.[17]

The mediocrity of the material, the unabsorbing nature of the films,
drew audiences' attention to their formal qualities: sceptical British cinemagoers were quick to spot the seams and joints, the places where the
movable backdrops, models and miniatures stood in for 'real' locations.
Staffell is convinced that if they hadn't been provoked by the shabby
quality of the stories they were presented with, they wouldn't have noticed
the artifice:

The audiences are not that naive, not that stupid, and I would
venture to suggest that had the subject-matter been what it should
have been they wouldn't have been wandering around saying 'How
did they do that?' They would be involved in the artists, in the

performance, in the story-line. They wouldn't have said, 'Oh, they're doing that with back projection or with magic lantern slides.' That's the kiss of death when you say that sort of thing. The public think they have been robbed.[18]

In hindsight, Independent Frame seems to sum up Rank's production endeavour as a whole. The story of the scheme is one of soaring ambition brought crashing down by lack of foresight, by bickering and by petty resentment. It seems worse than imprudent to invest more than half a million pounds in developing such a system and then not to find decent directors and stories, or not to finance properly the first films that were made with it: the system may have worked, but the films palpably did not. Although television picked up the pieces, and the BBC successfully set up its own application of the system,[19] Independent Frame, like so many Rank enterprises of the period, was eventually written off, a 'bad investment'. Perhaps the best film made using Rawnsley's technique was an early Children's Film Company offering, *Under the Frozen Falls*, which was shot on a shoe-string, with the technicians literally nailing bits and pieces together to make it work. Rawnsley's, after all, was a technicians' charter.

In recent years, in spite of the buffeting the industry has taken, it has become commonplace to say that British technicians are the best in the world. Everything from James Bond to Superman and Batman was shot at Pinewood. Rawnsley's old colleague Charles Staffell, veteran special effects man at the studios, later won an Oscar for his modification of back projection techniques. He has no doubts that Independent Frame worked, and that it exercises a lasting influence. The system could effect magical transformations, could enable filmmakers to turn barren bits of studio space into the interiors of country houses or HM prisons.[20]

Independent Frame's premature demise marked yet another missed opportunity for British filmmakers, who had shied away from it, fearing it would make robots out of them and that they would become 'cogwheels in the works, artistic servants in the machinery of modern times'.[21] Rank's recurring tragedy was that he always had the vision to sponsor such projects at the outset, but lack of money or loss of faith would prompt him to abandon the schemes before they had come to fruition. This was true of Independent Producers Ltd, of Independent Frame, and of his plans for a fully fledged British animation studio to knock Disney and Mickey Mouse off their perches.

DAVID HAND AND GAUMONT-BRITISH ANIMATION

Rank's attempts to set up an animation department to rival Disney failed to spawn a Mickey Mouse, a Donald Duck, or even a Pluto; Corny the

Figure 3 Cartoon figures from G-B Animation: Corny the Crow, Ginger Nutt and
Dusty the Mole

Crow, Ginger Nutt and Dusty the Mole, not to mention Ferdy the Fox,
were the best that his cartoonists could come up with, and they were never
embraced by the public in the way their American counterparts were.

In 1944, Rank had head-hunted David Hand, one of the top names in
American animation. In a career stretching back to 1919, Hand had been
employed with Popeye and Betty Boop's creators, the Fleischer brothers,
on their 'Out of the Inkwell' series, and with Walt Disney. At Disney, his
credentials were impressive: he was the supervising director of the first-
ever cartoon feature, *Snow White and the Seven Dwarfs*, and had worked
in the same capacity on *Bambi* and on the innovative wartime history of
aviation, *Victory through Air-Power*: a Titan of the industry, he was
generally reckoned to have the graphic and administrative skills to lay the
foundations for a British cartoon revival. Rank gave him a 5-year contract
and complete authority. Hand brought with him as assistants Roy
Paterson, a *Tom and Jerry* veteran from MGM's Animation Department,
and Ralph Wright, a 'storyman' from Disney, who had 'created' Pluto. The
trio had big plans. First, they ensconced themselves in Soho. Then they set
about recruiting artist-animators. They planned, eventually, to make cartoon films for world release, but would first cut their apprentices' teeth on
educational, religious, industrial and commercial shorts.

At the end of the war, the Gaumont-British Animation Department, as
Hand's outfit was called, was moved out of London to more spacious
country surroundings: they took over Odeon Theatres' wartime retreat,
Moor Hall, a country house in leafy Cookham, quickly installing their
elaborate equipment, and housing their young apprentices in dormitories.
Early, ambitious projects, none of which came to fruition, were to make
feature-length cartoons of Lewis Carroll's *The Hunting of the Snark*; to
adapt *The Wind in the Willows* in a dozen 10-minute episodes; and to tread
on Korda territory with an epic, animated version of *The First Men in the
Moon*, the novel by H.G. Wells.

A raw young apprentice at Cookham, later a successful television 'personality', was Bob Monkhouse, whose mother spotted a recruitment ad for G-B Animation in the local press. Monkhouse recalls being awestruck by Hand: 'He was one of the most impressive men I've met in my life . . . a super-executive.'[22] He remembers that in his time at Cookham, J. Arthur Rank came down to visit them only once. Rank was aloof and distant: 'He was a big, plain-spoken man who shook hands with us reluctantly.'[23] Also on the books was the artist George Henry Stringer, who had trained at Manchester Art School at the same time as L. S. Lowry. Soon, Hand's staff had ballooned to 120: 80 artists, 20 technicians, and 20 clerical and other workers. (At its peak, G-B Animation was employing more than 200.) There were 3,000 people working in the American cartoon industry. Hand claimed he could envision the day when there would be 5,000 in the British. However, he soon discovered his optimism was far from warranted – the operation quickly ran into difficulty. Just as Wesley Ruggles had been appalled by the primitive conditions he encountered at Shepperton Studios when he came over to direct *London Town*, and found that his 'glitzy' musical was gradually being sabotaged by rationing, lack of materials and rusty technicians, Hand discovered that the British animation scene was ragged at the edges. In June 1946, he wearily observed to the *Kinematograph Weekly* that 'equipment, building materials and other essentials for production are practically impossible to obtain', while remarking on how much the war had done to 'retard the natural development of the arts'.[24]

It took three years, Hand reckoned, to teach an artist how to animate. Only in late 1948 did his cartoons begin to appear in the West End. Originally, he had insisted that G-B Animation would not be making pastiches of Disney or Warner Brothers work, but would be evolving a specifically British style of cartoon, with British characters and British humour. This proved infinitely more difficult than he had envisaged. The British weren't 'so cartoon-minded' as the Americans, he claimed, pointing out that there were fewer 'funnies' in British newspapers than in their US counterparts. He turned down a suggestion from Rank that 'he should try to make animated cartoons out of the *Daily Mirror* strip characters', because he wanted to devise his own, original characters.

In a vain attempt to keep the studios ticking over while the apprentices mastered their craft, Hand kept the young animators busy, drawing maps for Rank's documentary series 'This Modern Age', making a variety of advertisements for everything from SP toothbrushes to Fox's Glacier Mints to Amami shampoo and Windsmore coats. The apprentices worked on professional projects for most of the day, but, Monkhouse remembers, spent up to four hours practising: under Roy Paterson's strict supervision, they were made to draw taps dripping or flags fluttering in the wind. It was arduous, uncomfortable work, sitting for hours on end, etching figures on glass panels which were illuminated from beneath by several hot and searing lights. The staff were on 13-week recurring contracts, and were paid a meagre £5 a week for their efforts. Out of their wage, they had to find the money for their bed and board. They slept in dormitories, and were all in mortal terror of the resident Moor Hall poltergeist, which caused ancient grandfather clocks to come crashing down staircases.

According to Monkhouse (who soon had himself transferred to the Sounds Department), Hand's ideal of a new, in-house style rapidly went out of the window: 'it was all Disney . . .'

The two main series G-B Animation managed to complete were 'Musical Paintbox' and 'Animaland'. A recent viewing of an episode of the latter, *The House Cat*, revealed the extent to which Hand and his colleagues depended on American prototypes. Shot in Technicolor, under the supervision of Ralph Wright, there is nothing whatsoever about this piece, other than a plummy, Oxford-inflected voice-over, to suggest that it was made in Britain. A colourful frenetic story of the domestic puss, *Felis vulgaris*, its pursuit of domestic mice (hardly an original theme) and its scraps with feral tom-cats, even the shape of the dustbins in the cartoon seems American. The same cannot be said for 'Musical Paintbox', which chooses specifically British themes: the episode *Canterbury Road* opens with the encouraging injunction 'To see your past, Use your Imagination', as a pair of doors part and we look into somebody's mind. Then we see a desert with a hole in the ground, a bucket and a placard saying 'Beware! Psychoanalyst at work'. There are images of such things as pigs on bicycles before we reach the main matter of the short, which is Canterbury pilgrims and their stories:

Alfred the Barrelmaker and Nicholas the Astrologer both loved the only girl for miles . . . Alice.

Canterbury Road seems stilted and enervated when compared with the brashness of its American cousins, or even of the Ralph Wright/ *Tom-and-Jerry*-inspired *The House Cat. A Fantasy on Ireland*, another of the 'Musical Paintbox' shorts, is similarly dull: a non-narrative, musical ramble round Dublin which moves into pastoral Ireland, eventually ending with some anthropomorphized potatoes, it deals in the crudest and most mawkish of national stereotypes.

When they were finally released in the cinemas, Hand's films were given a lukewarm reception. They were reasonable enough, but they lacked the madcap energy, inventiveness and lateral thinking of Warner Brothers, Disney, or MGM output. They were pale facsimiles of their Hollywood counterparts.

Regardless of their quality, Hand's cartoons would have been hard pressed to make back their money – in the period, a 10-minute cartoon cost £10,000 to £12,000 to produce – when there was no market for British animation outside the propaganda, education and instruction fields. As Hand's inveterate rival John Halas, whose work the American affected to despise, observed:

134

Due to double feature programmes, only a limited number of cinemas in Britain are showing cartoon films, apart from the new cinemas.[25]

Even where the cartoons were being shown, in Rank's Odeons and Gaumonts, they were too far down the bill to generate much revenue. (The system was heavily tilted in favour of first features, which always took the lion's share of the box-office receipts.)

Like Independent Frame, like the Independent Producers Ltd set-up, like a host of Rank's other projects, G-B Animation ended acrimoniously. There was a variety of reasons for this, not the least of which was the Rank Organization's predicament at the end of the 1940s (see chapter 6 on the ad-valorem tax). Hand had illicitly poached staff from his previous employers, Disney, and this combined with a general American antipathy to British films and the glut of animating talent that there was in the USA, meant that Hand's cartoons would never find a market on the far side of the Atlantic.

Hand's own enthusiasm for the project had quickly waned. Austerity Britain of the 1940s was hardly the best environment in which to launch an animation studio. Not only were there no outlets for the cartoons, they were impossibly awkward and expensive to make. Nearly all the materials had to be imported from America. Hand became more and more frustrated as he found that 'the wheels of industry were grinding slow'.[26] Although toys, games and books were marketed with the cartoons, they failed to wheedle their way into the public's affections.

Alan Wood reckoned that the outlay on the Moor Park experiment was in excess of £500,000. Precious little of that was recouped. As the Rank Organization lapsed into the red in the late 1940s, as workers were laid off, studios closed down and projects abandoned, it was inevitable that G-B Animation would go under. Sure enough, in the early spring of 1950, there were advertisements in the trade press announcing an auction where the discerning buyer could purchase some prime and very elaborate Technicolor animation equipment at knock-down prices. Hand's artists had abruptly been paid off. Moor Hall was sold to the British Tabulating Machine Company Inc. for a paltry £18,000, a sale price 'which did little to ease Rank's overdraft'.[27] Hand returned to America.

G-B Animation is typical of Rank's endeavours: all the spade work had been done, the equipment bought, the apprentices trained. By the end of 1948, Hand insisted that the worst was over, that 'the elaborate organization required in the making of cartoons had been built up'.[28] However, this time-consuming, expensive experiment was given little more than a year to prove itself. After the outfit folded, some of Hand's trainees would wend their way to Gerry Anderson to work on early episodes of 'Joe 90'; some were taken on by Halas and Batchelor. Mainly, though, they were lost to the industry. Paterson', Wright' and Hand's arduous training went for nothing. Had Rank waited till the mid-1950s, when television would have provided an outlet for his cartoons, G-B Animation might have succeeded. As it was, the operation seems ill-conceived, an idea out of its time. There was no demand for British cartoons, nor even in British theatres, and there was no mechanism whereby they could make money, however good they were. They did, though, contribute to Rank's 'prestige profile'.

'THIS MODERN AGE'

Throughout the world millions are homeless, millions live in appalling conditions. Every nation has come home to its own tragic housing problem.

('This Modern Age', no. 1, *Homes for All*, 1946)

Of all Rank's adventures in the film industry, none brought him more credit than his attempt to outdo America's documentary newsreel, 'The March of Time', with a magazine feature of his own, 'This Modern Age' (TMA). From its very first episode, *Homes for All*, released in September 1946, to its swansong four years and forty-one films later with *Turkey: Key to the Middle East*, 'This Modern Age' addressed pressing, often controversial issues with exemplary journalistic 'balance'. TMA's philosophy is summed up in a nutshell in its promotional leaflet for *Sudanese Dispute*:

Have the Sudanese the right to complete independence as a nation? Egypt says No, Britain says Yes . . . the British and Egyptian viewpoints are presented with complete impartiality and in a clear manner, so as to enable the onlooker to form his own opinion.[29]

Clarity, impartiality, detachment – these were the cornerstones of the series: the films were characterized by the same brand of patrician and mildly radical humanism which John Ellis suggests is at the core of the discourse of the 'quality film'.[30] With its gentle, paternal probing, TMA was a newsreel for the Attlee era. The opening image of *Homes for All* set the tone for what was to follow: soldiers marched home to Britain after the war, while a booming voice-over asked, in rhetorical fashion, whether there were houses for them to go to. Town planning, as Jill Craigie has suggested,[31] was a subject of intense public interest in bombed and blitzed 1940s Britain, and *Homes for All* plunged headlong into the debate of how the country should be reconstructed with a searing indictment of wasteful 'ribbon development', and a demand for social justice for all. The film celebrates house-building with a montage of workers busy constructing – building bathrooms, inserting window frames, fitting kitchens, smelting – all set to rousing music. The message is clear: there is no reason why modern, comfortable homes should not be available to all – the energy and ingenuity which went into war production should now be turned to the domestic front.

While it was common enough for privately or government funded documentaries, such as those made under the auspices of the Empire Marketing Board and the Crown Film Unit,[32] to tackle contemporary issues, it was most unusual for a commercial body, like the Rank Organization, to become involved in so specialized (and unprofitable) a field: for all its critical popularity, 'The March of Time' ran at a loss, and it was more or less inevitable that 'This Modern Age' would do the same:

> It is very rare for a short film to earn back enough to pay for its cost, for its share of the box-office receipts is too small, even when it is lucky enough to secure a good range of bookings. It has, moreover, to compete with American two-reel documentaries and shorts, or cartoons, which are often rented for a song or given away with a main feature.[33]

Rank's commitment to the series belies his reputation as a mercenary capitalist, out to hawk the British film industry to the Americans. Just as he had granted the Independent Producers complete creative (and fiscal) licence, he gave TMA's teams of producers and writers editorial control, even when they aired opinions in startling opposition to his own brand of true blue Tory politics. (Cynical contemporaries, noting that TMA's dates, 1946–50, neatly parallel those of the first Attlee government, suggest that the series was a 'sop to the Socialists', an attempt by Rank to keep in the good books of his (ruling) political opponents.[34] There is no evidence this was the rationale behind the TMA films.) Sergei Nolbandov, an émigré Russian law student, who had been kicking around Wardour Street since the early 1920s, was the supervising producer of the series. His associate, and literary editor, was Ivan Smith, although Smith later made way for J. L. Hodson, a well-known novelist and playwright. Echoing Lean's glowing remarks about the set-up at Independent Producers Ltd, Nolbandov observed: 'Few film producers – or newspaper editors – have as much freedom as we have.'[35]

The films kept to a strict format. They appeared at the rate of one a month, and were always twenty-one minutes (1,900 feet) long, with spoken commentaries of 1,600 words. Nolbandov had deliberately chosen to employ technicians from the feature rather than the documentary field, believing that this would give TMA the technical standard of feature films. The commentaries were generally read by Robert Harris, a former broadcaster and 'leading player at Stratford-on-Avon',[36] whose voice didn't have the booming, cannon-like quality of the commentator on 'The March of Time'. Music was provided by Muir Mathieson. The series quickly built up a following: within two years, it was being shown in twenty-three different countries. Nolbandov refused to allow the films to be changed in any way for export. A foreign language commentary was the only amendment he would countenance. Original footage was always shot on location rather than in the studios, 'whose atmosphere, the producers argue, is not true to life'.[37] Complementing this footage was the archive material: Nolbandov had agents scavenging the vaults of Wardour Street and of every major film library throughout the world, including Rank's own Central Film Library at Denham Studios, which could provide producers with everything from cat noises to images of lions and hyenas and collapsing houses.[38]

Every episode of TMA ended with the brave appeal: 'The Challenge Must Be Met in This Modern Age!' For all its critical and popular success, the quality of TMA was infinitely variable, as variable as the broad range of subjects it covered. Often, the commentaries struck a patronizing note. In TMA, no. 19, *Challenge in Nigeria*, the commentator observes: 'Many Africans have risen to distinction and today occupy important posts – police officers, barristers, high court judges',[39] while in TMA, no. 22, *Women in Our Time*, the commentator notes: 'Women are holding responsible positions as never before'[40] before going on to remark that 'it is women's beauty and graciousness which does so much to enrich our lives'. The two films reek of a kind of patriarchal, Anglo-Saxon condescension.

TMA's fetish for objectivity could see it lapse into blandness, but at its best the series was urgent and provocative. In TMA, no. 7, *Coal Crisis*, for example, the series examines the troubles faced in the mining industry now that it has come under public ownership: 'In taking over the mines the public has taken over a legacy of past misery and resentment.' While the voice-over emphasizes public responsibility and community action, the debt owed by the people to the miners, the visuals idealize the men in the pits in best Soviet fashion: there are some startling under-the-surface shots of miners bent double, shovelling coal towards the camera.

For its overseas jaunts, TMA would employ units of three: camera operator, assistant camera operator and researcher-writer. (The real struggle came in editing together original and archive footage and in laying on the soundtrack.) One of the most ambitious episodes of the series was no. 31, *India and Pakistan*, for which the crew travelled 8,000 miles and shot more than 50,000 feet of film. Justifying the expense of this extensive location work, Hodson observed: 'Even if the film was not finally made it was felt that we should secure a wealth of useful visual material that can be used in one way or another.'

Gerald Hanley, the project's researcher-writer, arrived in India bearing a letter to a prominent Indian political leader from the maverick Labour/ Conservative MP, future chairman of the Tote and 'Voice of Reason' in the *News of the World*, Woodrow Wyatt. Unfortunately, the letter was never delivered:

I had a personal letter to Mahatma Gandhi from Woodrow Wyatt MP. I looked forward to meeting the Mahatma whose effect upon India I had seen in wartime India, but he was assassinated the day after we arrived in Karachi from London [30 January 1948]. It was a strange opening to twelve months of travel across Pakistan and India, both countries still feeling the effect of the partition and Punjab massacres.[41]

India and Pakistan proved peculiarly difficult to film. As Hanley wrote back to head office in a memo half-way through shooting:

India as a film subject is endless – it just goes on – different peoples, climates, dress, religions, customs. The cameraman is like the man in the middle of the racing traffic – he does not quite know which way to turn – for India is so vast, so different – and each part of it is absorbing. The cameraman has to resist temptation to shoot everything he sees and must have a shot-line and story-line. Without that he just disappears into India which will lure any cameraman to bewilderment.[42]

(Post-colonial India had long been a source of fascination for J. Arthur Rank. Three years before he sent TMA to the sub-continent, he had posted Thorold Dickinson there on his behalf, to spend three months surveying the possibilities of feature film production on location in that country. Later, in 1958, Rank would sponsor *The Wind Cannot Read*, a Betty Box/Ralph Thomas picture, starring Dirk Bogarde, which was shot on location in India and Burma.)

Hanley and Co. may have been awestruck by their subject, but J. L. Hodson, back in London, was very disappointed with the visuals which the unit were sending home to England. He insisted he wanted a 'less historical and more newsy film'. Hanley protested that India and Pakistan were too vast a subject to do justice to in twenty-one minutes. 'This Modern Age', for all its much-vaunted attempts at giving both sides of any argument (as if there only ever were two sides), none the less had to simplify, reduce and sometimes even compromise its material to fit it into its slot and to ensure that it was not offensive. Nolbandov and Hodson received the assistance of the Foreign Office in setting up contacts and stories abroad. They were obliged to be careful not to denigrate the countries they portrayed, especially if these countries were potential customers. In *India and Pakistan*, therefore, part of Hanley's commentary needed to be revamped:

I [Hodson] spoke to Hanley. He thinks our sentence 'When will the two countries stop spending their resources by defending their borders against each other,' quite justified. Having regard to the hyper-sensitiveness of both countries, and the fact that the border situation may change while the film is still going the rounds in six or twelve months time, I think it may be best to take the sentence out.[43]

Most of TMA's offerings were not as ambitious or as expensive as *India and Pakistan*, but they made films about Japan ('On the atom bomb I rather doubt whether we can do much since my understanding is that all material shot at Hiroshima and Bikini was taken under American security control',[44] and about the Yaba Leper Colony in Nigeria ('It really is quite as gruesome as anything we have seen and it took Ted and Ian all their time not to be sick when they were shooting the injection of the inmates').[45]

In its brief history, the series dealt with various different aspects of British culture and society, examining the British on holiday, *When You Went Away*, and at leisure, *The British: Are They Artistic*, as well as touching on such diverse subjects as gambling and Antarctic whale hunts. The series had developed a loyal following and, when it was announced in late 1950 that TMA was to disappear, there was no shortage of defenders for the documentary.

Roger Manvell had long been championing TMA's cause in the pages of *Tribune*:

> One of the reactionary tendencies since the war has been to keep documentary off the public screens entirely, or to replace it with the worst type of so-called interest film . . . TMA challenges the average exhibitor's theory that the public hates the factual film, but he can do little about it since in this case the series is sponsored by the Rank Organization itself, and not, as in the past, by the Government. The standard of the series is very high, and in the latest issue, *Home and Beauty*, shows clearly and without unnecessary cultural whimsy how good design can make our domestic life pleasanter and better.[46]

Documentary filmmaker and writer Paul Rotha also bemoaned its passing:

> Few will deny that *This Modern Age* revealed Rank seriously trying to use the screens of his own and other people's cinemas for a serious purpose.[47]

There were calls for the series to be saved. They weren't heeded. For all that it won the Exhibitors' Poll in Britain four years running[48]; for all that it was more popular with British audiences than its great rival and precursor, 'The March of Time', and was even preferred to Walt Disney cartoons[49]; for all its influence as British propaganda throughout the world – a TMA film, *Rape of the Earth*, was shown to a UN conference on conservation and utilization of world resources[50]: it was not commercially viable. Spectators might have enjoyed seeing an issue of 'This Modern Age' as part of a supporting programme, but they were unlikely to come to the cinema for the documentary short's sake alone.

Having run up a huge deficit on his post-war prestige production, Rank eventually decided that he could no longer subsidize the series which he himself had devised. As he announced in his 1950 chairman's statement: 'We had received many compliments about this monthly production both in this country and from other parts of the world. We did not consider, however, that we were justified in continuing to operate this unit, in spite of the good work it was doing, when there was no reasonable prospect of our being able to recover the costs which were being incurred.'

TMA became a victim of Rank's swingeing cut-backs in production. Like Independent Frame and G-B Animation, its moment had been brief. 'The March of Time' took over a decade to establish itself. TMA proved itself in half that time. However, as long as documentaries and shorts were written out of the box-office equation, viewed by exhibitors as 'fillers', there would be no eroding the all-pervasive influence of the first feature. 'This Modern Age' rode on the coat-tails of Rank's big pictures. As they continued to fail at the box-office, they dragged the documentaries and cartoons down with them.

THE CHARM SCHOOL

In those days, audiences would go mad. They would even do so about a very good-looking man who opened a garden party: you just needed to say he was a Rank Organization star. Films were terribly exciting to people then. All these big stars, especially after the war years, were giving people release from things, from poverty, from shortages: suddenly you saw all those marvellous people being very romantic, and it became very important as a release for people.

(Olive Dodds, recalling her days as administrator of the Rank Charm School)[51]

Peggy Evans, Patsy Drake, Carletta Coburn, Patricia Dainton, Elspeth Grey, Sandra Martin, Margaret Thorburn, Sandra Dorne, Christopher Lee, Anthony Steel, Pete Murray, Carol Marsh, Diana Dors, Jill Ireland, Peggy Owens, Sonia Holm and a host of other good-looking, well-proportioned young actors and actresses with 'sparkling' personalities were put under contract by the Rank Organization, some of them passing through the famous 'Charm School', and most of them headed towards oblivion . . .

A sort of mixture between Lee Strasberg's Actors Studio and a London finishing school for young ladies, a place where you learned posture by balancing books on your head, where you trained for the film cameras by fighting a thousand fencing duels (fencing helps your poise and keeps you from blinking, useful skills for the screen), the 'Charm School' – the phrase was coined by an American journalist – represented Rank's bold attempt to mass-produce 'stars', an attempt which was conspicuously unsuccessful.

Stars are 'an economic necessity . . . a production value . . . an insurance value . . . a trademark value',[52] and the British film industry, some noticeable exceptions apart, has struggled to 'manufacture' them. The lack of recognizable 'marquee names' is frequently cited by the American 'showmen' as the reason for British film's failure to establish a foothold in the USA. Unlike the British industry, Hollywood has always made pictures whose leading players are instantly recognizable throughout the world. From 1910, when Carl Laemmle 'faked' stories of the death of Florence Lawrence, hitherto known as the 'Biograph Girl', and relaunched her career in one of his own pictures, giving the public her real name, right up till the 1990s, when studios reckoned that just to have Tom Cruise's name on a picture's billing automatically added millions to the box-office, regardless of what the film was about, the American industry has been as dominant in its projection and publicization of star personalities as in every other aspect of the film business.

In the early 1940s, Ted Black and Maurice Ostrer made a concerted attempt to fashion a British star system at Gainsborough through a planned programme of films in which they played the same artists in 'picture after picture'.[53] Lockwood, Granger, Mills, Mason, Roc and others were gradually established in the public mind. (In the 1930s, the celebrities of British cinema, with the possible exception of Jessie Matthews, were character actors – singers and comedians like Fields, Formby, Will Hay and Jack Hulbert.)

Ostrer, ever resourceful, inaugurated a 'bus panel' advertising campaign to get his players recognized, as well as encouraging them to wear clothes 'designed by famous houses', to do Lux toilet soap and Drene hair shampoo promotions, and to make personal appearances.[54] Rank's Charm School, however, had its origins not at Gainsborough, but at Riverside Studios, where Sydney Box had set up the 'Company of Youth' in December 1945. Box's intentions were simple – he took half a dozen young talents, put them under contract and kept them busy in 'bit' parts while they learned their craft. Box transferred the company to Gainsborough in 1946, when he was recruited by Rank.

Rank had already established a Contract Artists Department as a branch of 'Piffle' (Production Facilities (Films) Ltd), his central servicing organization. This was run by David Henley, a former general secretary of Equity and one-time colleague of the theatrical impresario Binkie Beaumont, who was well accustomed to dealing with actors. With the arrival of the Company of Youth, Henley broadened his activities, encouraging the Rank Organization to take hold of a large house in Highbury, North London, where it set up a small academy. Here, young contract artists could study screen acting when they were not required for film work.

As Henley's assistant Olive Dodds remembers, acting ability was not considered of paramount importance when it came to the recruitment of the starlets:

> We weren't so much concerned with acting talent. It was felt that in as far as you needed it for film work, it could be acquired. We looked first of all for faces, personalities, figures and so on: they had to be the typical heroine and hero.[55]

Dodds, Henley and Gainsborough casting director Weston Drury would occasionally spot a starlet in rep, or crossing the street, and would sign the young tyro up. Generally, though, it was through theatrical agents that the Charm School 'scholars' were found. Once under contract, a young actor or actress could expect to have his or her teeth straightened: 'Between us, we knew a good dentist: we sent them, and paid the bill'[56] and to be provided with a new wardrobe – Dodds had employed a full-time dress designer. 'It was almost like a very casual finishing school, but not a finishing school in the society sense: a finishing school of the presentation of oneself. So you learned to talk to people easily – bazaars, premières – you dressed up. You had pictures taken . . .'

At the school, which the starlets attended in a haphazard fashion, when they had nothing else that they were required to do, a stern elocutionist, formerly with the Royal Academy of Dramatic Art (RADA), Molly Terraine, who generally wore the same bizarre hat, with a crop of flowers on its top, put the actors through their paces. For novices with stoops and no acting experience, this was useful training. However, for the slightly more mature starlet, such as Anthony Steel, who had just come out of the army as a major, or Diana Dors, who reputedly had already been through RADA, the prospect of walking around a room with a book on one's head did not always appear alluring. As Christopher Lee, a somewhat macabre leading man, recalled in his autobiography, *Tall, Dark and Gruesome*: 'Molly took no impertinence or idleness, and she was a great elocution coach.'[57] Diana Dors was considerably more acerbic about Terraine, describing her to Barry Norman in 1982 as 'a dreadful harridan of a woman who struck fear and terror into everyone'.

In keeping with the Animation Department and 'This Modern Age', the Charm School suffered from one fundamental drawback. Just as there was no demand for either cartoons or documentaries, there was a marked lack of enthusiasm for employing the Charm School graduates. None of Rank's production companies was under any obligation to hire the starlets, even for 'bit' parts. Often, the Highbury actors and actresses were given no chance to put Terraine's lessons into practice: they served their apprenticeship, found they were not wanted and then left the industry. (Their contracts came up for renewal every year, and the turnover was swift.) The lucky ones were given walk-on parts, hauled into a production for three lines as a waitress or something equivalent. Rank's 'B' studios, also at Highbury, employed at least one Charm School novice per picture, and Sydney Box used the fledgeling talents whenever he could at Gainsborough Studios, but neither Two Cities nor any of the Independent Producers felt much inclined to give the starlets a chance. Resenting interference in their creative decisions and seeing 'central casting' as yet another sinister manifestation of the cold and clammy hand of 'Piffle', which already had them in thrall, they tended to avoid using the young contract artists as a matter of principle. Obviously, the Charm School hirelings, on basic yearly salaries and already contracted to Rank, were cheaper to hire than outside performers, but budget had never been the overriding consideration for the Independent Producers or for Del Giudice. Besides, producers preferred to do their own talent-spotting. As Olive Dodds regretfully puts it:

> The thing you discover in the end is that people like to discover their own stars. They don't want them handed on a plate.[58]

Although relatively few of Dodds and Terraine's charges managed to make the transition from pupescent Charm School apprentice to fully grown screen star (Diana Dors is often cited as the exception which proves the rule), the young contract artists served a useful secondary function for the Rank Organization. They swiftly discovered there was more to being a film star than appearing in front of the cameras. Pinewood casting director Weston Drury recalls that the starlets travelled the length and breadth of the land, opening garden fairs and bazaars, making personal appearances: 'The Organization got its money worth out of them by sending them where no one else wanted to go.'[59]

There were more than 60,000 applications to the Publicity Department for portraits of Rank stars per week. Theo Cowan, Rank's publicity impresario, daily dealt with a torrent of fan mail, processing around 350 applications a month for stars to appear at functions of one sort or another. He soon evolved an elaborate system for satisfying the public demand: 'We plan personal appearances like a military operation, and have the co-operation of several other departments – for instance, the travel specialists, the wardrobe and the hairdressers.'[60]

Planes, trains and cars were used to whisk the stars from the studios or from the theatres where they were performing to their engagements. The burdens put on Rank's leading lights were considerable. As Dirk Bogarde, one of the organization's top stars in the 1950s, recalls, with a measure of bad grace, he relied on Cowan to get him through 'the inanities of judging Beauty Queens, opening swimming pools in civic centres, giving bouquets to the Most Glamorous Grannies of Hull or Gipsy Hill' (Bogarde, 1978: 285). Sometimes it would seem that actors making personal appearances had actually stepped out of the screen:

Quite often you could do two personal appearances in an evening . . . you'd appear in one cinema at a town before your film had started and another one after it had finished. Sometimes this wasn't quite possible so they'd stop the film in the middle for you to come on to the stage and be introduced. The public never seemed to object, you know, to having the film broken up.

(From an interview with Donald Sinden by the author,
Chichester, 1992)

Fans were desperately keen to see their favourites in the flesh, but it was a question of supply and demand: if the requested star was already booked up, or unavailable, a young contract artist was sent in that star's stead, and was liable to be 'mobbed' in spite of his or her anonymity. (In the absence of pop stars, screen idols, even those who had never appeared in films, were fawned upon by fans. They were, to use Leo Lowenthal's phrase, 'Idols of Consumption', famous because they were famous, 'stars' simply by association with Rank.) Notice of the unknown starlet's arrival was given in the press beforehand. Olive Dodds made sure the starlet had the right clothes to wear, and money to spend. Terraine brushed up on the starlet's elocution, movement and poise. The starlet, who may have been languishing under contract, without the whiff of a screen role, was generally grateful for the publicity. The fans, for their part, would manage to overcome their disappointment at being presented with somebody they didn't instantly recognize, and would give the starlet a rousing, swooning welcome none the less.

On their days out, the young contract artists were transmogrified, made into Cinderellas. Stars for an afternoon, they may not have done anything to justify their celebrity: they may never have appeared in a film, but they were in demand all the same, living advertisements for the Rank Organization.

It was Dodd's conviction that anybody at all, provided they looked the right way, had personality and were prepared to learn, could become a star. In a period when there were few drama schools specializing in screen acting techniques and 'there were certainly no local government grants to help promising youngsters with fees',[61] an establishment like the Charm School served a useful purpose, providing publicity and a thorough grounding in voice and movement for its pupils – Rank had even made an arrangement with the Connaught Repertory Theatre in Worthing for the young actors to serve the occasional stint on the 'boards'. However, like Rank's other experiments, the Charm School was a good idea which ultimately did not work. Set up primarily to provide producers with a steady flow of young talent to tap, it was fatally undermined by the producers themselves. In Hollywood, stars under contract were assured of employment. In Highbury, this was not the case. Had Rank insisted that

145

the contract artists be given roles, filmmakers would have been forced to take the Charm School a little more seriously. As it was, the filmmakers were inclined to scoff at Terraine' and Dodds's antics, and recruited their actors from outside.

With little chance of being cast in reasonable screen roles, and with every chance of having to fester, doing next to nothing, the artists' morale was liable to sink. The Charm School's exclusive preoccupation with leading men and women was possibly misguided. A smattering of character actors would have introduced a little balance to the school, and reduced competition for the same roles. (After all, Rank's most successful star of the late 1950s was a comedian – Norman Wisdom.) There was something homogenized and bland about the crop of starlets, all uniformly good-looking, all wearing the same style of clothes, all photographed in identical light and poses by Cornel Lucas . . .

In 1950, as Rank's cut-backs continued apace, and as production was concentrated at Pinewood, the Charm School was disbanded. Only the actors making the organization a profit were kept under contract. Pete Murray, a Charm School alumnus whose career in films went nowhere, summed up the experiment disdainfully:

> The idea was that we would learn cinema techniques which really wasn't true at all. Really what it was was that they got a lot of pretty girls and maybe out of all those pretty girls, they found one who could act a little bit. . . . Really, for the main, it was an awful waste of time.
> (Pete Murray interviewed for the BBC documentary
> on the Charm School, broadcast in 1982)

HIGHBURY STUDIOS

> Were they drunk or sufficiently under the influence of drink to be driving to the public danger?[62]

One area of film production which the British had abandoned to the Americans after the abolition of the 'quota quickie' was the 'B' feature, the so-called curtain-raiser. In 1947, Rank revived this style of picture at Highbury Studios, a tiny film factory in North London, not far from Arsenal's football ground, where £20,000 movies were to be produced at the rate of one every five weeks, and where young British technicians were to be given the opportunity to refine their skills before being thrown into high-budget filmmaking. It was a short-lived operation, lasting only for two years until, in 1949, it took its place along with the other casualties of Rank's production crisis. However, in its brief lifespan, it was certainly successful within its own terms, providing early showcases for actresses such as Susan Shaw and directors such as Terence Fisher, and turning out its pictures on time and on budget. This was largely due to the efforts of the studios' supervisor, the resourceful and acerbic John Croydon, formerly an associate producer at Ealing. Croydon reacted to the cramped spaces, rickety equipment and restricted budgets with ingenuity. His method was to break down a script into its most minuscule elements, planning every shot in detail well before shooting began: he allowed no leeway for mistakes – retakes were as rare at Highbury as they had been in the straitened days of the 1930s. Generally, the key figure in each department, whether it be the camera operator or the art director, was grizzled and experienced. Newcomers started at the bottom and gradually worked their way up. There was no time for theory or for teaching. The studios were constantly in flux, with half of the restricted floorspace being used for filming while technicians struggled to construct sets for the forthcoming picture in the other half. (There was no erecting shop: all the sets had to be built on the floor.) The shortage of space made long shots a hazard. Often, the camera operator would find himself or herself wedged against the wall, struggling to put distance between the lens and the object it was aimed at. There were rarely more than four main figures featured in a cast. With such limited resources, Croydon endeavoured to use as many actors and actresses from the Charm School as possible. (He was contractually obliged to use at least one per picture. Highbury, as he put it, provided a 'severely practical' grounding[63] in the exigencies of film production for its often young employees.) At their best, Highbury films hinted at a new idiom, a low-budget style of filmmaking which was neither shoddy nor derivative of Hollywood.

The 1948 release *To the Public Danger*, for example, manages to combine elements of the public service film (warning viewers of the perils of drunk-driving) with an allegory about the *longueurs* of civilian life after six years of war. Taken from a Patrick Hamilton short story, it features two Charm School trainees (Dermot Walsh and Susan Shaw) in the leading roles, and also boasts an eccentric performance from Roy Plomley (later to devise *Desert Island Discs* for BBC Radio). The film tells of reckless, upper-middle-class Captain Cole, a neat amalgam of the old-fashioned 'bounder' and the post-war 'spiv', who drives through the English countryside in a large motor car at great speed, accompanied all the while by his permanently inebriated companion, played by Plomley, and who stops at every roadside pub and garage for liquid replenishment for both himself and the car. In one expansive GI-style lounge bar, Cole challenges a local couple to a game of bar billiards, wins easily, then invites the couple for a ride in his car. By now, Cole is very drunk, and his driving is erratic: trying to negotiate a tight corner, he knocks over, and presumes he has killed, a passing cyclist, but refuses to stop. After various altercations with the couple, and a short police chase, he has a frightening accident himself, 'pranging' his car against a large tree. The film ends with the camera tilting down the tree till it reveals the mangled remains of the car at the base. Directed by Terence Fisher, who was later to oversee most of Hammer's *Frankenstein* vehicles, and who would strike a profitable liaison with Christopher Lee, a former Rank Charm School leading man transformed into *Dracula, Prince of Darkness*, *To the Public Danger* broaches issues of class – public school Captain Cole's difficulties in coping with Attlee England, has strong performances by the two contract artists, and ends darkly, seeming to prefigure its director's later work. Socially relevant, narratively taut, and with the occasional flourishes of imaginative pro-duction design (notably the smashed-up automobile in the woods) this Highbury curtain-raiser showed what the studios could achieve with their meagre resources. Sadly, by 1949, when Rank was envisaging abandoning production altogether, the Highbury experiment came to an abrupt end. Neither cartoons nor documentaries nor 'B' features were profitable. It was inevitably that all three would be sacrificed as the Rank Organization found itself in a state of siege. Highbury ends up as yet another Rank footnote, an initiative taken with the long-term interests of the industry in mind which probably deserved to succeed but was smashed by short-term business demands.

RANK, MARY FIELD AND THE CHILDREN'S CINEMA CLUBS

I promise to tell the truth, to help others, and to obey my parents.
(The Odeon Children Club's Promise)

DO YOU WANT THE BEST IN LIFE FOR YOUR CHILD? GOOD BOOKS AND GOOD MUSIC FOR EXAMPLE? THEN WHY NOT GOOD FILMS?
(From Children's Club leaflets for parents)

The lingering image is of young Tom, pedalling into the wind, desperate to get to the station before the train leaves. *Tom's Ride*, Rank's first film for children, a 'short story with a pointed moral', bemused and excited its young audiences, combining a riveting chase sequence with a pious homily about property, theft and bicycles. Tom, the film's hero, yearns for a bike. As he sits in his local Odeon, watching Red Indians on their horses, all he can think about is the bike he craves. Outside the cinema, he finds a purse with a crisp £5 note in it. He is set to use the money to get himself a 'pair of wheels'. At the last moment, however, he is overcome by an attack of 'good citizenship', resolves to return the purse and its money to its rightful owner, and borrows his sister's bike, pedalling as fast as he can. He reaches the station just in time and manages to return the purse to the woman as she is on the point of boarding the train.

What was his prize for such exemplary behaviour? To the evident bewilderment of the children who saw *Tom's Ride*, there was no recompense. Tom got neither bicycle nor money for his efforts. At best, he could console himself with the thought that virtue was its own reward. Although children enjoyed the film, especially the chase sequence, they had nagging doubts about the moral message tagged on its end. It seemed to them unjust that Tom should get nothing for his honesty. What was the point in being honest if you didn't get anything for it?

The tensions between religion and business, philanthropy and commerce, which run throughout Rank's career in the film business, find their own peculiar application in his involvement with children's cinema clubs and films. On the one hand, he wanted to entertain the youngsters, lure them to the cinema at a tender age so that the habit stuck, and they would keep on coming as they grew older, thereby helping to bolster his box-office receipts: it was a good long-term investment to woo the audience in its infancy. On the other hand, Rank was genuinely fired with evangelical zeal, and was keen to inculcate youth with 'good Christian values'. After all, it had been his quest for projectors to liven up Sunday school lessons which had lured him into the industry in the first place.

British children liked the movies. At a Child Welfare Commission of the League of Nations, Oliver Bell, director of the British Film Institute, estimated that '700,000 children a week attended special matinees and there are now over 250 English theatres which go to the trouble of booking special films for their shows' (*Kinematograph Weekly*, 5 April 1938). However, adults weren't at all convinced that the cinema was 'good' for their offspring. Children's behaviour and tastes are a controversial field. In *The Age of the Dream Palace*, Jeffrey Richards charts the internecine strife, the myriad squabbles that took place through the 1930s between priests, politicians, teachers and every other self-styled guardian of public morality. In the 1940s, as patron of the Odeon and Gaumont Children's Cinema Clubs, and as the sponsor of Children's Educational Films, Rank was in the firing line of the children's film debate, with newspaper editorials accusing him of trying to run a sort of 'Hitler Youth', as sociologists wrote long and learned books, pointing out the way that the film clubs were 'poisoning the day-dreams' of their members. By an ironic reversal, Rank who had become involved with the Religious Film Society because he wanted to make films in opposition to Hollywood, was accused of cynical commercial opportunism himself. Not that Rank had started children's cinema clubs. They had been running for several years before he appeared on the scene. (Oscar Deutsch had pioneered children's film matinees in his Odeon theatres as early as 1937.) As Jeffrey Richards observes, Saturday mornings were chosen as the best time for showings: 'Schools were closed, cinemas unused and the children had their pocket money.'[64]

Deutsch's matinees demanded the same sort of Masonic vows from the young spectators that Rank would ask of his cinema club members:

I will be truthful and honourable and will always try to make myself a good and honourable young citizen. I will obey my elders and help the aged, the helpless and children smaller than myself. I will always be kind to animals.[65]

Rank's Odeon Children's Cinema Clubs officially opened in April 1943, on a Saturday morning, with 150 cinemas all holding the same elaborate ceremony, and with over 150,000 children making their 'club promises'. Rank celebrated the great day at the Odeon, Morden, where he had the comedian Arthur Askey in attendance. The first week's theme was 'personal hygiene'. Askey sang a song or two, and then announced a competition for the best essay on personal hygiene. The imaginative prize for the winner was cowboy star Gene Autry's hat.

The *Kinematograph Weekly* welcomed Rank's clubs with enthusiasm:

It is a grand movement, this club for the betterment of youngsters of both sexes. They learn nothing but what is for their ultimate good, and their parents profit by the knowledge that on a busy Saturday morning the 'kiddies' are in good hands, enjoying themselves and in safety.[66]

The film programme was only part of the proceedings. The clubs offered community singing lessons, model- and toy-making sections, needlework, amateur dramatics classes, road safety and first aid instruction. Membership was free. Although children were charged a small admission price, the clubs were budgeted to run at a loss. Rank ruled over them, a benevolent monarch dispatching birthday cards:

Every club member receives a birthday card from the club president which entitles free attendance with a friend at the following week's performance.[67]

Comedy, adventures and westerns were the staple fare on the film menu. To his credit, Rank never lost sight of his primary aim, which was to entertain the children: moral messages generally came wrapped in attractive packages. Initially, the films themselves were mainly American: although they were all scrutinized intently and sometimes even re-edited, they earned the disdain of at least one prominent sociologist. J. P. Mayer acidly remarked:

It would appear that either old westerns or old comical pictures are considered good, and what is more important, cheap enough for children.[68]

In his book *The Sociology of Film*, Mayer does not try to contextualize the film programme within the activities of the children's clubs as a whole, nor does he address the children's films which Rank was beginning to produce himself. Instead, he sneers from on high. He has done extensive research on the clubs, most of it sponsored by Rank, with whom he was initially friendly:

> In March 1944 friends introduced me to Mr J. Arthur Rank and the latter seemed to share my interest in a closer sociological investigation of film reactions . . . I gladly shelved my studies on political parties for a while. . . . Without Mr Rank's technical and financial facilities . . . these studies would not have been possible.[69]

Relations between Rank and Mayer cooled somewhat when it became apparent that Mayer was not particularly well disposed to the Saturday morning experiments. In the name of duty, Mayer had given up twenty of his own mornings to the clubs, sitting 'right among the children in order to be able to observe their behaviour, expressions and attitudes'.[70] There is nothing on record which says what the children made of this adult interloper in their midst. Mayer, a pipe-smoking Fabian with impeccable highbrow credentials, who quotes Nietzsche in the original German in his preface (and doesn't provide a translation) and who broadens his discussion of the children's clubs to encompass Greek and Elizabethan theatre, made no allowance for something as inconsequential as the children's pleasure in the films, instead castigating these Hollywood 'B' pictures and shorts for their 'moral and psychological shortcomings'.

The image of the academic surrounding by hundreds of bawling, brawling kids, taking copious notes whenever a boy or girl laughed or coughed, is at least faintly comic. Did Mayer have to take the club oath? Did he join in the club hymn?

> To the Odeon we have come.
> Now we can have some fun.
> We are a hundred thousand strong
> So how can we all be wrong?[71]

Did he obey the club's injunctions to wash his hands, say please, and not to push? He does not answer these questions. Enthusiastic about geographic and travel pictures, he deplores films involving submarines, guns and cowboys:

> Undoubtedly these serials are, from the point of view of the children, the highlights of the cinema clubs, but they are pernicious in their psychological effects, leaving the children at a high pitch of expectation for the next week's show, *poisoning their day-dreams* and, by an utterly artificial unreality, influencing their play.[72]
>
> (emphases added)

His criticisms are worth quoting at length. Both in his book and in a

Times editorial which he is acknowledged to have written, he launched his broadsides against the clubs:

> It is extremely doubtful whether children appreciate the 'good moral lessons' with which it is fashionable to conclude these films. . . . Even if it is intended to give pure entertainment, the child's power of visualization creates moral patterns. As matters stand, hundreds of thousands of children will soon be subject to an influence which in this regard is far below the level of the rules and standards of our educational system.
>
> (*The Times*, Saturday, 5 January 1946)

In his cultural, aesthetic and moral snobbery, his desire to 'destroy' pleasure, he anticipates some of the obfuscatory film theory later to characterize the influential *Screen* magazine in the 1970s and to set the tone for the way film has been taught within the academy. He conflates social and economic arguments, and uses his study of the children's clubs to damn the Rank Organization as a whole:

> What the school builds up in the week may be entirely nullified on Saturday morning. . . . This is naturally not the intention of those who run the children's clubs. They have the best intentions, but the task they undertake is beyond their spiritual, mental and technical equipment. In fact, *they do not know what they are doing*. . . . Here, clearly, is a case where an economic monopoly creates under the cloak of free enterprise mental attitudes which, in their present form, are detrimental to the community as a whole.[73]
>
> (emphases added)

Mayer infers that Rank is conducting subtle experiments on the children, inadvertently altering their states of mind, inculcating them with the lawless frontier values of the Saturday morning western series, or with the greed, avarice and lust that walk hand in hand with the crime film. As a socialist writing after six years of war against Fascism, Mayer is understandably suspicious of the crowd, of the sense of a mass movement given him by the children's clubs, with all that that entails in the stifling of individual response, but it is surely far-fetched to draw parallels between Rank's clubs and the Hitler Youth.[74] One gets the impression that Mayer was shocked by the brashness and cruelty of the youngsters: after his twenty mornings with the kids, he is driven to likening cinema to the bloody spectacle of Roman gladiatorial combat.

In his follow-up to *The Sociology of Film*, namely *British Cinemas and their Audiences*, Mayer shifts his emphasis away from the Pavlovian effects he reckons the cinema to have had on the clubs, and instead allows older fans their own voice: he solicited their letters by advertising in *Picturegoer*, and kept his own lofty interpolations to a minimum:

Our anonymous contributors speak for twenty million or more. They speak for many classes, for many age-groups, for men and women. It was felt that they should speak for once for themselves. Not through a critic who 'knows better'. Nor through the mouth of the 'superior' intellectual who by chance or choice went to a better school, to university to become a planner who then directs 'masses' according to the questions he thinks fit to ask and the answers he receives from mass polls. They are mostly his own answers.

(Mayer, 1948: introduction)

He would never have allowed the children 'to speak for themselves'. They were there to be observed. He did not think to ask them what their preferences were, or why they seemed to enjoy cowboy films more than the travelogues and Soviet pictures about young boys and tractors he would have recommended as suitably edifying material for the Saturday morning trip to the cinema.

Mayer's audience research at the Odeon and Gaumont Children's Cinema Clubs is complemented by the eccentric survey carried out by Mary Field, whom Rank had appointed chief of the Children's Film Department he had established in late 1943. Using tape recorders and infra-red cameras – for photography in the darkened theatres – Field and her colleagues set out to anatomize the Saturday morning audience, to record the children's every gesture, shuffle and cough; to label and categorize their likes and dislikes so that filmmakers could more precisely target their vehicles for club consumption. (Field had started her career in the 1920s on 'Secrets of Nature', a celebrated series of natural history films which is held as the great precursor of the work on television of a host of khaki-shorts-clad British naturalists, from David Attenborough's celebrated *Life on Earth* to the work of Bellamy and Co. She applied to the children the same kind of anthropological and minute scrutiny as she had to her stems and bushes.)

Unlike their parents, Field observed, children came to the cinema to take an active part in proceedings. She managed to distinguish seven different kinds of noise the kids might make in the course of a picture: the bad noise of boredom; the equally bad scream of (over-) excitement; the good healthy sound of intelligent excitement; healthy laughter; the good noise of interest; the coo of pleasure; and the complete silence. Field considered making films for children to be a deadly serious business, one that warranted this exhaustive and idiosyncratic level of research:

I know of nothing more calculated to inspire a sense of awe and responsibility than to see ten or twelve hundred children's faces with eyes lifted and riveted to what you are placing on the screen before them, influencing them, you hope, but are by no means certain, for good.[75]

153

All Children's Entertainment Films (CEF) work was controlled by a team of ten, with Field at the helm, which was based in London. Roughly, twenty production companies shot films for CEF on a freelance basis. (CEF had no producers under contract.) Units used included everybody from the National Film Board of Canada to Gaumont-British Africa. Initially, CEF pictures were given a rough ride by critics and filmmakers alike. Although they commissioned films from outside producers, the group kept those producers on a tight rein. Barry Delmaine, author/ director of the 1944 two-reeler *Here We Come Gathering*, with a quintes- sentially CEF theme, 'a story of schoolchildren helping in fruit-picking with the moral strongly marked',[76] had strong reservations about his own lack of editorial control. Field treated the filmmakers as functionaries, obliging them to conform to strict guidelines so as to ensure the right kind of audience noise:

> Assuming we technicians had any say in the morality 'plugged' in these films (which, at present, we do not), what should be our line? . . . at the moment the 'moral lesson' to be incorporated in each film is decided upon by a body known as the Youth Advisory Council. It is to be regretted that hardly any technicians are represented on this council and no children at all.[77]

As Delmaine's remarks suggest, there was an element of force-feeding in the CEF's activities; of giving children not what they wanted, but what was deemed by outsiders to be 'good for them'. The films needed to strike a fine balance between moralizing and entertaining. Too often, at least as far as journalists and technicians were concerned, they tended to err on the side of the former.

At the 1946 ACT conference, Field was taken to task. One technician said, 'The committee headed by Mary Field has no idea of what children want.' Another remarked that the films were made 'on a moral basis sixty years out of date'. And a third, summing up, said:

Mary Field does produce real stinkers.[78]

The Youth Advisory Council referred to by Delmaine helped to consti- pate CEF filmmakers' imaginations. It consisted of representatives from every conceivable lobby: there were mandarins from the BBC and the Church and the Home Office; there was even an observer from the Ministry of Education. Between them, the council members set the moral tone for the first of the CEF films. All the pictures were to set examples of 'good behaviour', and were to have themes of 'social significance', which were neither political nor overtly religious. Basic precepts to be taught by the films included kindness to animals and the social obligation of working for 'one's daily bread'.

Before Field and the CEF arrived on the scene, almost half a million children were already visiting the cinema, but could see only the kind of cowboy and submarine movie deplored by J. P. Mayer. The CEF aimed higher. Field, like Rank, had an ambitious vision. She wanted to rear a new kind of cinema audience. By moulding and educating children's tastes, she hoped she would 'raise' those tastes so that when the children became adults, they would be more demanding than their parents in selecting the type of features they wanted to see. This, in turn, would affect producers, who would 'raise' the level of their films to cater for the new, discriminating public. Field shared Rank's commitment to religious film. In the 1930s, she had spoken on several occasions at the religious film summer schools, where she had emphasized the value of the medium to teaching. She ingenuously remarked:

> The great contribution of the film to education is the way in which it widens experience. To see a film is the next best thing to visiting a place or watching a process.[79]

In the modern, industrial era, there had been an estrangement between city and country dwellers: certain children in Glasgow, Field noted, had never seen a sheep. As most of the setting and much of the imagery of the 'Good Book', as Rank was inclined to call the Bible,[80] was pastoral, films which attempted to bring rural scenes to urban cinemas could help religious understanding. (If you have never seen a sheep, concepts such as the 'Lamb of God' have diminished meaning.)

Field was helped in her desire to shoot the great outdoors by the severe shortage of studio space that the industry was suffering under in the mid-1940s: most of the children's films were made on outside locations, as a matter of necessity. (Hence the CEF fetish for films centred on fruit-picking and farm life, where youngsters, filling in for the men and women away at war, collected potatoes or raspberries.)

Originally, Rank, who had always had a penchant for the short, sharp 'lesson for the day', intended the average children's film to be about ten minutes long, and to contain one single, simple moral. However, it was soon found this was far too brief a length for a film to have any impact: one-reelers tended to get lost in the rest of the programme – they were no match for the cowboy flicks or gangster serials. It was soon decided to lengthen the films while cutting down on the moralizing. (Unsuccessful press screenings had seen hardened Wardour Street hacks choke in disgust at the earliest of the CEF work.)[81]

Ultimately, the children's films, like Rank's other wartime production endeavours, benefited from their epoch. When there was no certainty about anything, producers, as long as they weren't too muzzled by Youth Advisory Councils and the like, were far more inclined to take risks than they would have been in 'secure' times. As Rank himself put it when asked how defeat would affect his plans for the British cinema: 'If we lose the war, what difference does it make anyway?'[82] Profit, in the war years, was not the pressing consideration that it was in peacetime. (This was easy enough for Rank to claim when his theatres were packed full every night.)

By a neat stroke of irony, CEF, set up to educate and entertain children, was soon accused of exploiting them. Under labour laws, it was illegal to employ a child who was less than 12 years old. Field was thus reduced to scouring employment agencies for undersized teenagers, who didn't look their age. (Such rising luminaries as Anthony Newley, soon to play the Artful Dodger in Lean's *Oliver Twist*, and Jean Simmons, later to receive her 'break' in the same director's *Great Expectations*, were discovered in children's films.)

Field's policy had an international dimension. She imported pictures from abroad, commissioned foreign producers to make them, and also tried to export her own movies. She was in constant touch with the Soviet Union, one of the few other countries where films were being shot specifically for young audiences. To make pictures in languages other than English palatable to Saturday morning cinemagoers, she pioneered a 'story-teller' device:

> We agreed that the best way to make the English version would be to add an introduction, in this way introducing an English boy, who could tell the story to the audience by means of a commentary which could be superimposed on to the soundtrack and explain what the Norwegian was going to talk about in their own language. From this type of beginning we eventually developed an entirely new type of film production which, by means of a story-teller who was an integral part of the original script, would enable children of all nations to enjoy films, without any regard to the language in which they were originally produced.
>
> (Field, 1952: 75)

Such gems of European cinema as *The Mysterious Poacher* and *The Lonesome Climber* were thus brought to British screens.

CEF branched out into feature production with *The Boy Who Stopped Niagara*, and also provided a monthly newsreel, 'Our Club Magazine', which addressed topics directly relevant to club members, often featuring them at work or play. This was a frenetically paced series, which tried to be educative, but, worried that attention might flag, moved from subject to subject with a sometimes baffling and alarming rapidity. Upbeat, cheery music and an enthusiastic voice-over would carry the children through these breathless, high-minded 'shorts'.

> We start this magazine in Yorkshire to hear the Grimethorpe Village Choir singing 'Sweet and Low'. . . . Next we're going to an airfield near London where the Twickenham Model Aero-Club meet at

weekends to fly their model aeroplanes and gliders. . . . Model enthusiasts try to keep their models flying for as long as possible but whatever happens it is great fun![83]

The newsreels have the pattern of a school outing. From Twickenham Model Aero-Club, the magazine jumps to a wheat harvest in Norfolk. From there, it follows a mini-railway to Brighton before alighting briefly in Doncaster to watch a children's acrobatic troupe. As the young gymnasts do their somersaults and cartwheels, the voice-over intones: 'They're good, aren't they! And their ages are only between seven and eleven!'

One week, the magazine might feature a visit to London Zoo in the company of Tommy Handley, the ITMA man,[84] or a chastening few minutes at a hospital in Hampshire for crippled and lame children: 'The boys and girls who are nearly all the same ages as you, members, are taken outside to receive the treatment of the best doctor of all, Doctor Sun.'[85]

'Our Club' no. 58 has a few practical hints on cooking, and tries to teach 'the boys' the rudiments of puff pastry and shepherd's pie. From the mince and potatoes, it is but a small jump to Hans Christian Andersen's home town in Denmark, where there is a brief feature on glass-making. In 'Our Club' no. 28, a prize-winning pupil reads her essay about Worcester. 'Funny Bicycles', the 'Wood Carver' and 'Inside a Fire Station' (a section with clear echoes of Humphrey Jennings's classic Crown Film documentary, *Fires Were Started*) are the other elements in the episode. The magazines might have an international flavour, featuring Belgian evacuee children or the young prodigies in a Moscow art school. (Belgium and Russia predated the UK as producers of children's films, and Field had been able to make reciprocal arrangements with their two industries.)

Audiences were constantly changing as the children grew up. Field calculated that the clubs had a 'practically' new' membership every three years. It was therefore possible to reissue most of the CEF films. Although CEF fell victim to Rank's cutbacks of 1949–50, and was summarily closed down, the films remained in circulation (it took them up to fifteen years to go into profit) and the Saturday morning clubs stayed open.

Within a year of CEF's closure, the government provided funds for the setting-up of the Children's Film Foundation: J. Arthur Rank was pencilled in as chairman, and Mary Field was appointed the executive officer.

THE WAY WE LIVE

I went to see Mr Rank . . . I said why can't we have, instead of the 'B' pictures, which were awful, cheap American stuff that they got for nothing, why can't we have films that are about a serious purpose, as long as they're entertaining. Rank fell for this idea. He was rather pro it.[86]

As a microcosmic example of Rank's schizophrenia, of the contradictory impulses which tugged his film policy in opposite directions, the story of the production of Jill Craigie's 1946 drama-documentary *The Way We Live* assumes a significance far in excess of its relatively modest budget and credentials: this 'B' picture found its sponsor skewered on his usual dilemma, torn apart by the competing demands of art and business, the filmmakers and the front office.

Craigie, a former scriptwriter for the British Council, had approached Rank towards the end of the war, and had submitted a proposal to him for the making of a low-budget feature about the reconstruction of Plymouth, which had been on the sharp end of the blitz. As Angus Calder suggests, the city was utterly ravaged by German bombs:

> The housing 'casualty figures' for Plymouth came to exceed the total number of houses, as many were hit more than once. Several well-known hotels and about a hundred and fifty pubs were hit . . . thirty thousand people were homeless. As many as fifty thousand may have spilled out to sleep in the rural and sparsely populated hinterland of the town: in kind homes, in barns, in churches, in quarry tunnels, even in ditches and under hedges.[87]

Much to her surprise, Rank agreed to fund the project. Not only was she an inexperienced director, whose only previous film, *Out of Chaos*, a short about Henry Moore and the blitz, had been made for £7,000, but the subject she had chosen seemed resolutely downbeat. While books on art and architecture were bestsellers in the period, with everybody wanting a say in how post-war Britain should be rebuilt, there was none the less little evidence that this enthusiasm for town planning extended to the cinema. Craigie's desire to cast 'amateurs', Plymouth locals, in the leading roles did not bode particularly well. Nor did this early British attempt at neo-realism, at combining fact and fiction, real life with invented drama, seem to have much box-office allure. On the surface, Rank's personal decision to back the film seemed brave and admirable. With *The Way We Live*, he was chipping away at the sexism which characterized the post-war film industry. As Craigie recalls, it was well-nigh impossible for a woman director to get any kind of technical experience:

> I couldn't go into the cutting rooms or anything. . . . Carol Reed cut his teeth on 'B' pictures. David Lean, as you know, started as a tea-boy and went all the way up. I had no experience whatsoever, and you need a lot of experience to master the technical side.[88]

Rank's investment also hinted at a continuing political 'broad-mindedness'. Like 'This Modern Age', Craigie's fierce polemical picture came nowhere near to endorsing Rank's brand of patriarchal conservatism. *The Way We Live* was just the type of film the critics would hold up in cherished opposition to Rank's big-budget, 'international' prestige offerings: at £40,000, it was inexpensive, had a strong local identity, and addressed everyday issues. The very title, plain, descriptive, encapsulated Craigie's ambition, which was, quite literally, to tell how the British 'lived' in the aftermath of the upheaval of war, while interpreting 'what the artists and architects were saying to the public in that period'.[89] The film was made under the rubric of Two Cities. Del Giudice was Craigie's mentor: he had discovered her, one of his British 'tal-ents'. Unfortunately, Craigie had inadvertently stumbled into 'the very vicious war' [90] that was beginning to rage between Del Giudice and Rank's chief accountant and *éminence grise*, John Davis. To put it bluntly, Davis was trying to force Del Giudice out of the Rank Organization, ostensibly to save money and cut down on Two Cities extravagance. But he also wanted to consolidate his own power base. He saw Del Giudice as his main rival. Davis, at the helm of Odeon Theatres, had 'a very rotten trick' he could play on Del Giudice's films:

> He could put the films into the rotten cinemas at the wrong times to prove they weren't commercially successful. . . . He put *The Way We Live* on in the East End, where it got whistles and cat-calls. The theatre manager said to me, 'Oh, that's nothing! You should see what they did to *Henry V*. They threw tomatoes at the screen.'[91]

Davis was ruthless. According to Rank's daughter, 'he did not share my father's milk of human kindness',[92] and he had already done his best to scupper Craigie's production before it had even finished shooting. In the middle of the night, Craigie had been summoned from Plymouth to Rank's headquarters, where Davis had told her that the film would have to be abandoned. He had seen the rushes, and had decided that *The Way We Live* was not a commercial proposition.

Craigie desperately appealed to Rank to save the production. She showed him her extensive book of press cuttings. As a woman director, she had already become something of a cynosure with both local and national press:

> I had had an enormous amount of publicity just because I was a woman . . . all for the wrong reasons. 'Although she's in charge of forty men, she's very feminine' – this sort of terrible stuff.[93]

Furthermore, Craigie explained to the magnate, she had turned Plymouth upside down: the police were holding up the traffic; the City Fathers were involved. Even Lord Astor had given the project his blessing. The town's inhabitants were full of praise for Rank, flattered that he would want to make a film about their problems. As Craigie recalls, Rank and his accountant weren't of exactly the same frame of mind:

159

He [Rank] turned to Davis and said, 'You see, John: it can't be stopped.' And he was delighted![94]

Completing the film was only part of the battle. The next problem was how to ensure its release. After it was booed in the East End, Davis sent it for a trial run in Warrington, during 'wakes week', when the city was almost empty, and it did very little business there. Rank and Craigie's original intention, to release the picture as a 'B' feature in place of the cheap and second-rate Hollywood 'fillers' which exhibitors were obliged to use, was soon forgotten: *The Way We Live* became a pawn in the ongoing struggle between Davis and Del Giudice, with Davis determined that it should be suppressed. It was denied publicity, and would doubtless have sunk into oblivion had not an enterprising critic noticed a tiny review in the trade press, which described the film as 'intelligent, thoughtful, comprehensive'.[95] Lejeune, the critic in question, rallied her colleagues to the cause. They demanded to see the film and wrote about it at length in their columns. Thanks to their intervention, the film was given a proper distribution.

This whole tawdry episode lays bare tensions within the Rank Organization as a whole, tensions which find a full expression not only in the Davis–Del Giudice struggle, but within J. Arthur Rank himself. Crusading *News Chronicle* critic Richard Winnington, one of Craigie's most impassioned defenders, was quick to pinpoint the problem:

> This interesting sequence of events at once displays two truths. First the irreconcilability of Rank the producer of British films with Rank the exhibitor of Hollywood films, a contradiction that forces Mr Rank to reject with the right hand what he has made with the left. And second, that the critics are not, as Mr Rank would have it, entirely useless and destructive.[96]

The Rank Organization may have been a vertically integrated 'combine', with extensive production facilities and more than 600 cinemas, not to mention a bold and aggressive sales outfit. However, its ultimate reliance on exhibition (and hence on Hollywood output) to generate its profits meant that production, instead of being at the core of its activities, was secondary: it was more a servicing outfit than a filmmaking one. Throughout the mid- to late 1940s, Rank had ignored this anomaly, convinced that as British film's fortunes improved, production would gradually become self-sufficient. As Winnington notes, the source of his discomfiture was evident – his attempt to compete with Hollywood was financed by Hollywood: he depended on the receipts from American films to underwrite everything from *The Red Shoes* to Ginger Nutt cartoons. As soon as these receipts were endangered, so were his plans for reviving the industry from the bottom up through research, innovation and training, all loss-making areas.

For a few, brief post-war years, Rank oversaw a remarkable explosion of activity in every sphere of the British film business. The experiments charted here are but a small part of the overall expansion in the industry. He sponsored films and filmmakers all over the world. It is tragic that the unprecedented level of research and investment should leave so little of any permanence. By late 1950, the Charm School, 'This Modern Age', G-B Animation, Children's Entertainment Films and the Highbury Studios were all abandoned. Though not profitable in themselves, these institutions seemed to be laying the basis of a truly robust national film culture. After their demise, the Rank Organization lost the willingness to back controversial and uncommercial projects, whether they be Craigie's drama-doc, or Rawnsley's plans for Independent Frame. The crusading evangelical zeal which had driven Rank through the 1940s was seen to have dissipated: the 1950s were to be the 'Davis era'.

Perhaps the most crushing blow to Rank's film drive had been the ad-valorem tax of 1947.

6

THE BOGART OR BACON DEBATE

British Cinema and Society, 1946–50

The Government's new crisis programme on greater austerity was outlined by the Prime Minister in the Commons last night . . . he warned the country that it was about to fight another Battle of Britain. This battle could not be won by the few but only by the whole nation. The programme was a mixture of harder, longer, more directed work, increased exports and substantial cuts in imports.

(*Morning Chronicle*, 7 August 1947)

By the time the Second World War was over, Britain's debts were astronomical. It was estimated that the country had lost a quarter of its national wealth, some £7,000 million,[1] and its export trade was in tatters: every last bit of energy had been squeezed into the war effort. Resources were depleted. The Lend-Lease agreement[2] with the United States had been abruptly terminated on the defeat of Japan in August 1945, and Maynard Keynes had been sent scuttling off to Washington to negotiate for a low-interest loan. In order to secure the Vinson loan, the British had had to promise that they would make sterling 'freely convertible for all currency transactions'.[3] Of course, the British found this idea quite repugnant: to tamper with sterling was somehow to undermine that mystical 'sovereignty' on which they put so much store. But they were not in the position to quibble.

The country's post-war travails are a familiar story, charted in anthologies and histories from Sissons and French's *The Age of Austerity* to Arthur Marwick's scrutiny of *British Society since 1945*. The Attlee government's attempts to fashion a brave new world, though successful in substance, effecting wholesale and beneficial changes in everything from health to education, were constantly undermined by the bad weather, by the so-called dollar crisis, and by the country's last fitful gropings for the 'world influence' it used to take for granted. As David Marquand points out, even in 1947, when the country was paralysed by food, fuel and foreign exchange crises, and the balance of payments deficit was £600 million, 'over £200 million went on military expenditure overseas'.[4] The British

162

army had set itself up as some sort of police force, overseeing a 'return to order' in Europe, and maintaining a strong presence everywhere from Germany to Greece.

By the summer of 1947, the $3,750 million loan which Keynes had chiselled out of the reluctant American Treasury was almost exhausted. Britain had effectively run out of dollars. There was a pressing need to bolster exports while cutting down imports, especially those from America. This was to have dire consequences for Rank and the British film industry.

Part of the justification for Rank's protracted attempt to carve British films a niche in the American market had been his patriotic desire to prise dollars out of American audiences, and to bring them back home: he was doing his 'bit' for sterling and the export drive. Not that it was proving to be a very successful 'bit'. *Caesar and Cleopatra* and *Henry V* apart, British pictures were performing abysmally in the States, and the crippling over-heads of maintaining a sales organization like Eagle-Lion rapidly eroded any profits that were made. (Davis, as we shall see, repeated most of Rank's mistakes a decade later, when he masterminded the second wave of the Rank Organization's attack on the citadel of the US market: one of the quickest ways to ruin a British attempt on America is to spend a fortune on setting up offices and sales reps.) As Sidney Gilliat wryly observed in a recent memo:

> Certainly an expensive international selling machinery has *never* been necessary. Korda, with a very small decentralized organization, sold films well internationally, with just a foot in Paris, a room in Madrid, a telephone line to Munich, a man in New York, a toe in Cairo and so on.
>
> (Sidney Gilliat, memo to the author, 22 May 1991, p. 7)

Rank's Hollywood partners invariably let him down. Take, for example, the sad case of United Artists.[5] Back in 1944, Rank had arranged for United Artists to distribute a handful of his top pictures. A dusty ledger in their archive, quoting the pictures' rental earnings in the USA and Canada, shows that these films, whether through United Artists' languor or their own innate lack of marketability, were unmitigated disasters.

It was generally reckoned that a film had to earn $2 million in the USA and Canada before it could be termed a success.[6] Even the schlockiest 'B' feature emanating from the Hollywood studios could expect to make $500,000. Rank's pictures, however, lingered in depths a long way beneath this low-water mark; they were right down in the mud. *Mr Emmanuel*, a Two Cities 'prestige' offering, achieved rentals of $229,249. The Archers' *One of Our Aircraft Is Missing*, follow-up to their Oscar-winning *49th Parallel/The Invaders*, did surprisingly slow business, garnering $478,939 in a 3-year period from late 1942 to 1946. And *The Life and Death of Colonel*

163

Blimp, which was doctored by United Artists for its US release, managed a paltry $305,943. *Blithe Spirit*, despite its impeccable credentials – the Americans had already shown their enthusiasm for Noël Coward – reported a modest $452,152 in rentals. *The Way to the Stars*, rechristened *Johnny in the Clouds* in its American baptism, and reckoned by some to be the greatest of all the British war pictures, clocked in with a shockingly poor $63,434 for its first nine months of release, and *Man of Evil*'s rentals were a ludicrously low $17,285. It was little wonder that the Rank Organization kept quiet about its American receipts, mobilizing the twin blandishments of either 'disappointing' or 'encouraging' when quizzed by the Press on its US performances. Nor is it any wonder that Rank 'dropped' United Artists, making an alliance with Universal instead, in late 1945.[7]

Despite the erratic progress his films were making in America, Rank's standing in Hollywood had never been higher. His control of British cinemas made the studios as dependent on him as he was on them. As has already been hinted, the multiple threats of the rising popularity of television, the Supreme Court anti-trust legislation, and the loss of revenue from war-devastated European economies made Britain a key client for American filmmakers. Britain, however, was chronically short of dollars, and it didn't make sense to import Hollywood pictures when the country was dependent on American loans to keep the economy afloat in the first place. (In *The Hollywood Feature Film in Post-War Britain*, Paul Swann estimates that the amount spent by the British on American films and tobacco exceeded the sum total of the country's exports to the USA.[8] The government warned that only necessities could be imported.) There was quite literally a 'Bogart or bacon' debate,[9] with the Exchequer asking British people which they would more willingly forfeit, the food on their plates or the films at their local Odeon.

The film industry wasn't uppermost in the Attlee administration's mind. There were more pressing matters to attend to than the well-being of British production. Keeping the nation fed and warm were the immediate priorities, as was servicing the huge American loan. In intellectual circles, anti-Americanism was pronounced. The British reward for 'winning' the war was austerity and debt, and the USA was held at least partially responsible. The British may have been economically dependent on the Yanks, but they were keen to maintain their cultural independence.

At the time of its publication in 1944, the Palache Report's highlighting of monopolistic tendencies within the film industry had had minimal impact: one or two polite letters between Rank, the Chancellor and the Board of Trade and murmurings about the establishment of a state-owned cinema circuit seemed to have swept the matter away. By 1946, however, a delayed response to the report was suddenly made, with 'leftist' intellectuals, especially those associated with the ACT and *Tribune*, responding to

Palache, but carrying his relatively restrained critique of Rank several steps further.

FILMS: AN ALTERNATIVE TO RANK

The mass of the public remains as confused and misinformed as it has ever been about Rank's intentions towards the industry. They accept, without serious doubt, the fairy story which presents Rank as a doughty crusader bent on a large-scale invasion of Hollywood's own American territory. Few, if any, stop to ask themselves: why, if Rank is so determined to cut himself a large slice from Hollywood's cake, are the *gentlemen with funny names* over there always so friendly and accommodating to him.

(Mullally, 1946: 2; emphases added)

In 1946–7, three separate 'blasts' at Rank were taken by pamphleteers. First, there was Frederic Mullally's caustic critique of the Rank Organization, *Films, An Alternative to Rank*. Then there was Ralph Bond's *Monopoly*. And, finally, there was R. J. Minney's *Talking of Films*.

Mullally, a journalist on the *Tribune*, who also wrote under the name of Henry Fullerton, offers a tract dipped in vitriol, which eschews any analysis of Rank's part in the British film revival of the 1940s, instead putting its subject in the pillory, and hurling mud which he hopes will stick. Mullally's central thesis is that Rank, though insidiously passing himself off as a 'doughty crusader', is an unscrupulous and mercenary capitalist, whose ambitions for British film run no further than lining his own pockets.

Why aren't Britain's 25 million cinemagoers aware of the true nature of the 'man behind the gong'? Mullally blames the national Press – 'abundant space has always been found in its columns for Rank's apologists and publicity men'; the 'sluggish mental processes of the Board of Trade officials concerned'; and 'a conspiracy to keep the reading public ignorant of the threat which Rank's policy contains to the future of British films' (Mullally, 1946: 2). He invokes the language of Munich, 1938, casting the denizens of Hollywood, 'the gentlemen with funny names' as he calls them (perhaps unaware that this could easily be construed as an anti-Semitic slur), as Nazis: he talks of the 'appeasement' of the American film industry. And Rank is cast as a dictator, drunk on his own power, which he exercises 'without responsibility'. Hirelings and underlings are blinded by his opulence. In Mullally's diatribe, the mild-mannered magnate from Reigate undergoes an astonishing transformation. By the time he has come through the car wash, he is the devil incarnate, complete with everything but hooves, horns and prong.

In his monograph, Ralph Bond is less given to rhetorical flourish than Mullally, but reaches similar conclusions. Criticizing Rank's policy of

165

making high-budget, prestige films for the US market's benefit, Bond draws a parallel with war production. Would the government ever have built one super-tank instead of lots of serviceable tanks? Surely not, he protests: quantity was what was needed, mass production in films as in other spheres. British filmmakers had already displayed their 'quality': now they needed to learn to be more prolific. He draws the standard opposition between the British documentary tradition and Hollywood's whimsical superficiality:

> For this new spirit in British Cinema, much credit is due to the consistent and patient work of the documentary producers and technicians . . . it has often been said with much truth that the documentary film has become Britain's major contribution to the development of cinema.

> (Bond, 1946: 10)

Rank's brushes with American make-up earn his particular scorn:

> It is reported he [Rank] has acquired an interest in Westmore cosmetics and will distribute these in Britain in return for the services of the Westmore brothers as advisors on make-up for film artists. As Hollywood make-up seems to be aimed chiefly at eliminating every trace of individuality from the artist, we fail to see what benefit this deal will provide for British films.

> (Bond, 1946: 13)

R. J. Minney, in his *Talking of Films*, adds an economic dimension to the debate, pointing out that the dice are loaded against British filmmakers ever doing consistently well in the USA: the American circuits are always fully booked, and to show a British film would mean excluding one from Hollywood. He suggests it is altruism for US exhibitors to show British films, and altruism 'has no cash equivalent' (Minney, 1947: 24).

All three writers are united in the opinion that Rank is 'hogging' studio space with 'swollen epics', when independent producers, making films cheaply and quickly, would have a better chance of eroding the Hollywood stranglehold on British cinemas. All three are united in their disdain for Hollywood 'pot-boilers'. Mullally castigates the 'salacious immorality' of *The Wicked Lady*, which he likens to Hollywood 'trash'. Bond also uses the dustbin metaphor, talking of the way that America 'dumps' its pictures on the British market.

Elsewhere, Mullally takes his condemnation of Rank even further. Writing in *Tribune* a year earlier, he dismisses the multi-million-pound production programme that threw up movies ranging from *Colonel Blimp* to *Brief Encounter* as a sham, a smoke-screen to divert attention from Mr Rank's more nefarious activities. The investment in equipment, research, 'B' pictures, children's films, documentary newsreels and animation is likewise scorned as a tiny token gesture on the Rank Organization's behalf. According to Mullally's egregious analysis, Rank's protracted bid to set British cinema on its feet by cornering a part of the American market is nothing but a masquerade:

> His [Rank's] biggest profits come from the exhibition of American films, but someone has to supply his cinemas with the 25 per cent quotas, and so long as he enjoyed a considerable EPT [excess profits tax] cushion, he has nothing to lose by making £1,000,000 films instead of quota quickies. And see what he has to gain:- a) He disarms the anti-monopolists by *posing as the saviour* of the British film industry. b) He safeguards his American colleagues from the consequences of British Government intervention by maintaining the appearance of a virile and independent British film industry. c) By 'cornering' studio space, stars and technicians, he squeezes out the genuinely independent producers who alone can break down Hollywood's hegemony of the British box-office.
>
> (*Tribune*, 16 November 1945, p. 7; emphases added)

Mullally, Bond and Minney weren't prepared to give Mr Rank the benefit of any doubt. For them, he was the canker at the core of UK film. As far as they were concerned, Rank's tilting at the American market meant one of two things. Either he had hatched a plot with Hollywood, and would abandon British filmmakers at the earliest possible moment, allowing the Rank Organization to become an American satellite, or he was well intentioned, but misguided in his policy. Whatever the case, the result would be the same: British films would soon cease to reflect the British way of life:

> One shudders to think what sort of Britain will be put on the screen if any considerable proportion of our films are made by Hollywood companies, or their production influenced by American box-office considerations.
>
> (Bond, 1946: 24)

Preserving the 'British way of life' is an ambivalent project. At its most positive, it is about making British films with British stars and British stories, relevant to British people's lives, a laudable endeavour for an industry under the thumb of Hollywood. However, Mullally, Bond and Minney seem motivated by an almost xenophobic dislike of American culture (and imperialism) in particular, but of foreign influence in general. They take little consideration of audience preferences, of the fact that after the war British spectators continued to prefer pictures like *The Wicked Lady* (top box-office earner of 1946) and the 'worst excrescences of Hollywood' to the more culturally 'respectable' offerings of Ealing and the

Crown Film Unit. Rank argued that audiences needed to become accustomed to British films, that they would have to be gradually weaned away from Hollywood. By contrast, the trio of pamphleteers believed a wholesale transformation of British cinemagoing habits could be effected overnight. Moreover, they felt immediate action was necessary to stem the Hollywood tide. (Even in the grand year of British cinema, 1946, Hollywood held dominion over 80 per cent of Britain's screen time.) Two of the pamphleteers, Minney and Bond, were influential ACT members, and their distrust of Mr Rank's motives was shared by the union for which they spoke.

RANK AND THE ACT

Once, George Elvin, present of the ACT, was early for an appointment with J. Arthur Rank at Rank's suite in the Dorchester Hotel. While he waited for Rank to arrive, he made small talk with Rank's wife. She offered him a cigarette. He accepted. She dug deep into a gold handbag and rummaged around, eventually finding a gold cigarette case. She lit Elvin's cigarette with a gold lighter, and lit one for herself. Then, J. Arthur appeared, apologizing fulsomely for not being more prompt. At this point, Lady Rank dug again into her handbag. She pulled out a pair of gold scissors, with which she cut off the end of her cigarette, only half smoked, thereby saving the stub, which she put back in the gold cigarette case so that she could smoke it later. Elvin always used to tell this story, ending it by observing, 'That's how you become a millionaire: don't waste a thing.'[10] (The contradictory impulses that pulled Rank's film policy in opposite directions, that never-to-be-resolved tension between extravagance and frugality, seemed to extend to his private as well as public life.)

Although the ACT had been founded in precisely the same year – 1933 – as Rank had entered the industry via the Religious Film Society, there had been little friction between the respective parties early on: 'I don't think in the early days of the ACT he was very important',[11] said Sidney Cole, once its vice-president.

George Elvin and his brother Harold were key figures in the establishment of the ACT. They were from good union stock: their father was chairman of the Trades Union Congress (TUC). The Elvins sought to uphold Sidney Webb's famous precept that a union should exist 'to maintain and improve the wages and conditions of its members'. However, while serving as a pragmatic, representative body, protecting technicians' interests, the ACT also became a focus for film theory and debate. Its 'house' magazine, the *Cine-Technician*, filled its column inches with articles about aesthetics and politics. (In a sense, the ACT at play harked back to the Film Society of the 1920s, the organization set up by such diverse figures as Sidney Bernstein of Granada and Alfred Hitchcock, which would arrange private screenings of banned Eisenstein movies for wet Sunday afternoons or conduct symposia on the never-ending ailments of the British film industry.) Like the Film Society, the ACT had its quota of upper-class radicals: one of the union's earliest and most energetic members was that polymath of British film culture, Ivor Montagu. Journalist, filmmaker, editor, Montagu managed to combine his love of cinema and politics with an abiding passion for table tennis. (He was briefly president of the World Table Tennis Federation.) Another early and influential recruit was Anthony 'Puffin' Asquith, perhaps the most underrated director in British film history,[12] who shared his prime minister father's liberal politics, and would long be a tireless president and figure-head for the union. (In ACT mythology, Asquith and George Elvin are credited with rescuing the British film industry at the start of the Second World War by winning over Lord Beaverbrook to cinema's cause.[13])

In theory, relations between Rank and the ACT should have been cordial. Both claimed to have the interests of British film at heart, and the former had provided a continuity of employment for the latter's members. However, as Bond and Minney made clear, Rank's policy of trying to spend his way into America with prestige films was not one which the union agreed with. As early as 1945, George Elvin had expressed his alarm that Rank was being manipulated by his American partners.[14]

Furthermore, Rank's all-pervasive influence in Britain was chafing. On an ideological level, he was an unsympathetic figure. The sheer size of his operation led the ACT, which had a strong communist inflection, to characterize him as film's equivalent of a monopolistic factory-owner in Victorian times. The saga of *Caesar and Cleopatra*, a 'riotously extravagant venture', as ACT vice-president Sidney Cole described it, helped alienate the union, as did *London Town*, Wesley Ruggles' million-pound musical: monopolizing studio space, importing Hollywood stars – Rank's policy, if these films were the litmus test, was wasteful in the extreme. The ACT demanded increased productivity. Its basic argument was that the post-war British industry had the capacity to make at least 200 films a year. Rather than concentrating all available resources on a handful of super-pictures, it should be aiming for productivity. Sidney Cole, like the Bond–Mullally–Minney chorus, was quite categorical on this matter. In a 1946 article in the *Daily Worker*, he questioned Rank's strategy of making 'lavish and expensive films' for export; attacked his wheeler-dealing with Hollywood; and accused him of trying to extend his domestic monopoly into a 'fine big international cartel':

The future of British films? Well I know what it ought to be. Two hundred feature films a year of the same grand quality that we achieved during the war years. During those years, the British film industry grew up. It left behind its dubious past of shabby quota

169

pictures. Thrown back on its own ideas and resources and technicians, it produced scores of good films.[15]

Increased productivity would obviously be to the advantage of ACT
members: employment levels were bound to rise if more films were made.
The year 1936 had proved that Britain was indeed capable of passing the
200-feature mark. Cole conceded that some of the pictures made in that
particular production boom were dreadful, the worst of quota-quickiedom.
But, he argued, the same could be said of Hollywood: for every top-class
'A' feature to reach Britain, there was a low-grade 'B' filler left festering in
the States. More important than the individual quality of each and every
picture shot was the fact that the British would be competing with the
Americans. Until their hold on British screens was challenged, the British
would never have an industry worth the name.

Interviewed in 1991, Cole held to his opinions. The suggestions that
post-war British cinema was bound to fall into a rut, if only because it had
been deprived of its one staple genre, the 'war picture'; that inexpensive,
quickly shot British features were of limited appeal, and that there certainly wasn't an appetite for 200 of them; that some of them were liable to
be 'parochial' and hardly fit for export: these were met with scorn by this
doughty ex-editor from Ealing: 'Just by spending a lot of money and using
American stars, you can't guarantee success,' Cole still protests, 'you don't
have to be narrowly parochial, but if you start off by making films that are
within the cultural ambience of your community, you are more likely to be
successful.'[16]

While Rank saw the solution to British film's travails in creating a huge,
centralized organization, capable of servicing its filmmakers all down the
line, the ACT favoured a business based around hundreds of competing
independent producers, working swiftly, resourcefully and independently,
with government agencies providing the essential facilities such as studio
space and distribution. Rank's image as a benevolent Methodist, out to put
British cinema on the world map, was undercut by the union's rather more
sceptical portrayal of the magnate. To the ACT, Rank was a capitalist and
therefore not to be trusted. The values which he seemed to embody –
patriarchal religiosity, Toryism, Darwinian business ruthlessness – were
anathema. Now that the war was over, and there was a Labour government
in power, the union was more active in its lobbying against his 'undue and
overriding' influence.

If the ACT did not trust J. Arthur Rank, nor did Fleet Street.

RANK AND THE PRESS

Rank's treatment by the Press was infinitely variable. Throughout the
1940s, as Bond, Minney and Mullally complained that he was being

handled with kid-gloves by most of the newspapers, Rank protested that the critics were unfairly savaging his films. He exhorted them to show more patriotism, to give British cinema a psychological boost by lavishing a little praise on its pictures. Though they may have been prepared to do this during the war, the critics had quickly recovered their powers of vituperation, and weren't likely to be swayed by Rank's pleas. Rank was attacked on the left, in the pages of the *Daily Worker* and the *Tribune*, and on the right, most notably by the Beaverbrook empire, with whom he had an obscure and long-running feud.[17]

Sydney Wynne, Rank's chief of publicity, and a former journalist himself, recalls that Rank was an easy target:

> There were a number of left-wing journalists who were pretty nasty . . . who wrote pretty unfairly about Rank. Journalists as a whole don't like people who are very rich. They're suspicious of a millionaire. If a man's a millionaire, a miller and a movie magnate, they're trebly suspicious. They liked him enormously as a person though.[19]

Wynne, Ernest Bevin's son-in-law and an active, left-of-the-Labour-Party socialist himself, was convinced that his boss, for all his Tory bluster, had the best interests of the industry at heart: 'I believe that he was doing an absolutely essential job . . . and had these remarkable resources to be able to do it rather better than other people could.'[19]

However, Wynne concedes, there were times when Rank behaved like an old-fashioned, dictatorial press baron as he tried to bludgeon Fleet Street into submission. For instance, when Fred Thomas, editor of the influential trade magazine *Cinema-World*, had penned some not entirely flattering words about the miller/mogul, Rank had responded by withdrawing all his advertising from the magazine. As Rank was selling everything from lenses to cameras and laboratory facilities, this was a potentially crippling blow. Thomas beat a hasty retreat, proffering a fulsome apology in the following week's edition.

To counterbalance his rare attempts at terrifying journalists, Rank also went to some lengths to flatter them. Every year, on his behalf, Wynne used to organize a lavish lunch at the Dorchester Hotel. Here, the magnate would hold court as the hacks stuffed themselves on free food and drank their temperate hosts's health. Generally, for about three months after the December feast, Rank was assured of glowing coverage in the papers. Even R. J. Minney, who viewed the lunches as a blatant form of gastronomic bribery, never had quite the gumption to refuse his invitation to the annual 'bash'. Both journalists and film chief saw the irony in their once-a-year *rapprochement*. Wynne used to print up the menu for the feast in the form of a broadsheet. Emblazoned across the cover, in bold type, was the title: *The Hatchet Wielder's Gazette*.

Rank's influence on the British film industry in the post-war period seemed all-pervasive. It was little wonder he was a cynosure for Fleet Street: barely a week could go by without his striking some bold new deal with a Hollywood studio or acquiring yet another subsidiary company to add to his already lengthy list.[20] His tendencies towards 'monopoly' were examined by government committees, and came under increasing scrutiny in the House of Commons, where politicians from across the spectrum, with Bob Boothby, Woodrow Wyatt and Michael Foot to the fore,[21] held him up to censure. There were at least 25 million active cinemagoers in the country, all of whom must have been familiar with the bold bombardier banging the ceremonial gong. With its varied portfolio of financial interests and stable of contract stars, the Rank Organization was a subject of intense curiosity for economists and showbiz journalists alike. However, there still remained one important section of British society which was remarkably and mysteriously oblivious of Rank and all his offices: a 1946 survey carried out for the Rank Organization by a top market research company,[22] revealed that the country's 'opinion-formers', defined as the 'senior business executives' and 'higher-grade civil servants' who read *The Times* and the *Observer*, the *Economist*, the *Listener*, the *New Statesman and Nation*, and the *Tribune*,[23] knew startlingly little about the film industry. Britain's 'elite', rumoured to have their fingers on the nation's pulse, had been asked questions about the Rank Organization. Of these canvassed, 21 per cent had no idea Rank was involved in film production at all, and 75 per cent were ignorant of Rank's work in the profit-sapping but culturally respectable fields of newsreel, children's film and animation.

The survey's findings testify to an enduring disdain for the cinema held by the establishment. (Readers of *Picuregoer* – as they frequently proved with their well-informed letters to that magazine's editor – knew all about J. Arthur Rank, even if subscribers to the *New Statesman* and the *Economist* did not.) Rank tried to counter this indifference by upping his press and publicity budget to in excess of £1 million a year, and by arranging weekly press briefings[24] at his South Street offices. He set Sydney Wynne and the Publicity Department to work in devising 'a campaign comparable in size to prestige campaigns organized by leading industrial concerns such as the ICI'.[25]

However, regardless of the lengths he went to in order to woo British and American public opinion alike, all Rank's delicate arrangements were thrown into chaos by the ad-valorem tax of 1947.

THE AD-VALOREM TAX

The British may have set in motion a general reaction which could blast the hope of all trade revival all around the world.
(Eric Johnston, president of the Motion Picture Association
of America, on hearing of the ad-valorem tax)

The world-wide dollar shortage finally caught up with Britain in August of 1947, when the government announced a crisis austerity programme which, through longer working hours, savage cuts in imports and a prodigious export drive, was intended to save £144 million a year on food, £10 million on timber, £4 million on petrol and £5 million on luxury goods. Not only was Britain starved of dollars itself; most of its customer countries, to whom it could expect to export goods, were also in 'hock to the Yanks', and were not buying.

The ad-valorem tax on Hollywood films entitled the British Exchequer to 75 per cent of the movies' estimated earnings in the UK. In other words, as Eric Johnston put it, the British were trying to get 'a dollar's worth of film for a quarter'.[26] This was clearly unacceptable. Hollywood's response to the ad-valorem duty was swift and devastating: the tax had come into effect on 7 August 1947, a Finance Act having been speedily passed the week before to enable the Attlee government to impose such a draconian levy. Hollywood claimed the tax was illegal, 'against both letter and spirit' of the British/American reciprocal trade agreement, and entirely contrary to the spirit of the British Loan Agreement. (Part of the rationale for the Vinson loan to Keynes was that it would enable the cash-starved British to keep on buying American goods. Marshall Aid, shortly to follow, was similarly motivated.) By 8 August, Hollywood had put an embargo on its products: it wouldn't be sending any more films to Britain till the tax was lifted.

Rank's younger daughter Shelagh was married to an American and living in Hollywood when the government passed the infamous duty. As she recalls, there was a seismic shift in mood, a feeling of betrayal on the part of the studio executives. They had previously fêted Rank, seeing him as a vital figure in guaranteeing their continuing profits from the British market. Suddenly, they became much more frosty: all their kindness and hospitality abruptly ceased. Overnight, she found that she was being shunned:

> When I had my first child out there, you couldn't get into the hospital room with the flowers and what have you, and I don't think I bought any clothes for the dear little thing for about a year. But then that ad-valorem tax came, which was nothing to do with my father, but the Americans thought it was, and when I had my next baby, which was eighteen months later, it was quite a different story.[27]

John Woolf of General Film Distributors (GFD), also in Hollywood when news of the tax came through, remembers that the American film industry was stunned by the peremptory gesture. He was with Rank's old allies, Charles and Spyros Skouras of Fox, when they learned of the new measures. The brothers were furious. As far as they were concerned, the tax was a bombshell which was bound to have a catastrophic effect on both British and Hollywood production:

> The tax is something not only affecting our pockets, but the very roots of trading between our two countries. It's a question of principle as well as of dollars . . . what other industries have been discriminated against in this way?[28]

The ad-valorem tax was especially galling to Hollywood because the studios had been courting both Rank and the British government to prevent such a radical measure. Eric Johnston, president of the Motion Picture Association of America (MPAA), had already suggested a compromise plan to the British whereby some of Hollywood's earnings would be frozen in the UK:

> We had desired to meet the British half-way – by offering to block, during the dollar crisis, a substantial share of the earnings of American film companies in England. The proposal was submitted to responsible cabinet ministers . . . it would have benefited all and injured none.[29]

Although both British and American industries feigned shock at the tax, its introduction was an all too predictable consequence of Britain's beleaguered economy. Since the war had ended, the government had tried to keep a firm rein on imports. Hollywood films were a highly visible luxury. The Chancellor, Hugh Dalton, estimated that expenditure on tobacco and film accounted for 40 per cent of the country's total dollar imports. In the nine months from October 1944 to July 1945, the British had spent £13.3 million on American movies, and at least £70,000 on American film equipment. In the meantime, although Rank claimed that he was beginning to penetrate the US market, the dollar remittances accruing from his sales of films in America were tiny by comparison with the flow of sterling in the opposite direction: at his annual lunch to the critics in December 1945, Rank proudly announced that British films had made over £1 million in the export market over the past twelve months. (In other words, the British were spending roughly seventeen times as much on buying other people's movies as they were making by selling their own.)

While the post-war British film industry appeared robust (Odeon and Gaumont-British shares had risen by over 1000 per cent in value since 1940) the British economy was teetering on the brink of chaos. The excessive film imports rubbed salt in the wound of the American debt – audiences flocked to the cinemas, looking for relief from the austerity of their surroundings, but by spending money on Hollywood, contributed to that austerity: they were further exacerbating Britain's chronic dollar shortage. Still, prior to the tax, Rank's American prospects had seemed unusually rosy.

Up to 60 per cent of Hollywood's overseas earnings were at risk. Great Britain was as important to the American film industry as 'all the other countries of the world combined'.[30] Far better, *Variety* argued, for Hollywood distributors to make token and artificial concessions to the British, to allow Britain at least the illusion of a bridgehead in America, than to jeopardize American overseas profits. Joseph Seidelman, president of Universal, could even quantify the allowances he felt the USA could safely make: he reckoned that as long as the British were able to take from £2 to £2.5 million out of the US market,[31] with the prospect of more to come, the USA would be allowed by the Attlee government to hold on to the greater part of its nigh-on £20 million annual earnings. It was a case of offering sweeteners. The Americans didn't seem to perceive British films as a threat or to countenance the possibility that they could 'succeed' in the US market without this assistance. None the less, in 1946–7, the British film industry was treated with deference, with Arthur Rank seemingly the main beneficiary of the thaw in relations. Rank was viewed in Hollywood as the linchpin. His influence could protect the Americans from punitive government legislation, and his cinemas could provide an outlet for Hollywood pictures to continue reaching mass British audiences. In the summer of 1947, a matter of weeks before the duty was introduced, he and Davis were bullish about their new American prospects, buoyed up by the encouraging US performances of *Henry V* and *Caesar and Cleopatra*, and flattered by the alacrity with which the hard-bitten Hollywood moguls were prepared to jump into negotiations with them. Forever hinting in the trade press about opaquely struck deals which were going to net him a fortune, Rank was able to announce that he had secured play-dates for his films in the USA which would be worth $12 million a year,[32] a phenomenal figure in view of his previous American earnings. Meanwhile, Davis talked of an arrangement 'made with the five major circuits of America that they would play British films in terms and conditions precisely similar to those governing the screening of Hollywood product'.[33]

Finally, it appeared, after all its hiccups and false starts, the Rank Organization was about to establish itself as a major player in the US market. Rank could look back on several years of misadventure, confident that the tide was about to turn.

The misadventures had been many. As we have already seen, United Artists, his partners from 1944 to 1945, displayed all the resilience and imagination of snails in selling his pictures. Then there was the strange case of the raw stock shortage, another bone of contention between British and US industries: in 1945, the impact of various British movies at the American box-office was dulled and deadened when their release was held up by the shortage of stock on which to print them. *The Way Ahead, 2000*

Women and *The Demi-Paradise* were amongst the pictures affected.[34] (Although Hollywood had facts and figures to 'prove' the shortage, the British were convinced that this was yet another devious, underhand device for keeping their movies in quarantine.) Eagle-Lion, Rank's own world sales outfit, fronted by the irrepressible Teddy Carr, had been founded in a blaze of glory and publicity in 1944, but nobody seemed to notice that GFD were still in existence, and that, at least in America, the two companies were treading on each other's toes. In December 1945, Rank had struck a deal with the American railway-owner, Robert R. Young, which led to Young's setting up of Eagle-Lion Inc., an outfit renting Rank's pictures, but also making films of its own at its studios in Hollywood. Modest budget subjects, with typical 'B' titles such as *He Walked by Night*, or *Trapped*, or *Destination Moon*, these were released overseas by Rank.

To avoid confusion with Young's company, Rank's Eagle-Lion of America merged with GFD, coming under the rubric of the J. Arthur Rank Organization Incorporated (JARO Inc.). However, Eagle-Lion continued to exist as an overseas sales outfit, active everywhere but America, until 1950, when it too merged with JARO. From 1947 onward, when Carr had resigned, the company had been managed by Air Commodore 'Freddie' West, VC, who had long since entered the annals of history for his heroics during the First World War, when he tussled in the air with the most famous ace of them all, Manfred von Richthofen, the 'Red Baron',[35] and lost a leg in some feat of aerial derring-do. (There is a baffling proliferation of 'Eagles' of one sort or another in the Rank Organization's history. Quite apart from Eagle-Lion in its various manifestations, both Rank and Davis sat on the board of Eagle Star Insurance, one of Odeon's main city backers.)

After his unfortunate experiences with United Artists (see pp. 163–4), Rank had transferred his allegiance in 1945 to Universal, and in December of that year joined with his new partners to form United World Pictures (UWP). This was to be a $10 million company,[36] 50/50 financed by Rank and Universal, which would distribute eight films a year from Rank and a further eight from International, an exceptionally successful independent company formed in 1943 by Hollywood veterans Bill Goetz and Leo Spitz. Sadly, UWP's existence proved to be short-lived. The June 1946 Federal Court decision making block-booking illegal[37] threw the project into disarray: UWP had been set up precisely so that it could take advantage of block-booking. Still, Rank and Universal maintained their alliance: after Universal merged with International in 1946, becoming Universal-International (U-I), a new arrangement was made whereby U-I would sell Rank's films in tandem with its own. U-I were no more successful with Rank's movies than United Artists had been. (In 1946, Universal managed only $750,000 net of business with the British pictures.) As Joel Finler observes in his *Hollywood Story*, Rank's films and U-I's outpourings made the strangest of bed-fellows. In 1946–7, the prestige Independent Producers films were hitting American screens. *Odd Man Out*, *Black Narcissus* and *Great Expectations* 'appeared distinctly out of place along-side the bulk of U-I's own features. For the new look company once again found itself depending on cheap series like *Ma and Pa Kettle* and *Francis the Talking Mule* as well as a clutch of old Audie Murphy westerns'.[38]

Hitherto, whether sold under the auspices of Eagle-Lion, United Artists, Universal, United World Pictures, or Prestige Pictures, Rank's films had rarely done well in the United States. However, by the summer of 1947, the trend seemed to have been reversed. Hollywood was keen to do business with the British magnate: Paramount, Fox, RKO, Warner Brothers and MGM all guaranteed him play-dates, if only because they thought they were protecting their own interests by doing so. This new policy of molly-coddling the British proved controversial. After all, it ran counter to the ideology of 'free trade' and the 'open market'. To some, it was apostasy to suggest giving up American screen time to British pictures unless the British pictures earned the right to be seen: the wheeling and dealing between the Motion Picture Export Association (MPEA) and the British government, the idea of tinkering with the market and making way for 'outsiders', were considered unacceptable by the hard-bitten protectionists, many of whom seemed to feel that the British had engineered their economic crisis simply to cajole American exhibitors into releasing more of their movies. Paramount chairman Adolf Zukor was typically blunt on the matter:

> We are charged with draining the British Treasury although the earnings of American films in Britain are but small change compared with the millions that England receives from America for broadcloth, woollens, whisky and many other exports. . . . All of us know that a good picture, whether from Turkey, Yugoslavia or Tanganyika, can be shown here. The only test is whether or not the picture is good. . . . Hollywood makes pictures for the world. It has studied the wants of audiences everywhere and, in consequence, it makes the best pictures in the world. Britain makes them without even having America in mind. They haven't studied the wants of American markets as we have done traditionally, and therefore our films are, and will continue to be, superior.
>
> (Zukor, quoted in *Kinematograph Weekly*, 2 January, p. 18)

Zukor's curt dismissal neatly overlooks Rank's strenuous efforts at tailoring production for the American market, an endeavour which had led him to be attacked, and even reviled, for 'selling out' to Hollywood by the left-wing British press. Now, whether Zukor liked it or not, Britain's chronic dollar shortage demanded some nimble footwork from the US industry.

While the 1947 period of glasnost on the American circuits may have been superficial, motivated more by political and economic necessity than by any sudden enthusiasm for British pictures, Rank could plausibly argue that the very fact his pictures were 'getting through' would, in the long run, be to his advantage: metropolitan critics and audiences had already shown their liking for the work of the Archers and Cineguild in particular: with prolonged exposure, this 'niche' popularity might have been extended.

What are the difficulties that British films face in finding an American audience? In his look at movie audiences, *Immediate Seating*, Bruce Austin offers a 'propositional model of movie selection' (1989: 63) in which he lists the various elements a spectator takes into consideration before making the momentous decision of what to see. These range from advertising and publicity, through trailers and reviews, personal impact – the 'impact of other people's comments on an individual's movie attendance decision' (1989: 72), story and type, and production elements (such as director, screenwriter, and, most importantly, star) to production values, which Austin defines as the 'visual look of the film'. On almost every one of the above levels, British films in the USA were likely to suffer by comparison with Hollywood, regardless of Rank's tireless attempts to ease their reception. As far as advertising and publicity were concerned, the British were operating on a smaller budget. (Rank had upped his spending on press and publicity, but was hampered by a host of unforeseen events: wartime paper shortages meant that the British couldn't exploit the pictures to their best advantage, as did the Hearst Press's reluctance to carry either advertising or reviews of British films.) New York and Los Angeles critics may have been favourably disposed to Rank's prestige pictures, but this did not affect the vast bulk of American cinemagoers. By the same token, a single bad review from a noted critic could kill a film stone dead.[39] As far as production elements were concerned, British pictures were also at a disadvantage: British directors, screenwriters and stars remained largely unfamiliar to American audiences, who were liable to prefer Hollywood to Denham or Pinewood production values. By Austin's criteria, Rank's films started with an enormous handicap. As 'foreign product' – in spite of the shared language – they were likely to appeal only to the 'art audience'. (Not that this audience should be scoffed at. As Ealing comedies proved in the early 1950s, and as, for example, John Sayles's films continue to prove today, medium-budget 'art-house' movies can perform well, even without the benefit of a general release.)

Offered play-dates by all the major circuits, Rank was handily placed to avoid most, if not all, the pitfalls listed above, despite the general antipathy towards British films. He had been in consultation with the Breen Office, and had imported Hollywood stars and directors for several of his pictures.

In the American trade press, if not across the country as a whole, his profile was high. There appeared to be a genuine curiosity about British movies. Hollywood was offering unheard-of concessions.

Then, in a single fell swoop, the ad-valorem duty was introduced, and Rank's carefully laid plans went agley.

In late July of 1947, Rank was on his way back from America, aboard the *Queen Elizabeth*. He was due to see Stafford Cripps and Hugh Dalton, the President of the Board of Trade and the Chancellor of the Exchequer respectively, and was confident that he would be able to win the duo round to his point of view. He had reassured Hollywood that the government wouldn't take any precipitate action against American movies, and, on his arrival back in Britain, informed sceptical journalists that he expected British pictures to earn around $15 million in profits the following year.

Although the films duty, which came into effect on 7 August, was in no way exceptional, and could be seen as just another part of Attlee's ongoing battle to reduce imports and save dollars, it seemed to take Rank and Hollywood by surprise. Trade journals either side of the Atlantic began to buzz with talk of 'crisis' and 'trade war'.

Quite possibly, Dalton and Cripps hadn't anticipated the swift Hollywood embargo, and had overplayed their hand, convinced that the tax would frighten Hollywood into further concessions as it strove to protect the jewel in its export market. However, it soon became apparent that the Americans were not about to budge. They felt betrayed, and refused to send any more pictures to Britain until their grievances had been addressed and the tax repealed.

Quite apart from alienating Hollywood, the ad-valorem duty drove a neat wedge through the British industry: it destabilized production, frightening away investors, and brought to the surface all the old tensions between artists, technicians and the front office. On one very obvious level, the American embargo provided the British with a marvellous opportunity. George Elvin, president of the ACT, was understandably delighted by the tax and the reaction it provoked: now, with no new Hollywood films to fall back upon, it became a matter of necessity for the British to supply product to their own cinemas: instead of making expensive pictures for a hostile US market, they would have to cut budgets, up their productivity and cater for their own audiences. This was precisely the end Elvin and the ACT had been striving for – Dalton's duty guaranteed a production boom with a concomitant increase in employment levels for ACT members. Although Elvin had been demanding a 5-day, 44-hour week with improved wages for film workers, he suggested reversion to the 6-day week for the duration of the dispute, and was convinced that with ACT support, Britain was capable of making at least 150 films a year. Not everybody shared his optimism. In a survey of the studios at the time of the tax, a *Kinematograph Weekly* correspondent calculated that there was only

179

the capacity for eighty to a hundred films maximum. Elvin may have been happy with the embargo but his colleagues in the other film unions were aghast. The Cinematograph Exhibitors' Association (CEA) was up in arms, asking itself whether the government was out to destroy the British industry for good. Walter Fuller, general secretary of the association, fulminated:

> A devastating blow to the industry. It is the biggest threat to our future yet. . . . In the end there won't be enough cinemas open for our films to pay their way – which means our studios would close down.
>
> (*Motion Picture Herald*, 16 August 1947)

The National Association of Theatre and Kinematograph Employees, NATKE, was similarly downcast, with its leader, the Labour MP Tom O'Brien, accusing Dalton and Cripps of showing a callous disregard for the industry. Meanwhile, the American unions lobbied their British counter-parts hard, trying to persuade them to come out against the duty. However, there was such rancour and division within the British industry, and such unbridled enthusiasm for the tax on the part of the ACT, that this was never likely to happen.

It didn't take long for the film crisis to blow up into an international issue. Eric Johnston, president of the MPAA in succession to the formid-able Will Hays, was looking for an opportunity to stamp his own persona-lity on the industry. The furore around the Dalton duty gave him an early chance to creep from under Hays' shadow. He rapidly orchestrated the American embargo. In constant touch with President Truman and the State Department, he was able to bring heavy political and diplomatic pressure to bear on the Attlee administration. With the exhibitors and renters in uproar, clamouring for Hollywood pictures, it was by no means evident that the British would be able to withstand the American film blockade for long.

To cope with this new set of circumstances, Rank was obliged to fashion a completely different policy. He bitterly protested that any money saved by the Exchequer through ad-valorem would be lost many times over in the forfeited goodwill of the Americans. Rank's status in Hollywood had taken a bashing. The studios had vested their trust in him, believing that the British magnate, as president of the British Film Producers Association (BFPA), was a spokesperson for the government as well as for the industry. They had regarded his influence as comparable to that wielded by Eric Johnston. Now, it was revealed that he was helpless in the face of Dalton's precipitate action. His drive to woo America with 'prestige' productions began to come apart at the seams.

The American blockade posed the most pressing question of all for the

British industry. Did it have the capacity and skill to fill its own cinemas without the help of Hollywood?

SCARCE RESOURCES

> In spite of the grand boasts about future British products that might be attributed to J. Arthur Rank, the number per year of good British films could be counted on the fingers of little more than one hand. Flukes like *The Seventh Veil* were rare. Therefore the good films would correspond exactly with the number of good directors, none of whom at that time, thank God, were likely to be coerced into making a film which did not accord with his own taste: so each year one could reasonably expect: one film by Carol Reed, one film by David Lean, one film by Powell and Pressburger, one film by Launder and Gilliat, one fluke, one film by Anthony Asquith.
>
> (Mason, 1981: 154)

When the American embargo started in August 1947, Hollywood had 125 films in Britain that hadn't been shown to the public. Of these, 60 were classed as 'top features'. During the year, the British industry achieved a tally of 65 films itself, a marked improvement on 1946, which spawned only 44 pictures, but still nowhere near enough to keep the Odeons, Gaumonts and ABCs ticking over for long should the Hollywood siege continue. Once the Hollywood residue was exhausted, there were various short-term remedies to be taken, all to the disadvantage of the spectator, through which exhibitors could eke out a little more mileage from the available vehicles: single features, reissues and repertory seasons were obvious, if superficial, antidotes. However, if the British wanted to keep their cinemas open indefinitely, they were going to have to make up the shortfall themselves.

In post-war Britain, the national emphasis was on productivity, and the film industry's trials were far from unique: just as there was a 'coal crisis', lucidly described in an early episode of 'This Modern Age', there was a dire shortage of British film. Again, wartime rhetoric was thrown into action. Attlee warned the country that it would have to fight another 'Battle of Britain', this time not with Messerschmitts but against the twin forces of austerity and shortage.

A senior Rank executive recalls that a government representative approached J. Arthur Rank in person,[40] asking him to launch a film production drive in the 'national interest', and promising him protection from Hollywood. For four months, Rank had vacillated. Initially, he had been more concerned with protecting his American interests than in making a mass of films for the British market. In spite of the damage done to his reputation by the August duty, he still harboured hopes of exporting his films to the States. However, the trade embargo ensured that British films would have a free rein in their own market for just about the first time ever: with no Hollywood pictures to compete with, there was no reason why they should not establish themselves. Moreover, the Ranks were exemplary patriots. During the First World War, Joe Rank kept Britain fed by buying in vast stockpiles of flour from abroad.[41] During the Second World War, J. Arthur and his older brother, J. V. (Jimmy) Rank, did their 'bit' to ensure a plentiful supply of food on the Home Front: J. V. Rank was director of the Imported Cereals Committee of the Ministry of Food. Now, in this post-war crisis, as bread was rationed for the first time,[42] Rank stepped into the breach once more: in October 1947, he announced a hugely ambitious film production programme. Over the next twelve months, the Rank Organization undertook to make forty-three features, at a combined cost of £9,250,000, while continuing apace with its children's films, animation, newsreels and 'B' pictures. Rank boasted that his group had managed to avoid the worst of the raw materials and equipment shortages (this was not a claim his producers at either Gainsborough or G-B Animation would have agreed with[43]) and boldly proclaimed that while his films would be 'slightly less expensive' than hitherto, they would maintain the customary stamp of quality. Furthermore, Independent Frame was in the pipeline: by the summer of 1948, once David Rawnsley had put the finishing touches to this radical new method, he anticipated announcing an even more prolific production schedule.

With Rank's filmmakers moving into overdrive, and Pinewood working night-shifts, there was a sudden production boom, rivalling the one 'enjoyed' by the industry in the 1930s. As Denis Forman recalled in his *Films 1945–1950*:

> The spring of 1948 saw film production at its peak. Over seven thousand five hundred men and women were employed in the industry; every available studio was eagerly sought after, and the production schedules promised a crop of some seventy major films.
>
> (Forman, 1952: 11)

Again, however, this proved to be a shallow and short-lived revival, marked by the traditional internal dissent and fragmentation. The quota quickie may have been officially legislated out of existence by the 1938 Films Act, but several of the pictures produced as part of Rank's breakneck programme were ignominious failures, as much reviled and shunned as their 1930s quickie predecessors. By the end of 1949, the Rank Organization was in retreat, reeling under the weight of terrific production losses, and contemplating giving up production altogether. As Rank put it in his annual statement, sounding more elegiac than businesslike:

> Even if all our films had been of the quality that we hoped, the

unusually strong competition would have made it difficult to achieve satisfactory results. . . . Unfortunately many of the films we produced were not of the quality to ensure even reasonable returns. It can now be said that our plans to meet an unexpected and critical situation were too ambitious, that we made demands on the creative talent in the industry that were beyond its resources, and that as a result we spread our production capacity, in which I still have unshaken faith, too thinly over the films we made.[44]

It was the familiar tale, in a slightly modified form, of the conflict between art and business: Rank discovered that productivity, in itself, was no guarantee of success. Criticized for so long for his policy of making high-budget, prestige pictures, he was now similarly attacked for sponsoring mediocre, medium-budget pot-boilers.

The 1947–8 programme was certainly patchy. Brother and sister Sydney and Betty Box, frantically busy at Gainsborough Studios, turned out a wide range of films, everything from the popular 'Huggett' series, which emerged out of the film *Holiday Camp* (and for which Betty Box ran competitions in the *Daily Mirror*, allowing readers to vote for the names of the characters) to the mini-epics *The Bad Lord Byron* and *Christopher Columbus*. These last two, unlike Pascal's earlier efforts, were made to relatively tight budgets of around £200,000. *Lord Byron* inevitably fell foul of the Breen Office[45] and *Columbus*, despite the presence at the helm of Fredric March, failed to capture the public imagination. At Pinewood Studios, the Independent Producers chipped in with such films as *The Red Shoes*, *Oliver Twist* and *The Blue Lagoon*, but their golden moment was past, and they were already beginning to defect to Korda at the newly revitalized London Films. At Denham, Two Cities offered, among a sea of dross, Olivier's *Hamlet*. At Ealing, about to enter its classic comedy phase, successes such as *Kind Hearts and Coronets* and *Passport to Pimlico* were counterbalanced by the disappointing performance of the studio's most ambitious effort, *Scott of the Antarctic*.

The overall quality of his output may have been variable, but several excellent films were made at Rank's studios in the wake of the Dalton duty, and it was disingenuous for Rank to lay the blame for the crisis of 1949 on the filmmakers alone. As ever, it was an infinitely more complex story, in which the competing demands of shareholders, renters and exhibitors, not to mention the intervention of the government, the mercurial weather and just about every other variable, played a part.

What went wrong with the great production drive of 1947–8? In the first instance, Rank was 'betrayed' by the Attlee government: Harold Wilson, having taken over from Stafford Cripps as President of the Board of Trade, reneged on his predecessor's promise to protect the tender new crop of British films from Hollywood: in March 1948, he negotiated a truce with

Eric Johnston which confirmed Rank's nightmares, leaving his good, bad and indifferent pictures to compete with a stockpile of top American features. Inevitably, it was one-sided competition.

Under Wilson's new arrangement, US companies were able to remit back to the States no more than $17 million of their British profits: they were allowed (and encouraged) to invest the residue in the UK in such things as the travel and leisure industries, or to put their money into British film production. Wilson tagged on to the agreement an incentive for the American showmen to exhibit British films: for every dollar the British earned in US cinemas, Hollywood would be allowed to take the same amount in sterling out of the UK. Wilson was heavily criticized for making this concession, but justified the gesture by saying that British films were so unsuccessful in America that there was little danger of worsening Britain's dollar shortage. As he told the ACT conference in April 1948, very little revenue trickled back over the Atlantic from the States:

> Last year . . . the net earnings were only about four million dollars – and most of that was invested locally, so only about one million dollars were eventually remitted in cash.
>
> (*Kinematograph Weekly*, 15 April 1948, p. 19)

In his study of the British film industry in the 1940s, *Realism and Tinsel*, film historian Robert Murphy suggests that the Wilson–Johnston agreement was beneficial to both British and American industries: 'In retrospect it appears an adroit settlement of what had developed into a futile and mutually harmful dispute.'[46]

This was certainly not the way that Rank regarded the agreement. The Anglo-American dispute had lasted for barely more than six months. During this period, neither had the Hollywood embargo had the chance to bite (there were still more or less enough American films in Britain from before the Dalton duty to keep the cinemas busy) and nor had the British been given the time and protection to exploit the pictures made in the great production drive. The Exchequer can't have benefited – there were no new Hollywood films available to tax. Admittedly, Wilson was under heavy pressure from Eric Johnston, the MPEA and the State Department, not to mention the hordes of irate British renters and exhibitors, to resolve the dispute. However, by caving in so peremptorily, he denied the British industry its one chance to stand on its own feet, without being buttressed by Hollywood.

Wilson may have broken his predecessors' pledge to the Rank Organization that they wouldn't expose it to the horrors of full American competition, but, at least in his own eyes, he atoned for opening the floodgates to Hollywood by rapidly slapping on a 45 per cent quota level for British films. This, in its turn, infuriated Johnston and the Americans, who had believed the President of the Board of Trade when he had told the

House of Commons, in January 1948, that any quota level would be consistent with British production capacity. Johnston again felt he had been hoodwinked. He railed against the 45 per cent quota, claiming it was 'excessive, unnecessary and impossible of fulfillment' (*Kinematograph Weekly*, 24 June 1948, p. 3).

Over the past four years, from April 1944 to March 1948, Johnston pointed out, there had been an average of 449 films yearly in the British market: 310 American, 33 other foreign and 106 British. British studios were producing barely a quarter of the product they would need to keep their cinemas open. Wilson, had he kept to his word, would not have imposed a quota of more than 25 per cent. British exhibitors were equally perturbed by the quota: they were legally obliged to book almost every single film made in a British studio, regardless of quality. The rapacious distributors, including GFD, charged punitive rates for film hire.[47] The merry chaos of the late 1930s, when renters, showmen and producers all seemed to pursue diametrically opposed policies, was rekindled through Wilson's quixotic legislation. Once again, the British industry was fracturing, torn apart by internal dissent. Now, Rank was caught in the cross-fire. He was desperately trying to show his own films in his Odeons and Gaumonts. Putting on a brave face, he claimed that he was funning a self-imposed quota level of 60–65 per cent, and that his pictures were taking on average '£120 more per week than the best Hollywood films',[48] a figure the rest of the industry was hard pressed to believe. By the middle of 1948, there existed a state of undeclared war between Rank, the exhibitors and the government. As they had traditionally done when they did not like legislation or felt that it threatened their livelihoods, a great many exhibitors simply ignored it, defaulting on the quota levels and blithely continuing to show as many Hollywood films as they could. To Rank, this was perfidious betrayal. He had stuck his own neck out the previous year, at the time of the Hollywood blockade, and felt that he deserved to be supported by the British showmen:

> If it had not been for British film producers over the last 12 months, the CEA would have been in a very awkward position when the US put an embargo on pictures from that country. There was no resolution from the CEA thanking British film producers for making their position less arduous.
>
> (*Kinematograph Weekly*, 17 June 1948, p. 8)

The exhibitors saw no reason for gratitude to 'Uncle Arthur'. On the contrary, they felt that Rank was trying to bamboozle them into taking his films, regardless of the catastrophic effect that showing second-rate British features would have on their businesses. There was a particularly stormy CEA conference on the Isle of Man in June 1948, where most of the delegates now joined Mullally, Bond and Minney in casting their former benefactor as the Antichrist. By a typical quirk of irony, whereas he had been attacked in previous years by the ACT, *Tribune*, *Cine-Technician* and in the left-wing Press in general for not showing enough British pictures, now he was savaged by the CEA for trying to show too many:

> *Harry Mears*: 'Arthur Rank is virtually dictator of the industry . . . he ignores the CEA although he is a member of it . . . Rank already dictates to the press. You can see that for yourselves. You are not blind.' *Leslie Hill*: 'Mr Rank is working quickly. The old-timers are being booted out. There isn't a showman left at the top of the Rank Organization . . . there is no future for us while we are tied to Rank.' *Charles Metcalfe*: 'Nobody should be allowed the power wielded by Mr Rank today.'
>
> (Quoted from the 1948 CEA conference on the Isle of Man:
> *Kinematograph Weekly*, 24 June 1948, p. 21)

He also became a target for the right-wing Press. The *Financial Times* and the *Economist* were fiercely critical of his plans in late 1947 to have Odeon Theatres absorb the General Cinema Finance (GCF) Corporation. This meshing together of a main exhibition outlet with a production arm was, like his 1941 takeover of Gaumont-British and his subsequent boardroom shenanigans with Fox, deemed a piece of shoddy, underhand business, with the mogul putting his own interests before those of his shareholders:

> Rank certainly controls the group, but he exercises his control through a shareholding which is relatively small when compared with the vast holdings in debentures, preference shares, etc., by the public.[49]

Oscar Deutsch's original 1937 prospectus, issued when Odeon was first floated on the stock exchange, had stated categorically:

> THIS COMPANY WILL NOT ENGAGE IN FILM PRODUCTION, EITHER BY ITSELF OR BY ANY SUBSIDIARY COMPANY.

Rank chose to disregard the assurance. According to the *Financial Times*, not only was he behaving in a morally unscrupulous fashion, putting at risk shareholders' dividends by committing them to the perilous world of film production; the magnate had tried to slip the Odeon–GCF merger through without giving anybody the chance to scrutinize it – no balance sheet had been made available. The *Financial Times* commented as if personally aggrieved by the lack of information:

> Seldom has any deal involving the fortunes of a company with assets running into millions of pounds been put out in so perplexing a way. . . . From the terms of the notice issued to the Press over the weekend, the impression given is that this is merely an internal move

within the Rank Organization. . . . In fact, it is a vital change for Odeon and alters the company's entire investment status.[50]

Protesting that it was absurd 'that the activities of a company should be controlled indefinitely by the original prospectus', Rank argued that changing conditions demanded changing practices and that, in the wake of the American film embargo, when there was the threat of a serious shortage of Hollywood product, it was imperative to tie Odeon and GCF together: otherwise, all the pictures made with the backing of GCF[51] would pass to Gaumont cinemas (Gaumont-British and GCF were already financially affiliated) and the Odeon screens would be left bare.

Meanwhile, Rank's relations with his Hollywood partners had deteriorated drastically when he told them that although the Dalton tax had been rescinded, he would be unable to find space in his cinemas for more than twenty-five American pictures a year. Shareholders were alarmed that this would lead to a downturn in box-office returns, and more than ever rued the GCF-Odeon merger – Odeon was buying into a company which had already lost more than £2 million on film production, and still had £5.8 million to recoup on the films, not all of them complete, made as part of the ambitious, £9 million production programme of 1947–8.

In the period from the 1947 ad-valorem tax to his annual general statement two years later, when he told shareholders the full extent of the group's losses:

The group now has a bank overdraft of £16,286,581[52]

Rank was all at sea, at odds with right-wing Press and left-wing Press; at odds with his American partners; at odds with the ACT and the CEA. His best producers were quitting him. His research projects, everything from IMCOS to Independent Frame, were draining resources. Gradually, over these two painful years, his dreams of putting British film on the world map were abandoned. He grew to rely more and more on the goodwill of his bankers, the National Provincial, to keep him above water as his losses continued to accumulate.

Before addressing the major shift in Rank policy that the 1948–9 crisis engendered, before delineating the 'Davis era', when business aims at last triumphed over the organization's more liberal/philanthropic goals of the 1940s, it is necessary to address Rank's relations with the Attlee government in detail; to consider how he was affected by decisions made by the Board of Trade and the Exchequer, and to assess his ongoing battle with what was perhaps his greatest scourge, ET – the entertainment tax.

7

ET

The entertainment tax

I cannot help feeling that the entertainment duty has to come extent been used as a scapegoat for what has been an unsuccessful policy. And, of course, once that private enterprise, which has been singularly quiet about the entertainment duty in previous years, found this glorious new alibi under which the Government can be blamed for all their misfortunes, it was immediately taken up by the opposition press, who even forgot their criticisms of Mr Rank.

(Harold Wilson, speaking in the House of Commons,
December 1949)

While British filmmakers have always had an acute sense of their own importance, British governments, of whatever political hue, have tended to regard the industry and all its travails with a wry amusement or with a certain pinched sense of annoyance as the film lobbyists continue to bluster. Having commissioned numerous reports on the welfare of British cinema, and having been given frequent opportunities to intervene, to act on those reports, governments have tended to stay on the outside, to introduce piecemeal legislation and to watch from the sidelines as the industry withers. Harold Wilson, President of the Board of Trade in the late 1940s, a figure often (and largely mistakenly) praised for his occasional benevolent gestures towards the industry, applauded for overseeing the setting-up of the Eady Fund and the National Film Finance Corporation (NFFC),[1] stands as an emblematic figure – the British politician who enjoys a dabble in the film industry as light relief from the more onerous affairs of state. As he recalls in his *Memoirs: The Making of a Prime Minister*: 'Although far from the most important task for the Board of Trade, its responsibility for the film industry was one of the most exacting.'[2]

Doubtless, there were more pressing issues on the agenda than the well-being of British cinema. None the less, one can't survey the up-and-down trajectory of the film industry in the 1940s without at least a hint of regret at a missed opportunity. Between them, with the impetus of the wartime boom in audiences and the increasing 'respectability' of the British film, the government and the industry could surely have combined to 'set British

188

film on a sound footing'. The long-term repercussions of their failure to do so are still felt today, as little cabals of British producers pay visits to Downing Street, trying to convince uninterested prime ministers of the importance to national culture and economy of their medium, its unique ability to 'project Britain and the British way of life' as Michael Balcon would have it. For all their importuning, they are given morsels, a million pounds here and there, perhaps the occasional tax break,[3] and are told they must rely on private enterprise, and not state intervention, to revive the industry. Britain, the one country in Europe where cinema attendances have continued to rise throughout the late 1980s and early 1990s, where multiplexes have sprouted like mushrooms next to the supermarkets on the outskirts of all big towns, is able to provide few films of its own for the new generation of cinemagoers to see. If a film industry is understood as something which supplies continuity of production and employment, Britain – where the ingenuity does not go so much into the making of a picture as into its financing – has no industry. This is what makes the post-war failure of the Attlee government and the Rank Organization to supply a permanent base for British filmmakers so especially grating.

It wasn't that the 1946 Labour administration ignored the cinema. On the contrary, as we have seen, it sponsored a succession of investigations into the industry's shortcomings: there was the 1949 Portal–Plant Committee of Enquiry's assessment of the problems afflicting the *Distribution and Exhibition of Cinematograph Films*[4]; there were several shorter Board of Trade documents, including the 1948 'Gater' *Report of the Film Studio Committee*, which examined the feasibility of setting up a state-owned or state-run studio; there was the 1948 Cinematograph Act, with its 45 per cent quota level for British first features; there was the formation of the NFFC in 1948, through with the government helped sponsor (mainly Korda) production[5]; there was the establishment of the Eady Fund, diverting a proportion of British box-office receipts towards British production, in 1950[6]: all these measures suggest a willingness to diagnose and prescribe, and even to intervene. However, they were superficial palliatives, not lasting remedies. Rank's own struggle between the opposing forces of art and business was shared by the government: just as the magnate had difficulty in reconciling his desire to 'save' British production with the business imperative of maximizing box-office returns, the Attlee administration – and its Tory successors – were torn on the horns of their own dilemma; hard pressed to balance 'benevolent' interventionism with the lingering desire to fleece the already threadbare industry with an excoriating tax, one, in the long run, infinitely more damaging than even Dalton's duty.

Before addressing the effect ET – the entertainment tax – had on the British film industry of the late 1940s, it is worth sketching in its brief history.

189

Conceived as a short-term, wartime tax, ET was first levied in 1916. After the passing of the financial bill, 'New Duties', which facilitated its collection, the Chancellor of the Exchequer, Reginald McKenna, endeavoured to reassure alarmed exhibitors:

> Don't make a fuss, boys. This is a temporary tax. It will be abolished, I promise you . . . as soon as the war is over.[7]

The tax may have been intended as a short-term measure but, as A. P. Herbert has shown in his light-hearted history of ET, *No Fine on Fun*, the general attitude in Parliament was that people seeking entertainment in general and visiting the cinema in particular 'at a time like this ought to be made to contribute to the war'.[8] Politicians were notorious cinephobes, regarding film as a tawdry, immoral medium which deserved to be taxed.

> I have no sympathy whatsoever with the cinema entertainments[9]

was the response of Mr Tim Healy, MP to ET, while Mr Lough, MP averred that 'if somebody pays 2*d* for admission to these questionable forms of entertainment',[10] he or she should expect to be stung by the Exchequer. The tax was thus conceived as a tax on audiences. However, as Rank was quick to point out, the main burden fell on producers:

> This purchase tax . . . is basically designed to absorb spending power . . . and to restrict the sale of goods in short supply. In no case, so far as I am aware, has purchase tax been maintained on an article at a level which results in the manufacturer making a loss on the goods he manufactures.
>
> (Rank, quoted in *Kinematograph Weekly*, 10 November 1949, p. 8)

Needless to say, despite McKenna's reassurances, ET survived the Armistice, and continued to sap the industry throughout the 1920s and 1930s before escalating during the Second World War: in 1938, ET had waylaid the film industry and carried off £5.6 million, which represented 16 per cent on income, into Treasury coffers. In 1942, the wartime government doubled the rebate on entertainment tax at the expense of cinema, and by 1947 the tax had jumped an astonishing 700 per cent from its prewar levels, and stood at a staggering £41,390,000 during what was, admittedly, one of the most lucrative years (1946–7) in British film history. As attendances dropped, the tax subsided to a mere £39 million, out of a total box-office gross of £109 million, in 1948.

After the war, Rank bellowed and blew, whimpered and whined, using his every public platform to rail against the injustices of the tax, which he said was destroying him. Harold Wilson, not noted for his sympathy, tartly accused the magnate of using ET as a 'glorious new alibi' for a failed production policy, while Michael Foot, another of Rank's most outspoken parliamentary critics (who was associated with the *Tribune* and was also an ally of and journalist for Beaverbrook, who had long been suspicious of Rank), observed that the Yorkshireman had only started squealing 'wolf' when things started to go wrong. In the balmy days of 1945–6, according to Foot, when box-office receipts were at their peak, he had not complained at all. This wasn't strictly true: while Rank's criticisms of the tax were more muted during the prosperous years, when box-office results were good and production losses less pronounced, he was on record as early as May 1945 as saying, with Cassandra-like foresight:

> Very shortly, if it is not reduced at the earliest possible moment, the Treasury will discover that the Entertainment Tax is a golden egg, but the goose is in danger of being killed.
> (Rank, quoted in *Kinematograph Weekly*, 3 May 1945, p. 5)

As Alan Wood suggests in *Mr Rank*, Rank's policy of protesting about the tax in public at every given opportunity was counterproductive.[11] When a wealthy magnate at the helm of a seemingly profitable organization starts to moan that he is being ruined by taxation, he is hardly likely to elicit much sympathy, especially at a time when the nation as a whole is living through a period of intense shortage and rationing. None the less, Rank and Davis were always able to come up with startling facts and figures to underline the cruel injustice of the entertainment duty. For instance, Davis proclaimed that Hollywood's tax burden was less than half that borne by the British, while Rank used to tell the cautionary tale of *Henry V*:

> The film cost approximately half a million pounds and has been hailed in almost every country. . . . But although it went into production in 1943, and was first released in London in November 1944, it was only some weeks ago that the film recouped the cost of its negative. In the same period it has contributed more than £400,000 in Entertainment Tax.
> (Rank, quoted in *Kinematograph Weekly*, 8 December 1949, p. 9)

The Plant Report of 1949 was also highly critical of the effect the tax was having on the industry. Plant calculated that, taking ET into consideration, 'for every £100 worth of entertainment provided by the cinemas, the public have to pay £156 at the box-office, the Government taking the balance (Board of Trade, 1949: para. 57). Although Wilson had commissioned the Plant Report, he disregarded its findings, defending the entertainment tax robustly in the House of Commons:

> Most of us are agreed that whatever the taxation position at one moment or another, the financial position of this industry is not going to be made satisfactory purely by reducing taxation.[12]

Instead, he shifted the blame for Rank's production crisis of 1949 on to inefficient management, extravagance and poor scripts. Rank had slashed his costs all round, and even the top films of the 1947–8 production programme had not exceeded £250,000. However, the recent excesses of the industry were still vivid in the public memory. Apart from the obvious 'million-pound extravaganzas', *London Town* and *Caesar and Cleopatra*, other of his films had seemed excessively expensive to onlookers. *Men of Two Worlds*, directed by Thorold Dickinson at Two Cities, had cost £600,000, and the Archers' *A Matter of Life and Death* had clocked in at £650,000. In his bid to break into America, Rank had encouraged an image of profligacy. Whether fairly or not, British film had become associated with what the 1948 Gater Film Studio Committee called 'extravagance of production'.[13] Investors had been put off by the wastrel ways of some producers. By 1949, as ET began to bite, Rank was hard pressed to change his public image and to convince sceptical politicians and cinemagoers that he did indeed have a legitimate grievance. Entertainment tax, as the Plant Report confirmed, was bleeding the industry dry. Was the purpose of the tax, Plant asked, to destroy the film industry and thereby to free workers and resources for other, more pressing needs?

> A sufficiently heavy Entertainment Tax on cinema-going would have the effect of reducing attendances and revenues and would thus release productive resources which could no longer be profitably employed in the Cinematograph Industry for re-employment, inter-alia, in other export business.
>
> (Board of Trade, 1949: para. 60)

Was it, perhaps, to reduce the profitability of the British film market, and thereby to encourage producers to target overseas markets? Was it to reduce consumer spending among the British public? Plant infers that the tax was levied for none of these reasons: its purpose was simply to bolster the Treasury's coffers, regardless of the consequences for the industry. Although far from sympathetic to the vested interests of the two circuits, ABC and Rank, the report concluded that ET placed an insupportable burden on the industry as a whole. It drew attention to the disparity between the full rates of the tax which were raised on cinema, along with dog- and horse-racing, and the reduced rates paid by theatre, circus and football. The tax may indeed have been intended to be borne by the consumer/spectator, but most exhibitors found they couldn't afford to off-load the cost of the duty on to their customers. Under the tangled 'sliding scale' used to estimate the rate of tax on admission:

> the exhibitor was actually a penny better off when pricing a seat at 1*s* rather than 1*s* 3*d*, since the duty increased in one step at that point from 3½ to 7½*d*.
>
> (Board of Trade, 1949: para. 66)

192

In a sense, the industry's failure in the late 1940s was a failure of accountancy: there were still huge audiences. Box-office trade was brisk. But once Exchequer, renters and showmen had filched their shares of receipts, the barrel had run dry. There was nothing whatsoever left for the producers. As economist Nicholas Davenport observed in 1951:

> There must be something radically wrong with an industry with a total capitalization of £200 million which collects £109 million in cash from the public a year and yet cannot stand on its own financial feet. Laurence Olivier recently declared that British films pay very well but pay the wrong people.[14]

The Rank Organization's spectacular belly-flop of a collapse in the autumn of 1949, when it reluctantly revealed that its overdraft had escalated to £16,286,581 and that its trading profits had fallen by £4,321,453 (incorporating a production loss for the year of £3,350,000) with the result that the group showed an actual net loss of £746,747, almost brought the entire British industry to its knees. Rank's catastrophe met with wildly different responses from the Press. To the editor of the *Kinematograph Weekly*, the Rank results were a disaster to be laid forcefully at 'the doors of officialdom'.[15] To the *Tribune*, they marked a fitting epitaph for Rank's hubristic expansion. According to the latter's version of events, the production boom had failed because 'the emanation of bad taste and bad judgement from the top had acted as a deterrent to the engaging of original and talented producers'.[16] The *Tribune* editorial rings with that unmistakably supercilious tone adopted by the 'intellectual left' of the era when confronted with the 'dirty' forces of commerce or with a strain of film culture that did not conform to its tasteful/literary/(neo)realist/ documentary criteria. It was all too easy to sneer at Rank's lack of 'taste', taste being the preserve of *Tribune* and *Penguin Film Review* columists. Particularly distasteful to these arbiters was Sudney Box's output at Gainsborough Studios. Why, the *Tribune* journalist goes on to ask, did Rank choose to 'make such unmitigated flops as *Christopher Columbus* and *The Bad Lord Byron*'? In a muddled, blanket critique of the Rank Organization, the journalist (probably Frederic Mullally) blithely dismisses the entertainment tax as an irrelevance, and insists that Rank's misfortunes were brought upon himself, and were largely attributable to 'the exorbitant profits extracted from the industry by the exhibition, distribution and studio-owning sides'.[17] The fact that the Rank Organization was a combine, involved in both making and selling, and that the group, even with its renting and exhibition profits to bolster the figures, still managed to turn in a loss, seems to have eluded the journalist. In the *Tribune*'s eyes, Rank, though the biggest sponsor of British filmmakers, was the agent of the industry's misfortunes, not their victim:

Why did the Rank production programme fail so abysmally? Mr Rank with astonishing effrontery said 'It was because we made creative demands on the industry that were beyond its resources.' That is another way of saying he and his advisers are incompetent.[18]

And, although the *Tribune* had long lobbied for state intervention in the industry, with Rank on the rocks it now advocated the reign of the free market, suggesting that Rank was directly responsible for the farrago, and that his organization should simply be allowed to wither away, regardless of the jobs that would be lost and the chasm that would open up at the heart of the industry in his absence:

> We profoundly hope that the Government will not be bamboozled by this financial jugglery into pouring money into this bucket with a hole at the bottom.[19]

By contrast, the *Kinematograph Weekly*, which viewed Rank's tribulations as a 'tragedy for the British film industry', called for state intervention, accusing the government of causing the mess, and exhorting it to take responsibility for the consequences of its own actions.

Whether Rank or the Board of Trade, or a combination of the two, were to 'blame' for the crisis of 1949, Rank's attitude towards the industry was irrevocably altered. The various interventions of Dalton, Cripps and Wilson, the criticism of Rank by Parliament and in the Press, helped to change the hue of the Rank Organization, to move it rightward in the political spectrum: as Rank saw his 'philanthropic' endeavours crash around him, he was forced to make way for the policies of his ruthless accountant-lieutenant, John Davis, who had always been more interested in the bottom line of a balance sheet than in the quality of image on the screen that the money had paid for. Under Davis's tutelage, Rank was transmogrified, becoming a plausible facsimile of the monopolistic, money-motivated ogre that his detractors had long believed him to be. It was little wonder that within a year or so of his 1949 annual general statement, Rank had ceased to invest in the unprofitable but culturally laudable areas of research and production charted in chapter 5: 'This Modern Age', G-B Animation and Children's Entertainment Films had all folded by late 1950. As Stafford Cripps had noted at a dinner in honour of Rank in January 1947: 'I appreciate very fully the difficulties of giving a free and unhampered rein to artistic genius while at the same time keeping the operations of your enterprise within the bounds of commercial sanity.'[20] The struggle between 'commercial sanity' and 'artistic genius' was finally resolved, in favour of the former.

Arguably, the impact of the ad-valorem and entertainment taxes, and the benighted economic condition of post-war Britain, merely accelerated what was an inevitable process. Even without these dead weights to drag him down, Rank would have had to curb his ambitious production policy and to implement the kind of rigorous cost-cutting measures advocated by Davis. After all, not once, not even in the 'golden year' of 1946, had he managed to turn a profit on the films he himself made. His sudden about-turn of October 1947, when he heeded the 'patriotic' call, abandoning (or at least modifying) the idea of prestige production, and instead concentrating on making enough films to fill his own cinemas for the duration of the American blockade, seems, in hindsight, injudicious. As Richard Winnington put it:

> It was a laudable endeavour, but of course it could not be done. There were not enough competent writers, directors and producers to turn out so many pictures of good quality. In fact, quality was inevitably sacrificed to quantity.[21]

He had laid the basis for the production boom. He could offer his film-makers ample studio space and up-to-date equipment, including Independent Frame. But the filmmakers weren't up to scratch. Assessing the production boom, one is reminded of A. J. P. Taylor's famous remark about the British war machine at the start of the Second World War:

> The War machine . . . resembled an expensive motor car, beautifully polished, complete in every detail, except that there was no petrol in the tank.[22]

Speculating after the event serves little purpose. However, had the government encouraged and subsidized Rank's experiments in animation and newsreel, had it undertaken at least a modicum of responsibility for laying the foundations of an industry, 'things might have been different'. (By the same token, it was always going to be perilously difficult for Rank to establish the British film on the world map without a bridgehead in America.) In the end, Harold Wilson, pipe ablaze, galloped to the rescue, instituting the NFFC and overseeing the birth of the Eady Fund. He could quite legitimately claim to have 'saved' British production when Rank failed. (Rank himself acknowledged as much.) However, given Wilson's role in undermining the industry, he makes a less than satisfactory saviour.

Rank's was always an ambivalent enterprise. No account of his part in the industry in the 1940s can overlook his commitment to research, innovation and production, but, by the same token, no revision of his reputation can overlook the 'dark' business side which always complemented his naive and somewhat idealistic approach to film 'art'. ACT veteran Sidney Cole goes as far as to suggest that the Rank Organization suffered from a 'Freudian' malaise, with production taking the part of the 'unconscious', dark, mysterious, impossible to legislate for, and certainly repressed by the front office. (The analogy can be taken further: it often seemed that Rank's producers, especially Gabriel Pascal and those at

Independent Producers Ltd and Two Cities, had an 'Oedipus complex' in so far as their extravagance was slowly destroying the paternal organization within which they operated.)

In his doom-laden 1949 annual general statement to his shareholders,[23] one of the more depressing documents in British film history, Rank announced that he was planning films for no further ahead than the following June. Had it not been for Britain's chronic dollar shortage, which still threatened Hollywood imports and 'would make the future of the group's theatres a precarious one if it had to depend for product exclusively on the output of other studios',[24] and had it not been for the expenses bound to be incurred by an abrupt cessation of production, not to mention the upheaval as thousands lost their jobs, he would have abandoned filmmaking altogether. Obviously, as production was wound down, there wasn't the slightest chance of his (or anybody else's) theatres maintaining the 45 per cent quota level.

Harold Wilson, barely able to suppress his sense of glee at Rank's near-demise as a sponsor of British films, reduced the quota level to 30 per cent. As he did so, he implied that Rank's interest in British cinema had been purely peripheral. Disregarding Rank's series of grand patriotic gestures, he suggested that now that the group was no longer active in filmmaking, its theatres would doubtless try to revert to a diet of pure Hollywood: barely a year before, Rank had been calling for a 65 per cent quota, but Wilson questioned whether he had any interest at all in showing British films – the new quota level was intended to keep Mr Rank in line:

> It is, of course, extremely important to maintain a fairly high quota as an incentive, which it undoubtedly has been, to British production, and this is particularly important now in view of the changed position of the circuits, because the circuits – at least the ones owned by the Rank Organization – have no longer the same interest in displaying film produced in this country as they had when they themselves were a producing unit.[25]

With his typical, 'white-hot' ability for soundbites, Wilson himself had recently suggested that 'Export or Die!' applied as much to film as to any other industry.[26] Now, wise after the event, he suggested that Rank's great mistake was to 'try to export every film he made'.[27] He was fiercely critical that British film production as a whole had become so heavily dependent on the Rank Organization, and took a measure of pride in the fact that the NFFC (a.k.a. the Korda levy fund[28]) had filled the gap created by Rank's abdication of his place as the uncrowned king of the industry and was now 'helping many producers who for one reason or other had left the Rank Organization'.[29] (The NFFC'S production record was every bit as grim as Rank's: it lent millions of pounds and recouped hundreds.) Wilson was particularly proud of his plans for the Eady Fund; this was a levy on box-office receipts which would help finance a British Film Production Fund; would refill the coffers of the NFFC; and would also sponsor training – through a National Film School – and the Children's Film Foundation:

> I thought this one up while on holiday in Cornwall on a particular favourite walk of mine down to the beach, and succeeded in getting it through the Treasury . . . I was only too happy to father its title on the hard-working Treasury Official who turned my ideas into a detailed official scheme.[30]

As was widely acknowledged, Wilson's astute legislation kept the production industry alive. Although the Eady Fund would later be subject to abuse – it would end up underwriting 'runaway' Hollywood productions rather than sponsoring 'truly British' pictures – it still stands as one of the few practical interventions to benefit British cinema made by any government.

The debate about entertainment tax continued to rage. On a trip to America and Canada in the spring of 1950, Rank again used every available opportunity to condemn the duty. Back in Britain, politicians and journalists persisted in their attacks on the already winged magnate: Wilson and Michael Foot amongst others accused Rank of 'sour grapes'. Why, Foot asked, in the December 1949 films debate, hadn't Rank mentioned 'the terrible, cruel and harsh entertainments duty' when he announced his production drive in 1947? He called Rank the 'Rosencrantz of the industry'.[31] (Shakespearian imagery seemed to be much in vogue: at a *Kinematograph Weekly* forum on British films, Rank had attacked the organizers for not putting ET on the agenda. Any discussion of the industry which didn't address the duty was, or so the magnate insisted, like a production of 'Hamlet without the ham'.[32]) ET engendered a rare mood of consensus in the industry. It was something which exhibitors, distributors and producers could all feel aggrieved about. Rather than acknowledging that this unusual convergence of views amongst traditionally bickering parties was an indication of how damaging the tax had become, Wilson chose to see the new-found sense of harmony as something innately sinister:

> It is always potentially dangerous when industries that have been long divided and have been remarkable for their lack of unanimity come along with a new degree of unanimity to get something not from efforts by themselves but out of the taxpayer or consumer.[33]

He failed to recognize that, by causing producers to lose money, the duty had a counterproductive effect all the way long the line: (1) it reduced audiences – there were fewer first features to fill the theatres; (2) it reduced revenue to the Exchequer (ET was self-destructive – as it was a duty on the box-office, it managed to harm itself by scaring away audiences); (3) it exacerbated the dollar crisis, for as British production failed, spectators were bound to demand more films from Hollywood.

Whether or not he was overstating the impact of ET, whether or not his grand plan to sell British pictures to the Americans would have collapsed anyway, Rank began the new decade in disarray. Devoting less and less of his time to the film industry – since his brother Jimmy's death in 1952 he had been chairman and managing director of Joseph Rank Ltd and up to his neck in flour – he left the Rank Organization in the capable, if ruthless, hands of John Davis, erstwhile Odeon accountant, who, despite being one of the more reviled figures in British film history, managed to effect an astonishing turn-around in the group's fortunes, even if it was often at the expense of the 'quality' of the films made.

As an epitaph to this phase in the Rank Organization's history, the bold and expansive 1940s when Rank not only sponsored a whole series of enduring film 'classics', but attempted to set British cinema on the world map, Oliver Lyttelton's statement, in a House of Commons films debate, helps scotch the image of Rank as a reckless profiteer:

> The [Rank] monopoly which is complained of has provided the public with goods and services which cost it £4½ million more than it has received back from them and has also paid the Chancellor £9 million in Entertainment Duty. On these terms, I think the Chancellor could well do with a few more monopolies and so could the public.[34]

'A rich, portentous mixture of Beethoven, Chopin, Kitsch and Freud,' as Pauline Kael was later to call it, *The Seventh Veil* (1945), starring Ann Todd, established Sydney Box as a front rank producer.

Hamlet (1948) was one of the more successful 'prestige' pictures made under Rank's banner. Audiences, it seemed, were prepared to queue, even for Shakespeare. This picture shows the Odeon, Leicester Square.

Sydney Box's attempt at a prestige production. *The Bad Lord Byron* (1948), starring Dennis Price, had to be topped and trimmed before it met with the approval of the American censors.

Jack Warner and family survey the local brew with distaste in *The Huggetts Abroad* (1949). The Huggetts series, in many ways a forerunner of contemporary sitcom and soap opera, were among the more profitable offerings from Betty and Sydney Box at Gainsborough Studios in the late 1940s.

David Henley, head of Contract Artists, Stewart Granger, bestubbled leading man, and Greta Gynt, star of *London Town*, at a first night.

Diana Dors, the Charm School's top graduate, at an annual fair where the fans were given a chance to meet the stars.

Sidney Gilliat, who with Frank Launder founded Individual, one of the Independent Producer Limited Companies.

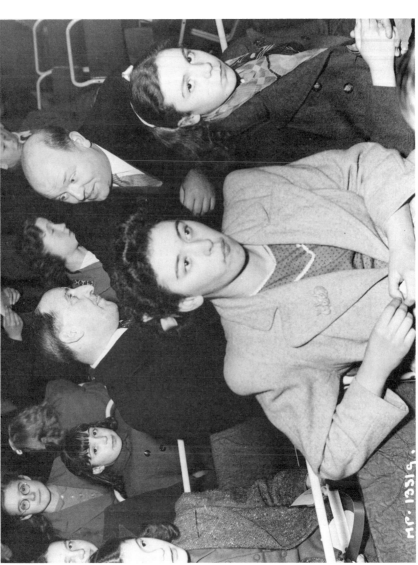

J. Arthur Rank and Sydney Box deep in discussion, in the midst of a Saturday morning 'Children's Club' screening.

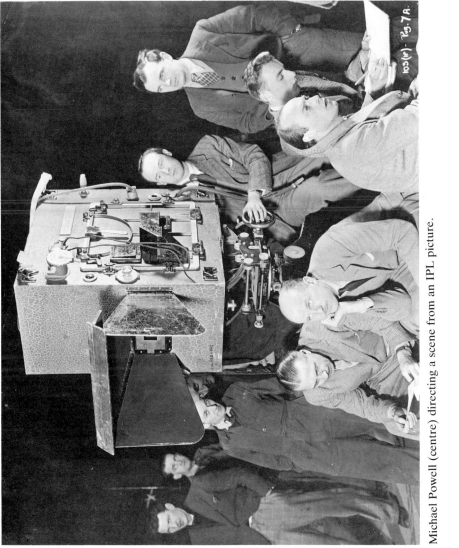

Michael Powell (centre) directing a scene from an IPL picture.

Betty Box, Britain's most prolific producer of the 1950s.

Trouble in Store (1954) was the first of the Norman Wisdom vehicles. Phenomenally successful, this picture helped cement Rank's recovery after the financial disasters of the late 1940s.

Sir John Davis, enthroned in his office at South Street.

8

RETRENCHMENT AND ECONOMY
Davis prunes

In 1945 the creative people were in charge. We made films the way we wanted and spent as we liked. The result was some of the best British films ever made. But we brought the Organization to bankruptcy. So in came the businessmen and accountants, who curtailed the creative people and restored solvency. Now, the creative people need some curb. But the businessmen get bitten with films. They think they know more about them than the filmmakers. They start to dictate the sort of pictures to be made, how they should be made, who should be in them, and even the background music.

(Ronald Neame, quoted in the *Daily Mail*, explaining why he left Rank, 18 December 1957)

Slapping a £150,000 maximum on feature film budgets, cutting executive salaries by 10 per cent, and laying off more than 200 workers at Pinewood, John Davis, Rank's doughty accountant, already managing director of Odeon Theatres, succeeded in halting what had appeared in the autumn of 1949 to be a precipitate decline in the group's fortunes, but did so at the expense of his boss's better nature: Davis shared none of Rank's indulgence towards filmmakers and their cronies. Rather than the fulcrum around which all other operations revolved, producers became little more than a servicing arm, whose primary function was to provide Odeon and Gaumont Theatres with pictures enough to fulfil their quota obligations.

Confronted with a £16 million overdraft, Rank, with Davis as virtual hatchet-man, had embarked on a three-pronged policy: his goals were now, and of necessity, no more ambitious than to reduce production commitments; to realize non-essential properties (in other words, to sell off anything not making an immediate profit); and to effect economies in overheads. It took less than a year for this good housekeeping to begin to pay dividends: Rank was able to announce in his 1950 statement to shareholders that a 'reduction of £3,365,545 has been made in bank loans and overdrafts, namely from £16,286,581 at the 25th June 1949, to £12,950,036 [*sic*] at the 24th June, 1950'.[1]

What had distinguished Rank's production crisis from its many forebears – from, for example, Korda's near collapse of a decade earlier, when the Prudential called in its loans[2] – was the extreme patience and indulgence with which his 'problems' were treated by his bankers. This obviously had something to do with Rank's own resources. He was, after all, a very wealthy man, and had effectively pumped £648,757 of his own money into Odeon Theatres Ltd to bolster its revenue reserves when the crisis struck in the form of forfeited payments due him from his shareholdings (*Kinematograph Weekly*, 10 November 1949, p. 8).

In spite of his production losses, Rank was a respected businessman who could lay his failures squarely at the door of the Attlee government, or could blame them on the excesses and shortcomings of his filmmakers. The National Provincial Bank, which doubtless shared the Tory magnate's suspicions of the Labour administration, accepted Rank and Davis's business expertise and trusted in their ability to fashion an effective rescue package, something they would never have done with Korda, Wilcox, Max Schach, or any of the host of improvident film mavericks from the 1930s. They were rewarded with this glowing homily from their grateful client:

I cannot allow this review to be concluded without referring to the help and encouragement we have received from our bankers. Our difficulties last summer were very great, aggravated as they were by the abnormal summer which adversely affected our theatre results and accentuated the production losses with which we had to deal. The support which we received, both at that time and in the months that followed, was magnificent. Our bankers gave us every possible assistance and this has done more than anything to assist us to recover the position.

(Rank's annual general statement to the shareholders, 1950)

However, the Rank Organization wasn't rescued by the banks alone.

'THE OUTSTANDING SERVICES OF MR JOHN DAVIS'[3]

He certainly has a pretty negative reputation, as being personally unpleasant and philistine, and bringing a ruthless accountancy philosophy into what began as a more liberal operation on Rank's part.

(Charles Barr)[4]

John Davis, like Joe Rank a workaholic with a capacity for working round the clock, is often luridly painted as a sort of pantomime villain of British film history, as the Visigoth let loose in the rarefied Romish corridors of the British industry. His negative reputation is not entirely unwarranted:

he managed, with seeming effortlessness, to antagonize a whole host of filmmakers, notably the free-thinking, free-spending 'artists' at Independent Producers. He could be said to have hounded Filippo Del Giudice out of the British film industry and into a pauper's grave. The stories of his prickliness and curmudgeonly behaviour at business meetings are legion – he once stopped a conference because somebody had turned up in a striped shirt: 'Go and change out of your pyjamas and we'll resume the meeting later' was his reported injunction. He was renowned for the cavalier fashion in which he hired and fired executives, and changed wives. He was feared, loathed and even despised at Pinewood Studios,[5] where he paid a weekly visit. He overhauled the Rank Organization's approach to production in the 1950s, and was far more likely to intervene, to trespass on producers' and directors' territory, than Rank had been the decade before. None the less, he was a highly appropriate figure to head the Rank Organization at a time when filmmaking was barely profitable, and when cut-backs, however brutal, were essential to the survival of the group: after all, the underlying conditions for filmmaking in 1950 were the same as they had been the year before. The entertainment tax had been neither rescinded nor reduced. The only concession Cripps had allowed the industry in his spring budget was ET relief for cinemas which combined 'live' performance with film exhibition. (This, as Rank was quick to point out, was not a particularly constructive move: it encouraged cinemas to obliterate their supporting programmes to make way for song-and-dance or comedy acts, and the supporting programme, Rank trumpeted, was 'the training ground of the industry'.) The startling disparity between the rates of ET levied on 'live' and film entertainment was a continuing source of frustration: during 1950, Rank contributed roughly £10.25 million to the Exchequer. Had his cinemas been taxed at the same rate as 'serious' theatres, his burden would have been lessened by over £8 million, and the difference might have enabled him to pursue the kind of ambitious production programme that he had mounted after the war. As it was, filmmaking was hardly viable. Rank still found 'the annual investment which is made in producing the negatives is greater than the return which can reasonably be anticipated from the markets available to British films'.[6]

He and Davis therefore switched their attention away from production, and instead began to focus on their renting and sales interests. In 1950, Rank undertook a punishing tour of every General Film Distributors branch in the country.[7] Manchester, Leeds, Cardiff, Glasgow, Newcastle – Rank visited every GFD salesman he could find. That the emphasis was on selling, not producing, was underlined when he stood down from his long-term position as president of the British Film Producers' Association (BFPA). His quitting his perch with the BFPA – an outfit with which his name had long been synonymous[8] – was symbolic of his much-diminished role in production. (Though the Rank Organization's filmmaking activities would soon revive, they would never again recapture the energy of the mid- to late 1940s, when Pinewood, Denham, Gainsborough, Ealing and Highbury were all running at full throttle. Even the tiny Gate Studios, owned by Rank personally and used for shooting GHW religious pictures, had been sold.)

One little incident, trivial in itself, seemed to signal a transformation in Rank's attitude towards experiment, innovation and risk. After the 1948 Cinematograph Act, the Board of Trade had set up a selection committee whose purpose was to view and recommend a certain number of 'independent' films for screening in the circuit cinemas of Rank and ABC. A typically well-intentioned gesture to ensure the independents of at least limited access to a mainstream audience, this provision was much resented by Rank, who insisted that he would hire any 'worthwhile' film on its own merits anyway, without having to be prodded by a tiresome government committee.

In 1950, Bernard Miles, the phlegmatic 'Walter' from *In Which We Serve*, and one of Britain's best-known character actors, had scripted, produced and directed *Chance of a Lifetime*, a low-budget, quasi-Ealing film, with a political sting in the tail, about a factory-owner, who, irritated by the complaints of his workers, allows them to take over the business and run it themselves. When first presented with the picture, Rank's 'bookers' turned it down, claiming that it lacked entertainment value. However, the Board of Trade's selection committee intervened, directing Odeon Theatres to give the film a screening. With the utmost reluctance, Rank complied. Needless to say, the film proved a flop, costing Rank, or so he claimed, 'substantial losses' in his London theatres. He was almost encouraged by its failure, which he saw as a testament to the skill of his bookers, who had had the acuity to reject it in the first place. Rank's critics, however, suggested that the film had been spurned initially because of its political content, not its lack of entertainment value. Furthermore, they weren't convinced that Rank hadn't engineered its poor box-office performance as part of his ongoing fight with the Board of Trade. Rank, sounding uncannily like the US exhibitors he had so despised a few years previously, protested that he and his bookers were impeccably even-handed, and would hire anything, regardless of where it came from, as long as they thought it might turn a profit. (It was no more surprising that British independents were suspicious of him than that he had been distrustful of the impartiality of the American showmen.) He took great pains to be fair to Miles's picture: the problem with *Chance of a Lifetime* wasn't its 'quality'; it was its commercial potential:

> I should like to make one thing clear. This film is not a bad film. It is sincerely and honestly made, and some of the acting in it is superb. It was, moreover, well received by the critics, some of whom gave it

high praise. It just lacked, in the opinion of our bookers, confirmed by public response, that *essential quality* which brings the public into the theatres and ensures that a profit and not a loss is made.[9]

This short paragraph hints at Rank's metamorphosis: the free-spending magnate who had entered the industry in the 1930s on a mission from God; the visionary patron who had sponsored such colossal loss-makers as G-B Animation, Independent Frame and *Caesar and Cleopatra* because he believed that it was in the long-term interests of the industry to do so; the Tory film tycoon who had received the warm approval of George Bernard Shaw himself – Shaw described him as 'a public-spirited and naturally honest spectator'[10]: he was now concerned, or so it seemed, with nothing more than the 'essential quality' of a film, the elixir which would bring him monetary success at the box-office, and was turning a cold shoulder towards Bernard Miles just as Gaumont-British Distributors had done to him back in 1935, when he was trying to get *Turn of the Tide* shown. Where had his sense of public spirit gone?

Rank, to the alarm of independent producers and exhibitors, had centralized control of Odeon and Gaumont-British, setting up a new body, Circuits Management Association (CMA) in 1948, to oversee the affairs of both. The terms of the 1948 Cinematograph Act prevented cross-bookings: Rank could not show films simultaneously in both circuits. None the less, as the Plant Report, delivered to Harold Wilson in November 1949, put it: 'The centralization of control of the two circuits meant that the fate awaiting a British feature film rested on two decisions',[11] one to be taken by ABC and the other by the CMA, which now dealt with all of Rank's bookings. As Rank's commitment to production waned, distributors fell back into their bad old ways: nothing much, the Plant Report inferred, had changed since the days of the Palache Committee five years previously. Renters dealing with independent pictures were as lethargic as ever, and had allowed 'exhibition arrangements to become stereotyped' by persevering with methods originally dictated by the wartime shortage of stock. Film base, Plant pointed out, was a 'dollar import' and hence in short supply: this meant that, during the war, fewer copies of films were made. (In the 1930s, a top feature could expect to be released in an issue of a hundred prints. By 1949, there were as few as forty prints of the average feature in circulation.) Fewer copies meant that it took longer for a given picture to be exhibited at every available outlet and hence delayed the time it took for the total receipts to wend their way back to the producer, a source of immense vexation to cash-starved independents. Although decreasing their workload, fewer copies also increased the influence of the distributors. As they were often involved in financing as well as renting movies, the distributors were able to maximize their earnings at the expense of the filmmakers, who depended on them both for sponsorship and sales. The

203

restrictive practice of barring, whereby circuits would only allow movies to be shown in their own cinemas, even in areas where there were larger or better theatres available, also slowed down returns. The industry exacerbated its own plight, and added to the misery caused it by the entertainment duty, by failing to sell its pictures as widely or as quickly as it could. To maximize returns, Plant advocated competitive bidding for films: whichever exhibitor offered the most for a movie should be allowed to show it. At a time when foreign markets did not appear at all lucrative:

> it would be no more than conservative budgeting to include *nothing* for overseas receipts in the estimates for the majority of British feature films produced throughout the post-war period.
>
> (Board of Trade, 1949: para. 54; emphasis added)

It was especially important to maximize domestic earnings. The Plant document stands as an important corrective to the notion that British cinema's problems of the late 1940s were entirely attributable to external factors such as the bone-headed interventions of the Board of Trade, the American embargo and the weather. The industry's problems were, at least to a degree, self-inflicted.

As audiences continued to slip away, Rank and Davis set out to enhance the cinemagoing experience, (rather than the films themselves) to woo them back:

> This industry is making a great effort to bring new patrons to our theatres. When they get there, don't treat them like sheep but give them a warm welcome – especially families. People dislike being herded about.[12]

The film as 'family entertainment': this was the Rank Organization's new goal as Britain moved out of Crippsian austerity and stumbled towards the promised land of Macmillan's 'soap-flake Arcadia'.[13] To lure the public away from the comforts of home and hearth and television, Rank and Davis launched a bold reform of the Circuits Management Association: the new, happy and hardy breed of cinema managers were to be trained, and retrained, and encouraged to compete with one another in a variety of schemes, for which they were presented with Silver Stars and Awards of Merit. For the Festival of Britain in 1951, the CMA organized a 'Miss Odeon and Gaumont Festival Girl' beauty contest, attracting over 3,000 entrants in the process. CMA even had its own version of the Charm School: in November 1950, Rank had opened the CMA Managers' Training Centre: based at the Gaumont in Finchley, this was essentially a boarding school where apprentice show*men* – cinema exhibition remained a resolutely chauvinist field – studied the theory and practice of luring an audience to a film which it does not necessarily know it wants to see. Gimmickry has always been at the heart of showmanship and there is an exhaustive thesis to be written about British showmen's japes over the years – the parades through city centres dressed in the costumes for the films which they were showing, the Dada-like 'events' aranged to alert the unsuspecting public to changes of bill at the local Gaumonts and ABCs. Rank entered fully into the spirit of showmanship. Every December, he would hand out prizes to the top cinema managers, and he is to be seen in the trade press of the period donning a series of colourful disguises. One year, he might be kitted out as a jockey. The next, he might be aping Nelson 'with one arm in a sling and a patch over his eye'.[14] For all his end-of-year japery, he was stern when cinema managers grew lax. There was one famous incident when he was driving through Plymouth and stopped to inspect a local theatre. Appalled by the condition it was in, he called out the manager from his office, gave him a stern dressing-down, and warned him that he wanted the cinema 'ship-shape' as soon as possible. The manager, obviously intimidated by the growling Methodist, readily complied, setting to work at once with mop and feather duster. It was only when Rank walked out of the cinema that he realized it was an ABC (and not one of his theatres at all).[15]

As the 1950s progressed, Rank and Davis, like the rest of the British and American film industry, were obliged to think of new ruses for dealing with the rise and rise of television, a medium with which Rank had a characteristically ambivalent relationship.

RANK AND TELEVISION

It is definitely not my view that television will harm the cinema. American experience is that, after the novelty period, it has helped other entertainments.

(Rank, speaking in November 1950)

One of Rank's more frequent complaints, outside unpatriotic critics and unfair taxes, was that he was constantly castigated as a 'monopolist', while BBC Television, which was protected by the state, and didn't have a single competitor, held exclusive sway over the airwaves, seemingly without a murmur of dissatisfaction from the ACT and the *Tribune*. Rank's own repeated pleas to the Postmaster-General for a licence to broadcast were turned down time and again.

Since 1941, when he acquired the key Metropolis and Bradford shares in Gaumont-British, Rank had held the controlling interest in Baird Television, a company with a slightly chequered history. Bought by Isidore Ostrer in 1932, it pioneered close-circuit relays in the 1930s, showing 'live' boxing as well as the 1939 Derby on television in West End cinemas, but had then fallen into receivership when Mickey Mouse took his bow,[16] and British television went into hibernation for the duration of the Second

World War. However, it had been merged with another company, Cinema-Television Ltd, in October 1940, and now he had taken it over, Rank was hard pressed to know whether it was an asset – television had obvious, if undeveloped, potential – or a hindrance: it was expensive to develop, especially when there was no guarantee that the government would grant him an experimental broadcast licence, let alone a commercial one.

As Asa Briggs has shown in his massive history of broadcasting,[17] Rank took a far more constructive approach to the new medium than most of his colleagues in the film business. As early as 1944, he was anticipating a 'substantial television market for old films', and envisioning a period when the two media would interact to mutual advantage; he predicted:

> Television might make films more popular than ever if our publicity people are clever enough.[18]

(In a sense, he was right: British cinema's perennial failure to broach the American market counted in its favour when it came to American television. Rank's pictures, many of them unreleased in US theatres, quickly gained a novelty/cult following on the small screen.) Rank was characterized by nothing so much as his ambivalences, profoundly troubled when it came to disentangling his business, art and religious commitments. Television was destined to vex further his already furrowed brow.

As television was largely quiescent from 1939 till the war was over, it is worth taking up the story of Cinema-Television in 1945. In that year, Rank informed Hollywood:

> We control Cinema-Television, which has done nothing since 1939, but we can produce a theatre-sized screen within three years.[19]

In those early days, Rank regarded television as a public, not a domestic, medium. Rather than families sitting at home, audiences would enjoy the experience of television in his theatres: with close-circuit broadcasts, television would complement cinema, offering an immediacy that film in the can could not provide. We have already seen how David Rawnsley envisaged using television to give 'live' plugs for forthcoming attractions, and even to relay entire films direct to cinema audiences:

> By the use of Independent Frame, it will be possible to televise an individual scene or scenes within a feature film, thus including in the film leading stars, who will play the scene in actual before the original background. . . . Leading stars will provide their *own trailers* before the actual settings by the use of Independent Frame . . . it is also fairly certain that by the use of Independent Frame, it will be practical to televise direct an entire film with the live artists, against pre-screened backgrounds.[20]

(emphases added)

The radar expert Sir Robert Watson-Watt's experiments with electronics, which attempted to devise a form of remote control for studio equipment, made Rawnsley's vision of 'live cinema' a possibility: Independent Frame sought, wherever possible, to curb accident and improvisation, and to make film production into a factory-like activity. Rehearsal, pre-planning and technical expertise were the bedrock of the method. (While Rawnsley's dreams of 'live cinema' never came to fruition, both British and American television in the mid-1950s experimented very successfully with 'live theatre'. In the USA, groundbreaking tele-plays such as Paddy Chayefsky's *Marty* and Rod Serling's *Requiem for a Heavyweight* offered a variety of raw, direct drama not found in the games shows or commercials which dominated the schedules. The same kind of impact was achieved a little later by Sydney Newman's 'Armchair Theatre', in which a host of British actors, writers and directors who, in earlier days, might have expected to pursue careers in cinema, were lured to television.)

Rank's desire to confine television to the large screen was understandable. Most feature films, after all, were designed to be 'big pictures', and Rank feared that compressing them into a small-screen television format might fatally undermine them. (Quite apart from their business rivalry with the medium, this was one of the reasons why producers were so loath to sell their pictures to television – they didn't want to see them 'diminished'.) As John Davis put it as late as 1954, when commercial television was already imminent:

> If they [films] are shown on the small screen they lose much of their quality and definition, and in fact give people the impression that films are not good. . . . Thus we depreciate the quality of our own goods.[21]

In the post-war years, Cinema-Television was a tantalizing prospect. Rank had concluded a deal with a Chicago-based company, the Rawland Corporation, for the manufacture of large-screen television equipment for commercial use in cinemas, and was waiting patiently for a licence to broadcast. He seemed to have every chance of success. As Ed Buscombe has recently pointed out, television was far from established as a popular domestic form – in late 1947, as few as 34,000 TV sets were in use in the UK, and only '0.2 per cent of homes' were equipped.[22] The BBC was short of product, limited both financially and in its transmitting capacity. Rank made overtures to the ailing corporation, suggesting they reach some mutually beneficial arrangement:

> Within four or five years of the end of the war, he [Rank] envisaged the BBC broadcasting direct to the public and the cinema industry

having its own television studios, where television programmes would be prepared for public showing. He did not foresee that a general diffusion of home television might spell doom for the cinema business.[23]

In the autumn of 1948, there were reports in the trade press that Rank was mooting a plan for 'the re-transmission of selected items from the BBC Television programme and special items from Pinewood Studios to CMA cinemas in the West End'.[24] Although the BBC was co-operative, if wary, as far as Rank's Cinema-Television experiments were concerned, it harboured the understandable fear that Rank, in the long run, would be more interested in broadcasting his own programmes to cinemas than in buying up old items from the corporation. This probably goes some way to explaining why the government afforded such extensive protection to Reith's old dominion. There was a strong suspicion that the BBC would quickly collapse in open competition with the film industry. A fragile, pupescent thing, it needed to be treated with great delicacy. (Furthermore, BBC executives didn't want television to become overly dependent on feature films.) Rank was continually frustrated in his attempts to wean a licence to broadcast out of the Postmaster-General, who might better have been described as the BBC's Protector-General. He was condemned to bear the ever-increasing expenses of Cinema-Television with no certain prospect of being able to give his new brainchild a proper commercial application. Still, Rank was a man of many paradoxes. Although his public utterances suggested he didn't believe television had a future as a domestic form, he none the less helped to defray the expenses of Cinema-Television through his sale of TV sets; he also controlled Bush Radio, one of the most consistently profitable of all his enterprises, which would provide the British public with 'tellies and wirelesses' for years to come. Moreover, as Olive Dodds, in charge of Rank's contract artists, recalls:

We didn't allow our people to do television in the early days at all. We regarded television as a rival.
(From an interview with Olive Dodds by the author, London, 1991)

In November 1948, the Postmaster-General had budged slightly, allowing Rank a permit for an 'experimental period', to pick up and relay BBC programmes, but did so only when he had been given assurances that Rank would sell movies to the BBC in return. Over the next four or five years, Rank carried out a series of 'test' broadcasts, relaying images the thirty miles from Pinewood Studios to a receiver and transmitter on the site of the burned-down glass emporium, Crystal Palace. Five main West End theatres were wired for reception of these images, as well as those carried from the BBC at Alexandra Palace. It was hard to tell whether the experiments were successful because there were no audiences to test them on:

> Unfortunately we have not been able to carry out experiments with large paying audiences in this country to secure knowledge of audience reaction as we have been, so far, unable to secure the necessary experimental licence.[25]

Ultimately, Cinema-Television proved to be a singularly ineffective weapon in the fight against domestic TV. After a belated debut in 1952, when close-circuit television relayed a 'live' fashion show to an Odeon cinema, and following a successful demonstration at a South African car show, 'Cintel' was aimed at a new market: drilling, capping, removal, canal work, gum improvement, flossing, filling and fluoride were the focuses for the next application of Cinema-Television:

> Rank believes that there is a big future for large-screen television outside the sphere of entertainment. . . . Dentists from 43 countries attending the International Dental Congress at the Royal Festival Hall in London this week are seeing larger than life demonstrations of the latest surgery techniques through the medium of the Cintel large-screen system.[26]

Dentistry was not the only field where Cinema-Television proved successful. In 1953, the Rank Organization collaborated with German television to arrange a big-screen transmission of a West Germany v. Austria football match. This sold out in Düsseldorf. However, such local triumphs would never be enough to sustain the company, particularly in view of the costs it was incurring. (The so-called 'Cintel' screen was the same size as the average cinema screen and was reckoned to cost between £10,000 and £15,000, which was a considerable outlay for a novelty with no proven commercial track record.)

As the 1950s progressed, Rank and Davis were forced to revise their opinion about domestic television. Instead of seeing it as an ally with which the film industry could work in perfect symbiotic harmony, or as something so insignificant as not to be worth worrying about, they were forced to acknowledge it as their main rival.

In *Sex, Class and Realism*, John Hill suggests that 'far from weakening the combines the 1950s was to witness an intensification of their monopoly power'.[27] While Rank and ABC, like the rest of the industry, suffered from diminished audiences and were forced to close several of their cinemas, 103 in Rank's case and 55 in ABC's – 'cinema closures overall amounted to 1,357' – the circuits' proportional control of the industry was thus bolstered, not reduced, by the first television decade. They were more entrenched and with a wider hegemony than ever. The successful independent producer Michael Relph testifies to the stranglehold in which ABC and Rank were able to hold British cinema throughout the 1950s:

> It is many years now since John Davis and Robert Clark (head of ABC) used to sit at opposite ends of the Film Producers' Association Board Table and dictate the policies of the British film industry to suit the interests of Rank and ABC. In the 50s, as an Independent Producer, I accepted that I was disenfranchised and took no interest in the politics of the industry.[28]

Still, even if Rank and ABC could congratulate themselves on their increased market share, that market was dwindling all the time. Even the 'dinosaurs', as Robert Murphy has described the circuits, were threatened with extinction, and had to fight to preserve their territory: there was a prolonged and bitter war waged between the film and television industries, with the former mounting a desperate rearguard defence of their interests and audiences against the encroachments of the latter. The 1950 Beveridge Committee Report on Broadcasting[29] had concluded that television's future was as a domestic, not a public/theatrical form. The film industry finally raised its head from the sand and acknowledged that television was hurting box-office attendances. While determining that it would not hasten its own demise by selling its choicest products to the new competitor, cinema sought ruses to win back its customers. (Adolescents, those in the 16-to-24 age bracket who had traditionally made up the backbone of the cinema audience, were now staying away in their droves.) Against this grim backcloth, the Rank Organization tried to lure families to its theatres in the adolescents' stead. The extensive renovation of CMA cinemas; the specialized training of cinema managers; the refusal, exceptional cases apart, to book 'X' films;[30] and the direction that production at Pinewood under Earl St John, a 'showman' himself, had taken during the decade: all underlined this new emphasis on the family audience. No account of the Rank Organization in the 1950s can overlook 'sweeties and ice cream', which began to account for a major part of the group's cinema profits. Rank, the self-proclaimed saviour of British film only a few years before, was called, in November 1952, to appear in court to defend one of his West End cinemas accused of defaulting on quota. (The very notion of defaulting on quota would have been anathema to the magnate in the late 1940s, when he regarded the quota levels with the same veneration as he afforded the Ten Commandments.) During the case, Rank issued his now familiar list of complaints and excuses, castigating entertainment tax and bemoaning the losses that cinemas were bound to sustain by trying to keep to the 30 per cent quota level. Even as he did so, he revealed that 'ancillary' earnings were becoming more and more important to the organization, with ice cream in particular playing a prominent part in the group's profits. He told a surprised court that he had made a profit of £1,151,000, considerably more than he had made from his films, on sales of ice cream in the previous year alone.[31]

Experiments in Vistavision and Cinemascope (as we shall see, a source of extreme grievance between Rank and Fox when it came to Victor Mature and *The Robe*); forays into 3D; the contemplation of stereo sound; the widening use of colour (in the bad old days of the 1940s, when Dr Kalmus kept an Edison-like grip on the exploitation of Technicolor, and when producers were forced to fight amongst themselves for access to Technicolor cameras, stock and lighting facilities – all in short supply – it wasn't easy for the British to exploit colour: however, by 1953, Rank's Denham Laboratories had the largest capacity in the world for processing Kalmus' rival, Eastman color): all these innovations, on screen and at confectionery counter alike, were designed to emphasize the 'specialness' of the cinemagoing experience as a stark contrast to the banality of staying at home and watching the 'box'. Charles Barr has written about British cinema's intense 'TV consciousness' in the decade,[32] its constant and denigrating references to its new, soul-destroying rival. Many British films of the period seemed to cast television as an instrument of the devil, as a medium which seeks to create 'fake community, fake togetherness', while the cinema, now surprisingly elevated to the status of traditional art/ culture, could boast that it provided 'authentic community'. (Using the terms of Richard Hoggart's influential *Uses of Literacy*, it seemed that cinema was trying to pass itself off as a kind of 'folk culture',[33] while scorning television as an instrument of numbing, meretricious mass culture, an ironic and even astonishing reversal given the contempt in which movies have traditionally been held by high cultural critics.) The 1953 Ealing vehicle *Meet Mr Lucifer* and Muriel Box's *Simon and Laura* of three years later are cited by Barr as exemplary telephobic texts: television may have its uses – relaying sports events, giving the weather – but it cannot be allowed to impinge on the 'more autonomous and full-blooded experience' provided by cinema.

The BBC had no desire to become a 'home cinema', but the corporation, along with its commercial counterparts from 1955 onward,[34] had a voracious hunger for films:

> In 1953, at a meeting with several trade bodies, the BBC listed its film requirements; sixty-six features a year for afternoon programmes, plus one feature a month for evening showing.
>
> (Buscombe, 1991: 202)

The film industry had already been elbowed out of the newsreel market. (Cinema newsreels had no chance of competing with live television relays: their death warrant had been signed by the 1953 Coronation, which Rank had filmed and rushed to his cinemas, but which the BBC had shown as it happened. It is little wonder that Rank's picture of the Coronation performed disappointingly in the American market. After live television relays, it can only have seemed reheated gruel.)

British cinema certainly wasn't going to give up its first features easily. The reluctance to sell pictures to television may have been mainly commercial as far as Rank and Davis were concerned. For the filmmakers, though, there was an added 'aesthetic' dimension to their determination to cling to their wares. It was believed, with a large measure of justification, that television editors had few qualms about mangling movies to get them to fit into the appropriate schedule slot. There was a notorious incident with an Anthony Asquith picture to give grounds to filmmakers fears:

> In the early days, the TV companies used to brutally cut movies. Asquith was very provoked when they ran a film of his called *Orders to Kill*, and it was cut. There was one cut which particularly annoyed Anthony because it destroyed the point of the film: it was a wartime film, about some people sent to Paris to locate and kill someone who has betrayed a resistance group. It was one of those situations where the least likely, the most harmless-looking person turned out to be the killer whereupon our hero shot him. As he died, the 'traitor' looked up and said 'Why?' This was very moving: it was later realized that a ghastly error had been made. This was cut![35]

Writers and directors were alarmed to see their pictures being trimmed, often without consultation, by unsympathetic or downright inept television staff. Such vandalism only stiffened the industry's resolve to hold on to its products.

There were fewer than 800,000 TV licences in Britain in 1951. By 1960, there were close to 11 million. In the same period, cinema attendances dropped from 1,635 million to a mere 501 million. As the decline continued unabated, it was inevitable that Rank, for all his bold post-war talk of cinema/television alliance, would join with ABC in lending support to the Sidney Bernstein-inspired organization, FIDO (the Film Industry Defence Organization), which sought to prevent producers from selling their movies to television. FIDO raised funds from a small levy on box-office receipts, and used these funds to pay filmmakers for entering into covenants which said they wouldn't sell their films to television. The image reached for by commentators to describe the outfit's activities is of Canute trying to repel the waves.[36] It was a forlorn endeavour. Rank paid lip-service to FIDO, although he wasn't officially participating in the system, but, hedging his bets as ever, bought a one-third stake in Southern Television, a sure sign that he had lost his faith in the long-term future of British film production.

As the Rank Organization carried on its erratic, sometimes profitable way through the 1960s and 1970s, its mission to 'save' British cinema would go on the wane. What had started in 1933 as a religious films outfit, and had become the backbone of British cinema by 1946, was now a fully fledged leisure conglomerate, with only a marginal interest in British film production.

9

RANK AND THE 1950s
The Xerox years

At the time of writing, in mid-1992, the Rank Organization has a stock market value of £1.8 billion and a workforce of 45,000. The company formed back in the 1930s to provide religious films for Sunday schools and Methodist halls has come full circle, and now garners a sizeable proportion of its profits through its gambling interests – Top Rank and Mecca bingo halls earned the group £40 million in 1991.[1] (Lest it be thought that Rank's memory has 'gone to the devil' as his successors plough money into casinos and dance halls, it should be pointed out that the Rank Foundation, established in 1953 to ensure that the group could never be taken over by non-British interests, continues to support a myriad different charities: between 1986 and 1989, it gave away £13,171,268, sponsoring everything from culture and education to animal conservation and medicine. The Rank Prize Fund awards grants for research in nutrition and opto-electronics. (After all, flour and film made the Ranks rich.) And the sterling work of the Religious Film Society is carried on by its spiritual and small-screen successor, the Christian Television Centre (CTVC): set up in Tooting in 1959 simply to teach the clergy how to appear on television without making asses of themselves, CTVC has mushroomed, and now boasts a state-of-the-art television studio at Bushey in Watford. Hundreds of hours of CTVC programmes are broadcast on British network television every year, and are watched by millions. Rank's cinema chain and distribution outfit are still going strong, netting the company more than £10 million in 1991. The organization maintains links with its old ally, Universal. Together with the American outfit, it has invested in a Florida theme park. Film production, in abeyance since the late 1960s, when Betty Box and Hugh Stewart were the last two Rank producers to leave Pinewood, has been more or less abandoned, and profits accruing from film and video alike are but a flea-bite in comparison with the money generated by what has become the mainstay of the group, namely Rank Xerox.

In a study of this nature, constrained by time and budget, it is not possible to do more than sketch Rank's fortunes, and the impact he had on

British film culture, from 1952, when he took over the family flour interests, till his death in 1972. Over this 20-year stretch, Rank became more
and more remote from the film scene. Hugh Stewart recalls:

> Rank was a very distant figure. I never saw him, except at the annual
> Christmas dinner and he didn't even come to that after a while.[2]

Betty Box offers an image of the magnate, like Churchill enjoying an
Indian summer in the 1950s, as a benevolent, grandfatherly man, pottering
from time to time on to the film set:

> He used to come and visit us, and I got my brace of pheasants every
> year . . . at the end of the season, we [producers] all got a brace of
> these pheasants. He was a very lovable person. I liked him, what little
> I saw of him. He was a dear.[3]

With Rank's time and energy consumed by the flour business, the reins
of the organization fell into Davis's hands. Though the 1950s were as
turbulent as any other decade in British film history, the organization, after
its near-catastrophe of 1949, managed an astonishing revival: its star had
miraculously risen again, albeit into a very different sort of ether.

REVIVAL

To many, the 1950s are the quintessential British film decade, and to skirt
over them in the manner I am about to do must seem peremptory at best,
heretical at worst. The 1950s, after all, are the era when the 'chaps',
Kenneth More, Jack Hawkins and an uncomfortable Dirk Bogarde, in
their immaculately polished brogues, perfectly pressed flannels and neatly
tailored tweed jackets, ruled the roost; when the intrepid John Mills was to
be seen scurrying across the desert in several war movies; when Britain
tapped a golden vein of comedy. France had *Cahiers du Cinéma*, Godard
and Truffaut. Britain, richer by far, could boast the 'Doctor' films, the
'Carry On' series and the Norman Wisdom comedies. If the French new
wave were railing against '*le cinéma du papa*',[4] the British were embracing
the cinema of great-grandpapa. Inanity and cheerfulness were the watch-
words, qualities found in abundance in one of the key films of the epoch,
where ancient cars bumbled their way from London to Brighton, and Kay
Kendall blasted at the trumpet, *Genevieve*.[5] (The film also starred Dinah
Sheridan, shortly to marry John Davis.) This was a vehicle with an
unhappy genesis – Hugh Stewart recalls it as 'one of the most detested films
ever made at Pinewood' and Olive Dodds remembers that Kendall,
Kenneth More and John Gregson, all under contract, 'came to me at one
time or another and said, "I want to be out of it",'[6] – but it was adored by
audiences. To detect a certain sea-change in the British approach to
production during this so-called 'age of affluence' and of mass production

and luxury goods, it is only necessary to chart the Independent Producers uncomfortable passage across the decade. Rank's free-spending artists of the 1940s found that their wings had been severely clipped: the prodigals, Powell and Pressburger, returned to the Rank fold after their sojourn with Korda, but only to make some of their dullest, most clunking pictures – the gulf between the mercurial brilliance of *The Red Shoes* and the heroic torpor of *The Battle of the River Plate* marks a wholesale transformation in the Rank 'aesthetic' since the balmy early days of Independent Producers Ltd when the Archers were let loose to do more or less as they pleased, even to build a stairway to heaven if they so wished. Anthony Havelock-Allan, who also returned briefly to Pinewood, remembers the 1950s as a difficult time for the 1940s visionaries:

> Arthur Rank by that time was beginning to do Norman Wisdom films . . . you were paralysed. British Lion didn't want much. I'd done three for Earl St John at Pinewood, and I remember the difficulty – only with the greatest difficulty did I get them done. You had two choices. Either you made comedies or you went to the Americans. You couldn't think of big subjects because there was no money. When you think of small subjects, then they're mostly local. And if they're local – nobody wants a film that is local. This meant a tremendous limitation on story ideas. Launder and Gilliat ran out of ideas. Powell and Pressburger split up. Mickey didn't do anything for a long time. David Lean didn't do much until Sam Spiegel took him into the American ambience with *Bridge on the River Kwai*. Otherwise his talent would have gone for nothing.[7]

As the Independent Producers struggled, filmmakers out of their time, a different style of production emerged at Pinewood, one that in its regulation and efficiency, if not its inspiration, was as close as Britain ever got to a Classical Hollywood Cinema.[8] Before looking at the 'classical' Pinewood regime of the 1950s, it is worth examining how the Rank Organization got itself out of its 1949 morass, and again put itself in the position to make pictures.

The 1940s ended with the Rank Organization £16 million in the red, and seemingly headed towards the reefs. However, Davis and Rank's fiscal pruning cut the overdraft quicker than anyone could have forecast. As early as 1950, the tide was beginning to turn as the two tore into the overdraft with relish, cost-cutting and 'rationalizing' away their debts. By 1951, the year when Davis became vice-chairman of the organization, the overdraft had been reduced to £9 million, and by 1954, it had dwindled to only £4 million.

The year 1954 was an exceptional one for the Rank Organization, one which helps modify the received wisdom that the 1950s saw the British film industry on a downward-sliding parabola throughout. Attendances were up in that year, no doubt a consequence of public disillusionment with BBC broadcasting. (In 1955, the birth of independent TV would lend a little more brio to television. In 1954, though, the BBC's continuing tendency to relay live classical music and Greek drama in prime time was grating the nerves of many viewers.) Despite the scourge of entertainment tax, which Tory chancellors proved as hungry to levy as their Labour predecessors,[9] production doubled in profitability, netting Rank close to £1 million. Most heartening of all, Rank's share of the total box-office take stood at over a third – £38 million out of £108 million spent overall.[10] Rank had come back from the brink of disaster, and could afford to gloat:

> With his back to the late summer sunshine, Mr Rank stood in his board room at South Street last week and modestly enjoyed the triumph of the road back.[11]

In early 1951, Rank had entered into a cabal with the National Film Finance Corporation (NFFC), which was also leaking money at an alarming rate,[12] to form one of the 'Groups'. British Filmmakers, a team of ten producer/directors, were contracted to shoot pictures at Pinewood for which GFD put up roughly three-quarters of the finance, with the NFFC providing the topping-up ('end') money. It wasn't a particularly happy experiment: few of the producer/director teams got on particularly well,[13] and they all resented their contractual obligation to plough any profits they made straight into a central kitty. None the less, as Davis later observed, without the NFFC, 'there would have been a complete financial collapse of British production' (*Financial Times Annual Review of British Industry*, 1954); for all its bureaucratic shortcomings, the NFFC enabled Rank to keep on making pictures, and by 1952 the organization was confident enough to embark on a production programme without this government crutch.

Rank's inexorable policy of rationalization had moved rather too rapidly for the ACT, who were appalled by his precipitate decision to close Denham Studios in late 1952. (The studios were briefly leased to the American Air Force but soon fell into desuetude.) Throughout the 1950s, relations between the magnate and the union continued to deteriorate. It was hardly surprising that the union was suspicious of Mr Rank: his swingeing cut-backs of 1949–50, and the mass redundancies that followed in their wake, inevitably put Elvin, Cole and Co. on their guard. Rank treated the ACT with a measure of impatience. In a 1951 letter to Elvin, he scolded the association, referring to:

> your union's lack of co-operation. Over many months your union's tactics have been abundantly clear. First a demand is made: at the conference table, your representatives are inflexible; and finally you refuse any form of arbitration.[14]

Davis and Rank were determined that the organization should not over-stretch itself as it had done, with such cataclysmic results, in the 1947–9 production drive. Righteously indignant, they felt that their efforts to restructure the business, to lure American money to Britain and to make co-production deals with Hollywood, were being hampered all the way along the line by the union, which was keen on nothing so much as foisting 'restrictions, restrictions, restrictions' on the film trade; it was trying to 'keep Hollywood directors out of the country',[15] and to protect the short-term interests of its members, namely their jobs and working conditions, at the expense of the long-term future of the industry. They seemed to expect the union to lie back and calmly take its medicine – studio closures, lay-offs – however bitter, and expressed an ingenuous amazement when Elvin and his followers rejected their prescriptions. Davis, for one, was not interested in expanding production simply to create jobs. He reckoned that 'creative talent' was in short supply, and what little of it there was had to be carefully harnessed. As he put it in the 1954 *Financial Times Annual Review of British Industry*:

> The production of a film is essentially creative and artistic, its success or failure lies in the producer's ability to weld the story and cast into an acceptable piece of entertainment for the masses. To be success-ful, a nice balance has to be struck between the commercial and artistic requirements.[16]

While he was certainly more meddlesome than Rank had been – any putative project needed to be approved by him in person – and while he was inclined to favour the formulaic over the original, there is little doubt that he was committed to maintaining at least some skeletal semblance of British film production, however haphazard and offensive to his accoun-tant's sensibility it might be. Havelock-Allan sums up Davis succinctly:

> A very fine businessman. He disliked the film business. It was against his training and all his attitude towards life. He was an extremely efficient man: the whole process seemed to him a very inefficient process, which indeed it is: it is as efficient as painting a picture. Anything that is a prototype – and every film is a prototype – is extremely inefficient.[17]

Under his tutelage, the 'very inefficient process' of filmmaking was streamlined, and producers were encouraged to tailor their wares to 'public demand', or at least Davis's perception of it. With one or two exceptions, such as Preminger's *The Man with the Golden Arm*, which were exempted on grounds of quality, the Rank Organization was wary about showing any of the new 'X' films in its cinemas. ('X' certificates had been introduced by the British Board of Film Censors in May 1950.) The family audience was put on a pedestal. As Davis continually made clear, he expected his filmmakers to cater for its needs and demands. Anything divisive that threatened family harmony or introduced grim 'realistic' elements which might be off-putting in the suburbs, was treated with an ill-disguised fear and contempt. Britain's new wave of the late 1950s, the angry brigade, filmmakers such as Lindsay Anderson, Tony Richardson, Karel Reisz and John Schlesinger, who meandered into the mainstream via Oxbridge, *Sequence* magazine, *Sight and Sound* and the 'Free Cinema',[18] earned Davis's particular opprobrium. Although Rank put up some of the money for Anderson's debut feature, the 'northern' – Britain's equivalent of the western[19] – *This Sporting Life*, in 1963, Davis did all he could to repulse the young turks:

> I do think that independent producers should take note of public demand and make films of entertainment value. The public has clearly shown that it does not want the dreary kitchen sink dramas.[20]

British film production of the 1950s, and Rank's output in particular, is held in very low esteem by the majority of film historians, who are wont to lump every film made in the decade together and then dismiss the whole bland and sticky mess. Robert Murphy's recent, and otherwise admirable, account of *Sixties British Cinema* epitomizes this trend. In an early paragraph, Murphy observes that 'British Cinema of the 1950s has a reputation for stagnant complacency', and then goes on to refer to the 'safe, innocuous films made at Pinewood' (Murphy, 1992: 31 *et seq.*). Notions of 'prestige' or 'quality' cinema had indeed gone out of the window. Filmmakers were no longer likely to be tailoring their pictures for the critics or addressing the 'agonies of the time'. (Consumer affluence in the 'You've never had it so good' decade seemed to deter producers and directors from tackling issues of social or political pith and import. Exceptions, such as *Sapphire* and *Violent Playground*, which dabbled rather unconvincingly with the problems of racism and juvenile delinquency, prove the rule.) However, in spite of the low regard in which British film culture of the 1950s was held by contemporaries such as Lindsay Anderson, who savaged the complacency of British filmmakers in two bad-tempered, curmudgeonly articles, 'Stand up, stand up' (1956) and 'Get out and push' (1957), and is still held today by Robert Murphy and others, in 1954 Davis was able to announce that Rank's pictures were doing better abroad than ever before. Over half their overall receipts were coming from foreign markets. This was quite a turn-around from late 1949, when the Plant Committee had observed that it would be sensible 'to include *nothing* for overseas receipts' when estimating what the majority of British feature films would produce in the post-war period (Board of Trade, 1949: para. 54).

Admittedly, America remained well-nigh impenetrable, but the rest of the world was warming to Pinewood fare. Norman Wisdom, a case in point, attracted big audiences in the most unlikely of countries: apart from his following in South America, Iran, Holland and Hong Kong, he was, astonishingly, a huge hit behind the Iron Curtain, especially in Albania, Czechoslovakia and the Soviet Union. As the comedian recalls, his army vehicle, *The Square Peg*, was much admired in the Eastern Bloc:

> Actually, I went to the Moscow Film festival. It was probably 1962. All the other American artists and stars were there, and they were showing various films at cinemas in Moscow, normally holding 1,000 or 1,500 or 2,000 people. And they showed my film in a stadium with 10,000 people and it was packed. I give you my word of honour.[21]

Truffaut, famously, is on record as complaining that the British are 'temperamentally incapable' of making movies, and it was the 1950s he seemed to be thinking of when he made his remark.[22] Still, it is worth observing that neither *The 400 Blows* nor *Jules and Jim* were ever shown in Moscow soccer stadia. Whatever the shortcomings in the eyes of the critics of 'formulaic' British filmmaking in the decade, a glib dismissal of a batch of films that broached cinemas in every continent of the world is hardly satisfactory. This foreign success may have been partly attributable to the overseas distribution set-up spawned by Eagle-Lion in the 1940s and to Rank's well-oiled publicity and selling machinery, but there is no denying that there was an appetite for British pictures all over the world (with the exception of the USA), however quaint and superficial they seemed to their detractors in the Press.

The 1950s brought new hazards. There were troubles with Cinemascope: to the exasperation of Fox and Spyros Skouras, Rank and Davis refused to install stereophonic equipment in any but a handful of their theatres, and inclined more to Vistavision than to 'Scope when it came to wide-screen gauges.[23] Skouras insisted that his blockbuster *The Robe*, a Roman extravaganza featuring Victor Mature in a toga, couldn't possibly be shown without stereo sound. The ensuing row occasioned a brief parting of the ways, soon patched up, between Rank and his old allies.[24] Besides the problems with Cinemascope, there were teething difficulties with 3-D. An early try-out of the new dimension caused chaos in Ireland:

> Following the loss of 2000 polaroid spectacles during the first run of *Bwana Devil* at the Theatre Royal, Dublin, plans to show 3-D films in Rank's Irish circuit cinemas have been scrapped . . . this decision had been taken because patrons deliberately destroyed the glasses or had refused to surrender them.
>
> (*Kinematograph Weekly*, 25 June 1953, p. 10)

These unfortunate blips apart, the new, severely curtailed programme of fifteen or sixteen Rank-made – as opposed to 'independent' – films at Pinewood was relatively successful. In 1952, as the Rank Organization emerged from the gloomy vale of its crisis years, Davis insisted that he, like Mr Rank, held British cinema close to his heart:

> Mr Rank and I decided, when we were struggling with our own problems at the height of our own crisis, that come what may, we would not be turned from the course on which we had started – to support British film production.
>
> (Davis, addressing the British Film Academy, May 1952)

In a modest way, he was true to his word, although his commitment to production didn't extend to innovation or originality. Production, now, became little more than a side-show, a tiny chip off the block of the Rank Organization's overall activities: Davis was set on 'diversification'. Before looking at his various forays into the leisure and entertainment industries outside cinema, it is, however, necessary to sketch in greater detail the filmmaking activities of the group in the mid- to late 1950s, when the Davis 'aesthetic' determined which films would be made.

PRODUCTION AT PINEWOOD

> Earl St John was a wonderful old drunk. He got locked into some cellars over one weekend. He was quite happy. It was a whole weekend. And he was a boy from Alabama. He was a real deep south American. He was huge. He was six foot six. And heavy and handsome. He was a wonderful man. But he didn't quite fit into the British filmmaking tradition.
>
> (Betty Box describing Earl St John, chief of production at Pinewood)

The cheery and bibulous Louisiana showman Earl St John was in charge of production at Pinewood throughout the 1950s, and it is little wonder that the studios, under the thumb of a former exhibitor taking his orders from an accountant, should so warmly have embraced the 'family way', making good wholesome fun – clean entertainment – its ultimate goal.

St John's antics as a showman in the 1920s, when he was running Paramount's British circuit, were legendary within the industry. To announce forthcoming attractions, he used to leap on to the stage, brandishing a whip, dressed like a lion-tamer in pale trousers, long boots and an oversized cowboy hat. His most famous coup, one of which he was justly proud, was turning the Prince of Wales away from a half-empty cinema. (He rang the newspapers to inform them of this well-calculated snub. The incident was fanned by publicity, and audiences for the film that was playing instantly doubled.) St John, like a farmer in a desert, used to pray for rain, which he knew would send dampened customers scampering to the box-office to get out of the downpour. He was often to be found marching up and down the queues forming at rival cinemas, denigrating the films that spectators were waiting to see while extolling his own crop. As a production chief, though, his judgement, sometimes blunted by his fondness for alcohol, was not always acute. (Although he was responsible for putting Norman Wisdom under contract, he didn't consider that Dirk Bogarde had a career as a film actor.) As an American, he had a specialized knowledge of the likes and dislikes of US audiences, and was used by Davis, who still had a hankering to break into the States, to vet scripts and ensure that they were suitable for 'Yankee consumption'. (This infuriated filmmakers, who knew fine well that few of their pictures ever reached the USA and that such tinkering couldn't help their reception.) Many producers felt that St John was too ready to defer to Davis, that he didn't have the gumption to argue his own case at board meetings. Havelock-Allan, for one, was not very impressed:

> He did what Davis told him to. He was an American who had been in the exhibition business at Paramount. Nice man, but not creative at all, not imaginative. He just did what he was told.
> (From an interview with Anthony Havelock-Allan, by the author,
> London, 1991)

Others felt that he put up a plucky fight in trying circumstances and didn't deserve to be dismissed as a 'yes-man'. After all, extracting money or promises from Davis was often a forlorn task:

> He really did try and he really did fight for us, but we always resented it because sometimes he came back with bad news. The bearer of bad news always gets his head chopped off.[25]

WISDOM AND THE DOCTORS

St John had plucked Norman Wisdom, the former flyweight boxing champion of the British army in India and stalwart of the army concert party, from under the noses of arch-rivals ABC, who were also keen to sign up the comedian – Wisdom was already an established stage and TV star. St John put Wisdom on a standard 7-year contract, but nobody at the Rank Organization knew what to do with their new acquisition. Ronald Neame directed a screen test for Wisdom, and wasn't impressed with what he saw. (Wisdom had to tell a youthful Petula Clark that her eyes were 'light as gossamer'. This phrase didn't afford him much comic mileage.[26]) In the first year of his contract, 1952, Wisdom wasn't used at all. In his second year, he was put in a formulaic £125,000 comedy for which nobody entertained high hopes. (Memories of Sid Field, the comedian star of the million-pound fiasco *London Town*, which lost the Rank Organization a small fortune, still rankled, and Davis didn't want to repeat the same mistake with Wisdom.) *Trouble in Store* was previewed at the Odeon,

Camden Town, and almost immediately, as Wisdom recalls, it became apparent that the film was going to be a hit:

> I remember that I was standing in the foyer, waiting, as the various people, John Davis, Earl St John, etc. came in, and they said, 'Oh, good evening.' Some of them said, 'Hello.' It was almost a brush-off. Then I went in and watched the film. I watched the people's faces mostly. And I couldn't believe it! I was so lucky. They were screaming with laughter. And the same people came out, Davis, St John etc., and they said, 'Oh, hello darling! Oh, you are wonderful. We were so proud of you. Oh, we think the world of you,' and all this sort of thing.[27]

Everything about *Trouble in Store* appealed to Davis. Just 'a simple black and white picture with no frills, but a heart in the right place',[28] it was cheap, clean and phenomenally popular. The Rank Organization was quick to take advantage of the comedian and to try to repeat this unexpected initial success. Jack Davies, Wisdom's scriptwriter, and Hugh Stewart, producer of most of the Wisdom films, were inventive and resourceful filmmakers, but they constrained the comedian. Stewart remembers that Wisdom had a yearning for 'straight' roles – that he wanted to play Hamlet or the Hunchback of Notre-Dame. However, he was condemned always to be the 'gump',[29] the woebegone, lovable little fellow in the cloth cap: whether he played a janitor or a nurse, a soldier or a milkman, the Wisdom persona – that familiar blend of comedy and pathos – remained inflexible. *Trouble in Store* broke all-time records: at the thirty London Gaumont cinemas where it opened, its receipts exceeded the previous best weekly take by more than £9,000.

John Davis, always keen to bring factory principles to bear, was quick to latch on to a formula. He felt that the Wisdom pictures, sure-fire winners, cut down the element of risk inevitable in any feature film production and lessened his dependence on the creativity of producers and directors. Wisdom movies were not, to borrow Havelock-Allan's phrase, 'prototypes': each new edition was merely a modification of the previous model. The same can be said for Betty Box's 'Doctor' films, which enjoyed a similar run of success. Box had read Richard Gordon's novel *Doctor in the House* on the train, and had thought that it would make a good feature. As with *Trouble in Store*, *Doctor in the House* wasn't a project for which the Rank Board held very great hopes:

> The day I started shooting *Doctor in the House*, I got a telephone call from Earl St John – it was the Tuesday – I was seeing the first day's rushes – and he said, 'Betty, I went to a board meeting yesterday and they're very worried about *Doctor in the House* . . . they don't like hospital films and they don't like titles with "Doctor" in them and

they'd like you to change the title. They think £120,000 is too much to pay.'[30]

Box scrimped and saved, hiring James Robertson Justice, his red beard and booming, bellowing bass, for a tenth of what she would have had to pay for her original choice for the role of the surgeon, Robert Morley. Like *Trouble in Store*, what was seen by the studio as a relatively modest offering outperformed the various blockbusters (including *The Robe*) which were then on release:

> *Doctor in the House* has uprooted all records at the Odeon, Leicester Square. . . . What does this fantastic success signify? I suggest that a large part of the result is due to the buoyant youthfulness of the film. Here is freshness. Here is vitality.
>
> (*Kine Weekly*, 22 April 1954, p. 5)

As in Wisdom's case, there was an immediate attempt to standardize the magical formula and recapture the same audience for a host of sequels. In all, six 'Doctor' films were made. Success, Box recalls, became something of a burden: any subsequent project she and her director-in-tow, Ralph Thomas, put up to the board had to be 'paid for' with a reprise of the 'Doctor' series:

> I could go to John Davis any time. He was a very easy person to talk to. But after I had made *Doctor in the House*, I was always loaded with that. I'd say, 'Look, I've a lovely subject I want to make. It's called *No Love for Johnny* and it's a political story.' Davis would reply: 'Well, politics, mmmnnn . . . but I tell you what – if you make another "Doctor" film you can do that one as well.' I was stuck with all these 'Doctors' I had to do. If I would be the golden girl and make them a 'Doctor', I could do whatever else I liked. No, I didn't want to do them. But I did them willingly in as much as they made money.[31]

The 'Carry On' series, which Rank distributed from the outset but also produced from 1967 onwards[32] was similarly, and proudly, formulaic. (Hugh Stewart remembers that whenever he asked Peter Rogers, the series' producer, what he was working on, Rogers would reply, 'Same story, different title.'[33])

Apart from its own, rather homogenized brand of family film comedy, the Rank Organization was also investing in the 'exotic', in international epics such as *El Cid* and *55 Days at Peking*,[34] was trying to lure independent or Hollywood 'runaway' productions to Pinewood, and was making a few high-budget movies aimed at the world market itself. When Betty Box wasn't hard at work on the 'Doctor' series, she was liable to be on location abroad, perhaps in Canada (*Campbell's Kingdom*), or India (*The Wind Cannot Read*), or France (*A Tale of Two Cities*). Abortively attempting to emulate Korda's success of the mid-1930s with adventures set in the British colonies, the organization started to sponsor expensive 'easterns', the antithesis to the 'northerns' being shot by Anderson, Schlesinger and Richardson. One of the original Independent Producers, Marcel Hellman, contributed with *North-West Frontier*, a rousing if unwieldy blockbuster starring Kenneth More, Lauren Bacall and the Indian sub-continent, which set out to make a full use of Eastman color, Cinemascope and imperial history. As one critic wrote:

I guarantee when you get home your TV screen will never have looked so small.

On a similar 'international' tack, the ill-starred *Ferry to Hong Kong*, made in the same year – 1959 – boasted one of Orson Welles's more eccentric performances and allowed C.A. Lejeune to demonstrate, in her *Observer* column, that she was still as bilious as ever:

There are two ways to make films that may prove acceptable to the foreign market. One is to make them with such indigenous truth that they are bound to be recognized by persons of discernment everywhere . . . the other way is to make them with the cosmopolitan conformity of a picture-strip, using types and clichés of screen behaviour that will perplex nobody in any country.

There was no doubt in Lejeune's mind that *Ferry to Hong Kong* fell into the latter category. (The film anticipates the otiose all-star extravaganzas of the 1960s, the international co-productions splitting at the seams with European and American actors, with which the studios would try to realize all their assets at once, pictures like *The Yellow Rolls-Royce* and *The VIPs*, or the movies Rank made with major US companies, such as *Heroes of Telemark* with Columbia, or *The Ipcress File* with Universal.)
In embarking on international co-productions, Davis had the appearance of an amateur alchemist stumbling after an elusive elixir:

The story went round Pinewood that Davis looked over the biggest successes of the past five years and deduced that they had an exotic title, an American leading man and a continental director . . . he decided these were the elements which make a successful film and he came up with the *Ferry to Hong Kong* . . . it was a dire flop!
(From an interview with Donald Sinden, by the author, Chichester, 1992)

After the trials of *The Way We Live*, Jill Craigie had foregone directing, but was working intermittently as a scriptwriter at Pinewood, where she contributed treatments for *The Million Pound Note* and *Windom's Way*, both of which ran against the grain of Rank's 1950s production. *Windom's Way*, the story of an English doctor (Peter Finch) in a Far Eastern hospital, broached political themes and was quietly critical of British colonialism. As the *Tribune*'s critic observed:

> If a film from Pinewood had been solely concerned with such issues as these, it would have indicated nothing short of a revolution, including the abdication of Rank, the deportation of John Davis and the exile of Earl St John.[35]

Not only in its film production but in its publicity drives, the Rank Organization was striking a new 'international' note. There was the famous occasion in the mid-1950s when Davis and publicity supremo Theo Cowan led a delegation of British stars in an assault on the Venice Film Festival, and Diana Dors stole innumerable headlines with her mink bikini. Norman Wisdom recalls that Rank sent him all over the world to publicize his films.

In 1959, there was a brief attempt to revive the frontier spirit of Independent Producers Ltd and Two Cities when Richard Attenborough, Jack Hawkins, Bryan Forbes, Michael Relph, Basil Dearden and Guy Green, all prominent 'talents' of the day, combined to form Allied Filmmakers (AFM), a production and distribution group that received some financial backing from Rank. The idea behind the new co-operative had come from Sydney Box, but illness forced him to drop out. In *Hollywood, England*, Alexander Walker describes the terms AFM struck with Rank:

> AFM liaised with the Rank Organization, which promised them a guarantee of £143,000, while the National Provincial Bank, who were Rank's financiers, guaranteed advances to AFM producers for up to five times this sum, to £848,000 . . . the distribution fee charged was $27\frac{1}{2}$ per cent for the first year, 25 per cent the second year; and of this AFM took 5 per cent and Rank the rest.
>
> (Walker, 1974: 102)

Like Independent Producers Ltd before them, Allied Filmmakers were granted internal autonomy and total artistic control. Although some excellent films, notably the classic *Whistle down the Wind*, came from the group, Allied Filmmakers soon fragmented and fell apart, caught in the vortex of 1960s British film culture, which was still perversely lop-sided, tilted in the favour of exhibitors and distributors but not producers.

DAVIS DIVERSIFIES

With results bolstered by *Trouble in Store* and *Doctor in the House*, 1954 had indeed been a good year for the Rank Organization, one in which Davis and Rank recaptured their confidence in British filmmakers and again began to talk about selling a 'reasonable number' of British films to the USA. However, the year marked yet another false dawn. Attendances diminished rapidly in 1955 and 1956. Although the top British pictures continued to show up reasonably well in competition with their American counterparts – 'Of the twenty-four best programmes which played our two circuits,' Rank told his shareholders in 1956, 'no fewer than ten came from British studios'[36] – the ever-increasing impact of television was beginning to hurt. Rank admitted as much when, in a bid to maintain profits, he upped attendance prices while beginning to close theatres.

Davis was actively looking for ways to branch out and spread the company's risks so that it would not be overly dependent on box-office receipts. Already, a substantial part of the group's profits was coming from the obscurer recesses of the industry, from such things as reconditioning and modernizing cinemas. (In the short term, as managers sought to 'improve' their theatres, television actually helped Rank, who was handily placed to win the majority of the refurbishment contracts.) As the *Financial Times* noted in 1955:

> Film production and distribution accounted for only about one-tenth of Odeon's 1954–55 profits. Apart from film exhibition, the main contributor to group profits is the manufacturing interests – British Optical and Precision Engineers and Cinema-Television, which controls Bush Radio. Last year, these subsidiaries' profits represented 30 per cent of the group's total.[37]

In the autumn of 1956, in what at the time seemed a prudent, if not spectacular, piece of business, Davis made an arrangement with the Haloid Company, a New York outfit which made and marketed the 'Rectigraph photocopying machine, the Foto-Flo high speed photocopying machine, xero copying equipment and supplies, and photographic and photocopy papers and chemicals'.[38] Under the terms of the deal, a new company, Rank Xerox Ltd, would have the right to manufacture and market this photocopying equipment everywhere outside the United States. Rank Xerox took time to get into its stride: in the early years, the equipment had to be developed and tested and marketed, and profits were not spectacular. Gradually, though, Xerox began to pick up momentum, and pretty soon it was making money at an alarming rate: all of Rank's other activities, including his film-related interests, appeared utterly inconsequential by comparison with this new copy-juggernaut. (It was once famously remarked that an independent television franchise provided a 'licence to print money'. By the same token, Rank Xerox made money as fast as it could copy the paper to print it on.)

By the late 1960s, the Rank Organization was known in the City as a 'one-product company', and that product wasn't anything to do with movies. In 1965, Rank Xerox's profits had jumped to £8.25 million, while all the rest of the group's activities combined to yield only £4.4 million. By 1969, the discrepancy was even more flagrant. Rank Xerox, at £46 million, was contributing close to 90 per cent of the group's overall, pre-tax profits, which stood at £52.2 million. Although Davis sometimes seemed openly embarrassed that what had started as a film company had been eaten up by its own photocopying subsidiary, he was also relieved to see Rank Xerox performing well; several other of the group's forays into new fields, notably Rank Records Ltd, were crashing failures, and Davis's benighted attempt to establish a British renting outfit in the USA was abandoned after only eighteen months: Rank Film Distributors of America, as this brave new venture was christened in a blaze of chauvinistic publicity in 1957, pro-voked a statement to the shareholders from Lord Rank – ennobled in 1958 – that sounded uncannily like his leaden attempt, a decade earlier, to blame his production crisis on a lack of talent in the industry:

> When we commenced this venture we were prepared for inescapable development losses for two or three years. . . . Unfortunately, it became clear that there was no reasonable prospect of achieving a profitable operation within this initial period, and it was decided to terminate our losses.[39]

These losses must have been considerable. Rank refused to give details of how much had been squandered in this second repulsed assault on the American market.

To compress twenty years of Rank history into a page or two: 1958 witnessed a dramatic downturn in the rate of Hollywood production. With so few pictures available, Rank merged the Odeon and Gaumont chains together, thereby putting an even tighter squeeze on independents seeking circuit release for their movies. Although he and Davis protested that their fortunes were 'inescapably bound up with the cinema industry, in which by far the greater proportion of our capital is invested',[40] they were doing their utmost to reduce their commitment to film. As they saw it, shorter working weeks and increased spending power were bound to lead to an increased demand for 'leisure', even if in fields outside cinema, and their job was to identify profitable new ventures, whether they be ten-pin bowling alleys, dance halls, or motorway service stations. Although Rank's films continued to perform respectably overseas, and although the best of them competed on equal terms with Hollywood's offerings in the domestic market,[41] the haemorrhage in film audiences – the leak had turned into a flood from mid-1957 onward – meant that production was barely profit-able, despite some long-overdue tax relief. (ET, already down to 15 per cent of the box-office, would be abolished altogether in 1960.) In 1959, Rank had increased his share in Southern Television from 33.5 to 37.6 per cent, confirmation – if any were needed – that he didn't think films could continue to pay.

In the 1960s, Rank and ABC's stranglehold on British exhibition con-tinued unabated. There were fewer outlets than ever, and the circuits continued to favour either American blockbusters or films in which they themselves had a stake, rather than independent British pictures. As Robert Murphy observes, the growing centralization of the Rank exhibition set-up helped to destroy local character and initiative without necessarily improving efficiency. After the overhaul of the cinemas in the early 1950s, when the industry still harboured hopes of defeating television, 'showmanship' itself went into decline, and the cinemas were allowed to deteriorate:

> Rank and ABC continued to prove themselves poor stewards of the nation's cinemas. Their modernisation programmes were always too little and too late.[42]

When Rank died in 1972, British production was, if anything, in a more parlous state than it had been forty years before, when he entered the industry.

DAVIS THE OGRE

Tales of the high-handed philistinism of the Hollywood bosses in the studio era are legion, and have been faithfully recorded by that army of scribblers which has grafted itself on to the American film industry like a prosthetic limb. However, just as British cinema lags behind the States in the quantity and opulence of its products, its moguls are deemed a pretty second-rate lot by comparison with the Louis B. Mayers and Sam Goldwyns. Sir John Davis, though, who stayed on as president of the Rank Organization until 1983, when he was already well into his seventies, has acquired a reputation for ruthlessness that puts many of his transatlantic counterparts into the shade:

> Within the confines of the Rank Organization Sir John controls a regime with which it is difficult to find an analogy except in the Byzantine court of Josef Stalin. Executives appointed to the board seem to have found this promotion merely the prelude to dismissal from the company and managing directors summoned to a monthly meeting attended in fear that they would be next for the chopping block.
>
> (*Spectator*, 27 September 1975)

It is, perhaps, symptomatic of British film culture in the 1970s that more attention seemed to be paid to Davis, and various conspiracies which he was accused of hatching, than to the few films that the Rank Organization was making. For instance, Davis's clumsy sacking of his chief executive, Graham Dowson, in 1975, ostensibly because Dowson did not marry his longtime companion; his controversial acceptance of a £15,000 pay rise in 1974, when the Rank Organization was laying off workers; and his 'inclination to call men back to London for a fifteen-minute briefing, even if they are on a beach the other side of Europe' (*Sunday Mirror*, 17 September 1972): these are accorded more space in the cuttings about Davis kept on microfiche at the British Film Institute than are any of his interventions in the film industry. Davis's lingering influence in the Rank Organization was based on his position as a trustee of the Rank Foundation which, until comparatively recently, controlled a majority of the group's voting shares, and he showed extreme reluctance to give up the reins of power. None the less, without Davis's business acumen, the Rank Organization would quite possibly have collapsed in the wake of its 1949 crisis. In the early 1950s, he helped 'rescue' British film, even if the manner of his rescue stuck in the craws of the filmmakers, and even if twenty years later, he was reviled for destroying the industry as Rank's production portfolio contracted alarmingly.

END-NOTE

This survey of Rank and the British film industry has sought to give the reader an idea of the range of activities the Methodist magnate was involved in; to move the focus away from the films themselves, and to look at the debates – social, economic and political – that were going on behind the screen. In hindsight, it seems half comic, half tragic, that all Rank's efforts to set the British industry on its feet should spawn nothing more than a photocopying company and a leisure conglomerate. Bingo halls and casinos help prop up a company which emerged from Methodist halls and Sunday schools.

To end on an appropriately bathetic note: without J. Arthur Rank's intervention, the British film industry, as I hope this book suggests, would have been in a far worse state, and might even have collapsed and folded in the mid-1940s, when he was the dominant influence in every sphere of British film culture. He remains the single figure in British film history who, however fleetingly, managed to create a fully fledged 'combine', not only providing continuity of employment for technicians, but allowing filmmakers an unheard-of licence, both creatively and in terms of budget. There was indeed 'Methodism in his madness'; there is no denying the benevolent effect he had on the industry in the immediate post-war years. For this, if nothing else, he deserves to be remembered as more than a mere appendage, a 'Mr Money Bags', in the ongoing, celebratory narra-tives of producers ranging from Korda to Puttnam, from Wilcox to Balcon. As Balcon himself observed, on the occasion of Ealing's twenty-first anniversary:

> No list of our blessings would be complete without mention of Mr J. Arthur Rank, Mr John Davis, and all the members of their Organization.[43]

GLOSSARY
SOME RANK FIGURES

BOND, RALPH Prominent ACT member and author of a stinging attack on Rank, *Monopoly* (1946). Born in 1906, Bond entered the industry in 1928. He became a producer, specializing in documentaries. Among his credits were *Today We Live*, *Unity is Strength* and *Power in the Land*.

BOX, BETTY Born Beckenham, Kent, 1920. Started her career as a commercial artist. During the Second World War, she was invited by her brother Sydney Box (q.v.) to join him in producing training, propaganda and documentary films for the war effort. These were made on behalf of the Ministry of Information, the War Office and the British Council. By the end of the war, Box had more than ten units working for her. She went with her brother to Gainsborough in 1946, where she took charge of production at Islington Studios. Among her many films in this period were *Miranda* (1948), directed by Ken Annakin, and several pictures in the popular 'Hugget' series. In 1950, she formed a partnership with director Ralph Thomas. Together, Thomas and Box made pictures at Pinewood throughout the 1950s and 1960s. Box's greatest success was with the 'Doctor' series. She also shot films on location in Canada, India and France, and prided herself in bringing her projects in on budget and on schedule. She was resolutely unpretentious. As she told *Cinema-TV* in 1974: 'I don't think film is a medium for social statement. Its *raison d'être* is to entertain. I don't think the mass audience is interested in films of social significance.' Her philosophy is shared by her husband Peter Rogers, producer of the 'Carry On' series, who worked early in his career for Rank's religious films outfit, GHW.

BOX, SYDNEY Prolific writer/producer. Born London 1907. Playwright, journalist and film publicist in the 1930s (he wrote an early volume [1937] on *Film Publicity*). Set up Verity Films in Drury Lane, London at the start of the Second World War and made a myriad propaganda and documentary shorts for government agencies. Shot *29 Acacia Avenue* with money advanced by Rank. The film was shelved (Rank disapproved of the hint of pre-marital 'impropriety') before being picked up by Columbia. After the phenomenal success of *The Seventh Veil*, shot on a shoe-string at Riverside Studios, Box was lured to Gainsborough, and took his 'Company of Youth' (forerunner of the Charm School) with him. Replacing the Black–Ostrer regime, he set out to make a minimum of twenty-five films a year at Shepherd's Bush and Islington, and almost had a nervous break-down in the process. The films, made under duress, were generally undis-tinguished. Even prestige offerings like *The Bad Lord Byron* and *Christopher Columbus* were shoddy, second-rate affairs by comparison with the work of the Archers and Cineguild a few years previously. Was married to Muriel Box, a former continuity girl to Powell and Pressburger who was later to direct *Simon and Laura* and *Street Corner* for Rank in the 1950s. Racked with ill-health throughout the latter part of his life. In *Hollywood, England* Alexander Walker observes that Box was the moving spirit behind the forming of Allied Filmmakers, an attempt to recapture the glories of the Independent Producers Ltd days, 'but illness caused him to drop out just as the group established itself, on 30 September, 1959'. Box died on 1 June 1983, in Western Australia.

CARR, E. T. 'TEDDY'   Rank's super-salesman, at the helm of Eagle-Lion. Born Britain, 1896. Educated at Manchester Grammar School. Joined United Artists as manager of its Birmingham branch in 1920. By 1922, he was general sales manager of United Artists. Before becoming managing director of Rank's world sales outfit in 1944, he had risen to giddy heights: he was managing director of the United Artists export operation as well as a director of Odeon Theatres Ltd and Odeon Cinema Holdings Ltd. Rank paid him an astronomical salary, but the attempt on the world market proved a failure, and there was some confusion as to where Eagle-Lion's role began and where Rank Film Distributors' ended. Often, they seemed to step on one another's toes.

COLE, SIDNEY   Former vice-president of the ACT and a persistent critic of the Rank Organization in the pages of the ACT journal, the *Cine-Technician*, and the *Daily Worker*. Born London, 1908. Educated at the London School of Economics. Entered the film industry in the 1930s, and quickly became established as one of Britain's top editors. Accompanied Thorold Dickinson and Ivor Montagu on a filmmaking expedition to Spain in 1938, during the Spanish Civil War. Edited Dickinson's *Gaslight*. Supervising editor for British National, Leslie Howard and Ealing. Associate producer at Ealing in the 1940s. In the 1950s, he moved into television, producing the popular 'Robin Hood' series.

CORFIELD, JOHN   Born Liverpool, 1893. Responsible for introducing Rank to Lady Yule (q.v.) and setting in motion the chain of events at British National which led his two patrons to finance *The Turn of the Tide*. A director of Pinewood Studios. After Yule and Rank went their separate ways in 1937, he stayed with Yule, helping to oversee British National's production programme.

COWAN, THEO   Born Letchworth, Hertfordshire, 15 November 1917. Left the army in 1945 with the rank of colonel. Joined the Rank Organization, gradually working his way up the outfit till he became deputy director of publicity. Expert at promoting stars and starlets and handling their affairs. When he died in September 1991, his obituary recalled a famous expedition he led to Europe in the mid-1950s: 'Cowan escorted a group of Rank artistes including Donald Sinden, Jack Hawkins, Belinda Lee, John Gregson, Diana Dors, James Robertson Justice and Eunice Grayson to the Venice Film Festival. Thanks in no small part to Cowan's judicious liaison between the bevy of stars and the Press, the publicity that resulted for the British contingent was unrivalled. It involved the inadvertent assistance of the Mediterranean Fleet and – on a more personal level – Diana Dors creating a sensation by appearing in a mink bikini.' Cowan left Rank to set up on his own in 1963.

CRAIGIE, JILL   Director. Made *Out of Chaos*, a wartime documentary about Henry Moore and the blitz. A protégée of Del Guidice, she was commissioned at the end of the war to make *The Way We Live* for Rank, much to John Davis's chagrin. Later she directed *Blue Scar* with money from the National Coal Board. Screenwriter for Rank in the 1950s, scripting *The Million Pound Note* and *Windom's Way*. Formerly married to Jeffrey Dell, screenwriter/novelist/producer, author of the 1930s satire on Korda and the British film industry, *Nobody Ordered Wolves* (1939).

CROYDON, JOHN   Ran Rank's 'B' picture Highbury Studios, 1947–9. Born London, 3 November 1907. Became location accountant for Gainsborough Studios, 1931; assistant studio manager for Gaumont-British, 1932–5; construction manager for MGM British, 1937–9; production manager for Irving Asher Productions, 1939–40; associate producer, Ealing Studios, 1943–7 (involved with films ranging from *Dead of Night* to *Champagne Charlie* and *Nicholas Nickleby*). After Highbury Studios closed down, he became production supervisor at Coronado Productions.

DAVIS, SIR JOHN   Born 10 November 1906. Educated at the City of London School. Davis was appointed secretary and accountant to the Odeon Group by Oscar Deutsch in 1937, and stayed with Odeon when

Rank acquired the company after Deutsch's premature death in 1941. Soon became managing director of the Rank Organization, and eventually chairman. From 1952 onwards, when Rank's brother died and Rank took over the reins of the family flour business, he was effectively running the Rank Organization. Renowned as a workaholic and for his occasional ruthlessness, he was behind the 1956 deal which led to the setting-up of Rank Xerox, soon to be far and away Rank's biggest money-spinner. Always a controversial figure. When he finally retired as Rank chief in 1983, Kenneth Fleet wrote in the *Daily Express*: 'the tragedy is that, except in all too brief spells, Rank has shown itself incapable of reinvesting those [Xerox] millions with much acumen or of managing its own cinema, leisure and industrial operations with much skill. For Rank's decline, John Davis must take the blame.' None the less, Davis was responsible for steering the Rank Group out of the financial morass in which it found itself in the early 1950s. When Davis died on 27 May 1993, aged 86, *The Times* remembered him thus: 'An ebullient, dictatorial figure who acknowledged four marriages but was reputed to have entered into six, Davis ruled the Rank Organization as a personal fiefdom and was directly responsible both for its successes and failures. He was loathed as much as he was admired and was notorious for the way he bossed around the Rank Organization's contract film stars and starlets; and for the cold-blooded manner in which he axed executives (*The Times*, Obituaries, 29 May 1993).

DEL GIUDICE, FILIPPO Born Trani, Italy, 1892. Studied at Rome University. Established a successful law practice. Left Italy in 1932 and fled to Britain to escape the Fascist regime. Gave Italian lessons before re-establishing his law practice in London and entering films as a contract lawyer. In 1937, with Mario Zampi, he formed Two Cities Films, which was later absorbed into the Rank Organization. In 1948, after leaving Two Cities, he set up Pilgrim Films, which sponsored pictures such as *The Guinea Pig* (the Boulting brothers), *Private Angelo* (Peter Ustinov) and *Chance of a Lifetime* (Bernard Miles). Died Florence, 31 December 1962.

DEUTSCH, OSCAR Born Birmingham, 1893. Son of a prosperous Hungarian scrap metal merchant. Entered the film industry in 1921, when he invested in W & F Film Services, a company which was later to grow into Gaumont-British. Founder of the Odeon chain. Deutsch was a deeply religious man who shared Rank's commitment to entertaining and educating children. When he died in late 1941, Rank inherited a large and prosperous circuit, the cornerstone of the Rank film empire.

DODDS, OLIVE During the Second World War, Dodds worked for Donald McCulloch, chairman of the Brains Trust. After experience as Bernard Miles's assistant on *Tawny Pipit*, she joined the Rank

Organization as second-in-command to David Henley, head of the Contract Artists Department, in 1945. She eventually took over from Henley, and stayed with Rank till 1960: 'David Henley left because they couldn't afford him. And I took over because they could afford me. By the time I left, they were dropping all the contract players unless they made a profit.' Dodds was administrator of the so-called Charm School. This was run by elocutionist and drama coach, Molly Terraine: 'Molly was very old-fashioned, a disciplinarian.' In the 1950s, once Balcon had joined the Odeon board, she supervised a change in the Rank policy towards contract actors, beginning to sign up character actors as well as leads.

FIELD, MARY   Born Wimbledon, 24 February 1896. Educated at Surbiton High School and Bedford College for Women, where she took her MA, gaining a distinction in Imperial History. She worked briefly teaching history and English before returning to university as a research scholar (she quickly became an expert on the Newfoundland fishing industry). Worked at Welwyn Studios as a continuity girl for Anthony Asquith. By the late 1920s, she was producing 'Secrets of Nature' shorts for British Instructional Films. Briefly flirted with the feature industry, directing a comedy on London life, *Strictly Business*, before returning to Gaumont-British Instructional to produce more episodes of her ground-breaking nature series, which was now rechristened 'Secrets of Life'. In the Second World War, she made official documentary films for the Ministry of Information before being drafted by Rank to head Children's Educational Films (CEF). In 1950, when Rank wound up CEF, she served on the British Board of Film Censors. The following year, she became executive officer of the Children's Film Foundation, which was set up with Eady Fund money and of which Rank was an honorary president. In 1958, she became a supervisor of children's programmes for ABC Television. Retired from ABC in 1963 and died in Worthing in 1968. Field's distinctions were manifold. She received an OBE in 1951; was president of UNESCO'S International Centre of Films for Children; was a fellow of the Royal Photographic Society, the British Kinematograph Society and the British Film Academy. She gives a full account of her time at CEF in her memoir, *Good Company* (1952).

GILLIAT, SIDNEY   Born Edgeley, Cheshire, 1908. Entered films as a reader. Gag man and assistant to popular comedian Walter Forde. Joined Gaumont-British as a junior writer in 1930. Teamed up with Frank Launder to write some of the most popular films of the era, including *The Lady Vanishes* and *Night Train to Munich*. Established successful producing/directing partnership with Launder at Gainsborough Studios, under the aegis of Ted Black. In the early war years, Launder and Gilliat turned out such hits as *Waterloo Bridge* and *Millions Like Us*. Launder and Gilliat, the individual team, joined Independent Producers Ltd in 1944. Gilliat died in June 1994.

GRANTLEY, LORD (RICHARD NORTON)   Born London, 1892. In the 1920s worked for the bankers Kuhn, Loeb. Joined United Artists in 1930 and from 1931 to 1933 was in charge of British production for them. In 1933, joined the board of British and Dominion, Herbert Wilcox's outfit, which distributed through United Artists. In 1936, he was installed as the first managing director of Pinewood Studios and in 1937 formed Pinebrook to make co-operative films there and so keep the studios busy. From 1938 to 1942, he was executive director of Denham and Pinewood Studios. He was chairman of Film Producers Association and member of the Board of Trade Films Council, 1938–9. His experiences in the British film industry, curtailed by a near-fatal car accident in the late 1930s, are recounted in his memoir, *Silver Spoon* (1954).

HAND, DAVID   Rank's animation supremo. Born Planefield, New Jersey, 1900. Studied at Chicago Academy of Fine Arts. Worked for the pioneer animator John Randolph Bry. In 1919, he animated *Andy Gump*. In the 1920s, he worked as an animator and director with Max Fleischer on the 'Out of the Inkwell' series. Made instructional films for Eastman Kodak. Joined Disney in 1930. Animator and director on more than sixty cartoons, including some of the 'Mickey Mouse' and 'Silly Symphony' series. Worked as supervising director of the first-ever Disney feature-length cartoon, *Snow White and the Seven Dwarfs*; also on *Bambi*, and on one of Disney's most innovative pictures, *Victory through Air-Power*. From 1944 to 1950, he was in charge of Gaumont-British Animation. On Rank's behalf, Hand and two American colleagues, Roy Paterson and Ralph Wright, tried to lay the foundations of a fully fledged British animation industry, but came up against insurmountable obstacles (see pp. 131–6). After G-B Animation closed down, Hand wanted to make 'B' features at Merton Park Studios with British crews and his own backing, but the ACT objected to his desire to be both producer and director, which they said would aggravate unemployment. He returned reluctantly to the USA. Died in October 1986, aged 86, in San Luis Obispo, California.

HAVELOCK-ALLAN, ANTHONY   Born 1905. Early career in the music business. From 1934 to 1937, worked as a producer for Paramount and for British and Dominion, becoming Richard Norton's second-in-command at Pinewood Studios. Joined with Filippo Del Giudice to produce *Unpublished Story* and *In Which We Serve*. Formed Cineguild with David Lean and Ronald Neame in 1943, and made films at Rank for

Independent Producers Ltd before quitting to form his own group, Constellation Films. Also produced pictures at Pinewood in the 1950s.

MINNEY, R. J.   Producer/journalist. Born Calcutta, 1895. Fiercely critical of the Rank experiment in his 1947 book *Talking of Films*. Producer under Maurice Ostrer at Gainsborough Studios in the early to mid-1940s, working on such projects as *Madonna of the Seven Moons*, *The Wicked Lady*, *The Magic Bow* and *Idol of Paris*. He edited *Everybody's Sunday Magazine* and *Strand Magazine*. Author of *Clive of India* and *Carve Her Name with Pride* (the story of Violette Szabo) and a biography of Anthony Asquith.

NOLBANDOV, SERGEI   Born 1895. Graduate in law, Moscow University. He co-wrote *Fire Over England*; was associate producer of *The Proud Valley* and *There Ain't No Justice*. Producer-in-chief of Rank's newsreel documentary series, 'This Modern Age'. Died 1971.

NORTON, RICHARD   *See* GRANTLEY, LORD

OSTRER, ISIDORE   Eldest of the Ostrer clan, which also included his brothers Mark and Maurice. President of Gaumont-British from 1929 till he sold out the vital shares in the Metropolis and Bradford Trust to Rank in 1941. In 1932, he had acquired control of Baird Television. Even before Rank's experiments with Cinema-Television, he pioneered close-circuit relays of boxing matches in West End cinemas, and also showed the 1939 Derby. Ventured into newspaper ownership, acquiring the *Sunday Referee* in 1931, and retaining control till it was merged with the *Sunday Chronicle* in 1939. Wrote several books on economic matters, including *Conquering Gold* (1932), which described the workings of the gold standard. Also published a volume of verse. Throughout his career, he remained chairman of the Lothbury Investment Corporation and the senior partner of the Ostrer Brothers merchant bank. Died in 1975, aged 86.

PASCAL, GABRIEL   Born Arad, Hungary, 4 June 1894. George Bernard Shaw's disciple, Pascal was one of the more flamboyant characters in British film history. He studied farming at the Hungarian National Economy College before serving as a lieutenant in the Hungarian Hussar Regiment in the First World War. He was briefly a member of the Imperial Burg theatre in Vienna before he formed his own company in Rome. Produced silent films in Italy. Was associated with the celebrated theatrical impresario Max Reinhardt. Began making his own films in Britain in 1936. After *Pygmalion* and *Major Barbara*, he struck a deal with Rank in 1943 for a three-picture programme, to comprise *Caesar and Cleopatra*, *St Joan* and *The Doctor's Dilemma*. *Caesar and Cleopatra*, made under the banner of Independent Producers Ltd, was the most expensive British film ever, and one of the most controversial. It was little wonder that the unions turned against Pascal, and Rank abandoned plans for the two sequels. As his wife Valerie Pascal recalls in her memoir, *The Devil and his Disciple* (1971), 'Gabriel was censured by the General Council of the Association of Cine-Technicians which ruled that he could work again in a British studio only under the severest of restrictions'. Pascal never did make another movie in Britain. His last picture, shot in Hollywood, was *Androcles and the Lion*. Died in 1954, aged 60.

RAWNSLEY, DAVID Born Sevenoaks, Kent, 1909. Production designer on innumerable British pictures, including *In Which We Serve* and *49th Parallel*, he was responsible for overseeing the development of Independent Frame, Rank's costly attempt at mechanizing film production.

ST JOHN, EARL Born Baton Rouge, Louisiana, 1892. Ran away from military academy in Alabama and, as legend has it, served as a pageboy to Sarah Bernhardt, who was touring the USA. Joined Mutual Film Company before the First World War and helped distribute early Chaplin pictures. In the 1920s, he was running Paramount's British circuit. When Odeon Theatres bought out Paramount Theatres in the UK, they inherited St John's contract. They kept him on. In 1939, he became personal assistant to John Davis. Was elevated to the position of production adviser to the Rank Organization in 1947, and from 1951 until his retirement in 1963 was Rank's executive producer, in charge of production at Pinewood.

WALKER, NORMAN Director of the film that lured Rank into the mainstream, *The Turn of the Tide*. An ex-army captain and industry veteran, who had been making films since the early 1920s, Walker served a stint as general manager of Denham and Pinewood Studios before becoming a director of GHW (Gregory/Hake/Walker), Rank's religious films outfit, for whom he directed the Technicolor religious epic *The Great Mr Handel*, most ambitious of all Rank's religious pictures.

WOOLF, C. M. The legendary and ruthless rentier of Wardour Street, Woolf was Rank's guide through the maze of the 1930s British film industry. At the start of the decade, he was working for Gaumont-British but in 1935 he split from the Ostrer brothers to form General Film Distributors (GFD). He had backing from Rank, and had been promised pictures to sell by *émigré* producer Max Schach, whose *Abdul the Damned* had been a runaway success at the British box-office, and Herbert Wilcox. However, when GFD was taken over by the General Cinema Finance

Corporation in 1936, he began to rely more and more on pictures from Universal. Died on New Year's Eve, 1942.

WYNNE, SYDNEY   Born London, 1909. In charge of publicity and PR at the Rank Organization in the post-war years. Special correspondent on the *Daily Herald*, 1934–8. Public relations officer with the gas industry, 1938–40. Director of public relations at the Ministry of Supply, and then recruited by the Rank Organization.

YULE, LADY   Eccentric philanthropist and millionairess who was active in the British film industry in the 1930s and 1940s. She inherited her money, an estimated £9 million, from her husband, Sir David Yule, who died in 1928. Sir David's fortune came principally from jute, but he was also a former director of the Midland Bank and a shareholder in the *Daily Chronicle*. Sir David and Lady Yule were first cousins. They married in 1900, and briefly lived together in Calcutta, where Sir David's business was based. The climate, however, didn't agree with Lady Yule, who contracted malaria, and refused ever again to spend prolonged periods in India. Lady Yule joined with Rank in forming British National in 1934, and helped finance *The Turn of the Tide* a year later. She was an original shareholder in Pinewood Studios, but sold her stake to Rank in 1937, at which time she bought out his interest in British National. Although she is sometimes credited with saving British film production at the start of the Second World War, when British National helped finance two Powell and Pressburger vehicles, her abiding interest in life was horses. She owned a stud farm in Hertfordshire, and was known as 'the fairy godmother of racehorses' because she refused to allow jockeys to use the whip on any of her animals. She kept her horses in great style. They had every modern comfort and convenience, including mechanically operated drinking troughs. British National ceased production in 1948. Lady Yule died in 1950, aged 76.

NOTES

INTRODUCTION OF FILM AND FLOUR

1 These notes are gleaned from the *Kinematograph Weekly*, 11 April 1946.
2 For further information about Bombadier Billy Wells and the body-builders who succeeded him as 'bangers' of the Rank gong, see Quentin Falk, *The Golden Gong* (London: 1985), and Geoffrey Macnab, 'Going, going . . . gone', *Sight and Sound*, January 1993.
3 Several of the figures I interviewed for this study, even those chary of the Rank Organization's influence on the British film industry, testified to the 'probity' and 'integrity' of J. Arthur Rank. This particular quote is taken from an interview with Sydney Wynne, formerly Rank's chief of publicity, London, September 1991.
4 For a discussion of David Low's debunking art, see A. J. P. Taylor, *English History 1914–1945* (Harmondsworth: 1976).
5 See Frederic Mullally (a.k.a. Henry Fullerton) in *Tribune*, 29 October 1943, for a typical attack on Rank.
6 See John Ellis, 'Art, culture, quality', *Screen*, Autumn 1978, for examples of criticisms of Rank in the 'quality press'.
7 See Angus Calder, *The People's War* (London: 1986), p. 367.
8 Quoted in a profile of Rank, *Time*, 19 May 1947.
9 This information about Rank's private life is taken from an interview with J. D. Hutchison, Rank's nephew and a former executive in the family flour business, London, July 1991.
10 ibid.
11 ibid.
12 From an interview with Rank's daughter, the Hon. Mrs Shelagh Cowen, London, September 1991.
13 ibid.
14 Quote taken from an interview with ex-Ealing editor and former vice-president of the ACT, Sidney Cole, London, September 1991.
15 See the first chapters of Charles Dickens, *Hard Times*, in particular the characterization of Mr Gradgrind.
16 Quoted in R. G. Burnett, *Through the Mill: The Life of Joseph Rank* (London: 1945), p. 108.
17 ibid., pp. 24, 25–34.
18 See Henry D. Rack, *Reasonable Enthusiast: John Wesley and the Rise of Methodism* (London: 1989), pp. 82–3, which quotes from Wesley's diaries of the late 1720s.
19 Glynn Hughes, *Yorkshire* (London: 1985), p. 68.

20 Rack, op. cit., p. 443.
21 Hutchison interview, op. cit.
22 Cowen interview, op. cit.
23 ibid.
24 Alan Wood, *Mr Rank* (London: 1952), p. 69.
25 Cowen interview, op. cit.
26 R. G. Burnett and E. D. Martell, *The Devil's Camera: Menace of a Film-Ridden World* (London: 1932), the opening dedication.
27 ibid., p. 9.
28 ibid., p. 10.
29 ibid., p. 12.
30 For examples of the Frankfurt School's disdain for mass culture, see Theodor Adorno's collection of essays, *Prisms* (London: 1967); Max Horkheimer, *The Eclipse of Reason* (London: 1947); and Leo Lowenthal, *Literature, Popular Culture and Society* (New York: 1961).
31 Adorno, op. cit., 'Perennial fashion – jazz', p. 127.
32 John Wesley, *A Short History of Methodism* (London: 1765), p. 11.
33 Adorno, op. cit., p. 123.
34 See Richard Hoggart's still influential *The Uses of Literacy* (London: 1958).
35 Burnett and Martell, op. cit., p. 16.
36 ibid., p. 15.
37 R. G. Burnett, *The Cinema for Christ* (London: 1934), p. 87. In the appendices the author offers a long list of films suitable for young people, including the short about Mussolini.
38 Quoted in Burnett, *Through the Mill*, p. 79.
39 See 'Rank Viewers' Reports', BFI Special Collection, held at the British Film Institute: 'During the early '30s, theatres now managed by Rank Leisure made a practice of viewing and reporting on every film offered to them. The reports were typed on to 8″ × 5″ cards and put into one gigantic alphabetical file' (BFI press release, 5 August 1982). Reports on approximately 15,000 titles, including *Cross Beams*, are in the collection. The viewers are as scathing about films made under Rank's banner as they are about any others.
40 Burnett, *Cinema for Christ*, p. 74.
41 Wood, op. cit., chapter on 'Religion and Lady Yule'.
42 ibid.
43 Information taken from an interview with Emeric Pressburger's grandson and biographer Kevin Macdonald, London, July 1991.
44 From a speech made by Norman Walker. The speech is quoted in the pamphlet for the Third Religious Film Summer School, *Religion in the Ordinary Cinema* (London: 1937), p. 14.
45 Cowen interview, op. cit.
46 From an interview with C. M. Woolf's son, Sir John Woolf, London, September 1991, in which he emphasized that Max Schach, the *émigré* producer, was responsible for persuading his father to 'set up on his own'. Schach promised to provide Woolf with pictures to distribute.

1 ON THE WAY TO AN EMPIRE

1 Quoted in *Kinematograph Weekly*, 26 November 1942, p. 24, as Rank sought to reassure his new shareholders that he held their best interests at heart.
2 Ralph Bond, *Monopoly* (London: 1946); see preface.
3 For a discussion of the state of British production in the 1930s, see Margaret

Street and Sarah Dickinson, *Cinema and State* (London: 1985); Jeffrey Richards, *The Age of the Dream Palace* (London: 1984); Rachael Low, *British Filmmaking in the 1930s* (London: 1985).

4 Michael Balcon, *A Lifetime of Films* (London: 1969).
5 Low, op. cit., pp. 199–208.
6 Richards, op. cit., pp. 34–45.
7 For a discussion of parallels between Dell's novel and Korda's set-up in the late 1930s, see Michael Powell, *A Life in Movies* (London: 1987).
8 James L. Limbacher, *The Influence of J. Arthur Rank* (London: 1971).
9 David Bordwell, Janet Staiger and Kristin Thompson, *The Classical Hollywood Cinema* (London: 1985), p. 314. The examination of 'The labor force, financing and mode of production' provides a useful point of reference for similar issues in the British industry of the 1920s and 1930s.
10 Richard Norton, *Silver Spoon* (London: 1954), p. 152. Norton (Lord Grantley) is an unusual figure in British film: he straddles the worlds of high finance – as a former banker at Kuhn, Loeb – and of film production: he knew Montagu Norman in both of his capacities.
11 See Herbert Wilcox's chatty autobiography, *25,000 Sunsets* (London: 1967), p. 107.
12 Quoted in *Kinematograph Weekly*, 15 December 1938, p. 1, in the wake of the film crisis.
13 Anthony Asquith's article, 'The tenth muse climbs Parnassus', *Penguin Film Review* 1, 1946: 17.
14 *Penguin Film Review* 4, 1946: 27–36. David Lean's piece is written to mark the release and reception of *Brief Encounter*.
15 ibid.
16 From an interview with Anthony Havelock-Allan, London, July 1991.
17 This phrase, apparently a cliché of the period, was used by Sydney Wynne, Rank's publicity chief in the 1940s, and quoted when interviewed by the author in London, September 1991.
18 John Russell Taylor, *Hitch* (London: 1978). Taylor discusses the strained relations between Hitchcock and Woolf in detail.
19 ibid.
20 ibid.
21 Havelock-Allan interview, op. cit.
22 *Kinematograph Weekly*, 6 January 1938, p. 7.
23 Norton, op. cit., p. 175
24 Low, op. cit., pp. 208–29.
25 Havelock-Allan interview, op. cit.
26 Norton, op. cit., p. 175.
27 ibid., p. 95.
28 Havelock-Allan interview, op. cit.
29 Norton, op. cit., p. 185.
30 Richards, op. cit., p. 37.
31 'Oscar and the Odeons', *Focus on Film* 22, 1975: 38–50, offers a useful survey of early Odeon history and Deutsch's part in it.
32 Tino Balio (ed.), *The American Film Industry* (New York: 1976a). See Douglas Gomery's essay, 'US film exhibition', pp. 218–28, in ibid.
33 See chapter 6 for a discussion of Rank's restructuring of the company and his disregard for Deutsch's 1937 promise to the shareholders not to involve Odeon in film production.
34 Tino Balio, *United Artists* (Madison, Wisc.: 1976b), pp. 221–4.

35 *Kinematograph Weekly*, 1 January 1942, p. 4.
36 Charles Barr (ed.), *All Our Yesterdays* (London: 1986). Robert Murphy's essay, 'Under the shadow of Hollywood', in ibid., p. 53, gives further information on the Gaumont-British takeover.
37 Low, op. cit., pp. 208–29.
38 *Kinematograph Weekly*, 26 February 1942, p. 3.
39 Low, op. cit., pp. 208–29.
40 Limbacher, op. cit., p. 19.
41 Norton, op. cit., p. 186.
42 ibid.
43 Patricia Warren, *Elstree: British Hollywood* (London: 1983).
44 From an interview with the Hon. Mrs Shelagh Cowen, London, September 1991.
45 From an interview with Sir John Woolf, London, September 1991.

2 WAR AND MONOPOLY

1 Winston Churchill, quoted in Angus Calder, *The People's War* (London: 1986), p. 15.
2 John Ellis, 'Art, culture, quality', *Screen*, Autumn 1978, pp. 42–7.
3 Roger Manvell, quoted in *Sight and Sound*, Spring 1946, p. 24.
4 ibid.
5 Ellis, op. cit., p. 44.
6 For a wider discussion of Rank's 'internationalism', see chapter 3.
7 Angus Calder, *Myth of the Blitz* (London: 1991). Calder talks of how the Battle of Britain has passed into popular myth, and now stands alongside St George, Arthur's Round Table and Botham's 1981 assault on the Australian bowling as a quintessential tale of Albion.
8 Quoted in a BBC documentary on *British Wartime Cinema*, broadcast in 1989 and presented by Christopher Frayling.
9 *The Pursuit of British Cinema* (London: 1984). Balcon was highly critical of Hitchcock for absconding to Hollywood at the outbreak of war. See Geoff Brown's essay, 'A knight and his castle', in ibid., p. 29.
10 Possibly an apocryphal story. Source: a telephone conversation with Nick Thomas, film historian and former editor of the St James Press *International Dictionary of Films and Filmmakers* in August 1991.
11 Michael Balcon, *A Lifetime of Films* (London: 1969).
12 *Kinematograph Weekly*, 9 January 1941, p. 30.
13 Calder, *People's War*, pp. 367–8, quotes from wartime social survey.
14 Guy Morgan, *Red Roses Every Night* (London: 1948a), p. 35.
15 *British Wartime Cinema*, op. cit.
16 Calder, *People's War*, p. 379.
17 ibid.
18 Calder, *Myth*.
19 Calder, *People's War*, p. 379.
20 Raymond Williams, *Keywords* (London: 1983). Williams charts the myriad different definitions of 'realism' across art and literature.
21 James L. Limbacher, *The Influence of J. Arthur Rank* (London: 1971), p. 10.
22 Motion Picture Herald, 2 February 1946.
23 From an interview with Anthony Havelock-Allan, London, July 1991.
24 Joel Finler, *The Hollywood Story* (London: 1988), section on Universal.
25 From an interview with Hugh Stewart, editor of *49th Parallel* and *The Man Who*

Knew Too Much, a leading figure in the Army Film Unit during the war and a key Rank producer at Pinewood in the 1950s, Denham, July 1991.

26 ibid.
27 From an interview with the Hon. Mrs Shelagh Cowen, London, September 1991.
28 For his study on *British Cinemas and their Audiences* (London: 1948), Mayer put an advertisement in *Picturegoer*, asking fans to respond to his questionnaire; the response was overwhelming.
29 *Kinematograph Weekly*, 11 January 1940, special supplement, p. G1.
30 *Picturegoer*, 16 March 1946, letters page.
31 See the opening of chapter 3 for a discussion of Rank and 'Sunday opening'.
32 Alan Wood, *Mr Rank* (London: 1952), p. 77.
33 David Bordwell, Janet Staiger and Kristin Thompson, *The Classical Hollywood Cinema* (London: 1985); see pp. 320–37 for a discussion of the Hollywood system.
34 Rank's leader in *The Times*, 25 January 1948, p. 4.
35 Michael Frayn in Michael Sissons and Philip French (eds), *The Age of Austerity* (London: 1986).
36 Havelock-Allan interview, op. cit.
37 Board of Trade, *Report of the Film Studio Committee* (London: 1948), para. 6; the so-called 'Gater' Report.
38 From an interview with Sidney Cole, London, September 1991.
39 Korda quoted in 'Conference on post-war trends of the British film industry', *Cine-Technician*, November–December 1943, p. 124.
40 Rank, quoted in *Kinematograph Weekly*, 24 August 1944, p. 4.
41 Margaret Street and Sarah Dickinson, *Cinema and State* (London: 1985).
42 Korda, quoted in *Cine-Technician* op. cit.
43 Board of Trade *Tendencies to Monopoly in the Cinematograph Films Industry*, (the Palache Report) (London: 1944).
44 Rank, quoted in *Cine-Technician*, November–December 1943, p. 124.

3 TILTING AT THE WORLD MARKET

1 Reported in *Kinematograph Weekly*, 3 October 1940.
2 From an interview with Betty Box and Peter Rogers, Beaconsfield, July 1991.
3 ibid.
4 ibid.
5 Dr Kalmus and his wife Natalie, who evolved Technicolor by superimposing two-colour images on top of each other, and developed the system into a 'three-color' process, insisted on being credited as 'color consultants' on every Technicolor film made between 1933 and 1949, the expiration date of their patent. Technicolor wasn't, therefore, widely used in Britain during the 1940s. It was awkward and expensive anyway, with the equipment in short supply. Castleton Knight's newsreel record of the XIVth Olympiad in London in 1948, *The Glory of Sport*, one of the Rank Organization's most ambitious Technicolor projects, commandeered equipment from Launder and Gilliat's *The Blue Lagoon* and David Macdonald's *Christopher Columbus*, which were then shooting – there simply weren't enough Technicolor cameras to go round.
6 For a discussion of Hollywood's 'celluloid imperialism', see Thomas Guback's essay 'Hollywood's international market', in Tino Balio (ed.), *The American Film Industry* (New York: 1976a), pp. 387–410.

7 Walter Benjamin, 'The work of art in the age of mechanical reproduction', in his *Illuminations* (London: 1982).

8 Guback, op. cit.

9 Alan Sked and Christopher Cook, *Post-War Britain* (London: 1984), p. 26.

10 Quoted in the film *Kings of the Road*, directed by Wim Wenders, 1976.

11 Margaret Street and Sarah Dickinson, *Cinema and State* (London: 1985), pp. 10–30, gives precise statistics.

12 ibid., p. 11.

13 ibid., p. 12.

14 Stephen Tallents, quoted in Philip Taylor, *Projecting Britain* (London: 1981), p. 121.

15 *Kinematograph Weekly*, 16 October 1941, p. 4.

16 Arthur Lucan had a surprising success as 'Old Mother Riley'. The series lasted from the late 1930s right through until 1952, when he/she took her bow in a grand finale co-starring Bela Lugosi.

17 The 1938 Films Act set lower quota requirements: this encouraged foreign investment in the industry but led to lower domestic levels of production.

18 Steve Woolley, head of Palace Pictures, quoted in Duncan Petrie's PhD thesis, 'Creativity and Constraint in British Cinema', University of Edinburgh (Sociology Department): 1990; published under the same title (London: 1991).

19 Bruce Austin, *Immediate Seating: A Look at Movie Audiences* (Belmont, Calif.: 1989).

20 Taylor, op. cit., p. 75.

21 ibid., p. 70.

22 ibid., p. 87.

23 ibid., pp. 70–5.

24 ibid., p. 70.

25 Red Kann's editorial from *Motion Picture Herald*, August 1947.

26 ibid.

27 Michael Balcon, quoted in *Kinematograph Weekly*, 11 January 1945, p. 163.

28 From an interview with Hugh Stewart, Denham, July 1991.

29 Sidney Cole, quoted in *Cine-Technician*, November–December 1943, p. 122.

30 Quote attributed to Winston Churchill.

31 Stewart interview, op. cit.

32 From an interview with Sidney Cole, London, September 1991. Cole explained that in the period leading up to *Gaslight*, he had been working with a film unit, including Thorold Dickinson and Ivor Montagu, shooting in Spain during the Civil War.

33 *Variety*, 12 February 1947: interview with Carol Reed.

34 *Motion Picture Herald*, spring 1932, review of the Gaumont-British picture, *Ghost Train*.

35 See *Picturegoer*'s letters pages from 1944 onward. The fans' mail is always sparky and contentious.

36 John Russell Taylor, *Strangers in Paradise* (London: 1983).

37 From an interview with Pinewood casting director Weston Drury, Windsor, October 1991. (To complicate matters, Drury's father, also called Weston Drury, preceded him as a casting director, working with Korda and Rank.)

38 Korda, quoted in Karol Kulik, *Alexander Korda: The Man Who Could Work Miracles* (London: 1975).

39 Paul Swann, *The Hollywood Feature Film in Post-War Britain* (London: 1987), p. 95.

40 A United Artists poster advertising the US release of *The Life and Death of*

Colonel Blimp.

41 Richard Norton, *Silver Spoon* (London: 1954), p. 69. Norton describes his problems selling Herbert Wilcox's pictures in the United States.
42 Frank Launder, quoted in *Kinematograph Weekly*, 8 April 1948, p. 14.
43 David Rose, quoted in *Kinematograph Weekly*, 27 January 1944, p. 5.
44 These figures are taken from notes made by the author at a lecture given by Ruth Vesey for the John Logie Baird Centre, University of Glasgow, spring 1990, on how Hollywood adapted its pictures for foreign consumption.
45 Guback, op. cit., pp. 387–410.
46 Information on Rank's 1945 trip to Hollywood is taken from James L. Limbacher, *The Influence of J. Arthur Rank* (London: 1971) and from *Kinematograph Weekly* and *Picturegoer* pieces by W. H. Mooring throughout July and August 1945. The quote comes from *Kinematograph Weekly*, 26 July 1945, p. 16.
47 W. H. Mooring in 'Rank puzzles Hollywood', *Picturegoer*, 4 August 1945.
48 Limbacher, op. cit., p. 10.
49 Red Kahn, *Motion Picture Herald*, July 1947.
50 George Elvin, *Kinematograph Weekly*, 27 September 1945, p. 36.
51 Rank, *Kinematograph Weekly*, 11 January 1945, p. 35.
52 Ronnie Neame, back from a fact-finding mission in the USA, quoted in *Kinematograph Weekly*, 6 June 1946, p. xv.
53 Robert Murphy, 'Rank's attempt on the American market', from James Curran and Vincent Porter (eds), *British Cinema History* (London: 1983), p. 167.
54 Norton, op. cit., p. 70.
55 Letter from Godwell Sears to Jack Warner, 14 August 1939, quoted in Rudy Behlmer, *Inside Warner Brothers* (New York: 1985), p. 100.
56 Tino Balio, *United Artists* (Madison, Wisc.: 1976b), pp. 196–201.
57 ibid.
58 ibid.
59 ibid.
60 *Kinematograph Weekly*, 17 February 1944.
61 ibid.
62 *Manchester Daily Dispatch*, 11 February 1944.

4 RANK AND HIS PRODUCERS

1 From an interview with Anthony Havelock-Allan, London, July 1991.
2 Dallas Bower's piece 'No celluloid utopia' appeared in *New Statesman*, 2 September 1944.
3 From an unpublished memo on Independent Producers Ltd written for the author by Sidney Gilliat, 22 May 1991.
4 Michael Powell, *A Life in Movies* (London: 1987), p. 670.
5 From an unpublished memo on 'Production Facilities (Films) Ltd' – Piffle – by F. J. Gilbert, formerly managing director of the outfit, in the BFI Special Collection.
6 Angus Calder, *The People's War* (London: 1986), p. 131.
7 Havelock-Allan interview, op. cit.
8 BBC documentary on *British Wartime Cinema*, broadcast in 1989 and presented by Christopher Frayling.
9 Havelock-Allan interview, op. cit.
10 Charles Barr (ed.), *All Our Yesterdays* (London: 1986), p. 1. Barr examines Ray and Truffaut's assertions that Britain and film do not go together.

NOTES

11 Board of Trade, *Tendencies to Monopoly in the Cinematograph Films Industry* (the Palache Report) (London: 1944), paras. 11–15.
12 Guy Morgan, 'Cash down and no credit', *Penguin Film Review* 6, 1948b: 17.
13 Havelock-Allan interview, op. cit.
14 From a profile of Del Giudice by John Barber, *Leader Magazine*, 21 June 1947.
15 Alan Wood, *Mr Rank* (London: 1952), pp. 128–44.
16 Del Giudice quoted in *Kinematograph Weekly*, 25 February 1943, p. 27.
17 For example, figures such as Michael Foot, Ralph Bond, Ivor Montagu, Sidney Cole and Frederic Mullally.
18 From an interview with Sir John Davis, London, June 1990, when he reminisced about Del Giudice, whom he held in very low regard.
19 See Michael Sissons and Philip French (eds), *The Age of Austerity* (London: 1986), for essays on the period.
20 Susan Cooper, 'Snoek piquante', in ibid., p. 35.
21 Harold Wilson, *Memoirs: The Making of a Prime Minister* (London: 1986), p. 104.
22 Josef Somlo, an Austrian *émigré*, later sacked from Two Cities himself, had been associated in the 1930s with Victor Saville Productions.
23 For extensive discussion on *The Way We Live*, see chapter 5, pp. 157–60.
24 Gilbert memo, op. cit.
25 Before being jettisoned from Two Cities, Del Giudice used every available platform to express his philosophy about film: see the *Daily Film Renter* or *Kinematograph Weekly*, 1944–7 for examples.
26 From an interview with Jill Craigie, Hampstead, June 1991, in which she suggested that Davis corrupted Rank's 'soul'. Craigie was one of Del Giudice's protégés, and held Davis in very low esteem.
27 A typical accountant's quote from Davis, *Kinematograph Weekly*, 11 April 1946, p. 4.
28 *Kinematograph Weekly*, 18 September 1947, p. 8.
29 Davis interview, op. cit.
30 Barber, op. cit.
31 Peter Price, 'The impresario urge', *Sight and Sound*, November 1950: 292.
32 Barber, op. cit.
33 Emeric Pressburger's diaries, January–March 1942; courtesy of Kevin Macdonald. The diaries are now in the British Film Institute.
34 Howard played the Scarlet Pimpernel, perhaps his quintessential role, for Korda.
35 *Kinematograph Weekly*, 6 August 1942, p. 3.
36 From 'Agreement Between Independent Producers Limited and General Film Distributors Ltd', drawn up by Richards, Butler & Co. in December 1942; courtesy of Kevin Macdonald.
37 ibid.
38 Powell, op. cit.
39 ibid.
40 George Perry, *Movies from the Mansion* (London: 1976), p. 93.
41 Gilliat memo, op. cit.
42 ibid.
43 ibid.
44 Havelock-Allan interview, op. cit.
45 Gilbert memo, op. cit.
46 From an interview with Betty Box, Beaconsfield, July 1991.

47 Adair's snipe is taken from his obituary for Ian Dalrymple, *The Times*, April 1989.
48 John Ellis, 'Art, culture, quality', *Screen*, Autumn 1978.
49 ibid.
50 Richard Winnington's drawings and criticism were collected in *Drawn and Quartered* (London: 1948); see p. 94.
51 ibid.
52 Gilliat memo, op. cit.
53 Havelock-Allan interview, op. cit.
54 From an interview with Hugh Stewart, Denham, July 1991.
55 From an interview with Oscar-winning special effects maestro Charles Staffell, Pinewood, September 1991.
56 Havelock-Allan interview, op. cit.
57 Ray Lewis, *Moving Picture Digest*, December 1946.
58 *Variety*, February 1947.
59 From Rank's Viewers' Reports (see Introduction, note 38).
60 From a contemporary report in the *Welwyn Times*, quoted in a letter written to the author by film historian Nick Thomas, August 1991.
61 Quoted in *Halliwell's Film Guide*, 6th edn (London: 1979), entry on *Caesar and Cleopatra*.
62 ibid., entry on *London Town*.
63 *Kinematograph Weekly*, 7 November 1946, p. 28, reveals that the Americans will delete sequences, trim, and add scenes of their own before releasing *London Town*.
64 Rank, quoted in *Kinematograph Weekly*, 7 June 1948, p. 8.
65 *Kinematograph Weekly*, 13 February 1947, p. 3.
66 From a transcript of an interview with Sidney Gilliat lent to the author by Kevin Macdonald, in which Gilliat rails against the iniquities of the Piffle Stories Department.
67 Staffell interview, op. cit.
68 Gilliat memo, op. cit.
69 Havelock-Allan interview, op. cit.
70 Gilbert memo, op. cit.
71 Gilliat memo, op. cit.
72 In the eyes of *Tribune* journalists, excess profits tax was used by the Rank Organization as an excuse for profligacy. By running up costs and cutting down profits, they denied the Exchequer its dues.
73 Havelock-Allan interview, op. cit.
74 Gilliat memo, op. cit.
75 Steven Silverman, *David Lean* (London: 1989), p. 89.
76 David Lean, 'Brief Encounter', *Penguin Film Review* 4, 1947: 37.
77 ibid.
78 Havelock-Allan interview, op. cit.
79 ibid.
80 Gilliat memo, op. cit.
81 The National Film Finance Corporation, which advanced a small fortune to British-Lion – Korda's distributors – was formed in the wake of the 1948 Cinematograph Act. For an analysis of circumstances surrounding its inception, see Margaret Street and Sarah Dickinson, *Cinema and State* (London: 1985).
82 Gilliat memo, op. cit.
83 Powell, op. cit.

84 Charles Barr, *Ealing Studios* (London: 1977).
85 Geoff Brown, 'A knight and his castle', in *The Pursuit of British Cinema* (London: 1984).
86 Quote made by Balcon to John Ellis, cited in 'Made in Ealing', *Screen*, spring 1975: 119, in which Sir Michael explains the voting patterns of his staff in 1947.
87 Betty Box interview, op. cit.
88 Stewart interview, op. cit. Stewart recalls that Balcon tried to foist an inept director, Slim Hand, on him for a film he was producing, just so that Ealing could be rid of Hand.
89 Brown, op. cit.
90 Roger Manvell, *Penguin Film Review* 4, 1947.
91 ibid.
92 Balcon to Ellis, op. cit. Balcon remembers his sojourn at MGM without affection.
93 Balcon quoted in *Kinematograph Weekly*, 14 January 1943, p. 49.
94 Kenneth Tynan, 'Ealing', *Films and Filming*, November 1955: 4.
95 From an interview with Olive Dodds, former head of Contract Artists at Rank, London, July 1991.
96 From an interview with Sidney Cole, London, September 1991. Cole was, and remains, deeply suspicious of Ealing's deal with the Rank Organization. He certainly doesn't share Balcon's point of view that Ealing was offered a 'model contract'.
97 Brown, op. cit.
98 John Davis, quoted in George Perry, *Forever Ealing* (London: 1981).
99 Ellis, 'Art . . .'.
100 Ray Seaton and Roy Martin, 'Gainsborough Studios', *Films and Filming*, May 1982: 11.
101 ibid.
102 Dilys Powell, quoted in the BFI dossier 'Gainsborough Melodrama'; see Robert Murphy and Sue Aspinall (eds) *Gainsborough Melodrama*, London, 1983.
103 Pam Cook in the BFI dossier 'Gainsborough Melodrama'; see ibid.
104 ibid.
105 Gilliat, in a letter to the author, June 1991.
106 From an interview with the Hon. Mrs Shelagh Cowen, London, July 1991.
107 Sue Aspinall in the BFI dossier 'Gainsborough Melodrama'; Murphy and Aspinall, op. cit.
108 BFI microfiche of reviews for *Caravan*.
109 Gilbert, op. cit.
110 *Kinematograph Weekly*, 2 May 1946, p. 4.
111 From 'Sydney Box', a profile by John Barber, *Leader Magazine*, 1 May 1948.
112 Betty Box interview, op. cit.
113 Profile of Box by Barber, op. cit.
114 Sydney Box, *Film Publicity* (London: 1937).
115 Betty Box interview, op. cit.
116 Muriel Box, *Odd Woman Out* (London: 1974), p. 176.
117 Betty Box interview, op. cit.
118 Pauline Kael, quoted in *Halliwell's Film Guide,* op. cit., review of *The Seventh Veil*.
119 Betty Box interview, op. cit.
120 ibid.; Box used to run competitions in the popular press where fans could win

prizes for devising new plot-lines for the 'Huggett' series.

5 RESEARCH AND INNOVATION

1 Quoted in *Kinematograph Weekly*, 21 March 1946, p. 24.
2 For a discussion of Watson-Watt's activities with radar during the Second World War, see Angus Calder, *The People's War* (London: 1986), pp. 458–9.
3 Michael Powell, 'Private and confidential' to J. Arthur Rank, 'Memorandum on a New Design for Films'. February 1945, courtesy of Kevin Macdonald.
4 ibid.
5 ibid.
6 David Rawnsley, 'Proposals for process film production', 4 August 1945 (private and confidential report on behalf of the Film Research Department); courtesy of Kevin Macdonald.
7 ibid.
8 ibid.
9 From an interview with Charles Staffell (a former colleague of Rawnsley), Pinewood, September 1991.
10 Rawnsley, 'Proposals'.
11 Joel Finler, *The Hollywood Story* (London: 1988), section on Warner Brothers.
12 Staffell interview, op. cit.
13 From an unpublished memo on Independent Producers Ltd written for the author by Sidney Gilliat, 22 May 1991.
14 From an interview with Betty Box, Beaconsfield, July 1991.
15 Rawnsley, 'Proposals'.
16 Rawnsley, quoted in *Kinematograph Weekly*, 6 January 1949, p. 8.
17 Staffell interview, op. cit.
18 ibid.
19 Rawnsley's partner Donald Wilson, involved with making the first Independent Frame pictures for Aquila, later joined the BBC.
20 See, for example, the film *Floodtide*: Staffell recalls that filmmakers were not allowed inside HM Prisons, but Independent Frame enabled them to get behind bars for the camera.
21 See booklet on Pinewood, published in 1965 to mark the thirtieth anniversary of the studios, and including a short piece, 'Pinewood blueprint', by Baynham Harris, technical consultant, which, while pointing out the drawbacks of Independent Frame, observes its residual benefits: 'Pinewood has developed the finest and most elaborate use of movie and slide back projection in the world. . . . Independent Frame may have faded from memories, but the tools that will now be available will at last become the servants, not the masters, of producers, directors and actors.'
22 From a telephone interview with Bob Monkhouse, a former apprentice at G-B Animation, June 1991.
23 ibid.
24 David Hand, writing in *Kinematograph Weekly*, 11 April 1946, p. 24b.
25 See the John Halas essay on 'Cartoons', in Oswell Blakeston (ed.), *Working for the Films* (London: 1947).
26 Monkhouse interview, op. cit.
27 From a tourist pamphlet on Moor Hall.
28 David Hand, quoted in *Kinematograph Weekly*, 9 September 1948, p. 19.
29 From a promotional leaflet in 'This Modern Age' files, in the Rank Film Archive at Alperton; courtesy of Derek Long.

30 See John Ellis, 'Art, culture, quality', *Screen*, Autumn 1978.

31 From an interview with Jill Craigie, London, June 1991.

32 For discussion of the Empire Marketing Board and the Crown Film Unit, see Ian Aitken, *Film and Reform: John Grierson and the Documentary Film Movement* (London: 1990).

33 Norman McKenzie, writing in the *New Statesman*, London, 1950.

34 Craigie interview, op. cit. Also see Geoffrey Macnab, 'Woman pioneer of the film industry', *Glasgow Herald*, October 1991.

35 *Kinematograph Weekly*, 26 September 1946, p. 23, and *Picturegoer*, 29 January 1949, p. 8.

36 ibid.

37 ibid.

38 From information on 'This Modern Age' in the Rank Film Archive (see n. 29). The Central Film Library at Denham was run by Sam Simmonds. It provided all manner of sound and image for Rank's filmmakers.

39 Commentary from 'This Modern Age', no. 19, *Challenge in Nigeria*.

40 Commentary from 'This Modern Age', no. 22, *Women in our Time*.

41 Hodson and Hanley quoted in files from the Rank Film Archive (see n. 29).

42 ibid.

43 ibid.

44 ibid.

45 ibid.

46 Roger Manvell, writing in *Tribune*, 23 August 1947.

47 Paul Rotha, writing in *Public Opinion*, December 1940.

48 Rank Film Archive on 'This Modern Age' (see n. 29).

49 ibid.

50 *Kinematograph Weekly*, 25 August 1949, p. 7.

51 From an interview with Olive Dodds, formerly head of Contract Artists at Rank and administrator of the Charm School, London, July 1991.

52 Richard Dyer, *Stars* (London: 1979). Christine Gledhill (ed.), *Stardom: Industry of Desire* (London: 1991).

53 Frank Launder talking about Ted Black, quoted in *Sight and Sound*, May 1950, p. 121.

54 *Kinematograph Weekly*, 24 January 1946, p. 43.

55 Dodds interview, op. cit.

56 ibid.

57 Christopher Lee, *Tall, Dark and Gruesome* (London: 1977). In this, his autobiography, Lee offers a first-hand account of the Charm School. See also Quentin Falk, *The Golden Gong* (London: 1985) and Barry Norman's documentary, *The Charm School*, broadcast in 1982.

58 Dodds interview, op. cit.

59 From an interview with Weston Drury, Windsor, October 1991.

60 Theo Cowan, 'Personal appearances', *Picturegoer*, 26 February 1949, pp. 10–11.

61 Dodds interview, op. cit.

62 See Terence Fisher's film, *To the Public Danger*, Highbury Studios, 1948.

63 Feature on Highbury Studios, *Kinematograph Weekly*, 18 December 1947, p. 73.

64 Jeffrey Richards, *The Age of the Dream Palace* (London: 1984), p. 83.

65 ibid.

66 *Kinematograph Weekly*, 22 April 1943; see also the previous issue, 15 April 1943.

67 *Kinematograph Weekly*, 8 August 1947.
68 J. P. Mayer, *The Sociology of Film* (London: 1946), p. 53.
69 ibid., p. 11.
70 ibid., p. 51.
71 ibid., p. 53.
72 ibid., p. 54.
73 ibid., p. 55.
74 *Kinematograph Weekly*, 8 August 1946, and a leader in *The Times*, 5 January 1946.
75 Mary Field, *Good Company* (London: 1952), p. 169.
76 Barry Delmaine on *Here We Come Gathering*, *Cine-Technician*, March–April 1946, p. 32. See also appendices to Field, op. cit. p. 169.
77 Delmaine, op. cit.
78 Report on the 1946 ACT conference in *Kinematograph Weekly*, 2 May 1946, p. 8.
79 Mary Field, 'Educational and interest films as background for the message of the Kingdom', *The Third Religious Film Summer School* (pamphlet: 1937), pp. 14–16.
80 From an interview with Hugh Stewart, Denham, July 1991. Stewart recalls that Rank once asked that the Bible be referred to as 'the Good Book' in a picture that Stewart was producing. Rank's interference in his producers' affairs ran to little more than this, although he did demand that no star ever be photographed with a drink in his or her hands.
81 Field, *Good Company*. *Kinematograph Weekly*, 1943–5, also offers accounts of early CEF screenings.
82 Rank quoted in Alan Wood, *Mr Rank* (London: 1952).
83 From a typical episode of 'Our Club Magazine', viewed by the author at the National Film Archive.
84 ibid.
85 ibid.
86 Craigie interview, op. cit.
87 Calder, op. cit., p. 211.
88 Craigie interview, op. cit.
89 ibid.
90 ibid.
91 ibid.
92 From an interview with the Hon. Mrs Shelagh Cowen, London, September 1991.
93 Craigie interview, op. cit.
94 ibid.
95 Richard Winnington, 'Rank versus Rank', *News Chronicle*, 27 July 1946.
96 ibid.

6 THE BOGART OR BACON DEBATE

1 Alan Sked and Christopher Cook, *Post-War Britain* (London: 1984), pp. 20–50.
2 ibid.
3 ibid.
4 David Marquand, 'Stafford Cripps', in Michael Sissons and Philip French (eds), *The Age of Austerity* (London: 1986), p. 69.
5 The material in the account that follows appears courtesy of film historian Mark Glancy, who had access to United Artists files and who kindly sent me

details of United Artists/Rank grosses.

6 ibid.

7 Tino Balio, *United Artists* (Madison, Wisc.: 1976b), p. 221. See also Robert Murphy, 'Rank's attempt on the American market', in James Curran and Vincent Porter (eds), *British Cinema History* (London: 1983), p. 168.

8 Paul Swann, *The Hollywood Feature Film in Post-War Britain* (London: 1987), and Margaret Street and Sarah Dickinson, *Cinema and State* (London: 1985), discuss Hollywood's impact on austerity Britain in much greater detail.

9 The phrase 'Bogart or bacon' was coined by Bob Boothby in the House of Commons, November 1945.

10 Elvin's anecdote was recalled by Sidney Cole in an interview with the author, London, September 1991.

11 ibid.

12 Nicholas Thomas, 'Anthony Asquith', in Nicholas Thomas (ed.), *International Dictionary of Films and Filmmakers*, Vol. 2, *Directors*, London/Chicago, 1991.

13 *ACTION: 50 Years in the Life of a Union* (London: 1983), p. 21.

14 *Kinematograph Weekly*, 27 September 1945, p. 36.

15 Sidney Cole, *Daily Worker*, 28 June 1946.

16 Cole interview, op. cit.

17 Beaverbrook and the Ostrer Brothers were on amicable terms. When Rank and Maurice Ostrer fell out, and Ostrer left Gainsborough, Beaverbrook took against Rank.

18 From an interview with Sydney Wynne, London, September 1991.

19 ibid.

20 For confirmation of this, read the trade press from 1942 onwards: Rank is ubiquitous.

21 Boothby, Foot and Wyatt were Rank's constant scourges in Parliament. (See *Kinematograph Weekly* reports of the various film debates in the House of Commons throughout the 1940s.)

22 *World Press News*, 27 March 1947: the market research company was Research Services Ltd.

23 ibid.

24 Wynne interview, op. cit.

25 *World Press News*, op. cit.

26 Eric Johnston, president of the Motion Picture Association of America, quoted in the *Kinematograph Weekly* and the *Motion Picture Herald*, August 1947.

27 From an interview with the Hon. Mrs Shelagh Cowen, London, September 1991.

28 *Motion Picture Herald*, August 1947.

29 *Kinematograph Weekly*, August 1947.

30 See, for example, Spyros Skouras in *Motion Picture Herald*, July 1947: *Variety*, March 1947: *Kinematograph Weekly*, 13 March 1947, p. 13.

31 *Kinematograph Weekly*, 8 May 1947, p. 11.

32 Rank, quoted in *Kinematograph Weekly*, 19 June 1947.

33 Davis, quoted in ibid., p. 14.

34 *Kinematograph Weekly*, 3 May 1947, p. 3.

35 See West's obituary in Daily Telegraph, Monday, 11 July 1988, for an account of his wartime exploits and part in the shooting-down of the Red Baron.

36 *Kinematograph Weekly*, 6 December 1945, p. 3.

37 The implications of this legislation are discussed at length by Thomas Guback, 'Hollywood's international market', in Tino Balio (ed.), *The American Film Industry* (New York: 1976a).

38 Joel Finler, *The Hollywood Story* (London: 1988), p. 210.
39 This reputedly happened with, for example, the 1988 Terence Davies movie, *Distant Voices, Still Lives*: the noted New York critic Vincent Canby gave the picture a bad review, and it sank, almost without trace.
40 From an interview with Sir John Davis, London, June 1990.
41 *The Master Millers* (London: 1955).
42 Sissons and French (eds), op. cit.
43 See chapter 4, 'Rank and his producers' and chapter 5, 'Research and innovation'.
44 Quoted from the chairman's annual general statement to the shareholders, Odeon: the J. Arthur Rank Organization, September 1949.
45 Sydney Box and Vivien Cox, *The Bad Lord Byron* (London: 1949), p. 12.
46 Robert Murphy, *Realism and Tinsel* (London: 1989), p. 222.
47 Board of Trade, *Distribution and Exhibition of Cinematograph Films* (the Plant Report) (London: 1949).
48 *Kinematograph Weekly*, 17 June 1948, p. 8.
49 *Financial Times*, 25 November 1947.
50 ibid.
51 *Financial Times*, 26 November 1947.
52 Chairman's annual general statement, op. cit.

7 ET

1 Andrew Roth, *Sir Harold Wilson, Yorkshire Walter Mitty* (London: 1977), p. 120.
2 Harold Wilson, *Memoirs: The Making of a Prime Minister* (London: 1986), p. 104.
3 At the time of writing, in the spring of 1992, the CBI and British film interests are lobbying for tax concessions.
4 Board of Trade, *Distribution and Exhibition of Cinematograph Films* (see Plant Report) (London: 1949).
5 See Margaret Street and Sarah Dickinson, *Cinema and State* (London: 1985).
6 ibid.
7 A. P. Herbert, *No Fine on Fun – A History of Entertainment Tax* (London: 1957), p. 15.
8 ibid., pp. 15–17.
9 ibid.
10 ibid.
11 See Alan Wood, *Mr Rank* (London: 1952), pp. 235–8.
12 Harold Wilson speaking in a House of Commons films debate, reported in *Kinematograph Weekly*, December 1949.
13 Board of Trade, *Report of the Film Studio Committee* (the Gater Report) (London: 1948), para. 9 (ii).
14 Richard Winnington and Nicholas Davenport, *The Future of British Films* (London: 1951), p. 5.
15 *Kinematograph Weekly*, 10 November 1949.
16 *Tribune*, no. 670, 11 November 1949, p. 1.
17 ibid.
18 ibid.
19 ibid.
20 *Kinematograph Weekly*, 23 January 1947, p. 3.
21 Winnington and Davenport, op. cit., p. 14.

22 A. J. P. Taylor, *English History 1914–1945* (Harmondsworth: 1976).
23 Available from Companies House. Quoted in *Kinematograph Weekly*, 10 November 1949.
24 ibid.
25 *Kinematograph Weekly*, 31 March 1950; see also 17 November 1949 and 22 December 1949.
26 *Kinematograph Weekly*, 23 June 1949.
27 *Kinematograph Weekly*, 17 November 1949, p. 9.
28 Korda died in 1956 still not having paid off all his loans from the NFFC.
29 For example, the various producers and directors who had defected to Korda from Independent Producers.
30 Harold Wilson, quoted in Roth, op. cit., p. 120.
31 *Kinematograph Weekly*, 31 March 1950.
32 *Kinematograph Weekly*, 15 December 1949, p. 6.
33 *Kinematograph Weekly*, 22 December 1949, p. 11.
34 Oliver Lyttleton speaking in the House of Commons (quoted in *Kinematograph Weekly*).

8 RETRENCHMENT AND ECONOMY

1 Chairman's annual general statement to the shareholders, the J. Arthur Rank Organization, 1950.
2 Karol Kulik, *Alexander Korda: The Man Who Could Work Miracles* (London: 1975).
3 Chairman's annual general statement op. cit. This is a phrase used by Rank.
4 From a letter to the author, June 1990.
5 From an interview with Charles Staffell, Pinewood, September 1991.
6 Chairman's annual general statement, op. cit.
7 *Kinematograph Weekly*, throughout the autumn of 1950.
8 ibid., 13 July 1950, p. 9.
9 Reported in the trade press, April 1950.
10 *Economist*, May 1950.
11 Board of Trade, *Distribution and Exhibition of Cinematograph Films* (the Plant Report) (London: 1949), paras 31–9.
12 *Kinematograph Weekly*, 20 July 1950, p. 36.
13 John Hill, *Sex, Class and Realism* (London: 1986), p. 5.
14 See, for example, the account of the CMA annual dinner, *Kinematograph Weekly*, 27 December 1951.
15 From an interview with Rank's nephew, J. D. Hutchison, London, July 1991: Rank used to tell this story 'against himself', but it highlights the concern in the early 1950s for improving cinemas to lure back spectators.
16 'A Mickey Mouse cartoon was the last thing seen on BBC television before the wartime shutdown.' See Ed Buscombe's essay, 'All bark and no bite', in John Corner (ed.), *Popular TV in Britain* (London: 1991).
17 Asa Briggs, *The History of Broadcasting*, Volume IV, *Sound and Vision* (London: 1979), p. 179.
18 ibid.
19 Rank, quoted in *Kinematograph Weekly*, 5 July 1945.
20 David Rawnsley's memo, 'Essential equipment for process film production', 1 February 1945, p. 45; BFI Special Collection.
21 John Davis, 'Efficiency and economy in British films', in *Financial Times Annual Review of British Industry* (London: 1954).

22 Buscombe, op. cit., p. 199.
23 Briggs, op. cit., p. 16.
24 *Kinematograph Weekly*, 21 September 1948.
25 Chairman's annual general statement, op. cit.
26 *Kinematograph Weekly*, 24 July 1952, p. 5.
27 Hill, op. cit., p. 37.
28 Michael Relph in *The Producer*, May 1987.
29 Buscombe, op. cit., p. 199.
30 Hill, op. cit., p. 49: 'Between 1951 and 1957, Rank Circuits exhibited only six (non-British) "X" films.' See also David Pirie, *Heritage of Horror* (London: 1975).
31 The case was discussed in the *Economist*, 6 December 1952.
32 Charles Barr (ed.), *All Our Yesterdays* (London: 1986); Barr's own essay on 'Broadcasting and cinema: screens within screens', discusses British cinema's paranoia about its small-screen cousin.
33 Richard Hoggart, author of *The Uses of Literacy*, was the moving spirit behind the Pilkington Committee, which shared the industry's scepticism about the 'triviality' of commercial television, albeit for very different reasons.
34 ITV was 'born' in 1955.
35 From an interview with Sidney Cole, London, September 1991.
36 See, for example, Harold Myers in *Variety*, 4 December 1963; David Robinson in the *Financial Times*, 14 April 1972; and Buscombe, op. cit. All use the Canute metaphor to describe British filmmakers trying to repel the waves of television.

9 RANK AND THE 1950s

1 Statistics gleaned from Roger Cowe, 'Xerox outflanks the rest of the muddle', *Guardian*, 31 January 1992. Subsequently is is rumoured that Rank is to sell off its film interests to service the massive debts incurred in buying the Mecca group.
2 From an interview with Hugh Stewart, Denham, July 1991.
3 From an interview with Betty Box, Beaconsfield, July 1991.
4 James Monaco, *The New Wave* (London: 1976).
5 As LWT's documentary/celebration of the 1950s, broadcast in January 1992, testifies *Genevieve*, along with *Doctor in the House*, has become embedded in popular memory as the quintessential film of its decade.
6 From an interview with Olive Dodds, London, July 1991, and Stewart interview, op. cit.
7 From an interview with Anthony Havelock-Allan, London, July 1991.
8 This assertion may seem far-fetched, but Rank production at Pinewood in the 1950s, in terms of production schedules, genre, budget, etc., was as close to the Hollywood factory system – at least as described by David Bordwell, Janet Staiger and Kirstin Thompson in *The Classical Hollywood Cinema* (London: 1985) – as Britain has ever been. In the 1940s, the golden moment of Independent Producers, the filmmakers were dominant. By the 1950s, though, their dreams and visions had become subordinate to the system.
9 In the March 1951 budget, for example, R. A. Butler made concessions to dog- and horse-racing, but not to films. Politicians remained as suspicious of the 'bastard muse' as they had been during the First World War.
10 Rank's annual general statement to the shareholders, 1954.
11 *Kine Weekly*, 23 September 1954, p. 7; from 1953, *Kinematograph Weekly*

changed to an abbreviated form of its earlier title.

12 *Kinematograph Weekly*, 1 February 1951, p. 34, discusses the setting-up of the NFFC.
13 Box interview, op. cit.; Betty Box recalls that the group was torn by internal dissent.
14 Rank, quoted in *Kinematograph Weekly*, 1 November 1951, p. 7.
15 ibid., 31 January 1952.
16 John Davis, 'Efficiency and economy in British films', in *Financial Times Annual Review of British Industry* (London: 1954).
17 Havelock-Allan interview, op. cit.
18 For discussion of kitchen sink films, see John Hill, *Sex, Class and Realism* (London: 1986).
19 Taken from a Charles Barr lecture at the University of East Anglia some time in the mid-1980s, when, as the author hazily recalls, Barr likened D. W. Griffith to W. G. Grace and the British 'northern' to the American 'western'.
20 Robert Murphy, *Sixties British Cinema* (London: 1992), p. 28.
21 From an interview with Norman Wisdom, Epsom, June 1991.
22 Charles Barr's introduction to *All Our Yesterdays* (London: 1986).
23 See *Kine Weekly*, 15 February 1954, p. 6. For more detailed discussion of the Rank–Fox scrap over Cinemascope, see Caroline Moorhead, *Sidney Bernstein* (London: 1984).
24 ibid.
25 Box interview, op. cit.
26 Wisdom interview, op. cit.
27 ibid.
28 *Kine Weekly*, 21 January 1954, p. 3.
29 As Wisdom recalls (interview, op. cit.) his persona as the 'gump', 'a short chap in a little grey tight-fitting suit for thirty shillings and a cap for one shilling', was conceived in a summer season at Scarborough, when Wisdom was doing a double act with conjuror and magician David Nixon. Nixon used to call the gump on to the stage (Wisdom pretended to be part of the audience). Although the double act soon ended, the costume and identity remained. See also Geoffrey Macnab, 'Laughter, plus pathos: the magic formula', *Glasgow Herald*, June 1991.
30 Box interview, op. cit.
31 ibid.
32 Quentin Falk, *The Golden Gong* (London: 1985), provides a full Rank filmography.
33 Stewart interview, op. cit.
34 Murphy, op. cit., p. 108.
35 From reviews of *Windom's Way* kept on microfiche at the BFI.
36 Rank's annual general statement to the shareholders, 1956.
37 *Financial Times*, 15 September 1955.
38 ibid., 10 September 1956.
39 Rank's annual general statement to the shareholders, 1959, contains this gloomy postscript on the second assault on the US market.
40 Rank, quoted in *Kine Weekly*, 25 September 1958, p. 6.
41 ibid.
42 Murphy, op. cit., p. 107.
43 Michael Balcon, quoted in *Kinematograph Weekly*, 18 October 1951, special supplement on Ealing's twenty-first anniversary, p. 9.

BIBLIOGRAPHY

BOOKS AND ARTICLES

ACTION: 50 Years in the Life of a Union, London, 1983.

Adorno, Theodor, *Prisms*, London, 1967.

Aitken, Ian, *Film and Reform: John Grierson and the Documentary Film Movement*, London, 1990.

Anderson, Lindsay, 'Stand up, stand up', *Sight and Sound*, Autumn 1956.

Anderson, Lindsay, 'Get out and push', in *Declaration*, ed. Tom Maschler, London, 1957.

Asquith, Anthony, 'The tenth muse climbs Parnassus', *Penguin Film Review* 1, 1946.

Austin, Bruce, *Immediate Seating: A Look at Movie Audiences*, Belmont, Calif., 1989.

Balcon, Michael, *Twenty Years of British Film*, London, 1947.

Balcon, Michael, *A Lifetime of Films*, London, 1969.

Balio, Tino, *United Artists*, Madison, Wisc., 1976b.

Balio, Tino, (ed.), *The American Film Industry*, New York, 1976a; revised edn, London, 1985.

Barr, Charles, *Ealing Studios*, London, 1977.

Barr, Charles (ed.), *All Our Yesterdays*, London, 1986.

Behlmer, Rudy, *Inside Warner Brothers*, New York, 1985.

Benjamin, Walter, *Illuminations*, London, 1982.

Blakeston, Oswell (ed.), *Working for the Films*, London, 1947.

Board of Trade, *Tendencies to Monopoly in the Cinematograph Films Industry* (the Palache Report), London, 1944.

Board of Trade, *Recommendations of the Cinematograph Films Council for New Legislation on Cinematograph Films*, London, 1947.

Board of Trade, *Report of the Film Studio Committee* (the Gater Report), London, 1948.

Board of Trade, Distribution and Exhibition of Cinematograph Films (the Plant Report), London, 1949.

Bogarde, Dirk, *Snakes and Ladders*, London, 1978.

Bond, Ralph, *Monopoly*, London, 1946.

Bordwell, David, Staiger, Janet and Thompson, Kristin, *The Classical Hollywood Cinema*, London, 1985.

Bower, Dallas, 'No celluloid utopia', *New Statesman*, 2 September 1944.

Box, Muriel, *Odd Woman Out*, London, 1974.

Box, Sydney, *Film Publicity*, London, 1937.

Box, Sydney and Cox, Vivien, *The Bad Lord Byron*, London, 1949.

Briggs, Asa, *The History of Broadcasting*, Volume IV, *Sound and Vision*, London, 1979.

Brown, Geoff, 'A knight and his castle', in *The Pursuit of British Cinema*, London, 1984.

Burnett, R.G., *The Cinema for Christ*, London, 1934.

Burnett, R.G., *Through the Mill: The Life of Joseph Rank*, London, 1945.

Burnett, R.G. and Martell, E.D., *The Devil's Camera: Menace of a Film-Ridden World*, London, 1932.

Buscombe, E., 'All bark and no bite', in John Corner (ed.), *Popular TV in Britain*, London, 1991.

Calder, Angus, *The People's War*, London, 1986.

Calder, Angus, *Myth of the Blitz*, London, 1991.

Cooper, Susan, 'Snoek piquante', in Michael Sissons and Philip French (eds), *The Age of Austerity*, London, 1986.

Corner, John (ed.), *Popular TV in Britain*, London, 1991.

Coster, Ian, *Friends in Aspic*, London, 1939.

Cowan, Theo, 'Personal appearances', *Picturegoer*, 26 February 1949.

Curran, James and Porter, Vincent (eds), *British Cinema History*, London, 1983.

Dalrymple, Ian, *Alexander Korda*, London, 1956.

Davis, John, 'Efficiency and economy in British films', in the *Financial Times Annual Review of British Industry*, London, 1954.

Dell, Jeffrey, *Nobody Ordered Wolves*, London, 1939.

Dickens, Charles, *Hard Times*.

Dickinson, Thorold, 'Indian Spring', *Penguin Film Review* 6, 1948.

Dyer, Richard, *Stars*, London, 1979.

Ellis, John, 'Made in Ealing', *Screen*, Spring 1975.

Ellis, John, 'Art, culture, quality', *Screen*, Autumn 1978.

Ellis, John, *Visible Fictions* (updated edn), London, 1992.

Falk, Quentin, *The Golden Gong*, London, 1985.

Field, Mary, 'Educational and interest films as background for the message of the Kingdom', *The Third Religious Film Summer School*, 1937 (pamphlet).

Field, Mary, *Good Company*, London, 1952.

Finler, Joel, *The Hollywood Story*, London, 1988.

Forbes, Bryan, *Notes for a Life*, London, 1977.

Forman, Denis, *Films 1945–1950*, London, 1952.

Gifford, Denis, *British Animation Films 1895–1985*, London, 1985.

Gilbert, F. L., 'Production Facilities (Films) Ltd', unpublished memo, 1981, held in BFI Special Collection.

Gilliat, Sidney, 'Independent Producers Ltd', unpublished memo, 22 May 1991, held by the author.

Gledhill, Christine (ed.), *Stardom: Industry of Desire*, London, 1991.

Gomery, Douglas, 'US film exhibition', in Tino Balio (ed.), *The American Film Industry*, New York, 1976.

Gomery, Douglas, *The Hollywood Studio System*, London, 1986.

Granger, Stewart, *Sparks Fly Upward*, London, 1981.

Greene, Graham, *The Pleasure Dome*, London, 1972.

Guback, Thomas, *The International Film Industry*, Bloomington, Ind., 1969.

Guback, Thomas, 'Hollywood's international market', in Tino Balio (ed.), *The American Film Industry*, New York, 1976.

Halas, John, 'Cartoons', in Oswell Blakeston (ed.), *Working for the Films*, London, 1947.

Halliwell's Film Guide, 6th edn, London, 1979.

Herbert, A. P., *No Fine on Fun – A History of Entertainment Tax*, London, 1957.

Hewison, Robert, *In Anger: Culture and the Cold War 1945–60*, London, 1981.

Hill, John, *Sex, Class and Realism*, London, 1986.

Hoggart, Richard, *The Uses of Literacy*, London, 1958.

Horkheimer, Max, *The Eclipse of Reason*, London, 1947.

Hughes, Glynn, *Yorkshire*, London, 1985.

Korda, Michael *Charmed Lives*, London, 1980.

Kulik, Karol, *Alexander Korda: The Man Who Could Work Miracles*, London, 1975.

Langley, Noel, *Hocus Pocus*, London, 1939.

Lean, David, 'Brief Encounter', *Penguin Film Review* 4, 1947.

Lee, Christopher, *Tall, Dark and Gruesome*, London, 1977.

Leigh, David and Jenkins, Simon, *Michael Foot: A Portrait*, London, 1981.

Lejeune, C. A., *Chestnuts in her Lap*, London, 1947.

Limbacher, James, L., *The Influence of J. Arthur Rank*, London, 1971.

Low, Rachael, *British Filmmaking in the 1930s*, London, 1985.

Lowenthal, Leo, *Literature, Popular Culture and Society*, New York, 1961.

Macnab, Geoffrey, 'Laughter plus pathos: the magic formula', *Glasgow Herald*, June 1991.

Macnab, Geoffrey, 'Woman pioneer of the film industry', *Glasgow Herald*, October 1991.

Macpherson, Don, *Traditions of Independence*, London, 1980.

Manvell, Roger, *Film*, London, 1946.

Marquand, David, 'Stafford Cripps', in Michael Sissons and Philip French (eds), *The Age of Austerity*, London, 1986.

Marwick, Arthur, *British Society since 1945*, London, 1982.

Mason, James, *Before I Forget*, London, 1981.

Mass Observation, *The Pub and the People, A Worktown Study*, London, 1943.

Mayer, J. P., *The Sociology of Film*, London, 1946.

Mayer, J. P., *British Cinemas and their Audiences*, London, 1948.

Minney, R. J., *Talking of Films*, London, 1947.

Minney, R. J., *Puffin Asquith*, London, 1983.

Monaco, James, *The New Wave*, London, 1976.

Moorhead, Caroline, *Sidney Bernstein*, London, 1984.

Morgan, Guy, *Red Roses Every Night*, London, 1948a.

Morgan, Guy, 'Cash down and no credit', *Penguin Film Review* 6, 1948b.

Morley, Sheridan, *A Talent to Amuse*, London, 1969.

Mullally, Frederic, *Films, An Alternative to Rank*, London, 1946.

Murphy, Robert, 'Rank's attempt on the American market', in James Curran and Vincent Porter (eds), *British Cinema History*, London, 1983.

Murphy, Robert, 'Under the shadow of Hollywood', in Charles Barr (ed.) *All Our Yesterdays*, London, 1986.

Murphy, Robert, *Realism and Tinsel*, London, 1989.

Murphy, Robert, *Sixties British Cinema*, London, 1992.

Murphy, Robert and Aspinall, Sue (eds), *Gainsborough Melodrama*, London, 1983.

Noble, Peter, *Spotlight on Filmland*, London, 1947.

Noble, Peter, *Reflected Glory*, London, 1958.

Norton, Richard, *Silver Spoon*, London, 1954.

Oakley, Charles, *Where We Came In*, London, 1964.

Osborne, John, *Almost a Gentleman*, London, 1991.

'Oscar and the Odeons', *Focus on Film* 22, 1975.

Pascal, Valerie, *The Devil and his Disciples*, London, 1971.

Perry, George, *Movies from the Mansion*, London, 1976.

Perry, George, *Forever Ealing*, London, 1981.

Perry, George, *The Great British Picture Show*, London, 1985.

Petrie, Duncan, J., *Creativity and Constraint in the British Film Industry*, London, 1991.

Pinewood, 1965 (a pamphlet published to mark the thirtieth anniversary of Pinewood Studios).

Pirie, David, *Heritage of Horror*, London, 1973.

Powell, Michael, 'Private and confidential' to J. Arthur Rank, 'Memorandum on a New Design for Films', February 1945.

Powell, Michael, *A Life in Movies*, London, 1987 (paperback); hardback edn 1986.

Price, Peter, 'The impresario urge', *Sight and Sound*, November 1950.

Rack, Henry D., *Reasonable Enthusiast: John Wesley and the Rise of Methodism*, London, 1989.

Rawnsley, David, 'Essential equipment for process film production', unpublished memo, 1 February 1945, held in BFI Special Collection.

Rawnsley, David, 'Proposals for process film production', unpublished memo, 4 August 1945, held in BFI Special Collection.

Rawnsley, David, 'Design by inference', *Penguin Film Review* 9, 1949.

Religion in the Ordinary Cinema, London, 1937 (a pamphlet published for the third Religious Film Summer School).

Richards, Jeffrey, *The Age of the Dream Palace*, London, 1984.

Richards, Jeffrey and Aldgate, Tony, *Best of British*, London, 1983.

Roth, Andrew, *Sir Harold Wilson, Yorkshire Walter Mitty*, London, 1977.

Seaton, Ray and Martin, Roy, 'Gainsborough Studios', *Films and Filming*, May 1982.

Silvermann, Steven, *David Lean*, London, 1989.

Sissons, Michael and French, Philip (eds), *The Age of Austerity*, London, 1986.

Sked, Alan and Cook, Christopher, *Post-War Britain*, London, 1984.

Street, Margaret and Dickinson, Sarah, *Cinema and State*, London, 1985.

Swann, Paul, *The Hollywood Feature Film in Post-War Britain*, London, 1987.

Taylor, A. J. P., *English History 1914–1945*, Harmondsworth, 1976.

Taylor, John Russell, *Hitch*, London, 1978.

Taylor, John Russell, *Strangers in Paradise*, London, 1983.

Taylor, Philip, *Projecting Britain*, London, 1981.

The Master Millers, London, 1955.

The Pursuit of British Cinema, London, 1984.

The Third Religious Film Summer School, 1937 (pamphlet).

Thomas, Nicholas, 'Anthony Asquith', in Nicholas Thomas (ed.), *International Dictionary of Films and Filmmakers*, Vol. 2, *Directors*, London/Chicago, 1991.

Tynan, Kenneth, 'Ealing', *Films and Filming*, November 1950.

Walker, Alexander, *Hollywood, England*, London, 1974.

Warren, Patricia, *Elstree: British Hollywood*, London, 1983.

Wesley, John, *A Short History of Methodism*, London, 1765.

Wilcox, Herbert, *25,000 Sunsets*, London, 1967.

Williams, Raymond, *Keywords*, London, 1983.

Wilson, Harold, *Memoirs: The Making of a Prime Minister*, London, 1986.

Winnington, Richard, 'Rank versus Rank', *News Chronicle*, 27 July 1946.

261

Winnington, Richard, *Drawn and Quartered*, London, 1948.
Winnington, Richard and Davenport, Nicholas, *The Future of British Films*, London, 1951.
Wood, Alan, *Mr Rank*, London, 1952.

JOURNALS AND NEWSPAPERS

American Cinematographer
Cinema/TV
Cine-Technician
Daily Film Renter
Films and Filming
Kinematograph Weekly
(from 1953, *Kine Weekly*)

Motion Picture Herald
News Chronicle
Picturegoer
Producer
Screen
Sight and Sound
Tribune

INTERVIEWS

Betty Box, Beaconsfield, July 1991
Sidney Cole, London, September 1991
Hon. Mrs Shelagh Cowen, London, September 1991
Jill Craigie, London, June 1991
Sir John Davis, London, June 1990
Olive Dodds, London, July 1991
Weston Drury, Windsor, October 1991
Anthony Havelock-Allan, London, July 1991
J. D. Hutchison, London, July 1991
Bob Monkhouse, London, June 1991 (telephone interview)
Peter Rogers, Beaconsfield, July 1991
Donald Sinden, Chichester, June 1992
Charles Staffell, Pinewood, September 1991
Hugh Stewart, Denham, July 1991
Norman Wisdom, Epsom, June 1991
Sir John Woolf, London, September 1991
Sydney Wynne, London, September 1991

OTHER SOURCES

BFI Special Collections, British Film Institute, 21 Stephen Street, London W1.
National Film Archive, 21 Stephen Street, London W1.
Rank Film Archive (courtesy of Derek Long and George Helyer), Unit 4, Abercorn Trading Estate, Manor Farm Road, Alperton HA0 1AN.
Rank Viewers' Reports, British Film Institute, 21 Stephen Street, London W1.

INDEX

Lyttelton, Oliver 198

Ma and Pa Kettle 176
Macaulay, Rose 105
McKenna, Reginald 190
Macmillan, Harold 4
Madeleine 108
Madonna of the Seven Moons 70, 117, 118
The Maggie 112
Maid of the Mountains 62
Major Barbara 36, 90
The Maltese Falcon 71
The Man in Grey 116, 117
Man of Evil 164
The Man Who Knew Too Much 23, 30
The Man with the Golden Arm 218
Mannock, P.L. 102
Manorfield Investments 33
Manvell, Roger 35, 97, 111, 140
March, Frederic 183
The March of Time 121, 136, 140, 141
Marriott, Moore 14
Marsh, Carol 141
Martin, Sandra 141
Martin, T.H. 41
Mason, James 64, 115, 117, 120
Mastership of Christ 14
Mathieson, Muir 137
Matthews. Jessie 17, 142
Mature, Victor 211, 220
Mayer, J.P. 40, 150, 151, 152, 154
Mayer, Louis B. 5, 51, 59, 112
Maxwell, John 30–3
Me and My Gal 26
Mears, Henry 186
Meet Mr Lucifer 211
Méliès, George 124
Men of Two Worlds 88, 192
The Men They Couldn't Arrest 62
Merton Park Studios 14
Metcalfe, Charles 186
Methodist Times 10, 11
Metro-Goldwyn-Mayer 30, 36, 40, 42, 75
Metropolis and Bradford Trust 30, 31, 33
Miles, Bernard 202
The Million Pound Note 225
Millions Like Us 92, 115
Mills, John 38, 115, 142, 215
Ministry of Aircraft Production 99

Ministry of Food 182
Ministry of Information 38, 44, 84, 118
Minney, R.J. 165, 166, 167, 185
Mrs Miniver 15
Mr Emmanuel 163
Molly and Me 61
Montagu, Ivor 169
Monkhouse, Bob 132, 134
Mooring, W.H. 72
Morden, Grant 24
More, Kenneth 215
Mother Riley 56
Motion Picture Association of America (MPAA) 54
Motion Picture Export Association (MPEA) 71, 176
Moyne Committee 75
Mullally, Frederic 165, 166, 167, 185
Murphy, Robert 77, 184, 210, 219, 229
Murray, Pete 141, 146
Musical Paintbox 134
The Mysterious Poacher 156

National Association of Theatre and Kinematograph Employees (NATKE) 180
National Film Board of Canada 169
National Film School 197
National Finance Corporation 108, 114, 188, 195, 196
National Provincial Bank 22, 26, 187, 200
Neagle, Anna 2, 67
Neame, Ronald 92, 108, 199, 222
Newley, Anthony 156
Night Train to Munich 92
Nobody Ordered Wolves 18
Nolbandov, Sergei 137, 138
Norton, Richard (Lord Grantley) 21

O'Brien, Tom 180
The Observer 35, 52
Odd Man Out 86, 176
Odeon Cinemas 22, 27, 28, 29, 31, 36, 42, 112, 186, 187
Okay for Sound 19
Oliver Twist 70, 95, 183
Olivier, Laurence 85, 89, 90, 183
One of Our Aircraft is Missing 91, 163
Orders is Orders 66
Ostrer, Isidore 30, 31, 32, 77
Ostrer, Mark 30